Java 2

BY EXAMPLE

A Division of Macmillan USA
201 West 103rd Street,
Indianapolis, Indiana 46290

Geoff Friesen

Java 2 by Example

International Standard Book Number: 0-7897-2266-6

Library of Congress Catalog Card Number: 99-66453

Printed in the United States of America

First Printing: January 2000

02   01   00   4   3   2   1

Trademarks

Warning and Disclaimer

Publisher
John Pierce

Acquisitions Editor
Todd Green

Development Editor
Susan Hobbs

Technical Editor
Thad Smith

Managing Editor
Thomas F. Hayes

Project Editor
Karen S. Shields

Copy Editor
Sossity Smith

Indexer
Rebecca Salerno

Proofreader
Jeanne Clark

Team Coordinator
Julie Otto

Media Developer
Jay Payne

Interior Designer
Karen Ruggles

Cover Designer
Rader Design

Copywriter
Eric Borgert

Production
Liz Johnston

Contents at a Glance

Table of Contents

About the Author

Geoff Friesen is heavily involved with Java technology. He has written numerous Java-based articles for *JavaWorld* (at http://www.javaworld.com) and *Windows TechEdge* (at http://www.windowstechedge.com) magazines (which have also appeared on the CNN and IBM Web sites), covering a range of topics from internationalization to Java Plug-in to the future of Java.

He was the chief developer on a project with EDS, where he integrated a smart card device, encryption, and digital signature generation Windows DLLs (written in C++) with Java applets via Java native interface technology. He has worked directly with the virtual machine and created his own disassembler for Java class files.

While writing this book, Geoff taught an introductory college-level Java course and an introductory university-level Java course. Many of the same concepts covered in those courses are also present in this book.

Dedication

To my parents, Bill and Mary, my sister, Sharon Larsen, her husband, Richard Larsen, and their children, Eric, Ryan, and Rebecca.

To my former university professor Dr. George E. McMaster, who introduced me to computer science and taught me how to write quality software; Dave Voorhis, who answered many of my personal computer questions over the years; Morgan Ross, who introduced me to Java; and Yvonne Baert for all of her encouragement and support in my pursuit of Java.

To my other close friends Chris Goudy, Clark and Hilda Sydor, Helen Stroud, Pastor Joe MacDonald, Lorraine Moore, Robert Lapensee, and the late Father Lucian Kemble, who was an inspiration in my life. Many thanks to all of you, and the many other people whose names could not be included because of space limitations.

Thank you.

Geoff

Tell Us What You Think!

As the reader of this book, *you* are our most important critic and commentator. We value your opinion and want to know what we're doing right, what we could do better, what areas you'd like to see us publish in, and any other words of wisdom you're willing to pass our way.

As a Publisher for Que, I welcome your comments. You can fax, email, or write me directly to let me know what you did or didn't like about this book—as well as what we can do to make our books stronger.

Please note that I cannot help you with technical problems related to the topic of this book, and that due to the high volume of mail I receive, I might not be able to reply to every message.

When you write, please be sure to include this book's title and author as well as your name and phone or fax number. I will carefully review your comments and share them with the author and editors who worked on the book.

Fax: 317-581-4666

Email: que_programming@macmillanusa.com

Mail: John Pierce
Publisher
Que
201 West 103rd Street
Indianapolis, IN 46290 USA

Introduction

Welcome to *Java 2 by Example*. You are about to embark on an exciting journey of adventure into the realm of Java technology. This is one journey that you will never forget.

Who Should Use This Book

You do not need a university degree to learn Java. Java is a very simple, yet sophisticated technology. All you need is curiosity, patience, and a desire to learn.

How This Book Is Organized

Java 2 by Example takes an example-oriented approach to teaching Java version 2 technology. Each chapter is peppered with many small examples, and most chapters conclude with a larger (and more useful) example.

This book is organized into five parts: "An Introduction to Java," "Exploring the Language," "Exploring the Class Library," "Case Study," and "Appendixes."

"An Introduction to Java" provides an introduction to Java, by way of Chapter 1, "Introducing Java." This chapter exposes you to what Java is and where it came from. You'll also learn about the Java Development Kit (JDK) and how to create a Java application and a Java applet.

"Exploring the Language" gives you an opportunity to learn all of the ins and outs of the Java language. Everything from basic language elements, such as comments and operators, to advanced concepts, such as packages, is presented in Chapters 2 through 9.

"Exploring the Class Library" gives you a chance to learn about string management, data structures, JFC and the AWT, multithreading, files, and streams. These concepts are covered in Chapters 10 through 17.

"Case Study" provides useful information for developing real-world Java programs. You'll learn how to plan, design, and implement Java software by way of the useful Contact Manager program that's presented in Chapter 18, "Contact Manager." Many concepts from previous chapters are used to bring Contact Manager into existence.

If you can master the habits that are presented in "Case Study," you'll save yourself wasted development time and have some fun in the development process.

A set of four appendixes and a glossary round out this book. Appendix A, "Reserved Words," contains a convenient table of the Java language's reserved words. Appendix B, "Operator Precedence," contains a convenient operator precedence table. The Java Development Kit's JAR tool is explored in Appendix

C, "JAR File Management." Finally, Appendix D, "Additional Resources," provides some additional resources that you might want to explore on your journey to mastering Java technology. This appendix even provides information on how to become a certified Java developer, a definite career enhancement. The glossary lists terms that are used throughout this book.

Conventions Used in This Book

This book follows certain conventions for indicating the syntax of various language elements (for example, comments, identifiers, expressions, statements, and so on), as well as for writing out method names.

Syntax

When learning a new language, it is important to understand the various ways in which the language's elements are combined into meaningful programs. This syntax needs to be formally written down by following certain conventions that show how elements are specified. The following conventions are observed:

- Syntax consists of literal text and non-literal text. Literal text is specified by placing this text between quote characters and must be entered by a developer exactly as it appears (without the quote characters). Non-literal text is specified by not placing this text between quote characters and is not entered by a developer. Instead, it serves as a placeholder for literal text that the developer must supply.

- Literal text consisting of two or more characters is placed between a pair of double quote characters (`""`). The double quote characters are not part of the literal text and are not entered.

  Example: `"while"`

  If a double quote character needs to be literally specified, it is preceded by a backslash character (`\"`). If a backslash character needs to be literally specified, it is doubled (`\\`).

- Literal text consisting of a single character is placed between a pair of single quote characters (`' '`). The single quote characters are not part of the literal text and are not entered.

  Example: `';'`

  If a single quote character needs to be literally specified, it is preceded by a backslash character (for example, `\'`).

- The vertical bar character (`|`) indicates a choice between two possibilities. A choice is usually surrounded by a pair of round bracket characters (`()`).

Example: (simple_statement ¦ compound_statement)

If the vertical bar character or a round bracket character needs to be literally specified, it is placed between a pair of single quote characters.

Example: '¦'

- The square bracket characters ([ ]) identify an option. Literal and non-literal text appearing between these characters is optional. The developer can choose to supply this text or not.

  Example: data_type variable_name ['=' expression] ';'

  If a square bracket character needs to be literally specified, it is placed between a pair of single quote characters.

  Example: '['

- Three period characters (...) indicate optional extraneous source code or the continuation of a comma-delimited list of elements.

  Example: "throws" exceptionName1 ',' exceptionName2 ',' ...

Method Naming

When a method name is specified, the name is written out with the data type names of its parameter list, surrounded by round bracket characters.

Example:

```
getParameter (String, String)
getCodeBase ()
```

Also, a space is placed between the method name and its parameter list to help improve source code clarity.

What's Next

It's time to turn our attention to the journey that lies ahead. By the time you get to the end of this book, you will have an incredible grasp of the Java language and be able to create some really interesting and useful software.

We begin this journey in Chapter 1 (which should come as no surprise). Let's get started!

Part I

An Introduction to Java

Chapter 1: Introducing Java

Introducing Java

When you encounter the word Java, what comes to mind? Do you imagine a delicious steaming cup of coffee? Does your mind reflect on a beautiful tropical island in the Indonesian island chain—a place where you might spend your next vacation? Or are you curious about a technology called Java that is causing quite a stir in the computer industry—a technology that has made Microsoft very nervous? If you are curious about this Java technology, you've picked up the right book. In this book, you'll learn how to use Java to create a new and exciting "breed" of computer programs.

Chapter 1 presents the following topics:

- What is Java?
- A brief history of Java
- The Java Development Kit
- Applications
- Applets

What Is Java?

A dictionary might define Java as a software technology that developers use to create portable, object-oriented, and secure computer programs.

Portable Java programs can be written and compiled once, and then run on any computer that supports Java. This concept is known as "write once, run anywhere." Portability helps you save development time because you don't have to write a separate version of your source code to target each computer that will run the compiled code.

Object-oriented Java programs are easier to write than non-object-oriented programs because translating real-world problems into source code is straightforward when using Java's object-oriented language features. As you'll discover, all Java programs take advantage of objects that send messages to each other. This is illustrated in Figure 1.1 where a few objects are shown sending messages back and forth. The objects are represented by circles, the messages are represented by lines, and each line has an arrow that points to the object receiving the message.

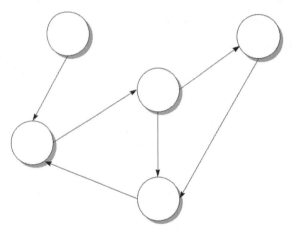

Figure 1.1: *Objects communicate with other objects by sending messages.*

Secure Java programs bring peace of mind to users. Because Java programs are automatically analyzed for security violations before being allowed to run, these programs are prevented from damaging the user's computer. Damage can take many forms: corrupting a computer's file system, "stealing" sensitive data (for example, a list of passwords), breaking video monitor hardware by changing the monitor's video signal parameters, and so on.

Java software technology is composed of four main entities: a computer language, a compiler, a virtual machine, and a class library.

Java Is a Computer Language

Developers specify the textual representation of a Java program by writing source code that "obeys" the rules of the Java computer language. The source code is then saved in text files with .java file extensions.

The Java computer language is similar to the C and C++ computer languages, from a syntactical point of view. Therefore, C and C++ developers should migrate to Java with ease. In the same breath, though, the Java computer language also has its differences from C and C++. Therefore, C and C++ developers will need to "unlearn" some C and C++ concepts when migrating to Java. For example, Java does not support the C/C++ concept of pointers (variables that contain the addresses of other variables).

Java Is a Compiler

Source code is read from text files and translated into byte code (instructions) by the Java compiler. This byte code is stored in class files (files with .class file extensions). If the compiler detects any rule violations, it will display one or more error messages and stop the compilation process. (A class is a blueprint that describes the structure of state and behavior for all objects that are created from the class.)

Java Is a Virtual Machine

The Java Virtual Machine—JVM for short—simulates a real computer. It is nothing more than an elaborate program that interprets each byte code instruction, selects a set of computer-specific instructions that correspond to each byte code instruction, and runs this set of instructions.

Virtual machine programs often contain code that serves as a virtual machine operating system. This code is known as the runtime. While the virtual machine interprets byte code, it communicates with the runtime to perform a variety of computer-specific tasks (such as allocating memory, accessing files, displaying information on the monitor, and so on).

Although the JVM and Java runtime are often discussed as two separate but connected entities, this book treats them as a single virtual machine entity.

Virtual machines make portability possible by serving as the only computer that a program needs to target. This means that Java programs never need to be "ported" to other computers. Only the virtual machine program (which is written in a computer-specific language such as C++) must be "ported."

Interpreting byte code is much slower than directly running computer code. This problem has led to the creation of Just In Time (JIT) compilers. While a virtual machine interprets byte code, it can tell which byte code runs more frequently than other byte code. The virtual machine can then tell the

JIT compiler to compile the more frequently called byte code into computer instructions, which the virtual machine will run without interpretation, greatly speeding up the Java program.

Java Is a Class Library

Java's class library contains many useful classes that developers can take advantage of to speed up their development time. There are many categories of classes in this library, including the networking, database, graphical user interface, multithreading, and data structure classes.

TIP

Always check the class library to see whether it contains what your program needs. If it does, then you save yourself considerable development time and avoid "re-inventing the wheel."

Putting all the entities of Java together, Figure 1.2 shows the process of building and running a Java program via the Java entities: computer language, compiler, virtual machine, and class library.

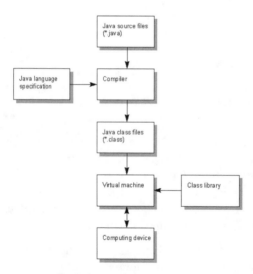

Figure 1.2: Building and running a Java program.

A Brief History of Java

The road to Java began in January 1991. Scott McNealy (the Chief Executive Officer of Sun Microsystems), Dr. James Gosling, Bill Joy, and several other people met at an Aspen, Colorado retreat to discuss a new era of personal computing.

At that time, computers were general-purpose computing devices. They ran large "monolithic" programs, such as word processors, spreadsheets, data-bases, desktop publishers, computer games, and communications tools.

Computer networks were starting to come into their own, but they were expensive, difficult to administer, and their real potential was still a few years away, when access to the Internet would become available to the general public and inspire greater interest in networks.

The visionaries at the retreat imagined a networked world of personal computing devices, such as electronic books and "intelligent" refrigerators that could suggest recipes based upon their contents. Because this networked world would be simpler to interact with than programming a typical VCR, the Sun people believed that a new (and profitable) market would form. And with Microsoft making inroads into Sun's workstation market, the chance for a new avenue of revenue was very compelling.

Within this networked world, objects would "flow" back and forth between different computing devices. These objects would contain properties and behavior for manipulating these properties. This code would run on any computing device connected to the network.

However, computing devices contain microprocessors, and each kind of microprocessor contains a different architecture and instruction set. How can an object adapt automatically to these different architectures and instruction sets? This is a difficult problem, but there is a simple solution.

Why not design a hypothetical-computing device and let this computing device run object code? Then, implement this computing device as a soft-ware program for each computing device that is attached to the network. The resulting software program is known as a virtual machine.

In June of 1991, Dr. Gosling began working on a language and a virtual machine. At the time, the project was called *Oak*, a name inspired by an oak tree that grew outside of Dr. Gosling's office window.

Unfortunately, attempts to market Oak failed. However, the mid-1990s brought hope to Sun with the introduction of the World Wide Web.

The Web makes it possible for anyone to publish information, via Web pages, for worldwide consumption. However, early Web pages were static entities. It was not possible to add dynamic content (such as embedding a spreadsheet program) to a Web page.

Oak was a perfect candidate for adding this dynamic content.

A hypothetical user would load a Web page (via a Web browser program) that specifies an "embedded" Oak program, and the Web browser would then download this program from wherever it resides on the Internet.

The browser would start the virtual machine and pass the Oak program to this machine where it would run. Figure 1.3 illustrates the process of embedding Oak programs within a Web browser.

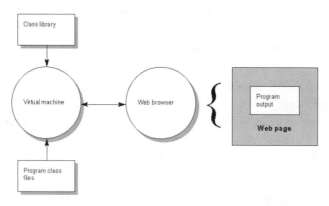

Figure 1.3: *Oak programs can be "embedded" within a Web browser.*

The virtual machine would be designed to interact with the browser to display the program's results within the Web page and obtain user input.

Therefore, a user with a Macintosh, a PC, or a UNIX machine could "surf" to the same Web page and experience an embedded program. It wouldn't matter that these three computers have different microprocessors and run different operating systems. As long as a virtual machine had been written for the computer and bundled with a Web browser, the Oak program would run unchanged on the virtual machine.

Because the virtual machine would perform elaborate verification and other security measures on programs before running them, a user's computer would not be the victim of malicious code. The virtual machine would detect malicious acts and not run the program.

Oak never had a chance to interact with Web browsers because, for marketing reasons, Sun decided to rename Oak. Oak became known as Java, and an agreement was made with Netscape Communications to embed a Java virtual machine within the popular Netscape Web browsers.

In May 1995, Sun officially introduced Java to the entire development community. Later that same year, Sun released a development kit for creating Java programs.

The Java Development Kit

The Java Development Kit (JDK) is Sun's toolkit for creating Java software. This toolkit is free to developers who would like to create Java programs.

The JDK contains useful tools (such as a compiler), a virtual machine, a class library, documentation, and examples. The various tools are known as command line tools because they are run from a command line within a DOS, UNIX, or some other command window.

JDK Versions

Many versions of the JDK have been released since 1995. These include versions from the original release 1.0.1 to the present 1.2.2.

Version numbers identify the significance of a release. For example, the transition from 0 in 1.0.1 to the right-most 1 in 1.1 represents significant JDK changes. However, the transition between the right-most 1 in 1.2.1 to the right-most 2 in 1.2.2 represents bug fixes only.

As this book is being written, version 1.2.2 is the most recent version of the JDK. Note: The examples in this book have been built and tested with JDK 1.2. However, these examples also should work with JDK 1.2.1 and JDK 1.2.2.

When version 1.2 was released, Sun decided to refer to this version as the Java 2 platform. Therefore, whenever the Java 2 term is mentioned, it refers to JDK versions 1.2, 1.2.1, 1.2.2, and to any future 1.2.x versions.

Obtaining and Installing the JDK

A free copy of JDK 1.2.2 can be downloaded from the Javasoft Web site (http://www.javasoft.com). To begin this process, click Products & APIs from the menu on the left side of the introductory Javasoft Web page. This click will take you to a page that lists JDK versions that are available for download. Select JDK 1.2.2 and follow instructions. One of the succeeding pages will prompt you to accept or reject the terms of Sun's license agreement for this JDK version. If you support this agreement, click the Accept button. You will then be taken to a Web page where you can download JDK 1.2.2.

The JDK is stored in a large installation file. (The JDK 1.2.2 installation file is around 20 megabytes in size.) You can either attempt to download the entire file, or download several smaller files that can be merged into the larger file (as explained by instructions on the download page). (The option of downloading multiple files is preferable if you have a slow Internet connection and your Internet provider is in the habit of dropping your connection after you've being connected to the Internet for one or more hours.)

After you've finished downloading or merging the JDK installation file, you can begin the installation process.

The installation file contains an installation program in addition to the JDK. Simply run this program and follow the onscreen instructions to install the JDK. For example, if you were to download the Windows release of JDK 1.2.2, you would end up with a file called jdk1_2_2-001-win.exe. Double-click this filename (from Windows Explorer) to start the installation program and follow the onscreen instructions.

A Tour of the JDK

The installation program creates several directories and copies files into these directories. One of the directories serves as the parent directory for all JDK directories. This directory is known as the JDK's installation directory.

Figure 1.4 shows the contents of JDK 1.2's installation directory, from a DOS window on a Windows 95 machine. (Note: This book uses the Win32 version of the JDK for its examples and figures.)

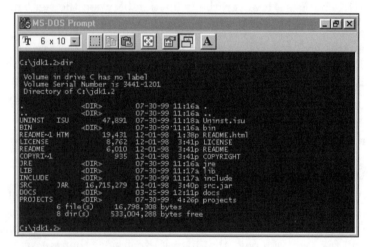

Figure 1.4: *The JDK 1.2 installation directory contains multiple files and directories.*

The README and README.html files describe the installed JDK. They are good places to start a tour of this toolkit.

The COPYRIGHT and LICENSE files contain important copyright and licensing information.

The Uninst.isu file contains information that is used when removing the JDK. (An older JDK version is usually removed before a more current version is installed.) Do not delete this file.

The src.jar file is a ZIP archive that contains the class library source code (a collection of files with .java file extensions). This source code is helpful for learning how the class library was constructed and to improve your skills as a Java developer.

The `bin` directory contains many useful tools. Three tools that are used throughout this book include the `javac.exe` compiler, the `java.exe` program for running applications, and the `appletviewer.exe` program for running applets. Another useful tool, discussed in Appendix C, "JAR File Management," is `jar.exe`. This tool is used to archive Java program files into a single file for easier distribution.

The `jre` directory contains a backup copy of the Java Runtime Environment (JRE) files. (The JRE is a runtime version of Java, as opposed to the JDK development version. In other words, unlike the JDK, the JRE contains no development tools, documentation, and examples.) These backup files can be used to repair damage to any runtime files in the runtime directory. (Because this book focuses on the JDK, the JRE will not be discussed any further.)

The `lib` directory contains library files that support the compiler (and other tools) and user-interface development. This directory also contains a file that is used in creating virtual machine applications. (Creating these applications will not be discussed because this topic is beyond the scope of this book.)

The `include` directory contains C-style header files that are used when working with the *Java Native Interface* (JNI) (a mechanism that "connects" class files to C/C++ libraries; because the JNI is beyond the scope of this book, it will not be discussed any further).

The `docs` directory contains documentation. However, because the JDK installation file does not include documentation, this directory is not automatically created, and documentation is not automatically installed by the JDK installation program. Instead, documentation must be downloaded separately, a `docs` directory must be manually created underneath the JDK installation directory, and the documentation must be manually installed into `docs`. The reason for this extra work is that the documentation is several megabytes in size. Placing everything into a single installation file would cause difficulties. After all, who wants to download 40+ megabytes in one shot!

Although not shown in Figure 1.4, the installation program can optionally install Java demonstration programs. If these programs are installed, a `demos` directory is created underneath the installation directory.

Finally, a `projects` directory has been manually created underneath the installation directory. The `projects` directory contains the various projects that are developed throughout this book. You might want to create your own `projects` directory underneath the JDK installation directory and, as you work through this book, organize your projects as separate directories within this directory.

Applications

An application is a standalone Java program consisting of one or more class files. Unlike applets, applications do not run within the context of a Web browser.

Application Structure

Every application contains a class file and a method (a named region of code that implements some kind of behavior) within this class file where execution begins. This class file is known as the main class file, and this method is known as the main method.

✔ For more information on methods, see "Methods," page 81.

EXAMPLE

The following source code illustrates the simplest possible application:

```
[ 1] // applicationName
[ 2]
[ 3] class applicationName
[ 4] {
[ 5]     public static void main (String [] args)
[ 6]     {
[ 7]     }
[ 8] }
```

Line 1 introduces what is known as a comment. Comments are used to describe source code. This comment identifies the name of the source file that contains this source code. The name is applicationName.java. When successfully compiled, a class file called applicationName.class will be created.

✔ For more information about comments, see "Comments," page 31.

Every application consists of at least one class specification. Classes are specified by the class reserved word followed by a name. Line 3 identifies applicationName as the name of this application's one and only class.

✔ For more information on classes, see "Declaring Classes," page 76.

Lines 4 and 8 specify brace ({ }) characters to mark the start and end of a class block (a region of source code that blueprints the structure of state [properties] and behavior [functionality via methods] for all objects that are created from the class).

Line 5 identifies a single method that is specified within the class block. This method is christened main and is specified as a public method, a static method, a void method, and a method that takes an array of String object arguments.

Don't worry if some of this does not make sense right now. It will become clear as you examine the Java language.

Building and Running Applications

The JDK java.exe tool is used to run applications. The name of the main class file (without the .class file extension) must be specified after java on the command line.

CAUTION

Including the .class file extension will cause java to display an error message instead of running the application.

An Example

EXAMPLE

To illustrate applications, let's build a text file viewer program. This program behaves like the DOS TYPE command or the UNIX CAT command. It displays the contents of various text files.

The following code listing specifies the viewer's implementation. This code is stored in a source file called view.java.

```
[ 1] // view.java
[ 2]
[ 3] import java.io.*;
[ 4]
[ 5] public class view
[ 6] {
[ 7]    public static void main (String [] args)
[ 8]    {
[ 9]       if (args.length != 1)
[10]       {
[11]          System.out.println ("syntax: view filename");
[12]          return;
[13]       }
[14]
[15]       FileInputStream fis = null;
[16]
[17]       try
[18]       {
[19]          fis = new FileInputStream (new File (args [0]));
[20]
[21]          int ch;
[22]          while ((ch = fis.read ()) != -1)
[23]             System.out.print ((char) ch);
[24]
[25]          System.out.println ("");
[26]       }
[27]       catch (FileNotFoundException e)
```

```
[28]     {
[29]             System.out.println ("File not found!");
[30]     }
[31]     catch (IOException e)
[32]     {
[33]             System.out.println ("Unable to read file!");
[34]     }
[35]     finally
[36]     {
[37]         if (fis != null)
[38]             try { fis.close (); } catch (IOException e) {}
[39]     }
[40]   }
[41] }
```

Now examine the code to see how it works.

Line 1 contains a pair of // (forward-slash) characters that introduce a comment.

Line 3 contains an import directive. Import directives are shortcuts that save you from having to enter package information.

✔ For more information on import directives, see "The Import Directive," page 200.

✔ For more information on packages, see "What Are Packages?" page 218.

Classes are identified by using Java's `class` reserved word and are given names—such as `view`. Classes can be made visible or invisible to other classes by using Java's `public` reserved word. The { and } (brace) characters in lines 6 and 41 identify a class block—an integrated group of variables and methods.

Lines 9 through 13 specify an If statement that checks to see if at least one command line argument has been passed to the application. This argument will identify the name of a file to be viewed. If no command line arguments have been passed, the `view` application displays an error message and exits. (If statements are discussed in Chapter 3, "Operators, Expressions, and Statements.")

Line 11 specifies a `System.out.println (String)` method call that outputs the contents of its `String` argument to the standard output stream. By default, the contents of this argument appear on the monitor.

✔ For more information on standard output streams, see "Streams," page 456.

Line 15 initializes a FileInputStream variable called fis to null. (Variables are discussed in Chapter 3 and null is discussed in Chapter 2, "Data Types, Literals, and Variables.")

Lines 17 through 39 specify an exception handler for dealing with file input/output problems.

✔ For more information about exception handling, see Chapter 8, "Exception Handling," page 185.

✔ For more information about files, see "Files," page 446.

A source file must be compiled into one or more class files before the program can be run. Figure 1.5 shows the javac.exe tool compiling the view.java source file.

```
C:\jdk1.2\projects\view>dir

 Volume in drive C has no label
 Volume Serial Number is 3441-1201
 Directory of C:\jdk1.2\projects\view

.              <DIR>        07-30-99  4:26p .
..             <DIR>        07-30-99  4:26p ..
VIEW~1   JAV         734  07-27-99  4:53p view.java
         1 file(s)           734 bytes
         2 dir(s)    535,822,336 bytes free

C:\jdk1.2\projects\view>javac view.java

C:\jdk1.2\projects\view>dir *.class

 Volume in drive C has no label
 Volume Serial Number is 3441-1201
 Directory of C:\jdk1.2\projects\view

VIEW~1   CLA         847  08-13-99  9:58a view.class
         1 file(s)           847 bytes
         0 dir(s)    525,303,808 bytes free

C:\jdk1.2\projects\view>
```

Figure 1.5: *Compiling* view.java *with the* javac.exe *compiler.*

CAUTION

The .java file extension must be specified when compiling an application's source file. The compiler will display an error message if .java is not specified.

CAUTION

The compiler displays an error message if the name of the application's .java file does not exactly match the name of the class in the source file. For example, the compiler would display an error message if the name of the class were View but the name of the .java file was view.

Figure 1.6 shows the java.exe tool running the text file viewer application. The contents of view.java are displayed.

OUTPUT

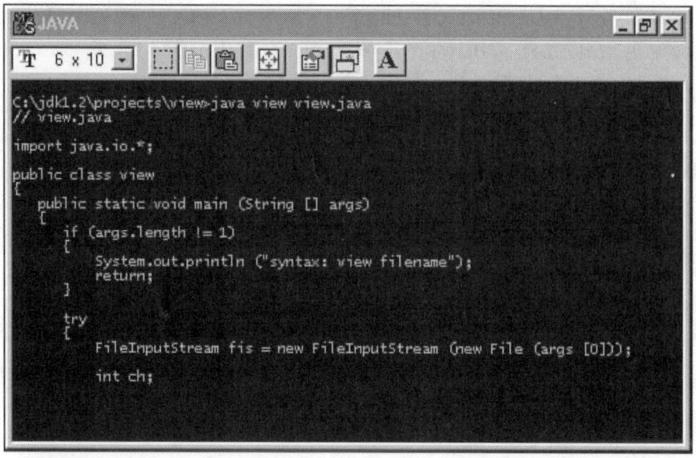

```
C:\jdk1.2\projects\view>java view view.java
// view.java

import java.io.*;

public class view
{
    public static void main (String [] args)
    {
        if (args.length != 1)
        {
            System.out.println ("syntax: view filename");
            return;
        }

        try
        {
            FileInputStream fis = new FileInputStream (new File (args [0]));

            int ch;
```

Figure 1.6: *Using* java.exe *to run the text file viewer application.*

Applets

Applets (those being Web browser–dependent Java programs consisting of one or more class files) are "embedded" within a Web page. Basically, when a user "surfs" to a Web page that contains the HTML specification for an applet, the Web browser examines this specification to discover the name of the applet's main class file. It then proceeds to download this class file by contacting the computer that contains this class file and requesting that the class file be sent to the Web browser. After the Web browser receives this class file, it will start the JVM, pass the class file to the JVM, and go about its business.

As this class file runs, it might reference other class files that are part of the applet. The JVM will "ask" the Web browser to contact the computer to download the additional class files on an as-needed basis.

Applets interact with Web browsers via the JVM. For example, applets display graphics within a rectangular applet area within the Web page. Actually, they don't directly display graphics. Instead, applet byte code passes graphics information to the JVM, which passes this information to the Web browser. Conversely, when a user clicks the mouse within the applet area, the Web browser passes this information to the JVM, which calls appropriate byte code within the applet to deal with this mouse click.

HTML Specification

The applet's HTML specification consists of three tags: <APPLET>, <PARAM>, and </APPLET>.

The <APPLET> tag starts an applet specification. This tag contains several attributes, including code, width, and height.

The code attribute specifies the name of the applet's starting class file. The width attribute specifies the width (in pixels or percentage) of the applet area. The height attribute specifies the height (in pixels or percentage) of the applet area.

The <PARAM> tag describes an applet parameter (a configurable entity that makes it possible to modify an applet after the applet's source code has been compiled). This tag contains two attributes: name and value.

The name attribute specifies the name of the parameter while the value attribute specifies the parameter's value.

Each parameter should be given its own <PARAM> tag. In other words, parameters do not share <PARAM> tags.

<PARAM> tags are optional. If an applet does not check for any parameters, <PARAM> tags are not specified. Even if an applet checks for parameters, the absence of one or more <PARAM> tags should not cause problems because the applet should properly handle this situation. (The applet could either work with default values or make decisions based on the absence of one or more parameters.)

An applet's starting class inherits a method from the Applet class called getParameter (String). This method is called with the name of a parameter (as an argument), and it searches through <PARAM> tags until it either finds a tag whose name attribute matches the parameter name argument or no match is found. If a match if found, the value attribute from the <PARAM> tag is read and returned from getParameter (String). Otherwise, a null value is returned to signal that no <PARAM> tag could be found.

<PARAM> tags do not have matching </PARAM> tags and they must be "sand-wiched" between the <APPLET> and </APPLET> tags.

The </APPLET> tag ends an <APPLET> specification.

Applet Structure

Every applet contains a class file that interacts with the Web browser. This class file is known as the main class file. However, unlike applications, there is no main method where execution begins. Instead, the Web browser indirectly calls an applet's methods at various times in response to a variety of activities.

The following source code illustrates the simplest possible applet:

EXAMPLE

```
[ 1] public class appletName extends java.applet.Applet
[ 2] {
[ 3] }
```

Line 1 specifies a single public class called `appletName` that derives capabilities from the `java.applet.Applet` class. (`Applet` is the name of the class, and `java.applet` is the name of a package—a section of the class library—that contains the `Applet` class file.)

These capabilities include four methods that a browser (indirectly) calls to manage an applet's life cycle: `init ()`, `start ()`, `stop ()`, and `destroy ()`.

The `init ()` method is called when an applet first begins its "life." You would place code within this method to initialize the applet. The `init ()` method is never again called during the "life" of the applet.

The `start ()` method is called immediately after the `init ()` method and every time a Web page containing an applet is revisited. You would normally place code to start threads (separate units of execution) within this method.

The `stop ()` method is called whenever a Web page containing an applet is replaced by another Web page, or just prior to a call to the `destroy ()` method. You would normally place code to stop background threads within the `stop ()` method.

The `destroy ()` method is called when a Web browser is terminating. You would place code within this method to perform global cleanup duties. Obviously, the `destroy ()` method is never called again.

For security reasons, applets are restricted in their activities. For example, applets cannot automatically send information to a user's printer. If they could, a malicious applet might attempt to print out hundreds of pages of paper, wasting paper and ink in the process. Applets are prevented from performing file operations and certain network activities, again for the user's protection.

Applet restrictions can be loosened by changing a browser's security settings. Furthermore, applets that are digitally signed (a complex security process) by their creators are allowed to access files, use the printer, and perform other sensitive tasks, provided that the user grants permission to the applet.

Building and Running Applets

The JDK `appletviewer.exe` tool is used to run applets. The name of an HTML file, that identifies the applet by using special HTML tags, must be specified after `appletviewer` on the command line. Applets also can be run from within Web browsers.

An Example

To illustrate applets, you can build a small image viewer applet that displays GIF and JPEG images.

EXAMPLE

The following code listing contains the image viewer's implementation. This code is stored in a source file called imageViewer.java.

```
[ 1] // imageViewer.java
[ 2]
[ 3] import java.applet.Applet;
[ 4] import java.awt.*;
[ 5]
[ 6] public class imageViewer extends Applet
[ 7] {
[ 8]    Image image;
[ 9]
[10]    public void init ()
[11]    {
[12]
[13]       String imageName = getParameter ("image");
[14]       if (imageName != null)
[15]          image = getImage (getCodeBase (), imageName);
[16]    }
[17]
[18]    public void paint (Graphics g)
[19]    {
[20]       if (image != null)
[21]          g.drawImage (image, 0, 0, this);
[22]    }
[23] }
```

Let's examine the code to see how it works.

Line 1 declares a comment while lines 3 through 4 declare import directives.

Lines 6 through 23 declare a class. Again, Chapter 4, "Encapsulation: Classes and Objects," discusses classes in detail.

Line 8 introduces a variable called image. This variable identifies the location of the bits and bytes making up an image.

✔ For more information about variables, see "Variables," page 38.

✔ For more information about images, see "Images," page 372.

Lines 10 through 16 specify an init () method. This method initializes the applet.

Line 13 calls the getParameter (String) (inherited from the Applet class) method to obtain the value of an applet parameter.

This method searches through the <PARAM> tags for a name attribute that matches the String argument. If a <PARAM> tag is found, the contents of the value attribute is returned by getParameter (String). Otherwise, a null value is returned.

Line 14 checks to make sure that `getParameter (String)` did not return a `null` value.

Line 15 calls the `getImage (String, String)` method (inherited from the `Applet` class) to get an image file associated with the value returned by `getParameter (String)`.

The `getCodeBase ()` method (also inherited from the `Applet` class) returns the name of the directory where the applet's class file and the image file are located.

Lines 18 through 22 specify a `paint (Graphics)` method. This method is called, indirectly by the Web browser, when it is time to update the applet area. `Graphics` identifies a *graphics context* (an object that represents a drawable surface, such as a video display or a printer).

✔ For more information on graphics and graphics contexts, see Chapter 14, "AWT, Part 1," page 347.

Line 21 specifies the `drawImage (Image, int, int, ImageObserver)` method to draw an image on a Web page.

A source file must be compiled into one or more class files before the program can be run. Figure 1.7 shows the `javac.exe` tool compiling the `imageViewer.java` source file.

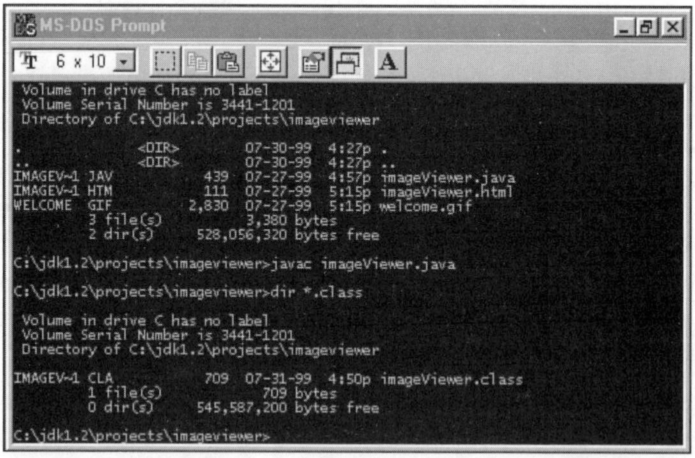

Figure 1.7: *Compiling `imageViewer.java` with the `javac.exe` compiler.*

CAUTION

The `.java` file extension must be specified when compiling an applet's source file. The compiler will display an error message if `.java` is not specified.

CAUTION

The compiler displays an error message if the name of the applet's .java file does not exactly match the name of the class in the source file. For example, the compiler would display an error message if the name of the class were ImageViewer while the name of the .java file was imageViewer.

Before the image viewer can be run, an HTML file needs to be constructed so that appletviewer.exe (or the Web browser) can load the applet's starting class file, start the JVM, and get things going.

The following code describes the HTML for the image viewer applet. This HTML is stored in a text file called imageViewer.html (or imageviewer.html—unlike .java and .class files, case does not matter when naming .html files).

```
[ 1] <applet code="imageViewer.class" width=215 height=100>
[ 2]    <param name="image" value="welcome.gif">
[ 3] </applet>
```

The <APPLET> tag identifies the applet's starting class file and describes the size of the applet area.

The name of the class file, specified by the code attribute, is imageViewer.class. The width of the applet area, specified by the width attribute, is 215 pixels. The height of the applet area, specified by the height attribute, is 100 pixels.

The <PARAM> tag identifies the name of the applet's single parameter and its value.

The name of the parameter, specified by the name attribute, is image. The value of the parameter, specified by the value attribute is welcome.gif.

Figure 1.8 shows the appletviewer.exe tool running the image viewer applet. A separate window displays the image.

OUTPUT

Figure 1.8: Using appletviewer.exe to run the image viewer applet.

Figure 1.9 shows a Netscape Web browser running the image viewer application and displaying the contents of `welcome.gif`.

Figure 1.9: *Using a Netscape Web browser to run the image viewer applet and view* `welcome.gif`.

What's Next?

Now that you've "sipped" some Java by way of this chapter's example programs, you may have acquired a taste for Java programming. You must understand the Java language before you can create Java programs. To that end, Chapter 2 will begin your education in Java language fundamentals.

Part II

Exploring the Language

2

Data Types, Literals, and Variables

The previous chapter introduced the Java language while examining application and applet source code. Before a Java program can be written, this language needs to be understood.

Starting with this chapter, the next several chapters explore most of the Java language. The only language topic not covered in these chapters is synchronization because this topic is covered in Chapter 16, "Multithreading."

Chapter 2 presents the following topics:

- What is a computer language?
- From ASCII to Unicode
- Comments
- Identifiers and reserved words
- Data types and literals
- Variables

What Is a Computer Language?

Billions of electrical signals flow through computer hardware as a computer program runs. These signals are the equivalent of precisely written computer instructions that are specified by a computer language.

Java, like other computer languages, specifies the basic entities of its language (such as comments, identifiers, reserved words, data types, literals, variables, and so on) and rules for combining these entities into meaningful source code.

Entities must be properly written out as source code according to the syntax and semantics rules of the Java language. An example of a syntax rule is ensuring that an integer only consist of a digit sequence. An example of a semantics rule is ensuring that an expression evaluates to an integer before using this integer as an index into an array. Violating either kind of rule results in compiler errors. For example, specifying 7X as an integer is a syntax error. Also, attempting to use a floating-point value as an array index is a semantics error.

From ASCII to Unicode

As you type keys on a computer's keyboard, the symbols that are assigned to these keys appear on the computer's monitor. These symbols have meaning to people, but are meaningless to computers.

Computers only manipulate binary digits (1s and 0s) and binary numbers (groups of binary digits arranged as *bytes*—8-bit quantities—and *words*—16-bit, 32-bit, 64-bit, or 128-bit quantities). (The term *bits* is commonly used as a synonym for *binary digits*. In fact, bits is a contraction of binary digits.)

Computers can manipulate symbols by manipulating the binary numbers that are associated with those symbols.

The combination of a binary number and a symbol's visual data is known as a *character*. A group of characters that completely define a written language's symbols is called a *character set*.

Creating a character set is an important task. The characters that constitute this set must completely define all symbols from a given written language (or languages). Because of its importance, the task of creating a character set is delegated to a standards committee.

Many years ago, the American National Standards Institute (ANSI) was given the task of creating a character set that would be used by all computing equipment within the United States and other countries. This character set would include letters A through Z, letters a through z, digits 0 through 9, punctuation, and some special symbols (such as the asterisk [*]).

ANSI ended up creating a standardized 7-bit character set called the *American Standard Code for Information Interchange* (ASCII). ASCII maps 128 binary numbers to 128 symbols. This character set is still being used.

Unfortunately, ASCII is not a complete character set for writing programs in any written language. Although ASCII works well with the written English language, it is not very accommodating to non-English written languages. For example, the accented characters that are part of the French and German written languages are not defined by ASCII. Also, many complex written languages, such as Chinese and Arabic, contain thousands of symbols. How could a character set that only has room for 128 entries possibly cope with all these symbols?

Several years ago, work began on a universal character set that would accommodate all the symbols from the Earth's major written languages. A lot of progress has since been made and the result is a standardized 16-bit character set called Unicode. Unicode maps up to 65,536 binary numbers to a maximum of 65,536 symbols. At present, slightly more than one-half of these binary numbers have been mapped.

For compatibility with ASCII, the first 128 characters of the Unicode character set are the ASCII characters. In other words, Unicode binary numbers 0 through 127 and ASCII binary numbers 0 through 127 map to the same symbols.

The Java language supports Unicode. The contents of a Java source file are examined by the compiler, and all non-Unicode characters are converted to Unicode before that source file is compiled.

This means that a developer can write source code using the native characters of his or her language. For example, the names of variables (discussed later in this chapter), methods, classes, interfaces, and packages (discussed in later chapters) can be specified using symbols that equate to letters and digits in any written language. This results in source code that is easier for the developer to write and read. However, operating-system support for displaying native characters as well as appropriate text-editor or word-processor software for entering and viewing these characters is still required.

For more information on Unicode, and to keep abreast of this standard, please visit the official Unicode Web site at `http://www.unicode.org`.

Comments

It is a very good idea to document your source code while you write this code. You should also update your documentation whenever you change this source code. Not only will source code documentation help others understand your code, it will also help you to remember what was going through your mind if and when you revisit your code at some future time.

Documenting Java source code is accomplished by taking advantage of comments. The textual information that you specify as part of a comment is completely ignored by the Java compiler. Therefore, comments do not result in any byte code being generated.

There are three kinds of comments: single-line, multi-line, and document.

Single-line Comments

A *single-line comment* spans a single line of text. This style of comment is introduced with the // characters. After the compiler detects //, all characters following // until the end of the current line are considered part of the comment.

EXAMPLE

The following code fragment illustrates a single-line comment:

```
// This is a single-line comment.
```

Multi-line Comments

A *multi-line comment* spans multiple lines. This style of comment begins with the /* characters and ends with the */ characters. All characters between /* and */ (including /* and */) are ignored by the compiler.

EXAMPLE

The following code fragment illustrates a multi-line comment:

```
/* This comment spans
   multiple lines. */
```

TIP

Multi-line comments are useful for commenting out portions of code during testing and debugging.

Documentation Comments

Like a multi-line comment, a *documentation comment* spans multiple lines. This style of comment begins with the /** characters and ends with the */ characters. All characters between /** and */ (including /** and */) are ignored by the compiler.

Documentation comments are useful for providing program documentation in the HTML format.

EXAMPLE

The following code fragment illustrates a documentation comment:

```
/** This is a documentation comment.  Although not shown
    documentation comments contain special instructions
    that are used by javadoc.exe when producing HTML. */
```

A source file containing documentation comments is passed to the JDK's `javadoc.exe` tool, which takes the contents of these comments and builds several HTML files. (The `javadoc.exe` tool is extensively documented in the JDK documentation.)

TIP

It is a good idea to include comments in your source code. Not only can they help other people to understand your code, they can help *you* understand your code six months after it was written.

Identifiers and Reserved Words

The Java language uses identifiers to name variables, methods, classes, interfaces, and packages. However, some of these identifiers are reserved for Java's exclusive use. These reserved identifiers are known as *reserved words*.

Identifiers

Identifiers consist of uppercase letters (A through Z, or equivalent uppercase letters in other languages), lowercase letters (a through z, or equivalent lowercase letters in other languages), digits (0 through 9, or equivalent digits in other languages), and a handful of special characters such as the dollar sign ($) and underscore (_). Furthermore, the first character must be a letter, a dollar sign (or other currency character), or an underscore (or other connecting punctuation character). Any other character will result in a compiler error.

The length of an identifier (that is to say, the number of characters that constitute an identifier) is limited only by the length of the line in which the identifier appears. (Java's compiler does not impose a limit on the length of a line.)

EXAMPLE

The following example illustrates valid identifiers:

```
$amount

_total

salary

counter6

number_of_tickets
```

EXAMPLE

The following example illustrates invalid identifiers:

`6tally`	An identifier cannot start with a digit.
`my*name`	An identifier cannot contain an asterisk.
`first name`	An identifier cannot contain a space.

Because Java is a case-sensitive language, identifiers that differ only in the case of their letters are treated as distinct. For example, count and Count are distinct identifiers because c and C are different characters.

Reserved Words

Reserved words are English words that describe certain language entities. For example, while is a reserved word that describes the notion of a While loop (discussed in the next chapter), whereas double is a reserved word that describes the notion of the double-precision floating-point data type (discussed later in this chapter). Reserved words cannot be used to name variables, methods, classes, interfaces, or packages.

> ✔ To see a table of Java's reserved words, see Appendix A, "Reserved Words," page 503.

Data Types and Literals

All computers process data. How is data specified in source code? The answer is to use a computer language's data types and literals.

Data Types

Java supports several data types that describe different kinds of data. These data types fall into two categories: primitive data types and reference data types.

Primitive data types are language-defined data types. Each primitive data type has a name, specifies how much memory is required to store a data item of that data type, and identifies a legal range of values from which a data item of that data type can be obtained. Table 2.1 lists Java's primitive data types.

Table 2.1: Primitive Data Types

Data Type	Size (Bits)	Data Item Ranges
boolean	1	true and false (expressed by the true and false reserved words)
char	16	0 through 65,535 (expressed by character literals—discussed later in this chapter)
byte	8	-128 to +127
short	16	-32,768 to +32,767
int	32	-2^{32} to $+2^{32}-1$
long	64	-2^{64} to $+2^{64}-1$
float	32	-3.4E+38 to +3.4E+38 (approximately)
double	64	-1.8E+308 to +1.8E+308 (approximately)

The Java language specifies a reserved word for each primitive data type. Developers use these reserved words to identify the data types of variables and method return values. Each reserved word is the same as the data type name.

Data items of some primitive data types can be directly converted to data items of other primitive data types without requiring the cast operator (discussed in the next chapter) by taking advantage of promotion rules. These rules apply to the byte, char, float, int, long, and short data types.

Basically, a data item of a primitive data type with fewer bits might be converted to a data item of a primitive data type with more bits without the need of a cast operator because no bits are lost. For example, a 32-bit int data item could be converted to a 64-bit long data item without a cast operator. The upper 32 bits of the 64-bit long data item would simply be stuffed with zeroes (positive data items only) or ones (negative data items only).

There are nineteen promotion rules. These rules can be summarized as follows:

- byte to short, int, long, float, or double

- short to int, long, float, or double

- char to int, long, float, or double

- int to long, float, or double

- long to float or double

- float to double

Attempting to convert a data item of a primitive data type with more bits to a data item of a primitive data type with fewer bits can result in loss of information. As a result, demotion rules are used. These rules apply to the byte, char, double, float, int, long, and short data types.

Basically, a data item with more bits (or a different internal representation such as floating-point versus integer) would be converted to a data item with fewer bits by using a cast operator because bits (or precision in the case of floating-point values) would be lost.

There are 23 demotion rules. These rules can be summarized as follows:

- byte to char

- short to byte or char

- char to byte or short

- int to byte, short, or char

- long to byte, short, char, or int

- float to byte, short, char, int, or long

- double to byte, short, char, int, long, or float

Reference data types are user-defined data types. Whenever you create a class, you are creating a reference data type. (Reference data types will be discussed in Chapter 4, "Encapsulation: Classes and Objects.")

The String data type, used to identify String data, is a special reference data type. Although String is not intrinsic to the language, it does have some language support. For example, the Java language provides an operator that concatenates two String data items together. If one of these data items is not a String, the non-String data item will be converted to a String data item before concatenation takes place. (String concatenation is discussed in Chapter 3, "Operators, Expressions, and Statements.")

Literals

Java makes it possible to literally embed data items in source code. Literal data items (literals for short) include Boolean true/false values, characters, integers, floating-point numbers, strings, and the `null` reserved word.

BOOLEAN LITERALS

A Boolean literal consists of the `true` or `false` reserved word.

The following example illustrates Boolean literals:
```
true
false
```

CHARACTER LITERALS

A character literal consists of a single character or an *escape sequence* (multiple characters that denote a single character) surrounded by single quote characters.

The following example illustrates character literals:

`'A'`	uppercase letter A
`'0'`	digit 0
`'\t'`	horizontal tab escape sequence
`'\r'`	carriage return escape sequence
`'\n'`	newline escape sequence
`'\u20ac'`	European Euro monetary symbol Unicode escape sequence

A Unicode escape sequence specifies a single Unicode character. This escape sequence consists of characters \u immediately followed by exactly four hexadecimal digits (digits 0–9, letters A–F, and letters a–f).

FLOATING-POINT LITERALS

A floating-point literal consists of optional digit characters followed by a decimal point character followed by optional digit characters followed by an optional *exponent* (an E or e character followed by a + or - character followed by digit characters) optionally followed by a lowercase letter f, an uppercase letter F, a lowercase letter d, or an uppercase letter D. If the f or F is specified, the data type is float. If the d or D is specified, the data type is double. If neither letter is specified, the data type defaults to double.

EXAMPLE

The following example illustrates floating-point literals:

6.5E+32   A floating point literal of data type double

7.5D   A floating point literal of data type double

0.0f   A floating point literal of data type float

INTEGER LITERALS

An integer literal consists of a sequence of digits optionally followed by a lowercase letter l or an uppercase letter L. If the l or L is specified, the data type is long. If the l or L is not specified, the data type defaults to int.

Integers can be specified in one of three formats: decimal, hexadecimal, or octal.

Decimal format is indicated by a non-zero digit followed by digits. Hexadecimal format is indicated by the characters 0x or 0X in front of a sequence of digits, uppercase letters ranging from A through F and lowercase letters ranging from a through f. Octal format is indicated by a zero digit followed by digits that range from 0 through 7.

EXAMPLE

The following example illustrates integer literals:

659L   A decimal integer literal of data type long.

0x4a   A hexadecimal integer literal of data type int.

0571   An octal integer literal of data type long.

STRING LITERALS

A string literal consists of zero or more characters surrounded by double quote (") characters.

EXAMPLE

The following example illustrates string literals:

`"This is a string literal."`

A string literal without characters is an *empty string*, as follows:

`" "`

THE NULL LITERAL

A null reference literal consists of the `null` reserved word.

The following example illustrates null reference literals:

`null`

EXAMPLE

Variables

Data items are stored in memory locations that are symbolically identified by name. These memory locations are known as *variables* because their contents can vary while a program runs. Variables can be classified as either simple variables or array variables.

Simple Variables

A memory location that holds a single data item at any one time is known as a *simple variable*.

DECLARATION

Simple variables must be declared before they are used. The format of a simple variable declaration is

`data_type identifier ';'`

where

`data_type` is either

- A primitive data type (specified by using the `boolean`, `byte`, `char`, `double`, `float`, `int`, `long`, or `short` reserved words)
- A reference data type

and

`identifier` is the simple variable's name.

CAUTION

Reserved words cannot be used as simple variable names.

INITIALIZATION

If a simple variable is not explicitly initialized, it will either be initialized to a default value (based upon the variable's data type) if the variable is used as a field variable (discussed in Chapter 4) or not initialized to a default value if the variable is used as a local variable (also discussed in Chapter 4). Table 2.2 lists the default values for field variables.

Table 2.2: Default Values for Field Variables

Data Type	Default Value
boolean	`false`
char	`'\u0000'`
byte	`0`
short	`0`
int	`0`
long	`0l`
float	`0.0f`
double	`0.0d`
String	`null`
reference	`null`

Simple variables can be explicitly initialized when they are declared.

The format of a simple variable declaration with explicit initialization is

`data_type identifier '=' expression ';'`

The assignment operator = is followed by an *expression* that must evaluate to a value whose data type matches `data_type`.

CAUTION

Boolean variables can only be assigned expressions that evaluate to the boolean data type.

Figure 2.1 illustrates simple variable declaration and initialization.

`int x = 65;`

4 bytes

Figure 2.1: *Declaring and initializing a simple variable.*

Each simple variable is given a unit of storage. The size of this storage is based upon the size of the variable's data type.

The following code fragment illustrates a variety of simple variable declarations and default/explicit initializations:

```
int x;
double rate = 4.5;
boolean first;
char grade_letter;
String name = "Dauphin";
```

Multiple simple variables can be specified within the same declaration by separating variable names with commas. Although each variable has its own name, all these variables share the same data type.

The following code illustrates declaration and initialization of multiple simple variables:

```
// Declare int variables x and y.  The x variable will be
// initialized to the default value 0.  The variable y will
// be explicitly initialized to 65.

int x, y = 65;

// Declare String variables country, province, and city.
// The country variable is initialized to Canada.  The
// province and city variables are initialized to the
// default null values.

String country = "Canada", province, city;
```

Array Variables

A memory location that references a contiguous sequence of memory locations (known as *array elements*), where each array element holds a single data item, is known as an *array variable*. All array elements share the same data type.

DECLARATION

Like simple variables, array variables must be declared before they are used.

The format of an array variable declaration is

data_type identifier '[' ']' ';'

or

data_type '[' ']' *identifier* ';'

where

data_type is either

- A primitive data type (specified by using the `boolean`, `byte`, `char`, `double`, `float`, `int`, `long`, or `short` reserved words)
- A reference data type

and

identifier is the array variable's name.

CAUTION
Reserved words cannot be used as array variable names.

---

identifier is either followed or preceded by square brackets (`[]`) to distinguish an array variable from a simple variable.

Array variables contain a reference to (that is, the address of) a sequence of storage locations that will hold the array's data items. Initially, this reference is null.

INITIALIZATION

Array variables need to be initialized before they can be used.

The format of an array variable declaration with explicit initialization is

```
data_type identifier '[' ']' '=' '{' expression ',' … ',' expression '}' ';'
```

or

```
data_type '[' ']' identifier '=' '{' expression ',' … ',' expression '}' ';'
```

The assignment operator = is followed by a comma-separated list of *expression*s (surrounded by brace (`{}`) characters). Each *expression* must evaluate to a value whose data type matches *data_type*.

Figure 2.2 illustrates array variable declaration and initialization.

```
int x [] = { 32, 56, -16 };
```

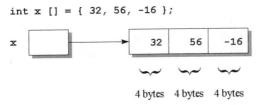

Figure 2.2: Declaring and initializing an array variable.

EXAMPLE

The following code fragment illustrates array variable declaration and initialization:

```
int x [] = { 45, 23, 32 };
```

Due to the dynamic nature of Java arrays, you cannot specify the number of elements between square brackets. For example, the following code fragment would result in a compiler error:

```
int x [3] = { 45, 23, 32 };
```

INDEXING

Array elements are *indexed* (accessed) by using an operator known as the index or subscript operator.

The index operator accesses an array element by specifying its numerical position within the array. (Numerical positions are integers.) The very first array element is located at position 0 and successive array elements are located at positions 1, 2, 3, and so on.

EXAMPLE

The following code fragment illustrates indexing:

```
int x [] = { 45, 23, 32 };
int i = x [1];
```

THE length PROPERTY

Arrays have a property that returns the size of the array (that is, the number of memory locations occupied by the array). This property is called length.

The format of specifying length is

```
identifier '.' length
```

where

identifier is the name of the array

and

a period (.) character separates the array name from the word length. This format can be interpreted as "fetch the value of the length property of the *identifier* array."

EXAMPLE

The following code fragment illustrates the `length` property:

```
String [] presidents = { "Washington", "Lincoln" };
int len = presidents.length;
```

Naming Variables

Variables can be named with any legal Java identifier that is not a reserved word.

Descriptive names should be chosen to identify variables. Some of these names might consist of multiple words.

There are two conventions for naming variables that consist of multiple words: using underscore characters to separate words (for example, `grade_letters`) and capitalizing the first letter of each word, except for the first word (for example, `gradeLetters`).

How you go about naming your variables is up to you, but be consistent, especially if somebody else will be reading your source code at a later date.

What's Next?

Now that you understand some simple language concepts (such as data types and variables), you need to learn how to make use of these concepts. For example, how do you combine literals and variables with operators to form expressions that produce new values? And how do you specify repetitive code, decisive code, and so on? The next chapter will clear up these mysteries.

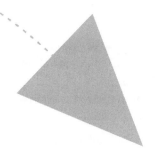

Operators, Expressions, and Statements

In the previous chapter, you started to explore the basics of the Java computer language. Specifically, you touched on the concepts of character sets, comments, identifiers, reserved words, data types, literals, and variables.

You still haven't gotten to the point where you can write Java programs. However, by the end of this chapter, you will have enough knowledge (with a small "nugget" of help in the form of a main method) to write a useful program that converts between Metric and non-Metric quantities.

Chapter 3 presents the following topics:

- Operators
- Expressions
- Mathematics
- Blocks
- Statements
- METRIX

Operators

Computer languages use operators to transform data items (known as *operands*) into new data items. For example, multiplying two numeric operands results in a new data item that represents the product of these operands.

Operators evaluate their operands according to a predefined evaluation order. For example, the division operator (/) evaluates its left-most operand before its right-most operand. As a second example, the post-increment operator (++) evaluates its operand before incrementing the operand while the pre-increment operator (++) increments its operand before evaluating the operand.

Unary, Binary, and Ternary Operators

Operators can be classified by the number of operands they require. These classifications include unary, binary, and ternary.

A unary operator transforms only one operand. The post-increment operator (++) is an example of a unary operator.

A binary operator transforms two operands. The addition operator (+) is an example of a binary operator.

A ternary operator transforms three operands. The conditional operator (?:) is an example of a ternary operator. (Incidentally, the conditional operator is the only ternary operator in Java's suite of operators.)

Prefix, Postfix, and Infix Operators

Operators also can be classified by where their operands are positioned, relative to the operator. These classifications include prefix, postfix, and infix.

A prefix operator is positioned before its operand. The negation operator (-) is an example of a prefix operator (such as -6).

A postfix operator is positioned after its operand. The post-increment operator (++) is an example of a postfix operator (such as count++).

An infix operator is positioned between its operands. The addition operator (+) is an example of an infix operator (such as total + 6).

Arithmetic Operators

The arithmetic operators perform various arithmetic operations on their operands. Each operator returns a value that contains the result.

ADDITION

The addition operator (+), a binary infix operator, adds two operands to produce a new value. Each operand must have a data type that is one of byte, char, double, float, int, long, or short.

The format of this operator is

```
operand1 '+' operand2
```

EXAMPLE

The following code fragment illustrates the addition operator:

```
int total = 0;
total = total + 79;

// total equals 79
```

SUBTRACTION

The subtraction operator (-), a binary infix operator, subtracts one operand from another operand to produce a new value. Each operand must have a data type that is one of byte, char, double, float, int, long, or short.

The format of this operator is

```
operand1 '-' operand2
```

operand2 is subtracted from *operand1*.

EXAMPLE

The following code fragment illustrates the subtraction operator:

```
int numItems = 63;
numItems = numItems - 1;

// numItems equals 62
```

MULTIPLICATION

The multiplication operator (*), a binary infix operator, multiplies two operands to produce a new value. Each operand must have a data type that is one of byte, char, double, float, int, long, or short.

The format of this operator is

```
operand1 '*' operand2
```

EXAMPLE

The following code fragment illustrates the multiplication operator:

```
double monthlyInterestRate = 0.005;
double accountBalance = 39568.0;
double interest = accountBalance * monthlyInterestRate;

// interest equals 197.84
```

DIVISION

The division operator (/), a binary infix operator, divides one operand by another operand to produce a new value. Each operand must have a data type that is one of byte, char, double, float, int, long, or short.

The format of this operator is

```
operand1 '/' operand2
```

operand1 is divided by *operand2*.

EXAMPLE

The following code fragment illustrates the division operator:

```
double total = 211.0;
double count = 5;
double average = total / count;

// average equals 42.2
```

If the denominator has the float or double data type and is equal to `0.0`, the division will result in a special value of either positive infinity or negative infinity (depending upon whether the numerator is positive or negative).

CAUTION

If the denominator is zero and both operands are of an integer type (such as byte, short, int, or long), the virtual machine throws an exception of data type ArithmeticException.

✔ To learn more about ArithmeticException, see Chapter 8, "Exception Handling," page 185.

MODULUS

The modulus operator (%), a binary infix operator, divides one integer operand by another integer operand and returns the remainder of the division. Each operand must have a data type that is one of byte, char, int, long, or short.

The format of this operator is

operand1 '%' *operand2*

EXAMPLE

The following code fragment illustrates the modulus operator:

```
int rem = 65 % 2;

// rem equals 1
```

CAUTION

If the denominator is zero, the virtual machine throws an exception of data type ArithmeticException.

POST-INCREMENT AND PRE-INCREMENT

The post-increment operator (++), a unary postfix operator, adds 1 to its integer operand. Before the increment is performed, the value of the operand is returned. The operand must have a data type that is one of byte, char, double, float, int, long, or short, and must not be a literal.

The format of this operator is

```
operand '++'
```

The pre-increment operator (++), a unary prefix operator, adds 1 to its integer operand. The value of the operand is returned after the increment is performed. The operand must have a data type that is one of byte, char, double, float, int, long, or short, and must not be a literal.

The format of this operator is

```
'++' operand
```

EXAMPLE

The following code fragment illustrates the postincrement and preincrement operators:

```
int count = 10;
int pre = ++count;    // pre equals 11
int post = count++; // post equals 11

// count equals 12
```

POST-DECREMENT AND PRE-DECREMENT

The post-decrement operator (- -), a unary postfix operator, subtracts 1 from its integer operand. Before the decrement is performed, the value of the operand is returned. The operand must have a data type that is one of byte, char, double, float, int, long, or short, and must not be a literal.

The format of this operator is

```
operand '--'
```

The pre-decrement operator (- -), a unary prefix operator, subtracts 1 from its integer operand. The value of the operand is returned after the decrement is performed. The operand must have a data type that is one of byte, char, double, float, int, long, or short, and must not be a literal.

The format of this operator is

```
'--' operand
```

EXAMPLE

The following code fragment illustrates the post-decrement and pre-decrement operators:

```
int count = 10;
int pre = --count;    // pre equals 9
int post = count--; // post equals 9

// count equals 8
```

UNARY MINUS AND UNARY PLUS

The unary minus operator (-), a unary prefix operator, negates the value of its operand. Negative operands are converted to positive operands and vice versa. The operand must have a data type that is one of byte, char, double, float, int, long, or short.

The format of this operator is

```
'-' operand
```

The unary plus operator (+), a unary prefix operator, doesn't do anything. (It is included for completeness.) The operand must have a data type that is one of byte, char, double, float, int, long, or short.

The format of this operator is

```
'+' operand
```

EXAMPLE

The following code fragment illustrates the unary plus and unary minus operators:

```
int w = 7;
int x = 3 - -w;
int y = w - +x;

// x equals 10
// y equals -3
```

Array Index Operator

The array index operator ([ ]), a unary operator, is used to access an array element and return its value.

The format of this operator is

```
identifier '[' operand ']'
```

identifier specifies the name of the array.

operand specifies an integer offset within this array. This offset is relative to zero because the first element in an array is always located at offset zero. *operand* must have a data type that is one of byte, char, int, long, or short.

EXAMPLE

The following code fragment illustrates the array index operator:

```
// Create an array variable that is composed of three int
// elements and assign integer literals 45, 23, and 32 to
// these elements.

int x [] = { 45, 23, 32 };

// Access the second element within the array by specifying
// the integer 1 with the [] index operator.  The value of
// this element will be assigned to int variable i.

int i = x [1];

// i equals 23
```

Assignment Operator

The assignment operator (=), a binary infix operator, assigns an operand to a variable.

The format of this operator is

```
identifier '=' operand;
```

identifier specifies the name of the variable.

The following code fragment illustrates the assignment operator:

```
boolean first;
first = true;
```

EXAMPLE

Bit Manipulation Operators

The bit manipulation operators manipulate the binary digits (bits) of their integer operands. Each operator returns a value that consists of the resulting binary digits.

BITWISE AND

The bitwise AND operator (&), a binary infix operator, compares its integer operands by comparing respective bit positions. If both bits are equal to 1 then the result bit is 1; otherwise, the result bit is 0. Each operand must have a data type that is one of byte, char, int, long, or short.

The format of this operator is

```
operand1 '&' operand2
```

The following code fragment illustrates the bitwise AND operator:

```
short x = 13 & 3;

// x equals 1
```

EXAMPLE

BITWISE INCLUSIVE OR

The bitwise inclusive OR operator (¦), a binary infix operator, compares its integer operands by comparing respective bit positions. If both bits are equal to 0 then the result bit is 0; otherwise, the result bit is 1. Each operand must have a data type that is one of byte, char, int, long, or short.

The format of this operator is

```
operand1 '¦' operand2
```

The following code fragment illustrates the bitwise inclusive OR operator:

```
short x = 13 ¦ 3;

// x equals 15
```

EXAMPLE

BITWISE EXCLUSIVE OR

The bitwise exclusive OR operator (^), a binary infix operator, compares its integer operands by comparing respective bit positions. If one bit is equal to 0 and the other bit is equal to 1 then the result bit is 1; otherwise, the result bit is 0. Each operand must have a data type that is one of byte, char, int, long, or short.

The format of this operator is

```
operand1 '^' operand2
```

The following code fragment illustrates the bitwise exclusive OR operator:

```
short x = 13 ^ 3;

// x equals 14
```

EXAMPLE

BITWISE SHIFT LEFT

The bitwise shift left operator (<<), a binary infix operator, shifts the bits in the left-most operand left by the number of bit positions specified in the right-most operand. For each shift left, a 0 bit is shifted into the right-most bit.

The format of this operator is

```
operand1 '<<' operand2
```

The following code fragment illustrates the bitwise shift left operator:

```
int x = -1 << 1;

// x equals -2
```

EXAMPLE

BITWISE SHIFT RIGHT WITH SIGN EXTENSION

The bitwise shift right with sign extension operator (>>), a binary infix operator, shifts the bits in the left-most operand right by the number of bit positions specified in the right-most operand. For each shift right, the left-most bit (the sign bit) is copied right. If this bit is 0, a 0 is copied one bit position to the right. If this bit is 1, a 1 is copied one bit position to the right.

The format of this operator is

```
operand1 '>>' operand2
```

The following code fragment illustrates the bitwise shift right with sign extension operator:

```
int x = -1 >> 1;

// x equals -1
```

EXAMPLE

Bitwise Shift Right with Zero Extension

The bitwise shift right with zero extension operator (>>>), a binary infix operator, shifts the left-most operand right by the number of bit positions specified in the right-most operand. For each shift right, a 0 bit is shifted into the left-most bit.

The format of this operator is

```
operand1 '>>>' operand2
```

The following code fragment illustrates the bitwise shift right with zero extension operator:

```
int x = -1 >>> 1;

// x equals 2147483647
```

EXAMPLE

Bitwise Complement

The bitwise complement operator (~), a unary prefix operator, toggles its operand's bit values (that is, 1s are converted to 0s, and 0s are converted to 1s).

The format of this operator is

```
'~' operand
```

The following code fragment illustrates the bitwise complement operator:

```
int x = -1;
x = ~x;

// x equals 0
```

EXAMPLE

Boolean Operators

The Boolean operators perform logical (that is to say true or false) operations on their Boolean operands. Each operator returns either a true or false value.

Boolean AND

The Boolean AND operator (&), a binary infix operator, performs a Boolean AND operation on its Boolean operands. Both operands are examined to see if they are true. If this is the case, the Boolean AND operator returns the Boolean true value. Otherwise, this operator returns the Boolean false value.

The format of this operator is

```
operand1 '&' operand2
```

EXAMPLE

The following code fragment illustrates the Boolean AND operator:

```
boolean x = true;
boolean y = false;
boolean result = x & y;

// result equals false
```

Boolean Inclusive OR

The Boolean inclusive OR operator (¦), a binary infix operator, performs a Boolean inclusive OR operation on its Boolean operands. Both operands are examined to see if they are false. If this is the case, the Boolean OR operator returns the Boolean `false` value. Otherwise, this operator returns the Boolean `true` value.

The format of this operator is

operand1 '¦' *operand2*

EXAMPLE

The following code fragment illustrates the Boolean inclusive OR operator:

```
boolean x = true;
boolean y = false;
boolean result = x ¦ y;

// result equals true
```

Boolean Exclusive OR

The Boolean exclusive OR operator (^), a binary infix operator, performs a Boolean exclusive OR operation on its Boolean operands. Both operands are examined to see if one of them is true while the other is false. If this is the case, the Boolean exclusive OR operator returns the Boolean `true` value. Otherwise, this operator returns the Boolean `false` value.

The format of this operator is

operand1 '^' *operand2*

EXAMPLE

The following code fragment illustrates the Boolean exclusive OR operator:

```
boolean x = true;
boolean y = false;
boolean result = x ^ y;

// result equals true;
```

Boolean NOT

The Boolean NOT operator (!), a unary prefix operator, performs a Boolean NOT operation on its Boolean operand. If the operand has the Boolean value `true`, this operator returns the Boolean value `false`. Otherwise, if this operand has the Boolean value `false`, this operator returns the Boolean value `true`.

The format of this operator is

```
'!' operand
```

EXAMPLE

The following code fragment illustrates the Boolean NOT operator:

```
boolean x = true;
boolean result = !x

// result equals false
```

Cast Operator

The cast operator ('(' data_type ')'), a unary prefix operator, converts the data type of its operand to another data type. Casting is used to demote one data type to another data type (that is to say, to convert a higher-precision value to a lower-precision value).

The format of this operator is

```
'(' data_type ')' operand
```

EXAMPLE

The following code fragment illustrates the cast operator:

```
int i = 3;
short x = (short) i;

// The 32-bit int value I is converted to the 16-bit short
// value x by chopping off the upper 16 bits of i.  Since
// those bits contain 0s, x also equals 3 after the
// conversion.
```

Conditional Operator

The conditional operator (?:), a ternary operator, evaluates a Boolean operand and, if this operand is true, returns the value of the operand after the ? character. Otherwise, it returns the value of the operand after the : character.

The format of this operator is

```
'(' operand1 ')' '?' operand2 ':' operand3
```

If operand1 evaluates to the Boolean value true, evaluate operand2 and return its value. If operand1 evaluates to the Boolean value false, evaluate operand3, and return its value.

CAUTION

The operands following the ? and : characters must have the same data types; otherwise, a compiler error occurs.

EXAMPLE

The following code fragment illustrates the conditional operator:

```
Boolean first = true;
String name = (first) ? "first" : "second";

// name equals "first"
```

Logical Operators

The logical operators perform logical operations on their Boolean operands. Although logical AND is similar to Boolean AND and logical OR is similar to Boolean inclusive OR, there is one difference.

The Boolean AND and Boolean inclusive OR operators evaluate both operands before returning a result, while the logical AND and logical OR operators might not evaluate the right-most operand.

SHORT CIRCUITING AND SIDE EFFECTS

Sometimes, it isn't necessary to evaluate both operands. For example, if the left-most operand is false and a Boolean AND operator is being used, why evaluate the right-most operand because the entire expression will evaluate to false? As a second example, if the left-most operand is true and a Boolean inclusive OR operator is being used, why evaluate the right-most operand because the entire expression will evaluate to true?

The logical AND operator does not evaluate the right-most operand if the left-most operand is false.

The logical OR operator does not evaluate the right-most operand if the left-most operand is true.

The technique of not always evaluating the right-most operand is known as *short-circuiting* and can improve performance by not executing code that doesn't need to be executed.

However, there is a problem with short-circuiting and that problem is known as the side effect problem, which is extraneous code that is executed during the evaluation of an operand.

EXAMPLE

The following code fragment illustrates a side effect (incrementing age) with the Boolean inclusive OR operator:

```
int age = 64;
boolean obtainPension = true | ++age > 64;

// age equals 65
```

EXAMPLE

The following code fragment illustrates a side effect (incrementing age) with the logical OR operator:

```
int age = 64;
boolean obtainPension = true || ++age > 64;
```

```
// age equals 64
```

In the first example, the age variable is incremented to 65, but in the second example, the age variable is not incremented. Depending upon the original program design guidelines, this could be a bug.

CAUTION

Avoid using the logical AND and the logical OR operators in expressions that have side effects because this can be the source of subtle and hard-to-find bugs.

LOGICAL AND

The logical AND operator (&&), a binary infix operator, evaluates the left-most operand to see if it is false. If false, evaluation ceases and the result is `false`. If the left-most operand is true, this operator evaluates the right-most operand. If that operand is false, the result is `false`. If that operand is true, the result is `true`. In other words, the result is `true` if both operands are true; otherwise, the result is `false`.

The format of this operator is

operand1 '&&' *operand2*

EXAMPLE

The following code fragment illustrates the logical AND operator:

```
boolean x = true;
boolean y = false;
boolean result = x && y;
```

```
// result equals false
```

LOGICAL OR

The logical OR operator (||), a binary infix operator, evaluates the left-most operand to see if it is true. If true, evaluation ceases and the result is `true`. If the left-most operand is false, this operator evaluates the right-most operand. If that operand is true, the result is `true`. If that operand is false, the result is `false`. In other words, the result is false if both operands are `false`; otherwise, the result is `true`.

The format of this operator is

operand1 '||' *operand2*

The following code fragment illustrates the logical OR operator:

```
boolean x = true;
boolean y = false;
boolean result = x || y;

// result equals true
```

Reference Data Type Checking Operator

The reference data type checking operator (`instanceof`), a binary infix operator, determines if an object is an instance of a class. A `true` value is returned if the object is an instance. Otherwise, a `false` value is returned.

The format of this operator is

```
object_identifier 'instanceof' class_identifier
```

object_identifier is the name of an object.

class_identifier is the name of a class.

The following code fragment illustrates the reference data type checking operator:

```
String s = "abc";
boolean result = s instanceof String;

// result equals true
```

Relational Operators

The relational operators determine the relative positions of their operands (on a numeric basis). These operators return Boolean `true` or `false` values.

LESS THAN

The less than operator (`<`), a binary infix operator, determines if its left-most operand is numerically less than its right-most operand. A Boolean true value is returned if this is the case.

The format of this operator is

```
operand1 '<' operand2
```

EXAMPLE

The following code fragment illustrates the less than operator:

```
int i = 6;
boolean result = i < 10;

// result equals true
```

Less Than or Equal To

The less than or equal to operator (<=), a binary infix operator, determines if its left-most operand is numerically less than or equal to its right-most operand. A Boolean `true` value is returned if this is the case.

The format of this operator is

operand1 `'<='` *operand2*

EXAMPLE

The following code fragment illustrates the less than or equal to operator:

```
int i = 6;
boolean result = i <= 10;

// result equals true
```

Greater Than

The greater than operator (>), a binary infix operator, determines if its left-most operand is numerically greater than its right-most operand. A Boolean `true` value is returned if this is the case.

The format of this operator is

operand1 `'>'` *operand2*

EXAMPLE

The following code fragment illustrates the greater than operator:

```
int i = 6;
boolean result = i > 10;

// result equals false
```

Greater Than or Equal To

The greater than or equal to operator (>=), a binary infix operator, determines if its left-most operand is numerically greater than or equal to its right-most operand. A Boolean `true` value is returned if this is the case.

The format of this operator is

operand1 `'>='` *operand2*

EXAMPLE

The following code fragment illustrates the greater than or equal to operator:

```
int i = 6;
boolean result = i >= 10;

// result equals false
```

Equal To

The equal to operator (==), a binary infix operator, determines if both operands are numerically equal. A Boolean `true` value is returned if this is the case.

The format of this operator is

```
operand1 '==' operand2
```

The following code fragment illustrates the equal to operator:

```
int i = 6;
boolean result = i == 10;

// result equals false
```

EXAMPLE

NOT EQUAL TO

The not equal to operator (!=), a binary infix operator, determines if both operands are numerically unequal. A Boolean `true` value is returned if this is the case.

The format of this operator is

```
operand1 '!=' operand2
```

The following code fragment illustrates the not equal to operator:

```
int i = 6;
boolean result = i != 10;

// result equals true
```

EXAMPLE

String Concatenation Operator

The string concatenation operator (+), a binary infix operator, concatenates its right-most `String` operand to its left-most `String` operand. If the right-most `String` operand is not a `String`, it is converted to a `String` before concatenation occurs.

The format of this operator is

```
operand1 '+' operand2
```

The following code fragment illustrates the string concatenation operator:

```
String one = "abc";
one = one + "def";

// one equals "abcdef"
```

EXAMPLE

Expressions

Developers create expressions out of one or more operators and their required numbers of operands. The JVM evaluates an expression and returns its value, which has a specific data type.

An expression is evaluated in such a manner that certain operators get to evaluate their operands before other operators. This is known as *precedence*. For example, the multiplication operator has a higher precedence than the addition operator because it is natural to perform multiplication before addition.

EXAMPLE

The following code fragment illustrates the precedence of an expression's operators:

```
int i = 8 + 3 * 2;

// i equals 14;
```

The multiplication operator gets first crack. It multiplies the 3 and 2 to produce 6 as a product. The addition operator is then allowed to add this 6 to the 8, producing a final value of 14.

Sometimes, it is not desirable to have a higher precedence operator evaluate before a lower precedence operator. In these cases, the parentheses characters (( )) are used to modify precedence. Placing part of an expression between parentheses causes that part to be evaluated before the rest of the expression. Furthermore, multiple parentheses can be nested inside of each other to further control evaluation order.

EXAMPLE

The following code fragment illustrates overriding the precedence of an expression's operators:

```
int i = (8 + 3) * 2;

// i equals 22;
```

The tables are turned! Because of the placement of the parenthesis operator, the addition operator is evaluated first.

✔ For a listing of Java's 47 operators, their precedence, and evaluation orders, see Appendix B, "Operator Precedence," page 505.

Mathematics

As you've just seen, Java supplies a variety of operators for performing various arithmetic operations. Of these operators, the division operator can generate some surprising results when used to divide floating-point values. These results are known as the IEEE 754 special values.

IEEE 754 Special Values

Back in the mid 1980s, the Institute for Electrical Engineering and Electronics (IEEE) released a standard that precisely describes the internal format of floating-point numbers. This standard also describes the ways in which floating-point operations are carried out.

What happens when an attempt is made to divide a positive floating-point number by zero, a negative number by zero, or even zero by zero? With the IEEE 754 standard, there is no guessing. Believe it or not, these floating-point operations are allowed to continue. However, the resulting values are treated as special floating-point values.

If you attempt to divide a positive floating-point number by zero, a special value is returned that is recognized as +Infinity. Conversely, if you attempt to divide a negative floating-point number by zero, -Infinity is returned. Finally, any attempt to divide zero by zero results in the return of a value recognized as NaN (Not a Number).

The +Infinity, -Infinity, and NaN character sequences are displayed if you try to call a System.out.println method to display the result of one of the aforementioned floating-point operations. For example, the following code fragment does just this:

```
System.out.println (1.0 / 0.0); // Outputs +Infinity
System.out.println (-1.0 / 0.0); // Outputs -Infinity
System.out.println (0.0 / 0.0); // Outputs NaN
```

On the other hand, if both of the division operator's operands are integers, an ArithmeticException object is thrown.

Precision

Some floating-point values (such as 1/3) require an infinite number of bits to be stored exactly. This is not possible on a computer with finite storage. Because all values must be stored using a finite number of bits, some loss of precision is bound to occur. This loss increases as calculations are performed. Sooner or later, you'll notice this loss as you use Java (or any other programming language) to perform floating-point calculations. With the exception of numerically intensive scientific software, you will probably never have to deal with this issue. (Dealing with loss of precision is the subject of university-level numerical analysis courses.)

The Math Class

I'm going to "jump the gun" on Chapter 4, "Encapsulation: Classes and Objects," by briefly introducing you to Java's Math class. This class provides what are known as class methods that you can call to perform a variety of mathematical operations.

You will find methods for performing trigonometry, calculating the square root of a number, determining the absolute value of a number, generating random numbers, and so on. Some of these methods will be used in later chapters.

In addition to these methods, Math provides a pair of read-only variables that represent the mathematical values of PI and the natural logarithm E. (The concept of a read-only variable is discussed in the next chapter.)

Because Math is a class and classes have not yet been discussed, no more will be said about Math in this chapter.

Blocks

When you write Java code, you'll often find yourself placing this code between a pair of brace characters ({}). These characters delimit what is known as a *block* (that is to say, a block of code).

There are different kinds of blocks. For example, a class block consists of field variable and method declarations, whereas a method block consists of statements. (You'll learn more about class blocks and method blocks in the next chapter.) However, there is a third kind of block known as a *statement block*. This block is used when describing statements.

A statement block identifies a region of source code that serves as the body of decision statements or loop statements. A statement block can consist of a single statement that is not surrounded by braces, or it can consist of zero or more statements surrounded by braces (although it is common to place two or more statements between braces).

You can nest statement blocks within statement blocks and create really complex statements.

EXAMPLE

The following code fragment illustrates a simple block:

```
// The following block computes the area of a circle.

{
    double PI = 3.14159;
    double radius = 25.5;
    double area = PI * radius * radius;
}
```

You can declare variables within statement blocks. As a rule, variables declared within an outer statement block are visible to code within inner statement blocks. But if an inner statement block declares a variable with the same name as a variable declared within an outer statement block, the variable within the inner statement block is said to hide the variable within the outer statement block. The visibility of variables declared within statement blocks is known as *scope*.

More will be said about statement blocks when statements are discussed.

Statements

Developers use statements to specify standalone units of executable code. Statements make it possible to declare variables, assign an evaluated expression's result to a variable of the same data type as the expression, iterate over a group of statements, make decisions, return from a method, and so on.

Decision statements and loop statements typically consist of a header followed by a statement block. The header, in the case of a decision statement, determines whether or not a statement block is executed. In the case of a loop statement, the header keeps track of the next loop iteration.

Assignment

The Assignment statement assigns a value to a variable.

The format of the Assignment statement is

```
identifier '=' expression ';'
```

identifier is the name of the variable.

expression is evaluated to obtain the variable's value. This value must be of a data type that matches *identifier*'s data type. (However, if *expression*'s data type occupies more bits than *identifier*'s data type, the cast operator, as discussed in Chapter 2, "Data Types, Literals, and Variables," is required.)

EXAMPLE

The following code fragment illustrates the Assignment statement:

```
short s;

// The value 300000 is interpreted as an int.  This value occupies four bytes.
// However, a short can only accommodate two bytes.  Therefore, some information
// will be lost when assigning 30000 to the short variable.  This means that a
// (short) cast operator is required.

s = (short) 300000;
```

Break

The Break statement exits from a Do-while loop statement block, a For loop statement block, a Switch statement block, or a While loop statement block.

The format of the Break statement is

```
"break" [label] ';'
```

label specifies where execution should proceed when dealing with nested loops (such as loops within loops) or Switch statements.

EXAMPLE

The following code fragment illustrates the Break statement being used to exit from a For loop statement block:

```
// Print the values of I from 0 through 5.

for (int i = 0; i < 10; i++)
{
    if (i >= 5)
        break;
    else
```

```
        System.out.println (i);
}
```

The following code fragment illustrates the Break label statement:

```
// Print the values of I from 0 through 0.  For each value
// of I, print the values of J from 0 through 1.

outer_for:     // A colon character must follow a label.

for (int i = 0; i < 4; i++)
    for (int j = 0; j < 4; j++)
        if (j == 2)
            break outer_for;
        else
            System.out.println ("i = " + i + ",j = " + j);
```

Continue

The Continue statement terminates the current iteration of a loop and continues with the next iteration of either the current loop or a labeled loop.

The format of the Continue statement is

```
"continue" [label] ';'
```

label specifies where execution should proceed when dealing with nested loops.

EXAMPLE

The following code fragment illustrates the Continue statement:

```
// Print the values of I from 0 through 5.

for (int i = 0; i < 10; i++)
    if (i > 5)
        continue;
    else
        System.out.println (i);
```

The following code fragment illustrates the Continue label statement:

```
// Print the values of I from 0 through 3.  For each value
// of I, print the values of J from 0 through 1.

outer_for:     // A colon character must follow a label.

for (int i = 0; i < 4; i++)
    for (int j = 0; j < 4; j++)
        if (j == 2)
            continue outer_for;
        else
            System.out.println ("i = " + i + ",j = " + j);
```

Do-while Loop

The Do-while loop statement iterates over a statement block, while a Boolean expression evaluates to true.

The format of the Do-while loop statement is

```
"do"
    statement_block
"while" '(' test_expr ')' ';'
```

This loop always iterates at least once because *test_expr* is evaluated at the bottom of the loop, after the block of statements have executed.

EXAMPLE

The following code fragment illustrates the Do-while loop statement:

```
int i = 0;

// Print the values of i from 0 through 9.

do
{
    System.out.println (i);
    i = i + 1;
}
while (i < 10);
```

For Loop

The For loop statement iterates over a statement block a specific number of times.

The format of the For loop statement is

```
"for" '(' init_expr_list ';' test_expr ';' advance_expr_list ')'
        statement_block
```

init_expr_list is a comma-delimited list of initialization expressions. Simple variables that are restricted to the context of the For loop statement can be declared within *init_expr_list*.

test_expr is an expression that is evaluated each time through the loop. If it evaluates to false, the loop exits.

advance_expr_list is a comma-delimited list of expressions that are used to advance variable values as the loop progresses.

EXAMPLE

The following code fragment illustrates the For loop statement:

```
// Print the values of i from 0 through 9.

for (int i = 0; i < 10; i++)
        System.out.println (i);
```

If

The If decision statement makes simple decisions.

The format of the If decision statement is

```
"if" '(' expression ')'
    statement_block
```

expression evaluates to either true or false. If true, *statement_block* is executed.

EXAMPLE

The following code fragment illustrates the If decision statement:

```
int bonus = 30;
int count = 550;

if (count > 500)
    count += bonus;

// count equals 580
```

If-else

The If-else decision statement makes two-way decisions.

The format of the If-else decision statement is

```
"if" '(' expression ')'
    statement_block1
"else"
    statement_block2
```

expression evaluates to either true or false. If true, *statement_block1* is executed. If false, *statement_block2* is executed.

EXAMPLE

The following code fragment illustrates the If-else decision statement:

```
char grade_letter = 'A';

if (grade_letter == 'A')
    System.out.println ("Congratulations");
else
    System.out.println ("Better luck next time.");

// Congratulations is output.
```

Nested If

The Nested If decision statement makes multi-way decisions.

The format of the Nested If decision statement is

```
"if" '(' expression1 ')'
    statement_block1
```

```
"else" "if" '(' expression2 ')'
    statement_block2
"else" "if" '(' expressionN ')'
    statement_blockN
"else"
    default_statement_block
```

expression1 is evaluated. If true, *statement_block1* is executed. If false, *expression2* is evaluated. If true, *statement_block2* is executed. If false, *expressionN* is evaluated. If true, *statement_blockN* is executed. If false, *default_statement_block* is executed.

The following code fragment illustrates the Nested If decision statement:

```
int toolCode = 3;

if (toolCode == 0)
{
    System.out.println ("Screwdriver");
    int quantity = 65;
    // Do something with quanity.
}
else if (toolCode == 1)
    System.out.println ("Hammer");
else
    System.out.println ("Unknown tool");
```

Return

The Return statement returns control from a called method to the calling method.

The format of the Return statement is

```
"return" [ expression ] ';'
```

Methods and the Return statement are discussed in Chapter 4.

Switch

The Switch decision statement makes multi-way decisions by comparing a specific integer value (not a `true` or `false` value) to multiple cases. As soon as there is a match, the block of code associated with a case is executed.

The format of the Switch decision statement is

```
"switch" '(' expression ')'
'{'
    "case" value1 ':'
        statement_block1
        "break" ';'
    "case" value2 ':'
```

```
              statement_block2
              "break" ';'
      "case" valueN ':'
              statement_blockN
              "break" ';'
    [ "default" ':'
              default_statement_block ']'
    '}'
```

expression is evaluated. (This expression must have a byte, char, int, long, or short data type.) If the integer value matches *value1*, *statement_block1* is executed. If the integer value matches *value2*, *statement_block2* is executed. If the integer value matches *valueN*, *statement_blockN* is executed. If neither value matches and the Switch decision statement provides a default, *default_statement_block* is executed.

EXAMPLE

The following code fragment illustrates the Switch decision statement:

```
char grade_letter = 'A';

switch (grade_letter)
{
    case 'A': System.out.println ("You're a genius!");
            break;
    case 'B': System.out.println ("Congratulations!");
            break;
    case 'C': System.out.println ("Not too bad!");
}

// You're a genius! is output.
```

The break reserved word identifies a Break statement. This statement is used to break out of the Switch statement block. Without this statement, execution would fall through to the next case and execute that code.

Throw

The Throw statement throws an object that describes an exception to the JVM. (The Throw statement is discussed in Chapter 8, "Exception Handling.")

Variable Declaration

The Variable declaration statement declares a variable and optionally assigns a value to the variable. Variable declaration statements were used in Chapter 2 to initialize simple variables and array variables.

While Loop

The While loop statement iterates over a statement block while an expression is true. This statement differs from the Do-while loop statement in that the While loop statement tests the expression at the top of the loop whereas the Do-while loop statement tests the expression at the bottom of the loop.

The format of the While loop statement is

```
"while" '(' test_expr ')'
    statement_block
```

EXAMPLE

The following code fragment illustrates the While loop statement:

```
int i = 0;

// Print the values of i from 0 through 9.

while (i < 10)
{
    System.out.println (i);
    i = i + 1;
}
```

METRIX

Have you ever needed to convert between a Metric and non-Metric quantity but couldn't remember the exact conversion formula? If you've been in this situation, you probably have wished for a computer program that could remember these conversion formulae and do the work for you.

METRIX is a Java application that converts between Metric and non-Metric temperatures and distances. Specifically, METRIX converts between degrees Celsius and degrees Fahrenheit. It also converts between miles and kilometers.

METRIX is deliberately limited to converting between the aforementioned quantities. For example, if you want to convert between pounds and kilograms, you'll need to add code to METRIX to make this happen. After all, I'm not going to deprive you of the joy of enhancing this program to suit your exact needs.

Setting Up METRIX

To set up METRIX, begin by double-clicking your MS-DOS icon (if you are using Windows), and go to a command prompt.

If you created a `projects` directory in Chapter 1, "Introducing Java," make `projects` your current directory. (If you do not have a `projects` directory, now is as good a time as any to create one.)

Assuming that projects is located within c:\jdk1.2\, enter the command cd \jdk1.2\projects to change to this directory.

From within your projects directory, create a directory called metrix (for example, md metrix). (If you prefer, you can create this directory entirely in uppercase. For example, you could issue the command md METRIX to create this directory. Case does not matter when it comes to directories.)

Download the file metrix.java from the Macmillan Web site, and place this file in your metrix directory.

Compiling METRIX

Compilation is a simple process. It involves running the javac.exe program and specifying the name of the source file as an argument to this program.

At the command prompt, enter the following line:

```
c:\jdk1.2\projects\metrix>javac metrix.java
```

CAUTION

The .java file extension must be specified when compiling an application's source file. The compiler will display an error message if .java is not specified.

If the compiler displays an error message, you might have typed Metrix.java or METRIX.java instead of metrix.java.

CAUTION

You must specify metrix.java and not Metrix.java, METRIX.java, or any other combination of lowercase/uppercase letters. The compiler is very sensitive to case and will display an error message if the class name (metrix) does not match the filename (metrix).

After compilation is finished, you should end up with a class file called metrix.class.

Figure 3.1 shows the compilation process.

Running METRIX

Congratulations! You successfully compiled metrix.java and are now ready to run metrix.class. All you need to do is fire up the java.exe program, and specify metrix.class as an argument to this program.

CAUTION

The .class file extension must not be specified; otherwise, the java.exe program will display an error message.

Figure 3.2 shows the process of running metrix.class with java.exe to display usage information.

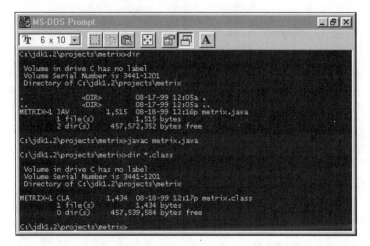

Figure 3.1: *Compiling* metrix.java *with the* javac.exe *compiler.*

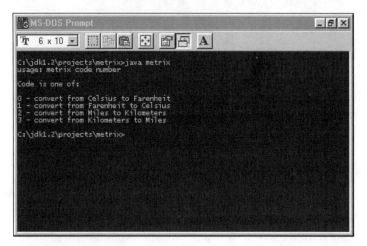

Figure 3.2: *Running* metrix.class *with* java.exe *to display usage information.*

Once you learn how to specify the correct number of command-line arguments (which you can ascertain from the usage information), you are ready to perform some actual conversions. Figure 3.3 shows the process of running metrix.class with java.exe to perform these conversions.

Potential Problems

METRIX requires the user to supply two numeric command-line arguments following java metrix. If either command-line argument is not numeric, METRIX throws a NumberFormatException object to the JVM which displays the error information contained within this object. If this happens, don't be disconcerted. Simply run METRIX a second time. (Exceptions are covered in Chapter 8.)

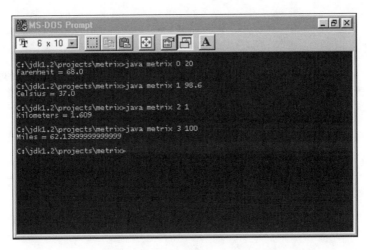

Figure 3.3: Running `metrix.class` with `java.exe` to perform conversions.

For example, the following command line shows the user attempting to pass abc instead of a number as the second command-line argument, which causes METRIX to throw a `NumberFormatException` object:

```
c:\jdk1.2\projects\metrix>java metrix 2 abc
```

Basically, you are telling METRIX that you want it to convert abc miles to kilometers. This is not logical and results in a `NumberFormatException` object.

Enhancing METRIX

The simplest enhancement task that you can perform on METRIX is to increase the number of conversions. For example, you could add the ability for METRIX to convert between pounds and kilograms.

A more involved enhancement task (and something you might want to look at after you've learned more about Java) is to give METRIX a graphical user interface. This would make it easier for the user to specify numeric quantities and perform conversions, without having to remember the arcane details of command-line arguments.

What's Next?

Now that you understand language fundamentals ranging from Chapter 2's comments to this chapter's statements, you can start to write some interesting programs (like METRIX).

However, until you learn about Java's object-oriented concepts, you won't be able to write very sophisticated programs. The next chapter introduces some of these object-oriented concepts.

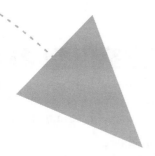

4

Encapsulation: Classes and Objects

Every Java program is built from classes and objects. These classes are blueprints that specify the properties and behaviors encapsulated (that is, integrated) into all resulting objects.

It is vital that you become familiar with classes, objects, and encapsulation because you'll be using these concepts in every Java program that you write.

Chapter 4 presents the following topics:

- Exploring OOP: encapsulation
- Declaring classes
- Providing fields and methods
- Objects
- Composition
- DEALERSHIP1

Exploring OOP: Encapsulation

The Java language is an object-oriented language. As such, it provides capabilities for creating and manipulating objects—the software equivalents of real-world entities such as trucks, employees, bank accounts, and so on.

Objects are dynamically created at runtime from classes that specify their composition. These classes encapsulate the properties and behaviors of all resulting objects. Figure 4.1 illustrates encapsulation via a real-world entity known as a pickup truck.

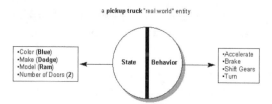

Figure 4.1: *Encapsulating a pickup truck.*

A pickup truck has properties consisting of color, make, model, number of doors, and so on. This entity also has behavior consisting of accelerating, braking, shifting gears, turning, and so on. When we discuss pickup trucks, we don't say to ourselves, "Let's go view some numbers of doors, colors, makes, models, accelerations, brakings, gear shiftings, and so on." No! We say, "Let's go view some pickup trucks." In other words, we talk about the encapsulation of a pickup truck's properties and behaviors by referring to the name of this encapsulated entity—pickup truck. (From a terminology perspective, note that I differentiate between the terms *object* and *entity* by referring to an object as the software equivalent of a real-world entity. Other than this, both terms mean roughly the same thing.)

Declaring Classes

An object-oriented program manipulates objects. Where do these objects come from? They are not manufactured out of "thin air." Objects are created from classes.

Every Java program, whether it is an application or an applet, must declare at least one class. It is not possible to write a Java program without classes. The format of a class declaration is

```
[ "public" ] [ "abstract" ¦ "final" ] "class" class_name
'{'
    // properties declarations
```

```
    // behavior declarations
'}'
```

Every class declaration requires a header consisting of at least the `class` reserved word followed by an identifier, `class_name`, which names the class. This identifier can't be a reserved word.

Class names are the nouns of a Java program (for example, `employee`, `vehicle`, `account`). They describe categories of objects.

A class block follows the class header. This class block begins with an open brace (`{`) character and ends with a close brace (`}`) character. Properties and behavior are specified within this block via variables (known as fields) and methods, respectively.

The `class` reserved word can be preceded by the `public` reserved word or either the `abstract` reserved word or the `final` reserved word.

By default, `class_name` is not visible to classes outside of its current package (that is, a class library). Specifying `public` causes `class_name` to become visible to all classes in all packages.

✔ For more information on packages, see Chapter 9, "Packages," page 217.

By default, `class_name` identifies a concrete class (that is, a class in which all method headers are followed by method blocks). Objects can be created from concrete classes. Specifying `abstract` turns `class_name` into an abstract class (that is, a class in which one or more method headers are not followed by method blocks). Objects cannot be created from abstract classes.

✔ For more information on abstract classes, see Chapter 6, "Polymorphism: Dynamic Method Binding," page 135.

By default, `class_name` can be used as the parent class of one or more child classes. Specifying `final` prevents `class_name` from being used as a parent class.

✔ For more on parent and child classes, see Chapter 5, "Inheritance: Superclasses and Subclasses," page 105.

The `abstract` and `final` reserved words cannot be specified together. If this were possible, a developer could declare an abstract class (of which no objects could be created) that could not be used as the parent class of concrete child classes. Such a class would be useless.

Java imposes no restrictions on the ordering of `public`, `abstract`, and `final`. You can specify `public abstract` or `final public` or `abstract public` or `public final`. Either specification is fine.

The following code fragment declares an `employee` class:

```
class employee
{
    // employee properties (represented by fields)

    // employee behavior (represented by methods)
}
```

Providing Fields and Methods

A class without properties or behavior is not very useful. You need to learn how to specify properties and behavior. In Java-speak, you need fields (properties) and methods (behavior).

Fields

A field variable identifies a single property and holds its value. Fields are declared within the class block that follows the class header. The format of a field declaration is

```
[ "public" ¦ "private" ¦ "protected" ]
[ "final" ] [ "static" ] [ "transient" ] [ "volatile" ]
        data_type field_name [ '=' field_initializer ] ';'
```

A field is declared by providing a data type (*data_type*) and a field name (*field_name*). The data type is either a primitive data type or a reference data type. The field name is an identifier that must not be a reserved word.

Field names, like class names, are the nouns of a Java program (for example, `color`, `model`, and `age`).

The following code fragment declares an `employee` class with two fields (`salary` and `name`):

```
class employee
{
    // employee properties (represented by fields)

    double salary;      // a primitive data type field
    String name;        // a reference data type field
}
```

A field can be initialized when it is declared. Initialization is indicated by specifying the assignment operator followed by a *field initializer* (an expression whose value is assigned to the field and has the same data type as the field's data type).

The following code fragment assigns a default value of `30000.0` to the salary field. (Perhaps the minimum salary for all employees at the company being modeled by an OOP program is 30,000 dollars. Because most employees earn this minimum, it makes sense to presume a salary level of 30,000 dollars for each new employee.)

```
class employee
{
    // employee properties (represented by fields)

    double salary = 30000.0;
    String name;
}
```

Every field has a certain level of visibility outside of its class. This level is controlled by the public, private, and protected reserved words.

A public field is visible outside of the class in which it is declared. A private field is not visible outside of its declaring class. A protected field is visible to every class declared within the same package as its declaring class and any child classes declared within any package. Finally, if public, private, or protected is not used, the field is visible only to classes declared within the same package as its declaring class.

EXAMPLE

Employees don't normally publish their salaries for anyone to read. The private reserved word hides this field from the outside world. However, the name field is not private because it doesn't matter who knows the employee's name. The following code fragment hides the salary field:

```
class employee
{
    // employee properties (represented by fields)

    private double salary = 30000.0;
    String name;
}
```

A field can be turned into a read-only field by using the final reserved word. After the field has been initialized, it cannot be modified.

CAUTION

Failing to initialize a final field at the time it is declared results in a compiler error.

EXAMPLE

The following code fragment introduces two read-only fields by using the final reserved word: UPPITY_MANAGER and LOWLY_WORKER. (With names like these, it kind of makes you wonder who would want to work for this particular company.) The names of these fields are specified using uppercase letters to distinguish them from non-read-only fields:

```
class employee
{
    // employee properties (represented by fields)
```

```
    private double salary = 30000.0;
    String name;

    final int UPPITY_MANAGER = 0;
    final int LOWLY_WORKER = 1;
}
```

The static reserved word differentiates between an instance field and a class field. An instance field, not declared with static, is unique to each class instance (that is, object) whereas a class field, declared with static, is shared by all class instances.

Each object is given its own copy of an instance field and can store its own unique value in this field. An instance field is created when its object is created and destroyed when its object is destroyed.

Only one copy of a class field exists. If one object modifies the value of this field, this value can be read by other objects. A class field is created when its class file is loaded and destroyed when its class file is unloaded.

EXAMPLE

The following code fragment introduces two read-only class fields using the static and final reserved words. Every employee object shares these fields. (The reasoning behind creating these fields as class fields is that UPPITY_MANAGER and LOWLY_WORKER are not specific to any employee. Instead, they are applicable to every employee. Why waste memory by assigning a separate copy of these fields to each employee object?)

```
class employee
{
    // employee properties (represented by fields)

    private double salary = 30000.0;
    String name;

    static final int UPPITY_MANAGER = 0;
    static final int LOWLY_WORKER = 1;
}
```

Java supports a mechanism known as *object serialization*. Briefly, this mechanism is used to save the property values of a program's objects (perhaps to a file) and restore these objects at a later time. In other words, a program can be paused and the computer turned off. Later, the computer can be turned on and the program re-started at the point where it was paused. The program will run as if nothing happened.

✔ For more information on object serialization, see Chapter 17, "Files and Streams," page 445.

The transient reserved word identifies a field that is not part of an object's persistent state. The value of this field is not saved when an object is serialized. For example, a counter field should not have its value saved and then restored when the serialized object is later re-created because the current value of the counter field is dynamically generated (perhaps by a thread) and not considered part of an object.

✔ For more information on threads, see Chapter 16, "Multithreading," page 415.

EXAMPLE

The following code fragment uses the transient reserved word to mark the counter field so that its value is not saved during serialization:

```
class employee
{
    // employee properties (represented by fields)

    private double salary = 30000.0;
    String name;

    transient static int counter;
}
```

The volatile reserved word identifies a field that can be modified in an asynchronous fashion (that is, at any time by different threads of execution.) When volatile is used, the JVM guarantees that the field's value is loaded from the field's memory every time this value is required, and any new value is saved to memory after being manipulated. These actions make it possible for threads to always have the most current value of the field to "play with." (Java does not currently make use of volatile but will probably use it in the future as its virtual machine architecture evolves.)

Methods

A method consists of a named group of statements that represent a behavior. Methods are declared within a class block. The format of a method declaration is

```
[ "public" ¦ "private" ¦ "protected" ]
([ "abstract" ] ¦ [ "final" ] [ "static" ] [ "native" ])
        return_data_type method_name '(' parameter_list ')'
        '{'
        '}'
```

A method is declared by providing a method name (*method_name*), a parameter list (*parameter_list*), and a return data type (*return_data_type*). The *method_name* is an identifier that names a method. This identifier cannot be a reserved word. Method names are the verbs of a Java program (for example, accelerate, eat, draw).

The *parameter_list* provides a comma-delimited list of parameter variable declarations that are surrounded by parentheses characters. Each declaration consists of a data type and a variable name. The parameter list corresponds to a method's argument list (a comma-delimited list of argument values) that is passed to the method when that method is called.

Parameter variables exist for as long as byte code within their declaring method continues to execute. After the method returns, these variables disappear.

CAUTION

Declaring parameter variables by specifying a data type name followed by a comma-delimited list of variable names (such as float x, y) instead of providing a comma-delimited list of data type names/variable names (such as float x, float y) results in a compiler error.

The *return_data_type* is the method's data type. This data type identifies the type of values that the method returns. If the method does not return a value, the return data type is marked with the void reserved word.

CAUTION

Forgetting to return a value from a method that has a non-void return data type or returning a value from a method that has a void return data type results in a compiler error.

The data type of each parameter variable and the return data type can be either a primitive data type or a reference data type.

The Return statement (briefly discussed in Chapter 3, "Operators, Expressions, and Statements") returns control from a called method to the calling method. This statement can either return a value or not; this depends on the method's return data type. If this data type is void, the Return statement cannot return a value.

The code fragment that follows declares two employee methods: getSalary () and setSalary (double). The getSalary () method uses the Return statement to return a value of data type double.

EXAMPLE

```
class employee
{
    // employee properties (represented by fields)

    private double salary = 30000.0;
    String name;

    transient static final int UPPITY_MANAGER = 0;
    transient static final int LOWLY_WORKER = 1;

    // employee behavior (represented by methods)

    double getSalary () { return salary; }
    void setSalary (double s) { salary = s; }
}
```

The return data type of getSalary () is double and the return data type of setSalary (double) is void. (Methods beginning with get and set are often referred to as accessor methods because they retrieve values from and set the values of private fields.)

Every method has a certain level of callability outside of its class. This level is controlled by the public, private, and protected reserved words.

A public method is callable from anywhere outside of the class in which it is declared. A private method is not callable from outside of its declaring class. A protected method is callable from every class declared within the same package as its declaring class and any derived classes declared within any package. Finally, if public, private, or protected is not used, the method is callable only from classes declared within the same package as its declaring class.

EXAMPLE

The following code fragment introduces a hidden calcBonus () method. This method is hidden because it is only called in the context of the getSalary () method. It will never be called from outside of this class. (Hidden methods are often known as *helper methods* because they help visible methods complete their tasks.)

```
class employee
{
    // employee properties (represented by fields)

    private double salary = 30000.0;
    String name;

    transient static final int UPPITY_MANAGER = 0;
    transient static final int LOWLY_WORKER = 1;

    // employee behavior (represented by methods)

    double getSalary () { return salary + calcBonus (); }
    void setSalary (double s) { salary = s; }

    private double calcBonus ()
    {
        double bonus = 0.0;

        // bonus calculation statements

        return bonus;
    }
}
```

The abstract reserved word identifies an abstract (as opposed to a concrete) method. Abstract methods have no code bodies. They are declared within abstract classes.

Each child class of an abstract parent class must provide a block of code for each abstract method that it inherits.

EXAMPLE

The following code fragment introduces an abstract method called getVacationPay (). This method is declared abstract because managers and workers receive vacation pay based on different formulae. Notice that employee also is declared abstract. The Java compiler requires any class containing an abstract method to be declared abstract.

```
abstract class employee
{
    // employee properties (represented by fields)

    private double salary = 30000.0;
    String name;

    transient static final int UPPITY_MANAGER = 0;
    transient static final int LOWLY_WORKER = 1;

    // employee behavior (represented by methods)

    double getSalary () { return salary + calcBonus (); }
    void setSalary (double s) { salary = s; }

    private double calcBonus ()
    {
        double bonus = 0.0;

        // bonus calculation statements

        return bonus;
    }

    abstract double getVacationPay ();
}
```

The final reserved word identifies a method that cannot be overridden in a child class. If a method should never be changed (by providing a different body of code) within a child class, this method should be declared final.

EXAMPLE

The following code fragment converts setSalary (double) into a final method. Any class derived from employee will not be able to override (that is, re-declare) the setSalary (double) method.

✔ For more information on method overriding, see Chapter 5, "Inheritance: Superclasses and Subclasses," page 105.

```
abstract class employee
{
```

```
    // employee properties (represented by fields)

    private double salary = 30000.0;
    String name;

    transient static final int UPPITY_MANAGER = 0;
    transient static final int LOWLY_WORKER = 1;

    // employee behavior (represented by methods)

    double getSalary () { return salary + calcBonus (); }
    final void setSalary (double s) { salary = s; }

    private double calcBonus ()
    {
        double bonus = 0.0;

        // bonus calculation statements

        return bonus;
    }

    abstract double getVacationPay ();
}
```

The static reserved word differentiates between an instance method and a class method. An instance method can access an object's instance fields as well as class fields, whereas a class method can only access class fields. Class methods are declared using the static reserved word. This is the only syntactic difference between instance and class methods.

The following code fragment introduces a private class field called numEmployees, which is initialized to zero. Two class methods, getNumEmployees () and incNumEmployees (), also are introduced to obtain the current value of this field and increment this field by a count of one.

```
abstract class employee
{
    // employee properties (represented by fields)

    private double salary = 30000.0;
    String name;

    transient static final int UPPITY_MANAGER = 0;
    transient static final int LOWLY_WORKER = 1;

    // employee behavior (represented by methods)
```

```
double getSalary () { return salary + calcBonus (); }
final void setSalary (double s) { salary = s; }

private double calcBonus ()
{
   double bonus = 0.0;

   // bonus calculation statements

   return bonus;
}

abstract double getVacationPay ();

private static int numEmployees = 0;

static int getNumEmployees () { return numEmployees; }
static void incNumEmployees () { numEmployees++; }
}
```

The numEmployees field is a class field because it does not contain employee-specific data. Instead, it contains data about all employee objects. In this case, that data describes how many employee objects are being manipulated by the program.

The native reserved word identifies a method whose code body is specified outside of Java, in a library written in C++ or some other computer language. Native methods are used to call *legacy code* (code previously written in older computer languages and widely used in a company, but not yet phased out) and provide this code with a modern user interface. (Native methods are beyond the scope of this book and will not be covered in any detail.)

The abstract reserved word cannot be used with final, static, or native. However, the final, static, and native reserved words can be specified in any order (for example, native static final).

LOCAL VARIABLES

Up to this point, we have seen that variables declared within a class are known as fields. We distinguished between instance fields and class fields. We learned that instance fields exist for the life of an object, whereas class fields exist for as long as their class files are loaded. We also learned that variables declared within a method's parameter list are known as parameter variables, and that parameter variables exist for the life of a method. There is a third category of variables that we have yet to see—local variables.

A *local variable* is declared within a method block or statement block. It can also be declared in a For loop header. This variable is local to the given block of code—it cannot be accessed from outside the block. Local variables exist for as long as their block continues to execute. As soon as the block ends, its local variables disappear.

The format of a local variable declaration is

```
data_type local_variable_name [ '=' local_variable_initializer] ';'
```

A local variable is declared by providing a data type (*data_type*) and a local variable name (*local_variable_name*). The data type is either a basic data type or a reference data type. The local variable name is an identifier that must not be a reserved word.

EXAMPLE

The code fragment that follows presents a print_strings () method that declares two local variables: a String array called strings (local to the method) and an int called i (local to the for loop). The method then proceeds to print out the contents of the String array.

```
void print_strings ()
{
    String [] strings = { "one", "two", "three" };
    for (int i = 0; i < strings.length; i++)
        System.out.println (strings [i]);
}
```

A local variable can be initialized when it is declared. Initialization is indicated by specifying the assignment operator (=) followed by a *local variable initializer* (an expression whose value is assigned to the local variable and whose value has the same data type as the local variable's data type).

Local variables must be initialized before their contents can be accessed. Failure to do this results in a compiler error.

CAUTION

Always initialize a local variable before attempting to access its contents. Failure to do this results in a compiler error.

OVERLOADING METHODS

Two or more methods might be declared in the same class with the same name but with different parameter lists. These methods are known as *overloaded methods*.

EXAMPLE

The following code fragment declares an abstract class called text. The first method is designed to draw the contents of the msg String object in some default drawing color. The second method does the same thing as the first method except that a drawing color can be specified.

```
abstract class text
{
```

```
abstract void drawText (String msg);
abstract void drawText (String msg, Color c);
```

}

It does not matter if the same or different return data types are specified (for example, void). The crucial thing to keep in mind when overloading methods is to specify different parameter lists (that is, number of and/or data types of parameters).

CAUTION

A method cannot be overloaded by declaring a second method with the same name, same parameter list, but a different return data type. Attempting to do this results in a compiler error.

Objects

Java programs create and destroy objects. The developer has complete control over object creation but has very limited control over an object's destruction.

Objects are manipulated by accessing their fields and methods. However, instance fields and methods are accessed differently than class fields and methods.

Creating Objects

An object is created from a class by using an object variable declaration statement. The newly created object is often referred to as a *class instance*.

The format of an object variable declaration statement is

```
reference_data_type object_name '=' "new" reference_data_type '(' argument_list
')' ';'
```

Every object has a reference data type (*reference_data_type*). This data type is the name of the class from which the object is being created.

Every object has a name (*object_name*). This name is an identifier that cannot be a reserved word. The JVM allocates a small region of memory (typically four bytes in size) to hold the address of (also known as a reference to) the object. For this reason, an object variable is often referred to as an *object reference variable*.

The assignment operator assigns the address of the newly created object memory to *object_name*.

The new reserved word allocates the object's memory. This memory holds the values of an object's instance fields. (The values of these instance fields differentiate one object from another object.)

When a class file is loaded (and before any object is created), a second region of memory is automatically allocated to hold class field values. This second region is kept separate from the memory that holds the instance field values because this second memory region is shared among all objects of a particular class. If one object modifies a class field, the new value is immediately available to other objects of that same class.

Finally, a third region of memory is allocated when a class file is loaded. This memory holds the byte code for the various methods declared within the class. Only one copy of this byte code exists in memory, and this byte code is shared among all objects of that class.

A constructor method follows new and initializes the object. This method consists of a class name (*reference_data_type*) followed by an *argument_list* placed between parentheses characters. (Constructor methods will be discussed in more detail at a later point in this chapter.)

EXAMPLE

The following code fragment creates an employee object and assigns its reference to the object reference variable e. (Assume that the abstract getVacationPay () method is not part of this class. If getVacationPay () is included, we cannot create an object from employee—remember, objects cannot be created from abstract classes, and employee would be abstract if it contained the abstract getVacationPay () method.)

```
employee e = new employee ();
```

Figure 4.2 illustrates the newly created employee object as it exists in memory.

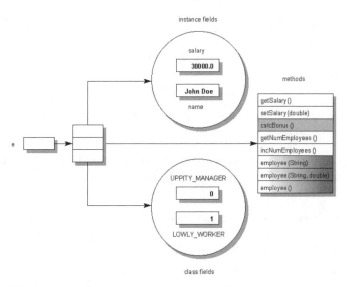

Figure 4.2: *The employee object as it exists in memory.*

The object reference variable e contains the address of three internal address variables that refer to the object's memory areas: instance fields, methods, and class fields. (You can think of the combination of instance fields, methods, and class fields as being an object.)

Each object gets its own set of instance fields. The values of these instance fields are what make one object different from another object.

Every object shares a block of code that implements the various methods. If every object was given its own block of code, a lot of memory would be wasted. (In Figure 4.2, the private calcBonus () method is shown in gray, while the three employee constructors are shown in a combination of white and gray.)

Every object shares a set of class fields. If one object changes the value of a class field, this new value is immediately available to all other objects created from the same class.

Accessing Fields

How is a field accessed? The access format differs based on whether the field is an instance field or a class field.

If the field is an instance field, the access format is

```
object_identifier '.' field_name
```

The *object_identifer* prefixes the field name to identify the object associated with the instance field. A period character (.) separates *object_identifier* from *field_name*.

EXAMPLE

The following code fragment creates an employee object, assigns its address to the object reference variable e, and displays the name field value via a call to System.out.println (String).

```
employee e = new employee ();
System.out.println (e.name);
```

If the field is a class field, the access format is

```
class_identifier '.' field_name
```

The *class_identifier* prefixes the field name to identify the class associated with the class field. A period character (.) separates *class_identifier* from *field_name*.

EXAMPLE

With class fields, you do not need to create an object prior to accessing these fields. The following code fragment displays the UPPITY_MANAGER field value via a call to System.out.println (String):

```
System.out.println (employee.UPPITY_MANAGER);
```

If a field is being accessed from within a method that is declared within the same class as the field, the format is

```
field_name
```

EXAMPLE

The following code fragment, taken directly from the employee class, shows the getSalary () method accessing the salary instance field:

```
double getSalary () { return salary + calcBonus (); }
```

Accessing Methods

How is a method accessed? The access format differs based on whether the method is an instance method or a class method.

If the method is an instance method, the access format is

```
object_identifier '.' method_name '(' argument_list ')' ';'
```

The *object_identifer* prefixes the method call to identify the object associated with the instance method. This is done so that the method identified by *method_name* will be able to access the object-specific instance fields. A period character (.) separates *object_identifier* from *method_name*.

EXAMPLE

The following code fragment creates an employee object, assigns its address to the object reference variable e, and calls the setSalary (double) method to initialize the salary field:

```
employee e = new employee ();
e.setSalary (50000.0);
```

If the method is a class method, the access format is

```
class_identifier '.' method_name '(' argument_list ')' ';'
```

The *class_identifier* prefixes the method call to identify the class associated with the class method. A period (.) character separates *class_identifier* from *method_name*.

With class methods, you do not need to create an object prior to calling these methods. The following code fragment calls the incNumEmployees () method to initialize the numEmployees field:

```
employee.incNumEmployees ();
```

If a method is calling a local method (that is, a called method within the same class as the calling method), the format is

```
method_name '(' argument_list ')' ';'
```

EXAMPLE

The following code fragment, taken directly from the employee class, shows the getSalary () method calling the calcBonus () local method:

```
double getSalary () { return salary + calcBonus (); }
```

Calling Methods

When a method is called, there are two ways in which arguments represented by variables can be passed: by value and by reference.

When a variable is passed to a method by value, only a copy of the variable is passed. The address of the variable is not passed. What does this mean? Basically, the method can manipulate the value via its corresponding parameter variable but can never modify the contents of the original variable. Variables whose data types are primitive data types (for example, short, double, boolean) are always passed by value.

When a variable is passed to a method by reference, the address of the variable is passed. Although the method "thinks" it is manipulating a parameter variable, it is really manipulating the original variable. Variables whose data types are reference data types are always passed by reference.

EXAMPLE

The following callDemo application illustrates the difference between call by value and call by reference:

```
class callDemo
{
    public static void main (String [] args)
    {
        int x1 = 3;
        method1 (x1);
        System.out.println (x1);

        int [] x2 = { 3, 2, 4 };
        method2 (x2);
        for (int i = 0; i < x2.length; i++)
        {
            System.out.print (x2 [i]);

            // The following If statement checks to see if
            // the last array element is being output.  If
            // it is not, a comma followed by a space is
            // output.  This is done to separate elements
            // on the same line.

            if (i != x2.length - 1)
                System.out.print (", ");
        }
    }

    static void method1 (int x)
    {
        x = 0;
    }
```

```
        static void method2 (int x [])
        {
           x [0] = 0;
        }
}
3
0, 2, 4
```

The value of x1 is not modified within method1 (int). The reason is that x1 is passed by value, not by reference. The x parameter variable only holds the value of this variable.

The first element within the x2 array has been changed from 3 to 0 within method2 (int []). The reason is that x2 is passed by reference. The x [] parameter variable holds the address of the x2 array. Modifying any array element via the parameter variable affects that element in the original array.

METHOD CALL STACK

Methods can call other methods. For example, the main method of an application can create an employee object and call its methods.

When a method is called, the JVM "remembers" the location of the byte code following the method call. This "remembering" allows the JVM to return execution to the instruction that follows the method call instruction.

The JVM "remembers" method calls by using what is known as a *method call stack* (a sequence of method call return addresses where the most recent method call return address appears at the top and the least recent method call return address appears at the bottom). The JVM returns from the most recent method call by removing the return address from the top of the stack, setting the new top of the stack to the next return address on that stack, and continuing to execute byte code beginning at the newly removed return address.

The method call stack also is used by the JVM's exception handling mechanism.

✔ For more information on exception handling, see Chapter 8, "Exception Handling," page 185.

THE CONSTRUCTOR METHOD

A *constructor* method is only used to initialize an object. The name of this method follows the new reserved word and consists of the class name followed by an argument list.

Constructor methods are declared like other methods except that they never return a value. Therefore, they are not declared with a return data type (not even void is specified).

CAUTION

Specifying a return data type in a constructor method declaration results in a compiler error.

The following code fragment adds two constructor methods to employee: employee (String) and employee (String, double):

```
class employee
{
    // employee properties (represented by fields)

    private double salary = 30000.0;
    String name;

    transient static final int UPPITY_MANAGER = 0;
    transient static final int LOWLY_WORKER = 1;

    // employee behavior (represented by methods)

    double getSalary () { return salary + calcBonus (); }
    final void setSalary (double s) { salary = s; }

    private double calcBonus ()
    {
        double bonus = 0.0;

        // bonus calculation statements

        return bonus;
    }

    private static int numEmployees = 0;

    static int getNumEmployees () { return numEmployees; }
    static void incNumEmployees () { numEmployees++; }

    employee (String empName)
    {
        name = empName;
    }

    employee (String empName, double sal)
    {
        name = empName;
        salary = sal;
    }
}
```

If a class does not declare any constructors, Java provides a default constructor that takes no arguments and does nothing. This constructor simply serves as a placeholder so objects can be created from the class.

Constructors can be declared with a public, private, protected, or default visibility. If a class declares private constructors, it is not possible to create objects from that class.

By default, a constructor has the same visibility as its class. For example, if a class is declared with the public reserved word, its constructors are publicly visible. If the class is not public, then its visibility is restricted to its package. The same holds true for its constructors.

Constructors are the only methods that can call other constructors. When calling another constructor, the name of the class cannot be used. Instead, a constructor must use a special reserved word called this.

EXAMPLE

The following code fragment adds a third constructor method to employee: employee (). This constructor calls the employee (String) constructor, via this, to initialize the employee's name to "John Doe":

```java
class employee
{
    // employee properties (represented by fields)

    private double salary = 30000.0;
    String name;

    transient static final int UPPITY_MANAGER = 0;
    transient static final int LOWLY_WORKER = 1;

    // employee behavior (represented by methods)

    double getSalary () { return salary + calcBonus (); }
    final void setSalary (double s) { salary = s; }

    private double calcBonus ()
    {
        double bonus = 0.0;

        // bonus calculation statements

        return bonus;
    }

    private static int numEmployees = 0;

    static int getNumEmployees () { return numEmployees; }
    static void incNumEmployees () { numEmployees++; }
```

```
employee (String empName)
{
   name = empName;
}

employee (String empName, double sal)
{
   name = empName;
   salary = sal;
}

employee () { this ("John Doe"); }
}
```

CAUTION

A constructor must use this to call another constructor. Specifying the class name instead of this results in a compiler error. For example, calling employee ("John Doe") instead of this ("John Doe") from within the employee () constructor results in a compiler error.

CAUTION

Only constructors can call other constructors. Calling a constructor from a non-constructor method results in a compiler error.

Java's this reserved word also is used to refer to fields from within a constructor (or any other method). This capability is useful when attempting to assign a parameter variable's value to a field when both the parameter variable name and field name are identical.

EXAMPLE

The following code fragment modifies the employee (String) and employee (String, double) constructors so that they use this to refer to the name and/or salary fields, allowing the values of same-named parameter variables to be assigned to these fields:

```
class employee
{
   // employee properties (represented by fields)

   private double salary = 30000.0;
   String name;

   transient static final int UPPITY_MANAGER = 0;
   transient static final int LOWLY_WORKER = 1;

   // employee behavior (represented by methods)
```

```
double getSalary () { return salary + calcBonus (); }
final void setSalary (double s) { salary = s; }

private double calcBonus ()
{
   double bonus = 0.0;

   // bonus calculation statements

   return bonus;
}

private static int numEmployees = 0;

static int getNumEmployees () { return numEmployees; }
static void incNumEmployees () { numEmployees++; }

employee (String name)
{
   this.name = name;
}

employee (String name, double salary)
{
   this.name = name;
   this.salary = salary;
}

employee () { this ("John Doe"); }
}
```

CAUTION
You cannot use this to assign parameter variable values to field references from within a class method because this refers to the current class instance, and class methods have no concept of a class instance.

Destroying Objects

Objects cannot be destroyed by a developer. The JVM is given this task to reduce the likelihood of memory leaks.

Programming languages like C and C++ give developers complete control over object creation and destruction. However, there are times when a developer does not provide code to properly destroy the program's objects. The memory allocated to these objects is never reclaimed, and this results in a memory leak. Over time, this leak gets worse, and the program eventually runs out of memory. When this happens, the program grinds to a halt. Obviously, this situation is not ideal for mission-critical software.

The JVM contains a garbage collector that runs at various times to destroy objects and reclaim memory.

Although the developer cannot destroy an object, he or she can indicate to the JVM that an object is no longer being used. This is accomplished by assigning the null literal to an object reference variable.

Assigning null to an object reference variable causes the JVM to decrement an internal reference count to that object. This reference count keeps track of all object variables that reference a particular object. (Each time an object reference variable references this object, the object's reference count is incremented.) After this reference count reaches zero, the object is marked for garbage collection. The next time the garbage collector runs, the object will be destroyed.

EXAMPLE

The following code fragment creates an employee object and assigns its reference to the object reference variable e. Later, it assigns null to this variable to inform the JVM that it no longer needs this object. The next time the garbage collector runs, it will destroy this object and reclaim memory.

```
employee e = new employee ();

// Additional statements

e = null;
```

Composition

You're making some vegetable soup. There are pieces of potatoes, carrots, and other vegetables floating in the broth. (Occasionally, one of the potato pieces winks at you with one of its eyes!)

You could model vegetable soup in software by creating a vegetable soup class, a potato class, a carrot class, and so on. The vegetable soup class could contain potato and carrot fields (among other fields). After you have created a vegetable soup object, this object's constructor could create potato and carrot objects, and assign their references to the potato and carrot fields. In other words, your vegetable soup object would be composed of potato and carrot objects.

As another example, an employee class could declare a String field called name. When an employee object is created, a String object is also created and its reference assigned to name. You could say that the employee object is composed of a name object (among other things).

Composition manifests itself through what are known as "has a" relationships. One object has another object that helps to define the first object. For example, the employee object has a name object (of data type String) that helps to define the employee (that is, an employee is an entity with a name, among other things).

Figure 4.3 illustrates composition by showing an employee object (referenced by object reference variable e) composed of a name object (in addition to the salary field).

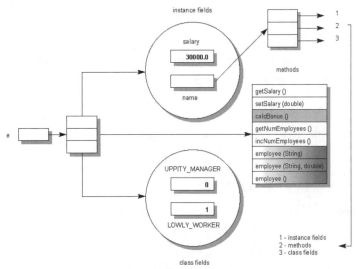

Figure 4.3: *The composite* employee *object.*

DEALERSHIP1

Imagine writing a program that simulates a vehicle dealership. Suppose that this program creates an inventory of vehicles, monitors sales of different types of vehicles, and so on.

You could write this program without using object-oriented techniques. However, you would probably find yourself spending more time writing the code than having fun playing with this code. Therefore, you might consider building your dealership program using the object-oriented techniques that have been presented in this chapter.

This chapter concludes with a dealership simulation called DEALERSHIP1. This application demonstrates classes, objects, private fields, accessor methods, constructors, and this. (Chapters 5, "Inheritance: Superclasses and Subclasses," and 6, "Polymorphism: Dynamic Method Binding," expand on DEALERSHIP1 by taking advantage of Java's inheritance and polymorphism capabilities.)

Setting Up DEALERSHIP1

To set up DEALERSHIP1, begin by double-clicking your MS-DOS icon (if you are using Windows), and go to a command prompt.

If you created a `projects` directory in Chapter 1, "Introducing Java," make `projects` your current directory. (If you do not have a `projects` directory, now is as good a time as any to create one.)

Assuming that `projects` is located within `c:\jdk1.2\`, enter the command `cd \jdk1.2\projects` to change to this directory.

From within your `projects` directory, create a directory called `dealership1` (for example, `md dealership1`). (If you prefer, you can create this directory entirely in uppercase. For example, you could issue the command `md DEALERSHIP1` to create this directory. Case does not matter when it comes to directories.)

Download the file `dealership1.java` from the Macmillan Web site, and place this file in your `dealership1` directory.

Compiling DEALERSHIP1

Compilation is a simple process. It involves running the `javac.exe` program and specifying the name of the source file as an argument to this program.

At the command prompt, enter the following line:

```
c:\jdk1.2\projects\dealership1>javac dealership1.java
```

CAUTION

The `.java` file extension must be specified when compiling an application's source file. The compiler will display an error message if `.java` is not specified.

If the compiler displays an error message, you might have typed `Dealership1.java` or `DEALERSHIP1.java` instead of `dealership1.java`.

CAUTION

You must specify `dealership1.java`, not `Dealership1.java`, `DEALERSHIP1.java`, or any other combination of lowercase/uppercase letters. The compiler is very sensitive to case and will display an error message if the class name (`dealership1`) does not match the filename (`dealerhip1`).

After compilation is finished, you should end up with a class file called `dealership1.class`.

Figure 4.4 shows the compilation process.

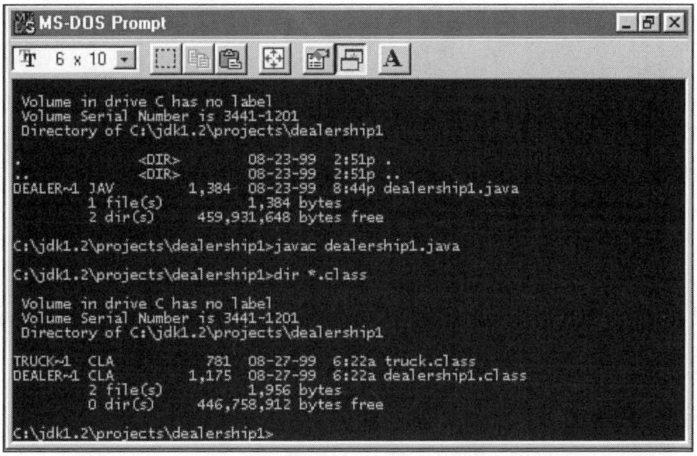

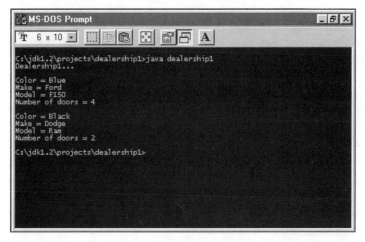

Figure 4.4: *Compiling* dealership1.java *with the* javac.exe *compiler.*

Running DEALERSHIP1

Congratulations! You successfully compiled dealership1.java and are now ready to run dealership1.class. All you need to do is fire up the java.exe program and specify dealership1.class as an argument to this program.

CAUTION

The .class file extension must not be specified; otherwise, the java.exe program will display an error message.

Figure 4.5 shows the process of running dealership1.class with java.exe.

Figure 4.5: *Running* dealership1.class *with* java.exe.

The properties of two pickup truck objects are displayed.

Potential Problems

As it stands, DEALERSHIP1 is pretty robust. However, if you decide to modify the code, you could run into some problems. Here are two possibilities:

- Forgetting to use `this` when referring to same-named fields will result in the object not being initialized.

- Attempting to call a constructor from within another constructor without using `this` will lead to a compiler error.

If you should encounter an error, don't panic. Instead, try to reason out the cause of this error, and then take appropriate action.

Enhancing DEALERSHIP1

You can enhance DEALERSHIP1 by creating an array of pickup truck objects. Use a For loop statement to iterate through this array, and call the various `get` accessor methods to obtain properties and display these properties during each iteration.

You can also enhance DEALERSHIP1 by thinking up some additional properties (for example, automatic/manual transmission—a Boolean?) and add them to truck. Don't forget to supply `get` accessor methods for these properties.

Remember, the sky is the limit as to what you can do with this program. (DEALERSHIP1 has been purposely kept simple to give you a chance to "get creative.")

What's Next?

Now that you've explored the first principle of object-oriented programming, encapsulation, it's time to turn your attention to the second principle, inheritance. You'll learn to either love inheritance (if your rich aunt passes on and leaves you lots of money) or hate inheritance (because it has a lot to do with onions and, well, you'll see).

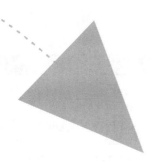

Inheritance: Superclasses and Subclasses

In the previous chapter, you learned that encapsulation is a very important principle of object-oriented programming. In this chapter, you will learn that the inheritance principle is equally important. With inheritance, you can organize your Java classes into hierarchical superclass/subclass relationships. The ability to inherit capabilities rather than "re-invent" the wheel is important from a code reuse and code maintenance standpoint.

Chapter 5 presents the following topics:

- Exploring OOP: inheritance
- Relating classes
- The root of all classes
- Multiple inheritance and interfaces
- Inheritance versus composition
- DEALERSHIP2

Exploring OOP: Inheritance

After the funeral, the family gets together to read the late Aunt Agatha's last will and testament. The solicitor puts on his glasses and starts to read the document. First comes the preamble, and then comes the good stuff. "Mr. Jones," says the solicitor, "you and your family have just inherited five million cheeseburgers!" Okay, that's inheritance. You can now turn to Chapter 6. Just kidding!

Inheritance, from an object-oriented perspective, is a little more involved than finding out how many dollars (or cheeseburgers) were bequeathed to you from your late Aunt. Inheritance gives you the ability to create a generalized class with generalized properties and methods, and a more specialized class that is derived from this class. The specialized class inherits everything from the generalized class. However, it can choose to override (replace) inherited capabilities and even add its own unique capabilities.

For example, everyone who works for a company is an employee of that company. Some employees might be sales persons, other employees might be accountants, and still other employees might be managers. Sales persons, accountants, and managers are related by the fact that they are all employees.

Figure 5.1 shows the relationship between sales person, accountant, and manager. Arrows point from sales person, accountant, and manager to employee, to show that they inherit state (such as employee number) and behavior (such as clocking in) from employee.

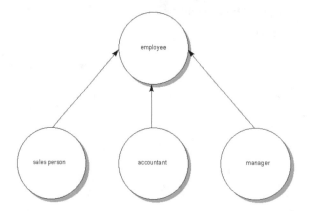

Figure 5.1: *Relating employee, sales person, accountant, and manager.*

People are the employees of a company. More specifically, people are the sales persons, accountants, and managers of a company. For example, Joe is an employee of some company. However, he is a specialized employee—a sales person. This is illustrated in Figure 5.2. The arrow points from Joe to sales person to show that Joe is a sales person.

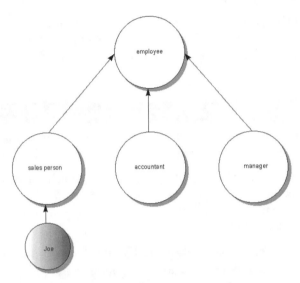

Figure 5.2: *Joe is a sales person employee.*

Some people can work multiple jobs. For example, Sally is an employee at the same company as Joe. However, she is both an accountant and a manager. This is illustrated in Figure 5.3.

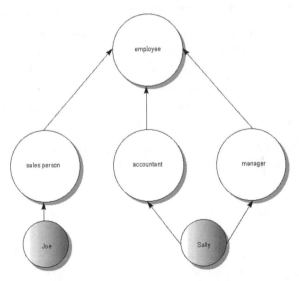

Figure 5.3: *Sally is both an accountant employee and a manager employee.*

The capability to inherit state and behavior from two or more entities is known as multiple inheritance. In our example, Joe inherits from only one entity, sales person, whereas Sally inherits from multiple entities, accountant and manager.

From an OOP perspective, employee, sales person, accountant, and manager are classes whereas Joe and Sally are objects of these classes. Thanks to inheritance, Joe is both a sales person (specifically) and an employee (generically).

Relating Classes

Chapter 4, "Encapsulation: Classes and Objects," mentioned that objects are not manufactured out of "thin air." Instead, they are created from classes.

Objects are related to other objects through inheritance by modifying the class blueprints from which these objects are created. These modifications suggest that one class extends the capabilities—the properties and behavior—of another class.

The following format is used to specify one class extending another class:

```
"class" class_identifier1 "extends" class_identifier2
'{'
'}'
```

The class that is extending another class (`class_identifier1`) is known as a *subclass* (or child class) whereas the class being extended (`class_identifier2`) is known as a *superclass* (or parent class). The extends reserved word appearing between both identifiers specifies this extension relationship.

The capability to extend a class conjures up the image of an onion. As you peel back each layer, another layer meets your eyes. In a similar fashion, if you peel back `class_identifier1`, you discover a layer called `class_identifier2`.

An object created from `class_identifier1` inherits the integrated properties and behavior of `class_identifier2` and integrates these properties/behavior with the integrated properties and behavior of `class_identifier1`.

EXAMPLE

The following code fragment declares a superclass called point3D and a subclass called sphere, which extends point3D:

```
class point3D
{
    private double x, y, z
}

class sphere extends point3D
{
    private double radius;
}
```

The x, y, and z fields could have been re-declared within sphere. (A three-dimensional point is located in three-dimensional space by its x, y, and z coordinates. A sphere is a three-dimensional point with a radius.) However, code would have been duplicated and the fact that a sphere is a three-dimensional point with radius would have been lost. (Remember: We are trying to model the real world using object-oriented programs. In the real world, a sphere with no radius is nothing more than a three-dimensional point.)

Suppose that we decide to create an object from the sphere class by issuing the following statement:

```
sphere s = new sphere ();
```

We end up with an object containing four private fields: x, y, z, and radius. This is illustrated in Figure 5.4.

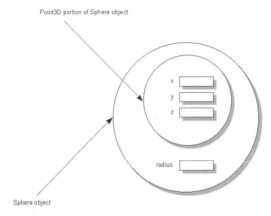

Figure 5.4: *The sphere object.*

The sphere object consists of two layers. The internal layer represents the integrated point3D state and behavior. The outer layer represents sphere's specialized state and behavior (that is, that state and behavior unique to spheres).

Because sphere's radius field is a private field, we cannot directly access this field. Instead, we need a pair of accessor methods to get and set this field's value. We also cannot directly access the x, y, and z fields, or even indirectly via accessor methods declared within sphere, because these fields are hidden within the point3D layer (by virtue of their being declared private).

CAUTION

Attempting to access the private fields of the superclass layer from a subclass results in a compiler error.

The capability to hide information within layers is known as *information hiding*. This capability can seem to be bothersome, but information hiding is applicable to our world.

Our world is based on layers. For example, the human body is a layer that surrounds organs. Organs are layers that surround tissues, blood vessels, and other entities. Tissue layers, blood vessel layers, and so on, surround cells. Carry this far enough and you end up with a layer of subatomic particles.

Suppose that you could expose everything making up a human body. All of the internal organs would appear on the outside and all their constituent layers would be turned inside out. (I really wouldn't want to see this.) The result would be chaos. (Obviously, this person wouldn't live very long.)

This idea holds when applied to object-oriented programs. Exposing all of each object layer's state and behavior and making it possible to manipulate all this state/behavior would only result in chaos. It is much better for a layer to hide that state and behavior not essential to other layers. (Knowing what to hide and what to expose is a very important task for each developer to cultivate.)

Calling Superclass Constructors

How do we initialize objects composed of multiple layers if we cannot access hidden fields within sub-layers? This is a good question and Java provides a good answer: call a superclass constructor via the super reserved word. The superclass constructor can then initialize its own hidden (and not-so-hidden) fields.

EXAMPLE

The following code fragment declares a superclass called employee and a subclass called salesPerson. It shows how super is used to call the employee (int, String) superclass constructor from the salesPerson (int, String, String) subclass constructor:

```
class employee
{
   private int employeeID;
   private String employeeName;

   employee (int employeeID, String employeeName)
   {
      this.employeeID = employeeID;
      this.employeeName = employeeName;
   }

   public int getEmployeeID () { return employeeID; }

   public String getEmployeeName () { return employeeName; }
```

```
}

class salesPerson extends employee
{
    private String territoryName;

    salesPerson (int employeeID,
                  String employeeName, String territoryName)
    {
        super (employeeID, employeeName);
        this.territoryName = territoryName;
    }
}
```

The following statement creates a new salesPerson object and assigns its reference to object reference variable s:

```
salesPerson s = new salesPerson (1000, "Joe", "West");
```

There is a lot of activity going on when we create a salesPerson object. Let's walk through this activity to find out what is happening.

The salesPerson class file is loaded into memory when the previous object creation statement is encountered (and if this class file is not already in memory).

Memory is allocated for the s object reference variable.

Memory is allocated for all salesPerson class fields (if there are any). This memory is then initialized to the values of these fields.

Memory is allocated for all employee layer class fields (if there are any). This memory is then initialized to the values of these fields.

Memory is allocated for all the instance fields within salesPerson and within the employee layer. All of these fields are initialized to default values.

The salesPerson (int, String, String) constructor is called. The first thing that this constructor does is to call its employee (int, String) super-class constructor by specifying super and passing the values of its employeeID and employeeName parameter variables (that is, 1000 and "Joe") as arguments to super. (The JVM knows which constructor to call based on the number and types of arguments being passed.)

The employee (int, String) superclass constructor initializes its private employeeID and employeeName fields. It makes use of this to refer to these fields so it doesn't end up assigning the values of the employeeID and employeeName parameters to the employeeID and employeeName parameters.

After the employee (int, String) superclass constructor completes, the
salesPerson (int, String, String) subclass constructor continues. It
assigns the territoryName parameter value (that is, "west") to its
territoryName field (by using this to differentiate between the current
object's territoryName field and the territoryName parameter).

At this point, the object is ready for use.

What happens if super has not been specified in the salesPerson (int,
String, String) constructor? In this situation, the compiler generates code
to call the employee () constructor. This code is placed before any other code.

During compilation, the compiler examines the employee class to see if
there are any constructors. If there are none, it automatically creates a
default no-argument employee () constructor.

When compiling salesPerson (int, String, String) and super is not specified, the compiler searches employee for an employee () constructor. If this
constructor is not found, the compiler reports an error.

CAUTION

Not specifying super in a subclass constructor and not providing either a no-argument
constructor or a default no-argument constructor in the superclass results in a compiler
error.

If specified, super must appear before any other code within a subclass constructor, super must only be called from within a subclass constructor, and
this and super cannot be used to call other constructors from within the
same subclass constructor. Compiler errors will result if any of these rules
are violated.

CAUTION

A superclass constructor call, via super, must be the first call within a subclass constructor. The superclass constructor call can only be made from within a subclass constructor. The use of this and super to call other constructors from within the same
subclass constructor is prohibited. Violating any of these rules results in compiler errors.

Method Overriding

A method declared in a superclass can be re-declared in a subclass by providing the same name, same parameter list, and same return data type, but
different method code. The subclass method is said to *override* the superclass method.

CAUTION

Overriding a superclass method by providing the same name and parameter list but providing a different return data type results in a compiler error.

When a subclass object is created and the overridden method is called, it is the subclass version of the overridden method that will be called—not the superclass version.

EXAMPLE

The following code fragment declares two classes, `rectangle` and `square`, and declares a `draw ()` method within each class:

```
class rectangle
{
    void draw ()
    {
        System.out.println ("I am a rectangle.");
    }
}

class square extends rectangle
{
    void draw ()
    {
        System.out.println ("I am a square.");
    }
}
```

In this example, both `rectangle` and `square` declare a `draw ()` method. If a `rectangle` object is created and then the `draw ()` method called, `"I am a rectangle."` will be displayed. However, if a `square` object is created and then the `draw ()` method called, `"I am a square."` will be displayed.

Overridden methods are important when it comes to the third OOP principle: polymorphism. More will be said about overriding in the next chapter.

Casting Classes

The inheritance relationship states that a subclass object is a kind of superclass object. Therefore, a subclass object reference can be assigned to a superclass object reference variable without casting. However, it is not possible to call any new subclass methods or access any additional subclass fields from the superclass reference variable, without casting back to the subclass reference.

EXAMPLE

The following code fragment declares an `animal` superclass and a `dog` subclass:

```
class animal
{
    void eats () { System.out.println ("Eating"); }
}

class dog extends animal
{
```

```
    void barks () { System.out.println ("Woof Woof"); }
}
```

We can create an `animal` superclass variable and assign a `dog` subclass object reference to this variable:

```
animal a = new dog ();
```

If we try to call `a.eats ()`, there are no problems because `animal` declares an `eats ()` method, which is inherited by `dog`:

```
a.eats ();     // No problems.
```

However, if we try to call `a.barks ()`, the compiler reports an error because `animal` does not have a `barks ()` method:

```
a.barks ();     // Error
```

We must cast the superclass reference back to a subclass reference before we can access subclass capabilities:

```
((dog) a).barks ();     // No problems.
```

CAUTION

Attempting to call a subclass method or access a subclass field from a superclass reference variable without a cast back to the subclass results in a compiler error.

Casting from a superclass reference back to a subclass reference, if not done properly, can lead to a specific runtime failure known as a `ClassCastException`. This failure can cause your program to terminate or behave erratically.

For example, suppose that an attempt was made to create an `animal` object and assign its reference to a `dog` reference variable. (The `(dog)` cast is necessary so the compiler will compile this statement.)

```
dog d = (dog) new animal ();
```

If you tried to run this code, a `ClassCastException` failure would occur. Why?

We know that a `dog` is a kind of animal, but is an animal a kind of dog? The answer is no. There are many kinds of animals: tigers, zebras, horses, bears, and so on.

Suppose that the `ClassCastException` failure did not occur in the previous statement. Now suppose we tried to execute the following code:

```
d.bark ();
```

The program would crash because there is no `bark ()` method declared within the `animal` class and we are trying to call this non-existent method via the `animal` object reference stored within the `dog` variable d. From the perspective of our world, we are trying to make every animal bark, not just a dog.

CAUTION

Assigning a superclass reference to an inappropriate subclass reference variable and attempting to call a subclass method or access a subclass field (which does not exist in the superclass) via this variable will result in a `ClassCastException`.

The Root of All Classes

A lot of thought was put into the design of Java. One area where this can be seen is in its extensive class library. This library contains many classes, but all these classes share something in common—they all inherit behavior from a root class called `Object`.

All classes implicitly extend the `Object` class. You do not need to supply `extends Object`. Not only does this reduce some typing, but it also solves a problem that we will examine when we explore interfaces.

The `Object` class provides eleven methods that any object created from any class can call. Classes can choose to ignore these methods or override them with class-specific behavior.

Class Information

`Object` declares a `getClass ()` method that returns an object of the `Class` data type. This `Class` object describes the class from which the object that called `getClass ()` was created. For example, the `Class` object contains methods that return arrays of constructor method names and their parameter lists, non-constructor method names and their return data types/parameter lists, field names and their data types, and so on.

EXAMPLE

The following application calls the `getClass ()` method on a `String` object to obtain an object that describes this class. After the class object has been returned, the `getName ()` method is called on the class object to return the name of the class:

```
// getClass.java

class getClass
{
    public static void main (String [] args)
    {
        String s = "abc";

        System.out.println (s.getClass ().getName ());
    }
}
```

`java.lang.String`

Notice that calls to `getClass ()` and `getName ()` are chained together by using multiple period characters. Java evaluates this "method call chaining" expression in a left-to-right order. For example, Java first calls `getClass ()` on the `String` object reference variable s. This call returns the class object that describes the `String` class. Java then calls `getName ()` on this class object to return the object's class name.

Cloning

`Object` declares a `clone ()` method that *clones* (duplicates) an object's field values.

There are two kinds of cloning, shallow and deep. *Shallow cloning* duplicates an object's primitive and reference field values but not the objects referenced by these reference fields. *Deep cloning* duplicates primitive and reference field values, and the objects that are referenced by these reference fields.

Every object that "wants" to be cloned must be created from a class that implements the `Cloneable` interface. This interface contains no method declarations; it is only used to identify a class that supports cloning.

`Object`'s `clone ()` method ensures that each object "wanting" to be cloned was created from a class that implements `Cloneable`. If this is not the case, `Object`'s `clone ()` method will throw a `CloneNotSupportedException` object.

If the object "wanting" to be cloned was created from a class that supports `Cloneable`, `Object`'s `clone ()` method will perform a shallow clone of the object's fields by creating a new object of the same data type as the object being cloned, copying the field values from the object being cloned to the new object, and returning a reference to the new object.

The following application demonstrates both forms of cloning: shallow and deep:

```
// cloneDemo.java

class engine implements Cloneable
{
    private int numCylinders;

    engine (int numCylinders)
    {
        this.numCylinders = numCylinders;
    }

    int getNumCylinders () { return numCylinders; }
```

```
     public Object clone () throws CloneNotSupportedException
     {
        return super.clone ();
     }
}

class vehicle implements Cloneable
{
   private String name;
   private engine e;

   vehicle (String name, engine e)
   {
      this.name = name;
      this.e = e;
   }

   String getName () { return name; }
   engine getEngine () { return e; }

   public Object clone () throws CloneNotSupportedException
   {
      vehicle newObject = (vehicle) super.clone ();

      if (this.e != null)
         newObject.e = (engine) this.e.clone ();

      if (this.name != null)
         newObject.name = new String (this.name);

      return newObject;
   }
}

class cloneDemo
{
   public static void main (String [] args)
   {
      vehicle v1 = new vehicle ("Halfton Pickup", new engine (6));
      vehicle v2 = null;

      try
      {
         v2 = (vehicle) v1.clone ();
      }
      catch (CloneNotSupportedException e)
      {
```

```
            System.out.println (e);
        }

    if (v1 == v2)
        System.out.println ("v2 is the same as v1");
    else
        System.out.println ("v2 is a duplicate of v1");

    String name1 = v1.getName ();
    String name2 = v2.getName ();

    if (name1 == name2)
        System.out.println ("name2 is the same as name1");
    else
        System.out.println ("name2 is a duplicate of name1");

    engine e1 = v1.getEngine ();
    engine e2 = v2.getEngine ();

    if (e1 == e2)
        System.out.println ("e2 is the same as e1");
    else
        System.out.println ("e2 is a duplicate of e1");

    if (e1.getNumCylinders () == e2.getNumCylinders ())
        System.out.println ("Number of cylinders match");
    else
        System.out.println ("Number of cylinders differ");
    }
}
```

```
v2 is a duplicate of v1
name2 is a duplicate of name1
e2 is a duplicate of e1
Number of cylinders match
```

OUTPUT

This example declares three classes: engine, vehicle, and cloneDemo. The engine class describes a vehicle's engine as consisting of a certain number of cylinders. The vehicle class describes a vehicle as consisting of a name and an engine. The cloneDemo class drives this application.

When the main method is called, a vehicle object is created and its reference assigned to v1. A second vehicle object is created and its reference assigned to v2. However, this second vehicle object is an exact duplicate of the object referenced by v1 (that is, it is not the same object as the object referenced by v1).

The following statement clones v1:

```
v2 = (vehicle) v1.clone ();
```

Because the clone () method returns an Object superclass reference, this reference must be cast back to the class of the object that called clone ()—vehicle.

The vehicle class declares a publicly visible clone () method. This method first calls its superclass clone () method which, in this example, is Object's clone () method.

Object's clone () method performs a shallow clone of all primitive fields within the vehicle class. Because there are no primitive fields, the address of a new vehicle object with no duplicate primitive fields is returned.

The address of this object is cast to vehicle and assigned to the newObject reference variable. At this point, shallow cloning is finished.

The vehicle class declares two reference fields: engine reference field e and String reference field name. The objects referenced by these fields contain their own primitive fields whose values need to be duplicated. This duplication occurs by creating new engine and String objects, and copying the values of the old engine and String objects to the new objects. However, there is no point in duplicating these objects if they don't exist (that is, the e and/or name field variables contain null values).

If e is actually referencing an engine object, the clone () method declared within the engine class is called. This method only calls its Object superclass method to clone its primitive field values. Because there are no reference fields declared in engine, there is no point in doing a deep clone. Therefore, engine's clone () method exits with the address of the duplicate engine object containing a duplicate number of cylinders value.

The address of the duplicate engine object is assigned to the e field of newObject—the new vehicle object.

If name is actually referencing a String object, a new String object is created and its address assigned to the name field of newObject. So why isn't clone () being called for String?

String does not override the clone () method. Because String inherits Object's clone () method, and because Object's clone () method is declared with protected visibility, there is no way that vehicle can call this method—protected methods are only accessible within the class in which they are declared as well as subclasses—even if these subclasses are declared in other packages.

Most of the time, you must call clone (). The reason for this has to do with child classes. If you do not call clone (), child classes will not be properly cloned. However, the String class is different. This class is declared as a final class. When any class is declared final, child classes cannot be derived (that is, extended) from parent classes. Therefore, when dealing with String, it is okay to create a new String object.

After initialization of newObject is finished, the address of this duplicate object is returned and assigned to v2 in the main method. A duplicate is born!

Equality

Java contains two mechanisms for determining equality: the equal to (==) relational operator and the equals (Object) method.

The equal to operator (==) is used to determine if either the contents of two primitive variables are equal or the references of two reference variables are equal (that is, both reference variables point to the same object). A Boolean true value is returned if they are equal; otherwise, a Boolean false value is returned.

The equals (Object) method is used to determine if the object contents of two reference variables are equal. A Boolean true value is returned if they are equal; otherwise, a Boolean false value is returned.

EXAMPLE

The following application uses the equal to operator (==) to prove that this operator distinguishes between primitive equality and reference equality:

```
// equality1.java

class equality1
{
    public static void main (String [] args)
    {
        int i1 = 10;
        int i2 = 10;

        System.out.println ("i1 = " + i1);
        System.out.println ("i2 = " + i2);

        if (i1 == i2)
            System.out.println ("i1 == i2\n");

        String s1 = "abc";
        String s2 = new String ("abc");

        System.out.println ("s1 = " + s1);
        System.out.println ("s2 = " + s2);

        if (s1 != s2)
            System.out.println ("s1 != s2");
    }
}
```

```
i1 = 10
i2 = 10
i1 == i2

s1 = abc
s2 = abc
s1 != s2
```

This example shows two techniques for creating a String object. The first technique appears to directly assign the "abc" string literal to String variable s1. However, behind the scenes, Java is actually creating a new String object and assigning its reference to s1, exactly like it is doing with s2. The references assigned to s1 and s2 differ, even though the contents of both objects are the same. Therefore, because the references are different and the == operator compares references, s1 is not equal to s2.

If the compiler finds multiple string literals with identical contents that are directly being assigned to String variables, it only creates one String object and gives each variable the same reference. Therefore, in the following code fragment, s1 and s2 refer to the same object so they are equal (as far as the == operator is concerned):

```
String s1 = "abc";
String s2 = "abc";
```

How can we compare object contents for equality? The answer is to make use of the equals (Object) method.

The following application uses the equals (Object) method to determine if two String objects with different references are the same:

```
// equality2.java

class equality2
{
   public static void main (String [] args)
   {
      String s1 = "abc";
      String s2 = new String ("abc");

      System.out.println ("s1 = " + s1);
      System.out.println ("s2 = " + s2);

      if (s1 == s2)
          System.out.println ("s1 == s2");

      if (s1.equals (s2))
          System.out.println ("s1.equals (s2)");
   }
}
```

```
s1 = abc
s2 = abc
s1.equals (s2)
```

Finalizing

Just before an object is destroyed, the JVM calls the object's finalize () method to give the object a chance to perform last-minute cleanup. This cleanup usually involves assigning null to all reference fields declared within the object's class. (Assigning null to a reference field causes the JVM to decrement a reference count on that field. After this reference count reaches zero, the object is automatically marked for garbage collection.)

The following application uses the finalize () method to set an employee object's name reference field to null. This marks that String object for garbage collection:

```java
// finalize.java

class employee
{
   private String name;
   private int id;

   employee (String name, int id)
   {
      this.name = name;
      this.id = id;
   }

   public void finalize ()
   {
      System.out.println ("Finalizing: " + id);
      name = null;
   }
}

class finalize
{
   public static void main (String [] args)
   {
      System.runFinalizersOnExit (true);

      employee e;

      for (int i = 0; i < 10; i++)
         e = new employee ("John Doe" + i, i);
```

```
        e = null;
    }
}
```

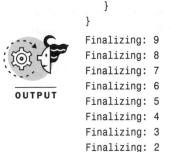

OUTPUT

```
Finalizing: 9
Finalizing: 8
Finalizing: 7
Finalizing: 6
Finalizing: 5
Finalizing: 4
Finalizing: 3
Finalizing: 2
Finalizing: 1
Finalizing: 0
```

There are a couple of things to point out about this program. First, the runFinalizersOnExit (boolean) method (declared as part of the System class) is called to "tell" the JVM to guarantee that all finalize () methods will be called prior to exit. (Normally, not all these methods are called.) Second, the order in which the finalize () methods are called varies from one JVM to another. In this example, the most recently created employee object is finalized before the very first created employee object.

✔ For more information on finalization, see Chapter 7, "Initializers, Finalizers, and Inner Classes," page 157.

Hash Codes

Hash codes are integer numbers that uniquely identify objects. These codes are used in partnership with Java's HashTable class.

To support hash code generation, a class overrides Object's hashCode () method. (Usually, this method is overridden in conjunction with the equals (Object) method.)

✔ For more information on HashTable and hashing, see Chapter 12, "Data Structures, Part 2," page 289.

Notification and Waiting

Object declares five methods that are used by multithreaded programs: notify (), notifyAll (), wait (), wait (long), and wait (long, int).

These notification and wait methods are used to synchronize access to critical data. They will be examined in a later chapter when multithreading is discussed.

String Representation

Every object is given the ability to create a string representation of its contents by inheriting `Object`'s `toString ()` method. This method returns a `String` object that describes these contents.

EXAMPLE

The following application attempts to print out the contents of the `toString1` object that is referenced by variable `ts1`:

```
// toString1.java

class toString1
{
    int i = 6;
    String name = "John Doe";

    public static void main (String [] args)
    {
        toString1 ts1 = new toString1 ();
        System.out.println (ts1);
    }
}
```

OUTPUT

```
toString1@f7bd4ae6
```

`System.out.println (String)` causes the previous characters to be displayed. However, they look a little strange.

The Java language provides the following feature. Whenever an object (regardless of class) is passed as an argument to a method that requires a `String` object argument, Java implicitly calls the `toString ()` method associated with the object argument. The `toString ()` method returns a `String` representation of the object.

If `toString ()` has not been overridden, this method returns a `String` object consisting of the object argument's class name, followed by an @ character, followed by a hash code that uniquely identifies the object.

However, it is possible to display more meaningful information, such as the names and values of the various fields. This can be done by overriding `toString ()`.

EXAMPLE

The following application attempts to print out the contents of the `toString2` object that is referenced by variable `ts2`. Instead of displaying the class name, an @ character, and a hash code, the contents of the `ts2` object is displayed:

```
// toString2.java

class toString2
{
```

```
    int i = 6;
    String name = "John Doe";

    public static void main (String [] args)
    {
        toString2 ts2 = new toString2 ();
        System.out.println (ts2);
    }

    public String toString ()
    {
        return "i = " + i + ", name = " + name;
    }
}
```

i = 6, name = John Doe

Take a look at the contents of the toString () method. Note the Return statement. This statement is returning the result of an expression that evaluates to the String data type. However, this expression might look a little strange. After all, it is attempting to concatenate an integer value to a string literal. What's going on?

When the Java compiler evaluates an expression containing the + operator, it evaluates the data type of its operands. If both data types are numeric data types, the compiler "knows" that the + operator is the addition operator. However, if one or both data types are reference data types, the compiler "knows" that this operator is the string concatenation operator.

If one of the operands has a numeric data type, the compiler generates byte code to convert this operand to a String object. However, if one of the operands has a non-String reference data type, the compiler calls this object's toString () method to return a String object. After this is done, both operands are String objects and string concatenation now takes place.

Multiple Inheritance and Interfaces

Earlier, the concept of multiple inheritance was defined as a means for an entity to inherit properties and behavior from multiple parents. For example, Sally inherits the capability to be both an accountant and a manager.

Unlike C++, Java does not support multiple inheritance. For example, it's not possible to say something such as this:

class a extends b, c

There is a good reason why Java does not support this concept—multiple inheritance is prone to problems.

Let's pretend that Java allowed a class to extend multiple classes. The following code fragment illustrates this situation:

```
class b
{
    int x;
    double y (int z) { return z + 3.5; }
    …

}

class c
{
    boolean x;
    char y (int z) { return (char) z; }
    …
}

class a extends b, c
{
    …
}
```

When the compiler is compiling class a, it is forced to make choices. "Do I include int x from class b or boolean x from class c? Do I include the double y (int) method from class b or the char y (int) method from class c?" The presence of two fields with the same name but different data types and two methods with the same name but two different return data types and different code bodies causes confusion for the compiler. Will the compiler create code that allocates four bytes for an integer or one bit for a Boolean? Will the compiler include the byte code for the y method from class b or the byte code for the y method from class c? Java solves these problems by forbidding multiple inheritance.

However, Java does provide a mechanism that you can use to take advantage of multiple inheritance while avoiding these problems—interfaces.

An interface is similar to an abstract class. However, unlike an abstract class, all methods declared within an interface must be abstract. Furthermore, it is only possible to declare read-only fields in an interface.

Although you can only extend one class, you can implement multiple interfaces to achieve multiple inheritance, as you will see. The format of an interface declaration is

```
[ "abstract" ] [ "public" ] "interface" interface_name
    [ "extends" interface_name2]
'{'
    // read-only field declarations
```

```
   // abstract method declarations
'}'
```

Every interface declaration requires a header consisting of at least the `interface` reserved word followed by an identifier that names the class. (The identifier can't be a reserved word.) In the preceding format, *interface_name* represents this identifier.

A block follows the interface header. This block begins with an open brace ({) character and ends with a close brace (}) character. Read-only fields and abstract methods are declared within this block.

The `interface` reserved word can be preceded by the `abstract` reserved word and/or the `public` reserved word.

All methods declared within an interface are abstract methods. This fact can be emphasized by prefixing the interface header with the `abstract` reserved word and/or prefixing each method declaration with the `abstract` reserved word. However, this is optional.

All read-only fields and methods declared within an interface are publicly visible. This fact can be emphasized by prefixing the interface header with the `public` reserved word and/or prefixing each field/method declaration with the `public` reserved word. However, this is optional.

EXAMPLE

The following code fragment declares a `shape` interface. This interface declares a publicly visible abstract `draw ()` method for drawing the shape. (Note that neither `public` nor `abstract` are specified to prefix `shape` or `draw ()`.)

```
interface shape
{
   void draw ();
}
```

An interface can inherit read-only variables and abstract method declarations from another interface by specifying the `extends` reserved word followed by another interface. This is useful for deriving more specialized interfaces from a generic interface.

EXAMPLE

The following code fragment declares a `shape3D` interface that extends `shape`. This interface declares a publicly visible abstract `volume ()` method for computing the volume of a three-dimensional shape. However, `shape3D` also has an inherited `draw ()` method:

```
interface shape3D extends shape
{
   double volume ();
}
```

Classes implement interfaces by specifying the `implements` reserved word followed by a comma-delimited list of interface names.

CAUTION

Forgetting to implement an interface method in a class that implements the interface results in a compiler error.

EXAMPLE

The following code fragment declares a `point3D` class and a `sphere` class. The sphere class extends `point3D` and also implements the `shape3D` interface:

```
class point3D
{
    private double x, y, z;

    point3D (double x, double y, double z)
    {
        this.x = x; this.y = y; this.z = z;
    }
}


class sphere extends point3D implements shape3D
{
    private double radius;

    sphere (double x, double y, double z, double radius)
    {
        super (x, y, z);
        this.radius = radius;
    }

    public void draw () { System.out.println ("Sphere"); }

    public double volume ()
    {
        return 4.0 / 3.0 * 3.14159 * radius * radius * radius;
    }
}
```

In this example, we are only implementing the single `shape3D` interface.

Inheritance Versus Composition

Inheritance deals with "is a" relationships. We say that one object is a kind of other object. For example, a sphere is a three-dimensional point with radius.

Inheritance works through layering classes within classes. When an object is created, the internal class structures are merged into a single structure.

Composition deals with "has a" relationships. We say that one object has a second object as part of itself. For example, an employee object has a String object that identifies the employee's name.

Composition works through composing classes out of other classes. When an object is created, the internal class structures are distinct building blocks that are separate from other class structures.

DEALERSHIP2

DEALERSHIP2 is an application that serves as a continuation of DEALER-SHIP1 (from the previous chapter). DEALERSHIP2 demonstrates super-classes, subclasses, super, and toString ().

Setting Up DEALERSHIP2

To set up DEALERSHIP2, begin by double-clicking your MS-DOS icon (if you are using Windows) and go to a command prompt.

If you created a projects directory in Chapter 1, "Introducing Java," make projects your current directory. (If you do not have a projects directory, now is as good a time as any to create one.)

Assuming that projects is located within c:\jdk1.2\, enter the command cd \jdk1.2\projects to change to this directory.

From within your projects directory, create a directory called dealership2 (for example, md dealership2). (If you prefer, you can create this directory entirely in uppercase. For example, you could issue the command md DEALERSHIP2 to create this directory. Case does not matter when it comes to directories.)

Download the file dealership2.java from the Macmillan Web site and place this file in your dealership2 directory.

Compiling DEALERSHIP2

Compilation is a simple process. It involves running the javac.exe program and specifying the name of the source file as an argument to this program.

At the command prompt, enter the following line:

```
c:\jdk1.2\projects\dealership2>javac dealership2.java
```

CAUTION

The .java file extension must be specified when compiling an application's source file. The compiler will display an error message if .java is not specified.

If the compiler displays an error message, you might have typed
`Dealership2.java` or `DEALERSHIP2.java` instead of `dealership2.java`.

CAUTION

You must specify `dealership2.java` and not `Dealership2.java`, `DEALERSHIP2.java`, or any other combination of lowercase/uppercase letters. The compiler is very sensitive to case and will display an error message if the class name (`dealership2`) does not match the filename (`dealerhip2`).

After compilation is finished, you should end up with a class file called
`dealership2.class`.

Figure 5.5 shows the compilation process.

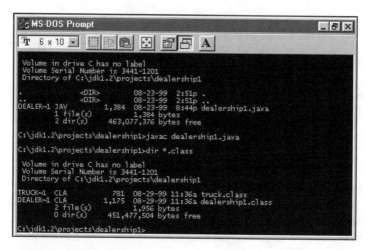

Figure 5.5: *Compiling* `dealership2.java` *with the* `javac.exe` *compiler.*

Running DEALERSHIP2

Congratulations! You successfully compiled `dealership2.java` and are now ready to run `dealership2.class`. All you need to do is fire up the `java.exe` program and specify `dealership2.class` as an argument to this program.

CAUTION

The `.class` file extension must not be specified, otherwise the `java.exe` program will display an error message.

Figure 5.6 shows the process of running `dealership2.class` with `java.exe`.

Various properties of a pickup truck object and a road hog motorcycle object are displayed. An inventory assessment of the various trucks and motorcycles in stock also is displayed.

Potential Problems

As it stands, DEALERSHIP2 is pretty robust. However, if you decide to modify the code, you could run into some problems. Here are two possibilities:

- Creating another vehicle-specific class and declaring getQuantity () or getUnitCost () in this class without using public will result in a compiler error. The error occurs because these methods are declared within the inventory interface with a default public visibility, and it is not possible to implement interface methods with less visibility.

- Creating vehicle objects is not an error. However, it makes more sense to create trucks and motorcycles because these concepts are more tangible than the "abstract" vehicle concept. (Abstraction will play an important role in the next chapter.)

If you should encounter an error, don't panic. Instead, try to reason out the cause of this error and then take appropriate action.

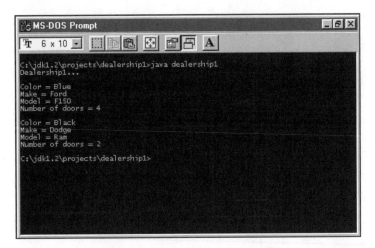

Figure 5.6: *Running* dealership2.class *with* java.exe.

Enhancing DEALERSHIP2

You can enhance DEALERSHIP2 by adding "set" accessor method declarations to inventory to set the quantity and unit cost of trucks and motorcycles. (These methods will need to be implemented within truck and motorcycle. Add private fields to these classes to hold quantity and unit cost values.)

You could also create a car class that inherits from vehicle and implements inventory methods. Create a variety of car objects and display the contents of these objects along with quantity, unit cost, and total cost.

For each object, calculate quantities and unit costs by calling the "set" accessor methods, and then use the "get" accessor methods to retrieve these values. Compute the total cost for each inventory item.

What's Next?

Now that you've explored the second principle of object-oriented programming, inheritance, it's time to turn your attention to the third principle, polymorphism. Of the three principles, polymorphism is often seen as the most difficult principle to grasp. However, polymorphism isn't that hard to grasp when discussed in a simplified manner.

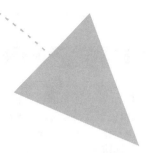

Polymorphism: Dynamic Method Binding

The previous chapter investigated the second principle of object-oriented programming: inheritance. This chapter examines the third and final OOP principle: polymorphism.

Of the three OOP principles, polymorphism can be the most challenging principle to learn because it is not as intuitive as either encapsulation or inheritance. However, as you'll discover, polymorphism really isn't that difficult to understand.

Chapter 6 presents the following topics:

- Exploring OOP: polymorphism
- Abstract classes
- Runtime type information
- Polymorphic interfaces
- Polymorphism versus data type/switch logic
- DEALERSHIP3

Exploring OOP: Polymorphism

Our world contains many kinds of animals, including monkeys, cows, and chickens. These animals share common behavioral concepts, such as eating. (Having grown up on a farm, it seems to me that eating is the only thing that animals like to do!) However, the actual eating behavior differs among the various species. For example, a monkey eats by holding a banana in its hand and chewing on the banana, whereas a cow eats by chewing grass with its mouth and a chicken eats by pecking grains off the ground with its beak.

From an OOP perspective, we can create an `animal` class that abstracts this common eating behavior, by providing an appropriate `eat ()` method. We can create `monkey`, `cow`, and `chicken` subclasses that override `animal`'s `eat ()` method in each subclass to specialize the manner by which each kind of animal eats.

At runtime, we can create an `animal` object reference variable a and a `chicken` object. We can assign the `chicken` object reference to a and call `a.eat ()`. Instead of calling `animal`'s `eat ()` method, the JVM calls `chicken`'s `eat ()` method. The JVM finds the correct `eat ()` method to call (that is, the `animal`, `monkey`, `cow`, or `chicken eat ()` method) by examining the object reference assigned to a. It then calls the `eat ()` method that is associated with this reference. Figure 6.1 illustrates a call to `chicken`'s `eat ()` method.

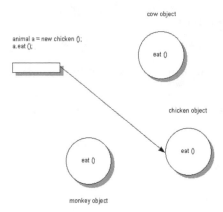

Figure 6.1: *Calling* `chicken`'s `eat ()` *method through* `animal` *object reference variable* a.

The mechanism that the JVM uses to locate and call the correct subclass method is known as *dynamic method binding*. (An object reference is dynamically assigned to a superclass object reference variable. This reference is examined to identify the object to which the subclass method is bound.)

What you've just been exposed to is polymorphism—the capability to use a superclass object reference variable to invoke subclass versions of overridden superclass methods.

Abstract Classes

Polymorphism deals with abstractions. For example, we might think in terms of animals eating, rather than chickens eating plus cows eating plus monkeys eating plus tigers eating, and so on. Thinking from an abstract point of view saves time. Coding from an abstract point of view reduces code size.

EXAMPLE

The following application illustrates polymorphism by allowing different animals to eat according to their own behaviors:

```
// animals1.java

class animal
{
    void eat () { System.out.println ("???"); }
}

class monkey extends animal
{
    void eat () { System.out.println ("Holding and eating banana!"); }
}

class cow extends animal
{
    void eat () { System.out.println ("Chewing grass with mouth!"); }
}

class chicken extends animal
{
    void eat () { System.out.println ("Pecking grains off ground!"); }
}

class animals1
{
    public static void main (String [] args)
    {
        animal [] animals =
        {
            new monkey (),
            new cow (),
            new chicken (),
            new animal ()
        };
```

```
        for (int i = 0; i < animals.length; i++)
            animals [i].eat ();
    }
}
```

OUTPUT

Holding and eating banana!

Chewing grass with mouth!

Pecking grains off ground!

???

We have a group of "happy" animals because they're all eating. But wait! There is something strange in the output. What are those three question marks?

Look carefully at the source code. Notice that a generic animal object is being created in the animals array. What is an animal object? Is it a monkey? No! Is it a cow? No! Is it a chicken? No! Is it a specific kind of animal? No! An animal object is an abstraction that identifies those properties and behaviors that are shared by all kinds of animals—such as eating.

We really shouldn't be able to create an animal object because it does not represent a specific kind of animal, such as cow, monkey, and chicken.

In Chapter 4, "Encapsulation: Classes and Objects," the concepts of an abstract class and abstract methods were introduced. These concepts identify classes that are generic (for example, animal) as opposed to classes that are specific (for example, monkey) and methods that are generic (for example, animal's eat () method) as opposed to methods that are specific (for example, monkey's eat () method).

CAUTION

Attempting to create an object from an abstract class results in a compiler error.

A class becomes an abstract class by prefixing the class reserved word with the abstract reserved word. A method becomes an abstract method by prefixing its return data type with the abstract reserved word. If a method is declared abstract, its declaring class must all be declared abstract.

CAUTION

Attempting to declare an abstract method without declaring the class as abstract (for example, abstract class ...) results in a compiler error.

EXAMPLE

The following application illustrates polymorphism by allowing different animals to eat according to their own behaviors. This time, it is not possible to create animal objects because animal is now an abstract class, by virtue of its abstract eat () method:

```
// animals2.java

abstract class animal
{
    abstract void eat ();
}

class monkey extends animal
{
    void eat () { System.out.println ("Holding and eating banana!"); }
}

class cow extends animal
{
    void eat () { System.out.println ("Chewing grass with mouth!"); }
}

class chicken extends animal
{
    void eat () { System.out.println ("Pecking grains off ground!"); }
}

class animals2
{
    public static void main (String [] args)
    {
        animal [] animals =
        {
            new monkey (),
            new cow (),
            new chicken ()
        };

        for (int i = 0; i < animals.length; i++)
            animals [i].eat ();
    }
}
```

OUTPUT

Holding and eating banana!

Chewing grass with mouth!

Pecking grains off ground!

Abstract classes can contain a mixture of abstract methods and concrete methods. For example, every kind of animal is either extinct or not extinct.

A method to test if an animal object represents an extinct kind of animal (such as the Dodo bird) could be placed in every animal subclass. However, this would be redundant and bloat the size of the program. It would be better to place this method in animal as a concrete method. Then, when an animal subclass object is created, its constructor could identify that kind of animal as being extinct or not.

EXAMPLE

The following application illustrates mixing concrete and abstract methods in an abstract animal class:

```
// animals3.java

abstract class animal
{
    private boolean extinct;

    animal (boolean extinct)
    {
        this.extinct = extinct;
    }

    abstract void eat ();

    boolean isExtinct () { return extinct; }
}

class monkey extends animal
{
    monkey (boolean extinct)
    {
        super (extinct);
    }

    void eat () { System.out.println ("Holding and eating banana!"); }
}

class cow extends animal
{
    cow (boolean extinct)
    {
        super (extinct);
    }

    void eat () { System.out.println ("Chewing grass with mouth!"); }
}
```

```
class chicken extends animal
{
   chicken (boolean extinct)
   {
      super (extinct);
   }

   void eat () { System.out.println ("Pecking grains off ground!"); }
}

class dodo extends animal
{
   dodo (boolean extinct)
   {
      super (extinct);
   }

   void eat () { System.out.println ("Pecking berries off trees!"); }
}

class animals3
{
   public static void main (String [] args)
   {
      animal [] animals =
      {
        new monkey (false),
        new cow (false),
        new chicken (false),
        new dodo (true)
      };

      for (int i = 0; i < animals.length; i++)
          if (animals [i].isExtinct ())
          System.out.println ("Animal is extinct.");
            else
                animals [i].eat ();
   }
}
```

OUTPUT

Holding and eating banana!

Chewing grass with mouth!

Pecking grains off ground!

Animal is extinct.

Runtime Type Information

Java provides an operator for determining the data type of an object (that is, the class from which the object was created)—`instanceof`.

The format of this operator is

```
object_identifier "instanceof" class_identifier
```

`object_identifier` is the name of an object.

`class_identifier` is the name of a class.

This operator returns a Boolean `true` value if `object_identifier` is an instance of `class_identifier`; otherwise, `false` is returned.

✔ For more information on `instanceof`, see Chapter 3, "Operators, Expressions, and Statements," page 45.

EXAMPLE

The following code fragment illustrates the `instanceof` operator:

```
String s = "abc";
boolean result = s instanceof String;
```

When this code fragment completes, the value of `result` is `true` because s references an object that is an instance of the `String` class.

The `instanceof` operator is required when casting an object reference variable from a superclass data type back to a subclass data type. If this is not done properly, a `ClassCastException` failure occurs.

EXAMPLE

The following application illustrates `instanceof`:

```
// shapes.java

abstract class shape
{
    abstract double area ();
}

class point extends shape
{
    private double x, y;

    point (double x, double y)
    {
        this.x = x; this.y = y;
    }

    double getX () { return x; }
    double getY () { return y; }
```

```
      double area () { return 0.0; }
}

class circle extends point
{
    private double radius;

    circle (double x, double y, double radius)
    {
        super (x, y);
        this.radius = radius;
    }

    double getRadius () { return radius; }

    double area () { return Math.PI * radius * radius; }
}

class rectangle extends shape
{
    private double length, width;

    rectangle (double length, double width)
    {
        this.length = length;
        this.width = width;
    }

    double getLength () { return length; }
    double getWidth () { return width; }

    double area () { return length * width; }
}

class shapes
{
    public static void main (String [] args)
    {
        shape shapeArray [] =
        {
            new circle (52.5, 32.6, 4.7),
            new rectangle (89.6, 78.3),
            new point (62.4, 45.7)
        };

        for (int i = 0; i < shapeArray.length; i++)
        {
```

```
                    if (shapeArray [i] instanceof point)
                    {
                        System.out.println ("Point");
                        System.out.println ("-----");
                    }
                    else if (shapeArray [i] instanceof circle)
                    {
                        System.out.println ("Circle");
                        System.out.println ("------");
                        System.out.println ("x = " +
                            ((circle) shapeArray [i]).getX ());
                        System.out.println ("y = " +
                            ((circle) shapeArray [i]).getY ());
                        System.out.println ("radius = " +
                            ((circle) shapeArray [i]).getRadius ());
                    }
                    else if (shapeArray [i] instanceof rectangle)
                    {
                        System.out.println ("Rectangle");
                        System.out.println ("---------");
                        System.out.println ("length = " +
                            ((rectangle) shapeArray [i]).getLength ());
                        System.out.println ("width = " +
                            ((rectangle) shapeArray [i]).getWidth ());
                    }

                    System.out.println ("Area = " + shapeArray [i].area ());

                    // Leave a blank line separator.

                    System.out.println ("");
                }
            }
        }
```

This application needs to use `instanceof` to determine an object's data type before it can cast the object back to its data type. The data type is required before any object-specific methods can be called (for example, the `getLength ()` method in the `rectangle` class).

```
Point
-----
Area = 69.39778171779854

Rectangle
---------
length = 89.6
width = 78.3
```

```
Area = 7015.679999999999

Point
.....
Area = 0.0
```

Notice anything strange about the output? The first line contains the word `Point`. If you study the code, should this word not be `Circle`? After all, the first shapeArray element reference points to a `circle` object.

Within the For loop statement, the first If of the Nested If decision statement checks to see if each shapeArray element is a `point`. Because the `circle` class is derived from `point`, a `circle` object is also a `point` object. (After all, a circle is a point with radius—the "is a" relationship.) Therefore, `instanceof` returns `true` because a `circle` object is also a `point` object.

This leads to an interesting situation. The second If clause within the Nested If decision statement that checks to see if the object is a `circle` is never executed, and neither are the method calls for `circle` objects. The moral of this situation is that care must be used in placing `instanceof` tests within Nested If statements. The `instanceof` that checks to see if an object is a superclass object should occur after the `instanceof` that checks if the object is a subclass object. For example, test to see if the object is a `circle` before testing to see if it is a `point`.

Polymorphic Interfaces

In Chapter 5, "Inheritance: Superclasses and Subclasses," you learned that interfaces are used to support the concept of multiple inheritance. However, they also are used to factor out the commonality found in different kinds of classes.

Suppose you own a very strange store that sells hammers and Camaro sportscars. Hammers and Camaros have nothing in common, at least nothing that comes to mind. However, there is commonality: Both items are inventory items.

Suppose you need to take inventory. What would your OOP program look like?

To start with, you might create abstract `tool` and `sportscar` classes to factor out the commonality of tools and sportscars. Then, you could derive a `hammer` class from `tool` and a `camaro` class from `sportscar` to identify a specific kind of tool and a specific kind of sportscar.

However, you also want to extend `hammer` and `camaro` from an `inventory` class so that inventory can be taken. You cannot do this because you are already extending from the `tool` and `sportscar` classes. (Java does not support multiple inheritance.)

You decide to create an `inventory` interface and force the `hammer` and `camaro` classes to implement that interface.

You decide to create an array of `tool` objects. (In addition to `hammer` objects, you might have `saw` objects and `drill` objects.) You then iterate through this array and call the `inventory` interface methods to take the inventory of all your tools.

You decide to create an array of `sportscar` objects. (In addition to `camaro` objects, you might have `corvette` objects and `firebird` objects.) You then iterate through this array and call the `inventory` interface methods to take the inventory of all your sportscars.

But isn't this a lot of work? Wouldn't it be better to create a single combined array of `tool` and `sportscar` objects? You'd save some code by combining these arrays.

Interfaces provide a solution to this problem. You can create an array of interface objects and iterate through this array.

EXAMPLE

The following application illustrates polymorphic interfaces:

```
// takeInventory.java

interface inventory
{
    String getItemName ();
    int getNumUnits ();
}


abstract class tool
{
}


class hammer extends tool implements inventory
{
    private String manufacturer;
    int numUnits;

    hammer (String manufacturer, int numUnits)
    {
        this.manufacturer = manufacturer;
        this.numUnits = numUnits;
    }

    public String getItemName () { return "Hammer"; }
    public int getNumUnits () { return numUnits; }
}
```

```
abstract class sportscar
{
}

class camaro extends sportscar implements inventory
{
   private String model;
   private String color;
   private int quantity;

   camaro (String model, String color, int quantity)
   {
      this.model = model;
      this.color = color;
      this.quantity = quantity;
   }

   public String getItemName () { return "Camaro"; }
   public int getNumUnits () { return quantity; }
}

class takeInventory
{
   public static void main (String [] args)
   {
      inventory [] inv =
      {
         new hammer ("Sears", 59),
         new camaro ("Z28", "red", 3)
      };

      for (int i = 0; i < inv.length; i++)
      {
          System.out.println ("Item name = " +
              inv [i].getItemName ());

          System.out.println ("Number of units = " +
              inv [i].getNumUnits ());
      }
   }
}
```

OUTPUT

```
Item name = Hammer
Number of units = 59
Item name = Camaro
Number of units = 3
```

Classes identify reference data types. Objects are created from classes. But what are interfaces?

An interface is not a data type but it sure acts like a data type. It is not a data type because you cannot create objects from interfaces. (After all, an interface consists of abstract methods and/or read-only field variables.) However, you can create an interface variable and assign the address of an object whose class implements that interface to this variable. (The interface variable, like an object reference variable, is only large enough to hold the address of an object.)

When an object reference has been assigned to an interface variable, only interface methods that have been implemented by the object can be called from that interface variable. In the previous example, the getItemName () and getNumUnits () methods are called from the inv interface array.

When interfaces are used in this fashion, they are known as *polymorphic interfaces*. In this situation, the only thing that matters is that an object created from a class that implements an interface can have its reference assigned to that interface's variables. As a result, tools and sportscars, animals, employees, and anything else that you can think of can share commonality. In fact, everything on this planet shares commonality: Not only do we all exist on this planet, we are all composed from atoms.

Polymorphism Versus Data Type/Switch Logic

Polymorphism is a natural part of our world. It's a good thing that this capability has found its way into OOP; otherwise, modeling this world would be a little more difficult.

How would we model the world if we did not have polymorphism at our disposal? If this were the case, we would need to fall back to an earlier technique that many developers have used in non-OOP languages to achieve polymorphic results: data type/switch logic.

Two sample applications are presented to illustrate the difference between polymorphism and data type/switch logic. The first example (animals4) uses polymorphism, while the second example (animals5) uses data type/switch logic.

EXAMPLE

The following animals4 application demonstrates polymorphism by way of several animal classes:

```
// animals4.java

abstract class animal
{
    abstract void makeNoise ();
}

class bear extends animal
{
```

```
    void makeNoise () { System.out.println ("Growls"); }
}

class chipmunk extends animal
{
    void makeNoise () { System.out.println ("Whistles"); }
}

class dog extends animal
{
    void makeNoise () { System.out.println ("Barks"); }
}

class animals4
{
    public static void main (String [] args)
    {
        dog joey = new dog ();

        animal [] menagerie = { new bear (), new chipmunk (), joey };

        for (int i = 0; i < menagerie.length; i++)
            menagerie [i].makeNoise ();
    }
}
```

```
Growls
Whistles
Barks
```

OUTPUT

Polymorphism works best when iterating through a collection of objects and calling a method that is common to these objects.

In the animals4 application, an animal array called menagerie is created. This array is initialized to three objects: a bear, a chipmunk, and a dog called joey.

A For loop statement iterates through this array and calls the makeNoise () method, which must be declared in the various animal classes.

At runtime, the JVM extracts an object reference from an array element and examines the object's data type. After it "knows" this data type, the JVM can call the appropriate makeNoise () method. Discovering the data type and calling the appropriate makeNoise () method happens behind the scenes.

Let's take a look at this same application without polymorphism.

EXAMPLE

The following `animals5` application demonstrates polymorphism without using Java's dynamic method binding mechanism. Data type detection and switch logic are used instead:

```java
// animals5.java

abstract class animal
{
    final static int BEAR = 0;
    final static int CHIPMUNK = 1;
    final static int DOG = 2;

    int animalType;

    animal (int animalType)
    {
        this.animalType = animalType;
    }
}

class bear extends animal
{
    bear ()
    {
        super (BEAR);
    }

    void growl () { System.out.println ("Growls"); }
}

class chipmunk extends animal
{
    chipmunk ()
    {
        super (CHIPMUNK);
    }

    void whistle () { System.out.println ("Whistles"); }
}

class dog extends animal
{
    dog ()
    {
        super (DOG);
    }

    void bark () { System.out.println ("Barks"); }
```

```
}

class animals5
{
   public static void main (String [] args)
   {
      dog joey = new dog ();

      animal [] menagerie = { new bear (), new chipmunk (), joey };

      for (int i = 0; i < menagerie.length; i++)
            switch (menagerie [i].animalType)
            {
               case animal.BEAR:
                     ((bear) menagerie [i]).growl ();
                     break;

               case animal.CHIPMUNK:
                     ((chipmunk) menagerie [i]).whistle ();
                     break;

               case animal.DOG:
                     ((dog) menagerie [i]).bark ();
            }
   }
}
```

```
Growls
Whistles
Barks
```

OUTPUT

Data type/switch logic offers the equivalent of polymorphism. However, the developer is responsible for providing several mechanisms.

Each participating class must be uniquely identified. The simplest identification mechanism is to associate an integer number with a class. However, specifying literal values makes the code harder to follow (and more prone to error). Therefore, it is better to provide final field variables that describe the various classes. In the example, the animal class declares BEAR, CHIPMUNK, and DOG.

If integer values are being used to differentiate among classes, each class will require an integer field to hold its own value. In the example, this field is called animalType and is declared in the animal class. It is then inherited by each subclass.

The constructor of each class (or some other mechanism) is responsible for initializing each object to an appropriate identifier. In the example, each object's animalType field is initialized to BEAR, CHIPMUNK, or DOG.

An array of `animal` objects is still created because subclass references can be assigned to superclass variables. (This is not a polymorphic concept.) In the example, a `menagerie` array of the `animal` data type is created.

A For loop statement iterates through the array's elements. A Switch statement examines the identifier (for example, `animalType`) to determine the object's class. An appropriate case is selected and execution proceeds. The array element is cast back to its appropriate subclass (for example, `bear`, `chipmunk`, or `dog`) and the class-specific method is called (for example, `growl ()`, `whistle ()`, or `bark ()`).

What's wrong with this code? It works, but there is a subtle problem. Suppose that we must add an additional `animal` subclass (such as a `tiger` subclass) to this application. We cannot just add a `tiger` subclass, create some `tiger` objects, and add them to the `menagerie` array. We also must create a `TIGER` final field variable with a unique value and an appropriate case to the Switch statement. This is not so bad with our simple example, but what happens if we have a much larger program consisting of hundreds of classes and many opportunities for adding or removing subclasses? The possibility of error increases. Because polymorphism's dynamic method binding capability does this for us, it is more appropriate to make use of this capability and forget about traditional data type/switch logic.

DEALERSHIP3

DEALERSHIP3 is an application that serves as a continuation of DEALERSHIP2 (from the previous chapter). DEALERSHIP3 demonstrates dynamic method binding, interfaces, abstract superclasses, and `instanceof`.

Setting Up DEALERSHIP3

To set up DEALERSHIP3, begin by double-clicking your MS-DOS icon (if you are using Windows) and go to a command prompt.

If you created a `projects` directory in Chapter 1, "Introducing Java," make `projects` your current directory. (If you do not have a `projects` directory, now is as good a time as any to create one.)

Assuming that `projects` is located within `c:\jdk1.2\`, enter the command `cd \jdk1.2\projects` to change to this directory.

From within your `projects` directory, create a directory called `dealership3` (for example, `md dealership3`). (If you prefer, you can create this directory entirely in uppercase. For example, you could issue the command `md DEALERSHIP3` to create this directory. Case does not matter when it comes to directories.)

Download the file `dealership3.java` from the Macmillan Web site and place this file in your `dealership3` directory.

Compiling DEALERSHIP3

Compilation is a simple process. It involves running the `javac.exe` program and specifying the name of the source file as an argument to this program.

At the command prompt, enter the following line:

```
c:\jdk1.2\projects\dealership3>javac dealership3.java
```

CAUTION

The `.java` file extension must be specified when compiling an application's source file. The compiler will display an error message if `.java` is not specified.

If the compiler displays an error message, you might have typed `Dealership3.java` or `DEALERSHIP3.java` instead of `dealership3.java`.

CAUTION

You must specify `dealership3.java` and not `Dealership3.java`, `DEALERSHIP3.java`, or any other combination of lowercase/uppercase letters. The compiler is very sensitive to case and will display an error message if the class name (`dealership3`) does not match the filename (`dealership3`).

After compilation is finished, you should end up with a class file called `dealership3.class`.

Figure 6.2 shows the compilation process.

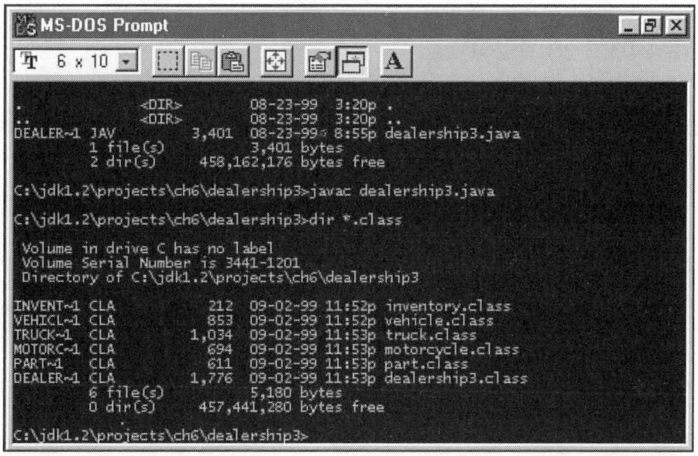

Figure 6.2: *Compiling* `dealership3.java` *with the* `javac.exe` *compiler.*

Running DEALERSHIP3

Congratulations! You successfully compiled dealership3.java and are now ready to run dealership3.class. All you need to do is fire up the java.exe program and specify dealership3.class as an argument to this program.

CAUTION

The .class file extension must not be specified; otherwise, the java.exe program will display an error message.

Figure 6.3 shows the process of running dealership3.class with java.exe.

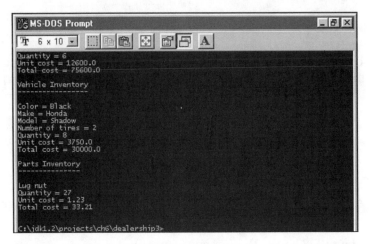

Figure 6.3: *Running* dealership3.class *with* java.exe.

Potential Problems

As it stands, DEALERSHIP3 is pretty robust. However, if you decide to modify the code, you could run into some problems. Here is one possibility. (This possibility is repeated from the previous chapter.)

- Creating another vehicle-specific class and declaring getQuantity () or getUnitCost () in this class without using public will result in a compiler error. The error occurs because these methods are declared within the inventory interface with a default public visibility and it is not possible to implement interface methods with less visibility.

If you should encounter an error, don't panic. Instead, try to reason out the cause of this error and then take appropriate action.

Enhancing DEALERSHIP3

You can enhance DEALERSHIP3 by turning it into a database application with a graphical user interface for data entry and display of information. However, before attempting to do this, you'll need to continue reading through this book to learn more about these concepts.

What's Next?

Now that you've explored the third principle of object-oriented programming, polymorphism, you need to learn how to properly initialize class fields and instance fields. You should also learn how to clean up objects before they are destroyed. These concepts are discussed in the next chapter, along with an interesting discussion on nesting classes within classes—a very useful technique that is used by Java's abstract windowing toolkit.

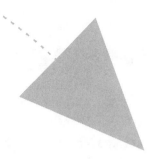

Initializers, Finalizers, and Inner Classes

Initializing objects is an important task. If this task is not properly carried out, objects will "begin life" in a "crippled" state. Java uses special language features known as initializers to handle this task.

Finalization complements the initialization task. When it's time for an object to "die," it should make every effort to "get its house in order." This task involves releasing any resources that the object is holding before it "dies." Java uses the finalizer language feature to give objects a chance to release resources before they are destroyed.

The Java language provides programs with the capability to nest classes (that is, declare classes within other classes). These nested classes are known as inner classes. (They are quite useful, as you will see.)

Chapter 7 presents the following topics:

- Initializers
- Finalizers
- Inner classes

Initializers

Initializers are special methods that initialize class fields and instance fields. They ensure that classes and objects are correctly initialized before a Java program "gets down to business" with whatever it has to do.

Because class fields and instance fields are different kinds of entities, they need to be initialized in different ways. It is for this reason that Java provides two different kinds of initializers—class field initializers and instance field initializers.

> ✔ For more information on `fields`, see Chapter 4, "Encapsulation: Classes and Objects," page 75.

Fields and Default Values

Fields are variables declared within a class block. Basically, there are two kinds of fields, class fields and instance fields.

A *class field* is shared by all objects created from the class that declares this field. If one of these objects changes the class field's value, the other objects are able to access the new value. In fact, a class's class fields exist long before any objects are created from that class.

An *instance field* is unique to an object. It is this uniqueness that sets objects apart. For example, a red car differs from a blue car based on its color property. Instance fields are created only when an object is created.

Unlike the C++ object-oriented language, Java guarantees that all its class and instance fields are initialized to default values before program code can access these fields. These default values are shown in Table 7.1.

Table 7.1: Default Values

Data Type	Default `Value`
boolean	`false`
char	`'\u0000'`
byte	`0`
short	`0`
int	`0`
long	`0l`
float	`0.0f`
double	`0.0d`
reference	`null`

Although the formats of these default values differ, they all share the following in common: The physical representation of default values consists of memory bits that are all set to zero.

Class Field Initializers

Class fields are created and initialized to default values just after the class file in which they are declared has been loaded into memory, and before any object from that class has been created. Let's take a look at an example.

EXAMPLE

```
class class0
{
    static int count;

    public static void main (String [] args)
    {
        System.out.println (count);
    }
}
```

OUTPUT

```
0
```

Before the main method begins to run, the JVM loads the class0 class file into memory. A region of memory is allocated for the main method's byte code, and a four-byte region is allocated for the count class field. The value of count is set to its default 0 value. This is illustrated in Figure 7.1.

Figure 7.1: *The class0 class as it exists in memory.*

The region inside the dashed lines is all that exists, as far as class0 is concerned.

Suppose that this class was slightly modified so that count was initialized to a value of 1, as in the following example. (This class has been renamed to class1 to make it easier to differentiate it from class0.)

EXAMPLE

```
class class1
{
    static int count = 1;

    public static void main (String [] args)
    {
        System.out.println (count);
    }
}
```

OUTPUT

```
1
```

After count has been initialized to its default 0 value, it is initialized a second time to a value of 1. This is illustrated in Figure 7.2.

Figure 7.2: *The* class1 *class as it exists in memory, after* count *is initialized to 1.*

What is responsible for initializing count to 1? It turns out that the compiler creates a special method called <clinit>, the class field initializer, that is responsible for initializing count.

For each class that declares at least one class field, the compiler creates a <clinit> method for that class and stores the byte code for this method in the resulting class file. If a class does not declare any class fields, the compiler will not create a <clinit> method for that class.

Essentially, the <clinit> method is a JVM method that takes no arguments and has the void return data type. This method is not declared in source code. In fact, it could never be declared in source code because the angle brackets cannot be used as part of a language identifier.

After a class file has been loaded into memory and its class fields initialized to their default values, the JVM calls <clinit> to initialize class fields to developer-supplied initial values—such as assigning 1 to count.

It is possible to initialize a class field using the value of a previously initialized class field, as shown in the following example:

EXAMPLE

```
// class2.java

class class2
{
    static int count = 1;
    static int total = 2 + count;

    public static void main (String [] args)
    {
        System.out.println (total);
    }
}
```

OUTPUT

```
3
```

After <clinit> has explicitly initialized the count field to 1, it initializes the total field to 2 plus the contents of the count field—1. As shown, the result is 3.

However, it is not possible for a class field to refer to a class field that follows it in source code. If this is attempted, the compiler reports an error, as shown in the following example:

EXAMPLE

```
// class3.java

class class3
{
    static int total = 2 + count;
    static int count = 1;

    public static void main (String [] args)
    {
        System.out.println (total);
    }
}
```

OUTPUT

```
class3.java:5 Can't make forward reference to count in class class3.
    static int total = 2 + count;
                           ^
```

As you can see, the compiler is complaining about a forward reference (an attempt to access a name before it has been declared).

Why is this a problem? This is a problem because the JVM has given count its default value of 0 and then, if allowed to proceed, would initialize total to 2, not 3 as the developer probably intended. After total was initialized to 2, count would then be initialized to 1.

Suppose that you need to take advantage of a complex initialization. For example, suppose you need to initialize total to the sum of integers ranging from 1 to 20 (inclusive). Java lets you do this by enabling you to use a class field initialization block (that is to say, blocks of code that initialize one or more class fields to non-default values).

A class field initialization block is declared within a class and prefixed with the static reserved word. This is illustrated in the following example:

EXAMPLE

```
// class4.java

class class4
{
    static int count = 1;
    static int total;

    static
    {
        for (int i = 1; i <= 20; i++)
            total += i;
    }

    public static void main (String [] args)
```

```
        {
            System.out.println (total);
        }
    }
}
210
```

This class field initialization block contains a For loop statement that iterates through the values from 1 to 20 and adds each value to total.

The int variable i that is declared within this block is a local variable. As soon as the <clinit> method finishes executing, this variable disappears. Local variable i and any other local variables that are declared within a class field initialization block cannot be accessed from outside that block.

When this class file is loaded, count and total are initialized to 0. After this is done, the JVM calls <clinit>. This method initializes count to 1, and then executes byte code to add the integers from 1 to 20 to total.

Any number of class field initialization statements (such as assigning 1 to count) and class field initialization blocks can be interspersed throughout a class. The compiler compiles this code and places it in <clinit>. Order matters! Class field initialization byte code is placed in <clinit> in the order in which the compiler processes it, from top to bottom. This is illustrated in the following example:

```
// class5.java

class class5
{
    static int count = 1;
    static int total;

    static
    {
        for (int i = 1; i <= 20; i++)
            total += i;
    }

    static int factorial5 = 1;

    static
    {
        for (int i = 1; i <= 5; i++)
            factorial5 *= i;
    }

    public static void main (String [] args)
    {
        System.out.println ("total = " + total);
```

```
        System.out.println ("factorial5 = " + factorial5);
        System.out.println ("e = " + e);
    }

    static double e = 2.71828;
    static
    {
        System.out.println ("HI");
    }
}
```

OUTPUT

```
HI
total = 210
factorial5 = 120
e = 2.71828
```

The JVM loads the class5 class file just before running the main method. The values of the count, total, and factorial fields are initialized to 0. The value of the e field is initialized to 0.0.

The JVM then calls the <clinit> method. The first thing that this method does is initialize count to 1. It then adds the values from 1 to 20 to the total field. After this is done, factorial5 is initialized to 1. The contents of the second class field initialization block are executed. This block computes 5! (five factorial). After factorial5 has been initialized to 120, the value of e (a special mathematical number) is initialized to 2.71828. Finally, <clinit> executes code in the last class field initialization block. This code causes the literal string "HI" to be displayed.

Class field initialization blocks can execute other kinds of Java code in addition to initializing class fields. They can even create objects and access their class and instance fields.

To prove that class field initializations and class field initialization blocks are executed before the main method, take a look at the output from the previous example. Notice that HI appears before any other output.

Instance Field Initializers

Instance fields, like class fields, are initialized to default values before they are accessed. However, whereas class fields are initialized just after the class file in which they are declared has been loaded into memory, and before any object from that class has been created, instance fields are initialized to these default values only after an object has been created. Let's take a look at an example:

EXAMPLE

```
// instance0.java

class instance0
{
```

```
    double rate;

    public static void main (String [] args)
    {
        instance0 i0 = new instance0 ();
        System.out.println (i0.rate);
    }
}
```

`0.0`

Before the `main` method begins to run, the virtual machine loads the `instance0` class file into memory. A region of memory is allocated to the `main` method's byte code.

Memory is allocated to reference variable `i0`. This memory is large enough (probably four bytes in size) to hold the address of several regions of memory.

The first region points to the object's instance fields. The second region points to shared class fields. The third region points to method byte code.

After memory has been allocated, the instance fields are initialized to their default values. Then, the `instance0 ()` constructor method is called to complete initialization.

If you look at the source code, you won't find an `instance0 ()` constructor. So where does this constructor come from? It turns out that if a class file does not declare any constructors, the compiler will create a default constructor that takes no arguments. This is illustrated in Figure 7.3.

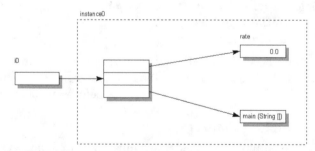

Figure 7.3: *The `instance0` class and `i0` reference variable as they exist in memory.*

In reality, `i0` refers to a list of addresses that point to various memory blocks. One of these addresses points to the instance field values that differentiate one object from another object. A second address points to the byte code associated with the methods that are declared in the object's class. A third address points to shared class fields. Because `instance0` declares no class fields, there is no block of memory for these fields (and no arrow pointing to this block in Figure 7.3).

Suppose that this class was slightly modified so that `rate` was initialized to a value of `6.5`, as in the following example. (This class has been renamed to `instance1` to make it easier to differentiate it from `instance0`.)

EXAMPLE

```
// instance1.java

class instance1
{
    double rate = 6.5;

    public static void main (String [] args)
    {
        instance1 i1 = new instance1 ();
        System.out.println (i1.rate);
    }
}
```

OUTPUT

```
6.5
```

After `rate` has been initialized to its default `0.0` value, it is initialized a second time to a value of `6.5`, as illustrated in Figure 7.4.

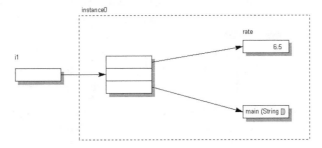

Figure 7.4: *The* `instance1` *class and* `i1` *reference variable as they exist in memory, after* `rate` *is initialized to* `6.5`.

What is responsible for initializing `rate` to `6.5`? The compiler creates a special method that initializes instance fields to developer-specified values. This method is called `<init>`, the instance field initializer.

Like `<clinit>`, `<init>` is a JVM method. However, there is a difference. Every constructor (such as `instance1 ()` in the previous example) is compiled into an `<init>` method. This means that a class declaration with three constructor methods would be compiled into a class file with three `<init>` methods.

Constructor methods are not given return data types, not even `void`. However, all `<init>` methods have a `void` return data type. Why? From a logical point of view, constructors do not return values. This is not their purpose. However, the JVM does not "think" in terms of constructors, just methods. Because <init> methods are the JVM equivalent of constructors, and because every JVM method has a return data type, void is used as the return data type for <init> methods.

To initialize an object, the JVM first initializes its instance fields to default values, and then calls the <init> method that matches the source code constructor call (based on number and data types of arguments). One of the first things that this method does is to initialize instance fields to developer-specified values (for example, assign 6.5 to rate). After this has been accomplished, the rest of the method's byte code is executed.

Class methods do not differentiate between objects. However, instance methods, including <init> methods, do differentiate. Because each object has its own unique set of instance fields, how does an instance method such as <init> differentiate between these field sets?

The answer lies with a special argument that is always passed as the first argument to an <init> (or any instance) method. This argument is an object reference (that is, the address of an object). Each reference points to a unique set of instance fields.

You've learned about using the reserved word this to call constructor methods and assign values to fields. This reserved word is a source code mechanism for referring to a specific object instance. In a sense, you could say that this is passed as the first argument to each <init> (and other instance) method. In other words, this serves as a bridge between different sets of instance fields and byte code methods that are shared amongst these fields.

It is possible to initialize an instance field using the value of a previously initialized instance field, as shown in the following example:

EXAMPLE

```
// instance2.java

class instance2
{
    double rate = 6.5;
    double balance = 50000.0;
    double monthlyInterest = balance * rate / 12.0;

    public static void main (String [] args)
    {
        instance2 i2 = new instance2 ();

        System.out.println ("balance = " + i2.balance);
        System.out.println ("monthly interest = " + i2.monthlyInterest);
    }
}
```

```
balance = 50000.0
monthly interest = 27083.333333333332
```

The `<init>` method that corresponds to the `instance2 ()` constructor is called. This method first initializes `rate` to `6.5`. It then initializes `balance` to `50000.0` and `monthlyInterest` to `27083.33`, the result of a calculation.

As with class fields, forward references are not allowed.

If you need to perform more complex instance field initialization, you can take advantage of instance field initialization blocks, (that is to say, blocks of code that initialize one or more instance fields to non-default values).

An instance field initialization block is declared within a class in a manner that is similar to a class field initialization block. However, the `static` reserved word does not prefix an instance field initialization block. This is illustrated in the following example:

```
// instance3.java

class instance3
{
    double interestRate = 3.5;
    double balance = 23000.0;

    double monthlyInterest [] =
    {
        0.0, 0.0, 0.0,
        0.0, 0.0, 0.0,
        0.0, 0.0, 0.0,
        0.0, 0.0, 0.0
    };

    {
        int i = 0;
        for (double rate = 1.0; rate <= 6.5; rate += 0.5)
            monthlyInterest [i++] = balance * rate / 12.0;
    }

    public static void main (String [] args)
    {
        instance3 i3 = new instance3 ();

        System.out.println ("balance = " + i3.balance);

        for (int i = 0; i < i3.monthlyInterest.length; i++)
            System.out.println ("Monthly interest for rate " +
                        (1.0 + 0.5 * i) + " equals " +
                        i3.monthlyInterest [i]);
    }
}
```

The instance field initialization block is used to pre-calculate the monthly interest values for a variety of interest rates.

OUTPUT

```
balance = 23000.0
Monthly interest for rate 1.0 equals 1916.6666666666667
Monthly interest for rate 1.5 equals 2875.0
Monthly interest for rate 2.0 equals 3833.3333333333335
Monthly interest for rate 2.5 equals 4791.666666666667
Monthly interest for rate 3.0 equals 5750.0
Monthly interest for rate 3.5 equals 6708.333333333333
Monthly interest for rate 4.0 equals 7666.666666666667
Monthly interest for rate 4.5 equals 8625.0
Monthly interest for rate 5.0 equals 9583.333333333334
Monthly interest for rate 5.5 equals 10541.666666666666
Monthly interest for rate 6.0 equals 11500.0
Monthly interest for rate 6.5 equals 12458.333333333334
```

A call to the `instance3 ()` constructor is a call to the `<init>` method. This method first initializes `interestRate`, `balance`, and `monthlyInterest` to 3.5, 23000.0, and an array of twelve 0.0 values, respectively. It then executes byte code to initialize the `monthlyInterest` array to values based on `balance` and a variety of interest rates.

The `int` variable `i` that is declared within the instance field initialization block is a local variable. As soon as the `<init>` method finishes executing, this variable disappears. Local variable `i`, and any other local variables that are declared within an instance field initialization block, cannot be accessed from outside that block.

Any number of instance field initialization statements (such as assigning 23000.0 to `balance`) and instance field initialization blocks can be interspersed throughout a class. The compiler compiles this code and places it in an `<init>` method. Order matters! Instance field initialization byte code is placed in `<init>` in the order in which the compiler processes it, from top to bottom.

However, there is a problem. Suppose that your class has two constructors. Which constructor gets compiled into the `<init>` method that initializes the instance fields? Let's see if we can answer this question with an example:

EXAMPLE

```
// instance4.java

class instance4
{
    int x;
    int y = 2;

    instance4 (int x)
    {
        this.x = x;
```

```
    }

    instance4 ()
    {
    }

    public static void main (String [] args)
    {
        instance4 i4 = new instance4 ();
        System.out.println (i4.y);
    }
}
```

2

So which constructor initializes y to 2? The answer is either constructor. It doesn't matter which constructor is called. Either constructor is compiled into an <init> method that initializes y to 2.

Mixing Class Field and Instance Field Initializers

Classes contain a mixture of class field and instance field declarations. What is the order of initialization when both kinds of fields are mixed? Actually, the order is easy to determine.

First, a class file is loaded into memory. As soon as this class file is loaded, memory is allocated for each method's byte code, and memory is allocated for all the class fields. The values of these fields are initialized to 0 (even though we interpret these default values as 0, 0.0, null, and so on).

Second, the <clinit> method is called (if present). This method contains byte code to evaluate developer-supplied expressions and assign resulting values to the class fields. The source code can contain a mixture of class field initialization statements and class field initialization blocks. This is all compiled into the single <clinit> method.

Initialization of the class is now complete. Initialization of objects is another matter.

The developer must supply a statement to create an object. This statement causes memory to be allocated for a variable that holds the object's address. The use of the new reserved word causes memory to be allocated for the object's instance fields. Finally, a constructor call is made to initialize the object.

As we've seen, a constructor is just "source code fluff." The compiler converts each constructor into an <init> method. Each <init> method contains byte code to initialize all instance fields. (This byte code is not supplied by the developer. It is implicitly generated by the compiler.) After this byte code executes, the rest of the byte code, corresponding to the source code that the developer supplied in the constructor, executes and object initialization completes.

The following example illustrates mixing class field and instance field initialization:

EXAMPLE

```
// mixed.java

class mixed
{
    int i1;

    static int i2;

    int i3 = 2;

    static int i4 = 4;

    {
        i1 = 6;

        System.out.println ("i1 assigned 6");
    }

    static
    {
        i2 = 8;

        System.out.println ("i2 assigned 8");
    }

    public static void main (String [] args)
    {
        System.out.println ("main entered");

        mixed m = new mixed ();

        System.out.println ("m.i1 = " + m.i1);
        System.out.println ("i2 = " + i2);
        System.out.println ("m.i3 = " + m.i3);
        System.out.println ("i4 = " + i4);

        System.out.println ("main exited");
    }

    {
        i1 += 6;

        System.out.println ("6 added to i1");
    }
```

```
   static
   {
      i2 -= 3;

      System.out.println ("3 subtracted from i2");
   }
}
```

```
i2 assigned 8
3 subtracted from i2
main entered
i1 assigned 6
6 added to i1
m.i1 = 12
i2 = 5
m.i3 = 2
i4 = 4
main exited
```

Initialization and Inheritance

We have looked at initialization as it applies to a class that is not derived from any other class. However, there are some issues that we need to examine when inheritance is involved. To get things started, let's look at an example:

```java
// inherit0.java

class parent
{
   int a = 5;

   int b;

   static double c = 2.0;

   static long d;

   {
      System.out.println ("a = " + a);
      System.out.println ("b = " + b);
   }

   static
   {
      System.out.println ("c = " + c);
      System.out.println ("d = " + d);
   }
}
```

```
class child extends parent
{
   int w;

   static int x = 2;

   double y = 3.5;

   static boolean z = true;

   {
      System.out.println ("w = " + w);
      System.out.println ("y = " + y);
   }

   static
   {
      System.out.println ("x = " + x);
      System.out.println ("z = " + z);
   }
}

class inherit0
{
   public static void main (String [] args)
   {
      child c = new child ();

      System.out.println ("c.a = " + c.a);
      System.out.println ("c.b = " + c.b);
      System.out.println ("parent.c = " + parent.c);
      System.out.println ("parent.d = " + parent.d);

      System.out.println ("c.w = " + c.w);
      System.out.println ("child.x = " + c.x);
      System.out.println ("c.y = " + c.y);
      System.out.println ("child.z = " + c.z);
   }
}
```

This example consists of three classes: parent, child, and inherit0. The inherit0 class creates a child object and displays the contents of the various fields.

OUTPUT

```
c = 2.0
d = 0
x = 2
z = true
a = 5
```

```
b = 0
w = 0
y = 3.5
c.a = 5
c.b = 0
parent.c = 2.0
parent.d = 0
c.w = 0
child.x = 2
c.y = 3.5
child.z = true
```

Take a good look at the output. Notice that the `parent` class fields are initialized followed by the `child` class fields. Then, the `parent` instance fields are initialized followed by the `child` instance fields. Now look at this initialization in detail.

The JVM loads the `inherit0` class file and starts executing the `main` method byte code. The first thing that the `main` method byte code does is construct a `child` object called `c`. This construction requires several steps.

As soon as the `child` class is referenced, the JVM loads the `child.class` and `parent.class` files. (The `parent.class` file is loaded by virtue of being `child`'s superclass.) After these class files have been loaded, the JVM allocates enough memory for all class fields declared in `parent` and in `child`.

The `parent` class `<clinit>` method is called to initialize the `parent` class fields. After this method returns, the `<clinit>` method in the `child` class is called to initialize its class fields. At this point, all class fields have been initialized.

Memory is allocated for the `child` variable `c` and memory is allocated for all instance fields in both `parent` and `child` layers. All fields are initialized to zero by the virtual machine.

The `<init>` method that corresponds to the `child ()` constructor is called. The first thing that this method does is to call the `<init>` method in the `parent ()` class. The first thing that `parent`'s `<init>` method does is to call the `<init>` method in the `Object` root class.

When `Object`'s `<init>` method returns, `parent`'s `<init>` method initializes all its instance fields to the developer-supplied values, and executes the contents of instance field initialization blocks. Any developer-supplied byte code is then executed (that is, byte code compiled from developer-supplied constructor source code). After this method returns, `child`'s `<init>` method initializes its instance fields and executes its instance field initialization blocks. Any developer supplied byte code is then executed.

An <init> method begins with one of two calls: a call to another <init> method within the same class (analogous to calling another constructor within the same class via this) or a call to another <init> method within the superclass (analogous to calling another constructor within the superclass via super). For this reason, the super or this constructor call must be the first source code that appears within a constructor, if either call is specified.

✔ For more information on super, see Chapter 5, "Inheritance: Superclasses and Subclasses," page 105.

If a child class does not specify a super call, this call will still be generated by the compiler, and the byte code will be placed at the front of the corresponding <init> method. However, in this case, code will be generated to call a no-argument constructor in the superclass. If this constructor does not exist, the compiler will report an error.

Initialization order is important when inheritance is being used. The child class <init> method is always called first. However, the first code in this method either calls another <init> method in the child class (that is, one constructor calls another constructor in the same class) or an <init> method in the superclass.

The superclass <init> method either calls an <init> method in the same class or an <init> method in its superclass. This continues until Object's <init> method is called. (There will always be an <init> method in each subclass that calls the superclass <init> method.) Therefore, <init> method calls "bubble up" to Object. After Object completes its <init> method call (which currently does nothing because there are no class or instance fields within Object—at least not in the Win32 version of the JDK), the <init> method in its immediate child class continues executing by initializing its instance fields. The rest of its byte code is then executed. This process continues until control is finally returned to the child class <init> method that originated this process. This <init> method initializes its instance fields, and then executes the rest of its byte code.

So why is this order used? The idea is to ensure that all superclass layers have completed initialization before subclass layers are initialized. It is then possible for a subclass constructor to refer to superclass fields, and know that these fields have been initialized.

Fields, like methods, can be overridden. When this happens, the super reserved word can be used to refer to a field in a parent class and make it accessible to the child class. This capability is illustrated in the following example:

EXAMPLE

```
// inherit1.java

class parent
{
    int a = 2;

    static int b = 5;
}

class child extends parent
{
    int a = 3;

    static int b = 6;

    int getA () { return super.a; }
}

class inherit1
{
    public static void main (String [] args)
    {
        child c = new child ();

        System.out.println ("c.a = " + c.a);
        System.out.println ("c.a (in superclass) = " + c.getA ());

        System.out.println ("parent.b = " + parent.b);
        System.out.println ("child.b = " + child.b);
    }
}
```

OUTPUT

```
c.a = 3
c.a (in superclass) = 2
Parent.b = 5
Child.b = 6
```

It is possible to access subclass fields from a superclass constructor. If this happens, the subclass fields will not be initialized. This could seriously affect an object's "sanity." Therefore, you should not do this. However, just to be nasty, I'm going to show you how. I'm doing this so you can see why it should be avoided. Check out the following example:

EXAMPLE

```
// inherit2.java

class parent
{
    parent ()
    {
```

```
            System.out.println ("parent: x = " + ((child) this).getX ());
            System.out.println ("parent: y = " + ((child) this).y);
        }
    }

class child extends parent
{
    private int x = 5;

    int getX () { return x; }

    int y = -2;
}

class inherit2
{
    public static void main (String [] args)
    {
        child c = new child ();

        System.out.println ("x = " + c.getX ());
        System.out.println ("y = " + c.y);
    }
}
```

```
parent: x = 0
parent: y = 0
x = 5
y = -2
```

OUTPUT

Accessing subclass fields from superclass constructors results in retrieving the default values. You should never do this because subclass fields are not initialized until after the superclass constructor finishes, and the subclass constructor "does its thing." If you do this, you are just begging for trouble.

Finalizers

Finalizers are methods that objects can use to release resources before they are destroyed. The garbage collection part of the virtual machine is responsible for calling finalizers. The actual finalizer method is called finalize (). This method is inherited from the Object class. As you will see, this method is not always called, and should only be used for certain tasks.

Garbage Collection

You can create objects via the new reserved word. However, you cannot destroy these objects. Java does not give developers the chance to destroy objects because, all too often, a developer forgets to properly destroy these objects. Besides, not having to worry about destroying objects is one less hassle for developers, and is one more way in which to ensure a program's robustness.

The JVM maintains a table of reference counts for each created object. Each time the object's address is assigned to some variable (for example, String s = "abc" ;), the reference count is incremented. Each time this address is replaced by the null value (for example, s = null;), the reference count is decremented.

The JVM runs a low priority thread of execution known as the garbage collector. (Threads will be discussed in a later chapter.) The garbage collector examines this table of reference counts and notes those objects whose counts are set to zero. For each object with a zero reference count, the garbage collector calls the object's finalize () method. After the finalize () method returns, the garbage collector re-checks the reference count for this object. If this count is still zero, the garbage collector destroys the object by freeing its memory.

Because the garbage collector re-checks an object's reference count after finalize () returns, it is possible to prevent an object from "dying." However, the object should be allowed to "die." Another object can always be created. Besides, the code for preventing an object from "dying" can complicate an understanding of the program's flow.

The finalize () Method

Every object inherits the finalize () method from the Object class. By default, this method does nothing. However, it can be overridden to respond to an object's impending destruction.

The finalize () method does not return a value. What's the point? The object is "dying." Therefore, the return data type of finalize () is void.

Let's look at an example to see how finalize () is used:

EXAMPLE

```
// finalize0.java

class finalize0
{
    int id;

    public static void main (String [] args)
    {
        finalize0 f0 = null;
        for (int i = 0; i < 10; i++)
            f0 = new finalize0 (i);
    }
}
```

```
public void finalize () throws Throwable
{
   System.out.println ("Finalizing " + id);
   super.finalize ();
}

finalize0 (int i)
{
   id = i;
}
}
```

The last line of a `finalize ()` method should call the superclass `finalize ()` method to give that layer a chance to clean up. This is accomplished by calling `super.finalize ()`.

OUTPUT

There is no output. This program does not call the `finalize ()` method. Why?

The garbage collector thread runs at various times. There is no guarantee that this thread will even run during the life of a short program. Because the garbage collector is the only entity that can call `finalize ()`, this method will not be called if the garbage collector has not run.

If you would like to see `finalize ()` being called, change the terminating value of the For loop statement from `10` to some large number like `50000`. Because so many objects will be created, the garbage collector is bound to run at some point. (The act of overwriting the address value in `f0` causes the reference count assigned to the previously created object to drop to zero.)

Is there a way to ensure that `finalize ()` will be called for each object that is destroyed? Yes, there is a way. You need to call a special method that is part of the `System` class. This method is called `runFinalizersOnExit (boolean)`. This method takes a `boolean` argument that indicates if these finalizers should be executed. If this argument is `true`, the finalizers will be run, as shown in the following example:

EXAMPLE

```
// finalize1.java

class finalize1
{
   int id;

   public static void main (String [] args)
   {
      System.runFinalizersOnExit (true);

      finalize1 f1 = null;
```

```
        for (int i = 0; i < 10; i++)
            f1 = new finalize1 (i);
    }

    public void finalize () throws Throwable
    {
        System.out.println ("Finalizing " + id);
        super.finalize ();
    }

    finalize1 (int i)
    {
        id = i;
    }
}
```

OUTPUT

```
Finalizing 9
Finalizing 8
Finalizing 7
Finalizing 6
Finalizing 5
Finalizing 4
Finalizing 3
Finalizing 2
Finalizing 1
Finalizing 0
```

This time, the finalizers are called. As you can see, they are called in reverse order. The most recent object to be created is the first object to be destroyed.

Unfortunately, there are multithreading problems with the runFinalizersOnExit (boolean) method. Therefore, this method has been marked for deprecation. This means that you should not use it in your programs.

The runFinalization () method is part of the System class and suggests that the virtual machine make every effort to run finalizers. However, this does not mean that any finalizers will be executed.

If the finalize () method might not always be called, what is it good for? It turns out that the finalize () method can serve as a "fall back" if the object did not explicitly release a resource that it allocated. For example, if an object's constructor opens a file, this file is owned by the object until it closes that file. If the object does not attempt to close this file before it "dies," other objects might not be able to access this file. Therefore, placing a file-closing method call in the object's finalize () method can serve as a safeguard. If the program runs long enough, the garbage collector will run at some point and call the finalize () method. The file will be closed.

If an exception occurs in a `finalize ()` method, this method will not complete executing any cleanup code after the exception occurred. (Exceptions are discussed in the next chapter.)

Inner Classes

Classes can be declared in other classes. These classes are known as *inner classes*, and are used to enforce a relationship between a pair of classes. The inner class is a "helper" class that assists the outer class in doing its work.

Inner classes have complete access to the field and method members of the outer class, even if those members are declared `private`. However, the outer class can only access those inner class fields and methods that are not declared `private`. Furthermore, it is possible to declare the inner class `private` so that only the outer class can communicate with the inner class. (It also is possible to declare the inner class `public` or `protected`—they may also be declared `abstract` or `final`.)

Inner classes minimize naming conflicts at the class name/ interface name level. When a class is declared inside another class, the compiler takes the outer class name, appends a dollar-sign character to that name, and appends the inner class name to the dollar sign.

For example, if a source file already has a class name called x and another class name called y, and an inner class called x is declared in y, the compiler will generate class files `x.class`, `y.class`, and `y$x.class`.

There are two kinds of inner classes: *static inner classes* (analogous to class fields and class methods) and *instance inner classes* (analogous to instance fields and instance methods).

Static Inner Classes

A static inner class is associated with the outer class—not an object created from the outer class. It is declared with the `static` reserved word. Because a static inner class is only associated with the outer class (and not an instance of the outer class), it cannot access any outer class instance fields or instance methods.

Static inner classes can declare class and instance fields, as shown in the following example:

EXAMPLE

```
// inner0.java

class outerClass
{
    static int a = 1;
```

```
    static class innerClass
    {
        static int b = a + 1;

        int c = 3;
    }
}

class inner0
{
    public static void main (String [] args)
    {
        System.out.println ("a = " + outerClass.a);
        System.out.println ("b = " + outerClass.innerClass.b);

        outerClass.innerClass ocic = new outerClass.innerClass ();
        System.out.println ("c = " + ocic.c);
    }
}
```

Before an instance field, declared within a static inner class, can be accessed, a static inner class object needs to be created. This object is created by prefixing the static inner class name with the outer class name and a period character. (This is required because all outer class objects share a single static inner class object.)

```
a = 1
b = 2
c = 3
```

OUTPUT

Instance Inner Classes

An instance inner class is associated with an object created from the outer class. It is not declared with the static reserved word. Because an instance inner class is only associated with an outer class instance, it can access outer class instance fields and instance methods (as well as outer class static fields and static methods).

Instance inner classes can only declare instance fields, as shown in the following example:

EXAMPLE

```
// inner1.java

class outerClass
{
    static int a = 1;

    class innerClass
    {
        int b = a + 1;
```

```
        }
    }

class inner1
{
    public static void main (String [] args)
    {
        System.out.println ("a = " + outerClass.a);

        outerClass oc = new outerClass ();
        outerClass.innerClass ocic = oc.new innerClass ();
        System.out.println ("b = " + ocic.b);
    }
}
```

Before an instance field, declared within an instance inner class, can be accessed, an instance inner class object needs to be created. This object is created by prefixing the instance inner class name with an outer class object variable name and a period character. (This is required because each outer class object has its own unique inner class object.)

```
a = 1
b = 2
```

Anonymous Inner Classes

Situations will arise where you will need to create a child class that extends a parent class and override one or more parent class methods. However, you will only need to create a single object from this class. As you can probably guess, this is overkill. Is there a better way to deal with this situation? You bet!

It is possible to anonymously extend a parent class, override appropriate parent methods, and create an object in one single step—take advantage of anonymous inner classes (that is to say, inner classes without class names).

Anonymous inner classes, although a little disconcerting when first encountered, are very convenient and not that difficult to work with. And, because you don't have to supply a class name for an anonymous inner class, you reduce the likelihood of introducing a class name that conflicts with another inner class name.

The following example illustrates anonymous inner classes:

```
// inner2.java

abstract class animal
{
    abstract void talk ();
}

class dog extends animal
```

EXAMPLE

```
{
   void talk () { System.out.println ("Bark!"); }
}

class inner2
{
   public static void main (String [] args)
   {
      new dog ().talk ();

      new animal ()
      { void talk () { System.out.println ("Meow!"); }}.talk ();
   }
}
```

This example illustrates two things. First, we went to a lot of trouble to create a dog class that inherits from animal. We created a dog object so that its talk () method could be called. Second, we decided that we needed a cat object. Rather than explicitly create a cat class, we implicitly created this class, implemented the abstract talk () method from animal, and called this method. (Although it looks like we created an object from the abstract animal class, we did not. Objects cannot be created from abstract classes.)

OUTPUT

```
Bark!
Meow!
```

Unlike static inner classes and instance inner classes, the compiler generates a number (starting at 1) for use as the inner class name. In this example, the compiler generates three class files: animal.class, inner2.class, and inner2$1.class.

Anonymous inner classes are often used with the Abstract Windowing Toolkit (AWT) adapter classes. We'll look at this use of anonymous inner classes when we discuss the AWT in a later chapter.

What's Next?

Programs normally execute flawlessly. However, situations can arise when something goes wrong. For example, a program tries to open a file on a floppy disk, but there is no disk in the floppy disk drive.

Programs must be carefully written to handle these exceptional situations (that is to say, exceptions to the normal flow of the program's execution); otherwise, the program will fail—and the user will probably feel like throwing a brick through the developer's living room window!

The next chapter discusses Java's exception handling mechanism. In it you will learn about exceptions and how to write code that correctly responds to and recovers from exceptions.

Exception Handling

As a rule, programs perform flawlessly. However, there are times when programs fail. As a developer, part of your job is to produce programs that properly handle failure. After all, why should users pay for software that terminates at the first sign of failure, causing unsaved data to be lost? Vehicle manufacturers issue recalls when major defects are discovered in their products. However, defective programs are never recalled. Maybe it's time for a change.

You can guard against failure by taking advantage of Java's exception-handling mechanism. This mechanism, if it's used properly, can help you write robust code.

Chapter 8 presents the following topics:

- Dealing with failure
- Throwing exceptions
- Catching exceptions
- Cleaning up
- Exceptional issues
- CALC

Dealing with Failure

Why do programs fail? How were failures handled in the past? What are exceptions and errors? What is exception handling? Why exception handling? These are all good questions. Let's find some answers.

Why Do Programs Fail?

Programs fail when they are either unable to acquire needed resources or when their code is flawed. A failure resulting from an inability to acquire a resource is known as an *external failure*, whereas a failure resulting from flawed code is known as an *internal failure*.

External failures occur when a program tries to obtain some resource that is missing, is in short supply, or is being used by another program. An example of the first scenario is an attempt to open a file, but the file does not exist. An example of the second scenario is an attempt to allocate a certain amount of memory, but the amount of available memory is insufficient to satisfy this request. An example of the third scenario is an attempt to open a file that has already been opened by another program, and this program is not prepared to share the file. When an external failure occurs, the program experiencing the failure is not at fault, but it bears the responsibility for properly handling this failure.

Internal failures occur when a computer tries to run program instructions that are fundamentally flawed. An example of internal failure is a calculation that results in a division by zero failure when certain values are passed to this calculation. Another example of internal failure is an attempt to access an object's fields or call its methods via a null reference. When an internal failure occurs, the program experiencing this failure is at fault. An internal failure should never occur because the developer should have invested some time in planning a program's code to prevent internal failures, before writing the source code.

How Were Failures Handled in the Past?

Before object-oriented programming came into being, methods were known as *functions*. Functions were written to return values to indicate whether they succeeded and, if they failed, to identify the failure.

A function would typically return a zero integer value to identify success and a negative integer value to identify a specific kind of failure. This return value was commonly known as an *error code*. The responsibility for interpreting this error code and properly responding to this failure was entrusted to the function that called the failed function.

There are three problems with using error codes: ignoring the error codes, obscuring code flow, and increasing the size of the program.

Developers can write source code that ignores error codes. Because error codes are not examined, there is no way to tell that a failure has occurred. Ignoring one failure can lead to other failures. For example, suppose that a function attempts to open a file, fails, and returns an error code. Now suppose the function that called the open function does not check the error code to see if something went wrong. Instead, it runs merrily on its way and tries to read something from the file. Obviously, the read attempt will not work (there is no open file). Suppose that this read instruction is located in a loop that keeps repeating the read instruction until a certain value is read. Because this value will never be read, this loop keeps iterating without stopping, resulting in a locked-up program. The program must be terminated from the operating system, resulting in the loss of any unsaved data.

Error-handling code can obscure code flow. Tracing through the program's source code is harder with all of the decision and other statements that detect and handle errors.

Error-handling code can increase the size of a program. For example, a program that copies one file to another file might contain file open, file read, file write, and file close functionality. Error-handling code would be required to deal with those situations when a file could not be opened (for reading), a file could not be created (for writing), a file could not be read from, a file could not be written to, and a file could not be closed. The amount of error-handling code for responding to these possible failures could easily surpass the amount of file-copying code.

The problems with the traditional failure-handling model led to the creation of the exception-handling model. This model is based on a paper called "Exception Handling for C++ (revised)," written by Andrew Koenig and Bjarne Stroustrup (the father of C++). (This paper was first presented in April 1990 at the USENIX C++ Conference in San Francisco.)

What Are Exceptions and Errors?

When a failure happens while a Java program is running, the program typically creates an object that describes the failure. This object is known as an *exception*, which reports the exceptional state of the program. This exception is passed to the JVM, which locates program code that can handle the exception (that is to say, it can recover from the failure). (For certain kinds of failure, the JVM—not the program—creates the exception, and then attempts to locate program code to handle this exception.)

It is possible (although unlikely) that the JVM could fail. For example, the JVM could "discover" that there is insufficient available memory to allocate to a large array. In this situation, the JVM creates a very special kind of exception that describes this failure. This exception is known as an *error*.

If the JVM cannot locate program code to deal with this error, it will immediately terminate the program.

A FAMILY OF CLASSES

All exception and error classes are descendents of the `Throwable` class. As a result, they inherit the fields and methods that are part of `Throwable`.

`Throwable` contains a private `String` field that holds a description of the program's failed state. This field is initialized by indirectly calling an appropriate `Throwable` constructor at the time the exception is created (remember the `super ()` constructor call). (If this field is not initialized, it will contain the `null` reference value.)

`Throwable` contains a public `getMessage ()` method that returns the contents of this field. This method is often called from an exception handler to obtain a description of the failed state.

`Throwable` contains a public `printStackTrace ()` method that builds an error message consisting of the exception object's class name, program state information, and the contents of the method call stack. This information is sent to the standard error stream. The destination of this stream is either a command-line console (applications) or a Web browser's Java console (applets).

✔ For more information on standard error streams, see Chapter 17, "Files and Streams," page 445.

Two classes are derived from `Throwable`: `Exception` and `Error`.

THE Exception CLASS

The `Exception` class is the root class for Java's family of exception classes.

Listing 8.1 provides a complete hierarchy of those exception classes defined in JDK 1.2. Subclasses are shown below and to the right of superclasses.

Listing 8.1: Java's `Exception` class hierarchy.

```
Exception
    AclNotFoundException
    ActivationException
        UnknownGroupException
        UnknownObjectException
    AlreadyBoundException
    ApplicationException
    AWTException
    BadLocationException
    ClassNotFoundException
    CloneNotSupportedException
        ServerCloneException
```

```
DataFormatException
ExpandVetoException
GeneralSecurityException
    CertificateException
        CertificateEncodingException
        CertificateExpiredException
        CertificateNotYetValidException
        CertificateParsingException
    CRLException
    DigestException
    InvalidAlgorithmParameterException
    InvalidKeySpecException
    InvalidParameterSpecException
    KeyException
        InvalidKeyException
        KeyManagementException
    KeyStoreException
    NoSuchAlgorithmException
    NoSuchProviderException
    SignatureException
    UnrecoverableKeyException
IllegalAccessException
InstantiationException
InterruptedException
IntrospectionException
InvocationTargetException
IOException
    ChangedCharSetException
    CharConversionException
    EOFException
    FileNotFoundException
    InterruptedIOException
        MalformedURLException
    ObjectStreamException
        InvalidClassException
        InvalidObjectException
        NotActiveException
        NotSerializableException
        OptionalDataException
        StreamCorruptedException
        WriteAbortedException
    ProtocolException
    RemoteException
        AccessException
        ActivateFailedException
        ConnectException
        ConnectIOException
        ExportException
```

Listing 8.1: continued

```
                SocketSecurityException
                  MarshalException
            NoSuchObjectException
            ServerError
            ServerException
            ServerRuntimeException
                  SkeletonMismatchException
            SkeletonNotFoundException
            StubNotFoundException
            UnexpectedException
                  UnknownHostException
            UnmarshalException
        SocketException
            BindException
            ConnectException
            NoRouteToHostException
        SyncFailedException
        UnknownHostException
        UnknownServiceException
        UnsupportedEncodingException
              UTFDataFormatException
        ZipException
              JarException
    LastOwnerException
    NoninvertibleTransformException
    NoSuchFieldException
    NoSuchMethodException
    NotBoundException
    NotOwnerException
    ParseException
    PrinterException
        PrinterAbortException
        PrinterIOException
    PrivilegedActionException
    PropertyVetoException
    RemarshalException
    RuntimeException
        ArithmeticException
        ArrayStoreException
        CannotRedoException
        CannotUndoException
        ClassCastException
              CMMException
        ConcurrentModificationException
        EmptyStackException
        IllegalArgumentException
```

```
                        IllegalThreadStateException
                        InvalidParameterException
                        NumberFormatException
                         IllegalMonitorStateException
        IllegalPathStateException
        IllegalStateException
                        IllegalComponentStateException
                        InvalidDnDOperationException
        ImagingOpException
                        IndexOutOfBoundsException
                        ArrayIndexOutOfBoundsException
                        StringIndexOutOfBoundsException
        MissingResourceException
        NegativeArraySizeException
        NoSuchElementException
                          NullPointerException
        ProfileDataException
        ProviderException
        RasterFormatException
        SecurityException
                        AccessControlException
                        RMISecurityException
                         SystemException
                        BAD_CONTEXT
                        BAD_INV_ORDER
                        BAD_OPERATION
                        BAD_PARAM
                        BAD_TYPECODE
                                COMM_FAILURE
                        DATA_CONVERSION
                        FREE_MEM
                        IMP_LIMIT
                        INITIALIZE
                        INTERNAL
                        INTF_REPOS
                            INV_FLAG
                        INV_IDENT
                        INV_OBJREF
                        INV_POLICY
                        INVALID_TRANSACTION
                        MARSHAL
                            NO_IMPLEMENT
                        NO_MEMORY
                        NO_PERMISSION
                        NO_RESOURCES
                        NO_RESPONSE
                        OBJ_ADAPTER
                            OBJECT_NOT_EXIST
```

Listing 8.1: continued

```
                PERSIST_STORE
                TRANSACTION_REQUIRED
                TRANSACTION_ROLLEDBACK
                    TRANSIENT
                UNKNOWN
            UnsupportedOperationException
    ServerNotActiveException
    SQLException
        BatchUpdateException
        SQLWarning
    TooManyListenersException
    UnsupportedFlavorException
    UnsupportedLookAndFeelException
    UserException
        AlreadyBound
        BadKind
        Bounds
        Bounds (different from the previous)
        CannotProceed
        InconsistentTypeCode
        Invalid
        InvalidName
        InvalidName (different from the previous)
            InvalidSeq
        InvalidValue
        NotEmpty
        NotFound
        PolicyError
        TypeMismatch
        UnknownUserException
            WrongTransaction
```

Most, but not all, exception class names end with the word Exception.

THE Error CLASS

The Error class is the root class for Java's family of error classes.

Listing 8.2 provides a complete hierarchy of those error classes defined in JDK 1.2. Subclasses are shown below and to the right of superclasses.

Listing 8.2: Java's Error class hierarchy.

```
Error
    AWTError
    LinkageError
        ClassCircularityError
        ClassFormatError
```

```
            UnsupportedClassVersionError
      ExceptionInInitializerError
      IncompatibleClassChangeError
          AbstractMethodError
          IllegalAccessError
          InstantiationError
          NoSuchFieldError
          NoSuchMethodError
      NoClassDefFoundError
      UnsatisfiedLinkError
      VerifyError
  ThreadDeath
  VirtualMachineError
      InternalError
      OutOfMemoryError
      StackOverflowError
      UnknownError
```

Most, but not all, error class names end with the word Error. (ThreadDeath is the exception—yes, I know, this is a bad pun!)

What Is Exception Handling?

When a failure is detected (such as file not found), program codes create an object from an appropriate exception class and then pass this object to the JVM—a task known as *throwing an exception*. The JVM must search for appropriate code (within the same program) that can handle that exception.

The search begins in the failing method. If that method specifies an exception handler (that is to say, exception-handling code) designed to process exceptions of the same data type as the exception that needs to be handled, the search ends, and the exception is handled.

However, if an exception handler is not present, the JVM searches backwards through the method call stack until a method is located that can handle the exception. After the exception handler has been found, the exception is passed to the handler, and the handler handles the exception.

The tasks of finding an exception handler and passing the exception to this handler are known as *catching an exception*.

What happens if an exception handler cannot be found? This is a serious problem. Non-GUI (Graphical User Interface) applications and the JVM are terminated, whereas GUI applications and applets can continue running, but they run with the possibility of internal corruption and are not considered reliable.

Why Exception Handling?

One of the problems with the old failure-handling model was not using that model. However, the exception-handling model was designed to be used. External failures must either be handled or documented within source code if they are not handled. On the other hand, a program is not required to handle an internal failure because a properly written program does not generate internal failures.

Obscurity was another problem with the old failure-handling model. Error-handling code was interspersed with source code, resulting in source code that was hard to read. The exception-handling model separates a program's code from exception handlers, making it easier to trace through the source code.

The size of error-handling code was a third problem because the amount of this code could really increase the size of a program. However, the extra amount of code that exception handling adds to a program is considerably less.

Throwing Exceptions

Code that throws an exception based on an external failure needs to be placed within a Try statement whereas code that throws an exception based on an internal failure does not need to be placed within a Try statement.

Exceptions come in two flavors: checked and unchecked. Java's Throw statement makes it possible to throw checked or unchecked exceptions. Checked exceptions must be specified via a method's Throws clause.

The Try Statement

A Try statement surrounds a block of statements (possibly including other Try statements) that have the potential for throwing exceptions based on external failures. The statements within this block are "tried" to see if an external failure occurs.

The format of a Try statement is

```
"try"
'{'
    // One or more Java statements
'}'
```

A Try statement is prefixed with the `try` reserved word and is followed by a block of statements that have the potential to throw exceptions. Any variables created within this block have a scope that is restricted to the block. As a result, attempts to access these variables from outside of the block result in compiler errors.

The following code fragment attempts to open a file called abc.dat and connect it to an input stream. (Don't worry about what input streams are—they will be discussed in a later chapter. For now, an input stream is only being used to illustrate an exception based on an external failure.)

```
try
{
    FileInputStream fis = new FileInputStream ("abc.dat");
}
```

The FileInputStream (String) constructor contains code that attempts to open the file called abc.dat and associate this file with an input stream object. If this file is not found (or cannot be opened for some reason), this external failure forces the FileInputStream (String) constructor to create a FileNotFoundException object and throw this exception to the JVM.

If an exception is not thrown from within a Try statement, execution flows out of this statement and continues with the first instruction that follows Try.

If an exception is thrown, and an exception handler is located, after the exception handler finishes running, the Try statement will not resume running. For all intent and purpose, the Try statement is finished after an exception is thrown. There is no way to resume its unexecuted code.

Checked and Unchecked Exceptions

An exception that is based on an external failure is known as a *checked exception*. The compiler checks to see if this exception is being handled or explicitly specified as not being handled. For example, any exception that is created from FileNotFoundException is a checked exception.

An exception based on an internal failure is known as an *unchecked exception*. The compiler does not check to see if this exception is being handled because programs can be written to avoid internal failures. For example, a division-by-zero internal failure results in an unchecked exception of data type ArithmeticException. As a second example, an attempt to access an array element using a negative index or an index that is greater than or equal to the length of the array is an internal failure that results in an unchecked exception of data type ArrayIndexOutOfBounds.

ArithmeticException and ArrayIndexOutOfBounds are classes derived from RuntimeException. Any exception that is created from RuntimeException (or a derived class) is an unchecked exception.

The Throw Statement

A Throw statement creates and throws checked or unchecked exceptions. However, this statement should only be used to throw checked exceptions.

The format of a Throw statement is

```
"throw" exception ';'
```

A Throw statement is prefixed with the throw reserved word and followed by a newly created object that describes the failed state of the program.

EXAMPLE

The following code fragment throws a FileNotFoundException object (the object is initialized with a description of the program state when this failure occurred):

```
throw new FileNotFoundException ("Could not find abc.dat");
```

The Throws Clause

A Throws clause describes all the checked exceptions that can be thrown from within a method, by way of a comma-delimited list of exception class names tacked on to the end of the method header.

The format of a Throws clause is

```
"throws" exceptionClassName1 ',' exceptionClassName2 ',' …
```

EXAMPLE

The following code fragment specifies a Throws clause that lists FileNotFoundException as the exception data type of exceptions that can be explicitly thrown from within the main method:

```
public static void main (String [] args) throws FileNotFoundException
{
    FileInputStream fis = new FileInputStream ("abc.dat");
}
```

Because of the Throws clause, the FileInputStream (String) constructor call does not need to be placed within a Try statement. In other words, the main method is passing the buck to the JVM. ("This isn't my problem, let somebody else worry about it!")

Also, the FileNotFoundException object is thrown indirectly. There is no Throws statement defined within the main method, but there is a Throws statement either directly within the FileInputStream (String) constructor or within a method that is called from within this constructor.

CAUTION

Throwing a checked exception from a method that does not specify a Throws clause, or a Throws clause with that exception listed, will lead to compiler errors.

Catching Exceptions

Once an exception has been thrown, either directly by program code or indirectly by the JVM, this exception must be handled. Handling an exception is accomplished by providing an appropriate Catch clause.

It is possible to specify multiple Catch clauses immediately after a Try statement. This makes it possible to catch several kinds of exceptions in a single location and reduce exception-handling code clutter.

Situations might arise where you want to re-throw the same exception or throw a different kind of exception from within a Catch clause, as you'll shortly discover.

The Catch Clause

A Catch clause serves as an exception handler for either its preceding Try statement or some other Try statement that is reached through method calls in the preceding Try statement. The format of this clause is

```
"catch" '(' ExceptionClassName objectName ')'
'{'
    // One or more Java exception statements
'}'
```

A Catch clause is prefixed with the catch reserved word and is followed by a block of exception-handling statements.

The parameter list specifies a single parameter. This parameter consists of a data type (ExceptionClassName) and a name (objectName). The data type identifies the name of the exception class. The name identifies the exception object variable that is passed to the Catch clause exception handler.

CAUTION

ExceptionClassName must be either the Throwable class name or the name of a class that inherits from Throwable. Specifying any other class name results in a compiler error. Furthermore, specifying more than one parameter in the Catch clause parameter list also results in a compiler error.

EXAMPLE

The following code fragment specifies a Try statement surrounding code that attempts to open a file called abc.dat and connect an input stream to this file. However, if abc.dat does not exist, the FileInputStream (String) constructor throws an exception of data type FileNotFoundException:

```
try
{
    FileInputStream fis = new FileInputStream ("abc.dat");
}
catch (FileNotFoundException e)
{
    System.out.println (e.getMessage ());
}
```

The Catch clause that immediately follows the Try statement contains a parameter, FileNotFoundException, that matches the data type of the exception thrown by the constructor. Because the Catch clause immediately follows Try, it gets first crack at handling the exception.

CAUTION

Placing statements between a Try statement and a Catch clause results in a compiler error.

The Catch clause calls the getMessage () method that's inherited from Throwable. This method returns program state information including the name of the file that could not be opened: abc.dat.

Multiple Catch Clauses

It is possible to specify multiple Catch clauses after a single Try statement. This results in the ability to catch different kinds of exceptions in one location.

EXAMPLE

The following code fragment is taken from the view example application that was presented in Chapter 1, "Introducing Java." This code fragment consists of a Try statement that attempts to open a file, attach this file to an input stream, read each character from this input stream, output that character to the standard output device (that is, the video monitor or a file), and close the file associated with the input stream. It also contains a pair of exception-handling Catch clauses.

```java
FileInputStream fis = null;
try
{
    fis = new FileInputStream (new File (args [0]));

    int ch;
    while ((ch = fis.read ()) != -1)
       System.out.print ((char) ch);

    fis.close ();

    System.out.println ("");
}
catch (FileNotFoundException e)
{
    System.out.println ("File not found!");
    try
    {
       fis.close ();
    }
    catch (IOException ioe) {}
}
catch (IOException e)
{
    System.out.println ("Unable to read file!");
```

```
    try
    {
        fis.close ();
    }
    catch (IOException ioe) {}
}
```

Note the two primary Catch clauses. The first Catch clause handles
FileNotFoundException objects that might be thrown by the
FileInputStream (String) constructor. The second Catch clause handles
any IOException object that might be thrown from the read () method.

CAUTION

Specifying two or more Catch clauses with the same parameter data type after a Try
statement leads to compiler errors.

There is one problem with this example: redundant code. Not only is the
file associated with the fis input stream closed from within the Try statement, it is also closed from within each Catch clause.

If the Try statement succeeds, the file is closed from within the Try statement.
If a FileNotFoundException or IOException object is thrown, it is not possible
to come back to the Try statement and close the file after executing the appropriate Catch clause. Therefore, the file closing code must be duplicated within
each Catch clause. This is most distressing because the code is bloating. How
can this problem be solved? The Finally clause solves this problem in an ele-
gant fashion, as you will discover when the Finally clause is discussed.

Can the order of multiple Catch clauses be switched? For example, could
the Catch clause that catches IOException objects be specified before the
Catch clause that catches FileNotFoundException objects? In this case, the
answer is no.

IOException is a superclass of FileNotFoundException. If IOException is
specified before FileNotFoundException, a FileNotFoundException object
would be caught by the IOException Catch clause. The reason this happens
has to do with polymorphism. Because a FileNotFoundException is a kind of
IOException, the JVM would pass the FileNotFoundException object to the
IOException Catch clause handler.

The compiler does not like dead code. Because the Catch clause that handles FileNotFoundException objects would never be executed, the compiler
would generate an error.

CAUTION

Placing a Catch clause with a superclass exception data type before a Catch clause
with a subclass exception data type leads to compiler errors.

Throwing Exceptions from Catch Clauses

It's possible to throw an exception from within a Catch clause. Why would you want to do this?

Suppose that you are in charge of building a class library, to be used by a variety of applications. You are given a specification for the library's contract (that is, the part of the library that is callable from outside of the library). The contract consists of public class names (including exception class names), public field names and data types, public method names along with their return data types and parameter lists (that is, number of parameters and data types for these parameters), and the formats of exception objects. You are told that you can implement the library in any way you see fit as long as you do not violate the contract.

An application creates an object from one of your classes and calls one of the object's methods. However, the application passes one or more invalid arguments to the method.

Your method calls an internal method (from within a Try statement) and passes these arguments to that method. This internal method doesn't "like" the arguments and throws an exception. This exception is based on a private exception class that is solely used by the library.

The Catch clause that follows the Try statement handles the exception. However, your method cannot proceed. It needs to inform the application that something went wrong. You cannot re-throw this exception to the application because it is based on a private exception class, and the contract clearly defines other exception classes. Therefore, you create an exception from an exception class that is defined by the contract, populate this object with appropriate data, and throw this exception from within the Catch clause. The application will deal with the problem.

Cleaning Up

While learning about multiple Catch clauses, you saw an example of code that creates a `FileInputStream` object and initializes this object (via a call to the `FileInputStream (String)` constructor). This code was placed inside a Try statement. You also saw a call to the object's `close ()` method specified in three places: the Try statement and the two Catch clauses. (After all, the file associated with the stream must be closed before it can be re-opened.) This redundant cleanup code can be avoided by taking advantage of the Try statement's Finally clause.

The Finally Clause

A Finally clause serves as a cleanup handler for a preceding Try statement. The format of this clause is

```
"finally"
```

```
'{'
    // One or more Java statements
'}'
```

A Finally clause is prefixed with the `finally` reserved word and is followed by a block of cleanup handling statements.

After the last statement in either the Try statement or a Catch clause (if specified) has been executed, the code within a Finally clause (if specified) is executed.

EXAMPLE

The following code fragment is similar to the view example application that was presented in Chapter 1. This code fragment consists of a Try statement that attempts to open a file, attach this file to an input stream, read each character from this input stream, and output that character to the standard output device (that is, the video monitor or a file) and close the file associated with the input stream. It also contains a pair of exception handling Catch clauses and a cleanup Finally clause.

```
FileInputStream fis = null;

try
{
    fis = new FileInputStream (new File (args [0]));

    int ch;
    while ((ch = fis.read ()) != -1)
        System.out.print ((char) ch);

    System.out.println ("");

    return;
}
catch (FileNotFoundException e)
{
    System.out.println ("File not found!");
}
catch (IOException e)
{
    System.out.println ("Unable to read file!");
}
finally
{
    try
    {
        fis.close ();
    }
    catch (IOException ioe) {}

}
```

It doesn't matter how the Try statement exits (the Return statement or a thrown exception); the Finally clause will still close the file associated with the `fis` input stream before the method terminates.

If an exception is thrown within a Try statement and a matching Catch clause is not found within the same method, the code within a Finally clause (if present) runs before the JVM searches for an exception handler. In other words, the JVM cannot leave the method until the Finally clause has been run.

Throwing Exceptions from Finally Clauses

Like Catch clauses, a Finally clause might throw an exception. However, this could be dangerous. For example, code within a Try statement throws an exception. There is no Catch clause following the Try statement to handle the exception. The JVM will have to search the method call stack for a method containing an appropriate exception handler. However, because the Try statement is immediately followed by a Finally clause, the Finally clause will execute before the exception handler is located. The Finally clause executes some code that results in an exception, and decides to throw this exception. This thrown exception replaces the exception that was thrown from within the Try statement. Therefore, an exception is lost, and the original failure is not handled.

CAUTION

If a Try statement throws an exception and there is no local Catch clause to handle the exception, the Finally clause could throw another exception, causing the original exception to disappear.

Exceptional Issues

What happens when something fails inside a constructor? How do exceptions work in an inheritance situation with superclasses and subclasses? How is a brand new exception class created and used? Should checked exceptions be handled where they occur, or should they be passed to a calling method? Finally, why is it a bad idea to derive exception classes from `RuntimeException`?

Constructors and Exception Handling

What happens when a problem is detected within a constructor? The constructor cannot return a value to indicate this problem. The object is created but left in an improperly initialized state. Initializing a publicly visible field to a certain value and having the caller check this field for the value after the object has been created would solve this problem, but this solution is poor programming practice. A better solution utilizes exceptions.

A thrown exception will allow the caller to detect a failure within the constructor and identify the state of the constructor when that failure occurred. Objects created from within the constructor will automatically be marked for garbage collection.

The following code fragment consists of a contrived application that demonstrates throwing an exception from a constructor.

This code fragment creates a class called fred (for want of a better name). The constructor iterates through one hundred iterations via a For loop statement. Each value of the For loop statement's loop counter is displayed. After ten values have been displayed, execution pauses for the user to press a key (via System.in.read ()—discussed in a later chapter). After the user presses a key, execution continues.

System.in.read () can throw an IOException object. (This is due to System.in.read () having the ability to read from either the keyboard or a file.) Rather than handle this exception from within the constructor, the decision is made to throw the exception and terminate the creation of the object.

The fred () constructor requires a Throws clause that lists IOException. The main method also has a Throws clause that lists this exception because it passes the buck.

```
import java.io.*;

class fred
{
    fred () throws IOException
    {
        for (int i = 0; i < 100; i ++)
        {
            System.out.println (i);

            if (i % 10 == 0)
                System.in.read ();
        }
    }

    public static void main (String [] args) throws IOException
    {
        fred f = new fred ();
    }
}
```

Exceptions and Inheritance

A superclass method can declare a Throws clause with a list of checked exceptions. A subclass method that overrides this superclass method also can declare a Throws clause. However, the subclass method's Throws clause cannot list exceptions that are not listed within the superclass method's Throws clause.

CAUTION

Listing exceptions in a subclass method's Throws clause that are not listed in a superclass method's Throws clause is a compiler error.

Rolling Your Own Checked Exceptions

There might come a time when you need to define a new kind of checked exception. When this happens, you would derive a new class from the Exception class. (You also could derive this class from a class derived from Exception—except for RuntimeException or any of its derived classes—if the new class describes an exception related to an existing family of exceptions.)

For example, suppose that your computer is connected to sensors that monitor the core temperature of a nuclear reactor. (I know, this is far fetched!) If the core temperature rises past a certain temperature, you need to use controls to raise the control rods out of the reactor core. If the core temperature drops below a certain temperature, the reactor is shutting down. Regardless of what happens, you need to take appropriate action.

Does the core temperature rising past a certain temperature qualify as a checked exception? You bet. This is a failure that is external to a program.

Let's create a new exception class for our nuclear reactor example and call this class TemperatureException.

TIP

Any exception classes that you create should end in the word Exception. This is a convention that helps people who are reviewing your source code to identify exception classes.

Listing 8.3 contains a code fragment that specifies a TemperatureException class.

Listing 8.3: The TemperatureException class.

```
[ 1] class TemperatureException extends Exception
[ 2] {
[ 3]     private double temperature;
[ 4]
[ 5]     TemperatureException ()
[ 6]     {
[ 7]        super ("Control is broken!");
[ 8]     }
[ 9]
```

```
[10]      TemperatureException (String s)
[11]      {
[12]         super (s);
[13]      }
[14]
[15]      public void setTemperature (double temperature)
[16]      {
[17]         this.temperature = temperature;
[18]      }
[19]
[20]      public double getTemperature ()
[21]      {
[22]        return temperature;
[23]      }
[24] }
[25]
```

Line 1 introduces this class and shows that it is derived from Exception.

Lines 5 through 8 introduce a no-argument constructor. This constructor simply calls the Exception superclass constructor and passes a (hopefully) generic description of the program state when the exception occurs. In this case, this constructor passes a Control is broken! description. (The Exception () constructor will forward this description to the Throwable class where the description is stored in Throwable's private String field, as previously mentioned.)

Lines 10 through 13 introduce a second constructor that takes a single argument: a description of the program state. This constructor forwards the description to Exception, which forwards the description to Throwable.

These two constructors are complementary. There are times when you want to create a generic exception that contains a standard message so you do not need to invent new messages. Therefore, you would want to use the no-argument constructor. However, at different times you would want to override this standard message and supply a customized message. This requires a constructor that lets you specify this customized message.

The Throwable class only provides a single String field for describing an exception. However, you might want the ability to create additional fields to further define state. Obviously, you cannot add these fields to Throwable. However, you can certainly add these fields to your exception class. Line 3 introduces an additional field called temperature. This field will hold the actual core temperature of our reactor when it goes critical.

Good object-programming practices call for keeping most fields private and providing accessor methods that get or set the values of these fields. Lines 15 through 18 specify a set accessor method that sets the value of the private field, whereas lines 20 through 23 specify a get accessor method that gets the field's value.

Let's create and deal with `TemperatureException` objects in an application. This application will monitor core temperature and generate `TemperatureException` objects when the temperature becomes critical.

Listing 8.4 contains a code fragment that specifies the application's `NuclearReactorMonitor` class. The line numbers in this code fragment are a continuation of the line numbers in Listing 8.3.

Listing 8.4: The `NuclearReactorMonitor` class.

```
[26] class NuclearReactorMonitor
[27] {
[28]     static double coreTemperature = 10000.0;
[29]
[30]     public static void main (String [] args)
[31]     {
[32]        try
[33]        {
[34]            monitorReactorCore ();
[35]            return;
[36]        }
[37]        catch (TemperatureException e)
[38]        {
[39]            System.out.println (e.getMessage ());
[40]            System.out.println ("Core temperature has reached: "
[41]                                + e.getTemperature ());
[42]        }
[43]        finally
[44]        {
[45]            System.out.println ("Shutting down reactor!");
[46]        }
[47]     }
[48]
[49]     static int applyControl ()
[50]     {
[51]        return (int) (Math.random () * 3);
[52]     }
[53]
[54]     static double fluctuation ()
[55]     {
[56]        double amount;
[57]
[58]        amount = Math.random () * 100;
[59]
[60]        if (Math.random () < 0.5)
[61]            amount = -amount;
[62]
[63]        return amount;
[64]     }
```

```
[65]
[66]    static void monitorReactorCore () throws TemperatureException
[67]    {
[68]        while (true)
[69]        {
[70]            coreTemperature += fluctuation ();
[71]
[72]            if (coreTemperature > 15000.0)
[73]            {
[74]                switch (applyControl ())
[75]                {
[76]                    case 0: coreTemperature = 10000.0;
[77]                            break;
[78]
[79]                    case 1: TemperatureException te =
[80]                               new TemperatureException ("Control is
➥jammed!");
[81]                            te.setTemperature (coreTemperature);
[82]                            throw te;
[83]
[84]                    case 2: TemperatureException te2 =
[85]                               new TemperatureException ();
[86]                            te2.setTemperature (coreTemperature);
[87]                            throw te2;
[88]                }
[89]            }
[90]
[91]            // If core temperature drops below 9000 degrees ...
[92]            // ... reactor is cooling down and will stop nuclear ...
[93]            // ... reaction.
[94]
[95]            if (coreTemperature < 9000.0)
[96]                break;
[97]        }
[98]    }
[99] }
```

Line 28 specifies a static field called coreTemperature. The value of this field represents the current core temperature. It is initialized to a (ridiculous) value of 10000 that represents a safe temperature.

Lines 30 through 48 specify the main method. This method contains a loop that continuously monitors the reactor core temperature by calling the monitorReactorCore () method.

Suppose that an exception is thrown from monitorReactorCore (). In this case, the JVM needs to search for an appropriate exception handler. An appropriate handler is located immediately following the Try statement. This Catch clause handler is located in 37 through 42.

The Catch clause handler receives the `TemperatureException` object that was thrown in `monitorReactorCore` () and proceeds to display program state information. It calls the inherited `getMessage` () method to obtain a description of the exception and the `getTemperature` () method to obtain the core temperature when the exception occurred. After this information has been displayed, it's time to clean up (that is, get rid of some radioactive fallout).

The Finally clause in lines 43 through 46 is responsible for cleanup. In this case, it informs us that the reactor is shutting down.

The Finally clause is executed whether or not an exception occurs. Common cleanup code can be placed in one location, reducing code size and the possibility of error.

Lines 49 through 52 specify a method called `applyControl` (). This method is called when the core temperature rises above a critical value. The idea behind this method is to control this problem and restore the core temperature to an acceptable temperature.

The `applyControl` () method returns one of three random values. A zero value indicates that the control restored the core temperature. A one value indicates that the control jammed and could not do its work. A two value indicates that the control is broken. ("I really should have chosen metal instead of plastic but Congress only gave me enough money for plastic!")

Lines 54 through 64 specify a method called `fluctuation` (). This method is called to generate a random core temperature fluctuation. This fluctuation ranges from -99 to 99 degrees.

Lines 66 through 98 specify the `monitorReactorCore` () method. This workhorse method does the actual monitoring.

The method header in line 66 specifies a Throws clause that lists `TemperatureException` as a checked exception class.

The `monitorReactorCore` () method is capable of throwing a checked exception of data type `TemperatureException`. Therefore, the call to `monitorReactorCore` () must either be placed within a Try statement (and it is) or the `TemperatureException` class must be listed in the `main` method's Throws clause. (There isn't a Throws clause attached to the `main` method header because the program will handle the exception within the `main`.)

The `monitorReactorCore` () method attempts to solve a core temperature problem by applying a control. However, if this control does not work, there is nothing that `monitorReactorCore` () can do. It must seek assistance from some other location within the program. Therefore, it throws a `TemperatureException` object. Because this object is created from a checked exception class, the exception must be listed within the method's Throws clause.

Lines 68 through 97 specify what appears to be an infinite loop. However, this loop can be exited in one of two ways, as will be seen.

Line 70 calls the `fluctuation ()` method to return a random temperature. This temperature is added to `coreTemperature`.

Line 72 checks to see if this core temperature has exceeded the critical value of 15000 degrees. If it has, corrective action must be taken.

Lines 74 through 88 attempt this corrective action via the Switch decision statement.

Line 74 calls the `applyControl ()` method. If this method returns zero, `coreTemperature` is reset to 10000 degrees and the Switch statement exits. (You can now breathe a sigh of relief!)

If this method returns a value of one or two, we are in serious trouble.

If a value of one is returned, the control is jammed. A `TemperatureException` object is created and indicates a jammed control. The current value of `coreTemperature` is stored within this object so an exception handler can display this value.

If a value of two is returned, the control is broken. Again, a `TemperatureException` object is created. However, the `TemperatureException ()` constructor is called and it creates an appropriate description of the program state. This state is augmented with the current value of `coreTemperature` via a call to `setTemperature (double)`.

In either case, a Throw statement is used to throw this exception. The JVM picks up this object and searches for an exception handler. It will find such a handler in the `main` method where appropriate action will be taken.

If the core temperature falls below 9000 degrees, a Break statement in line 96 will exit the loop and the method. The reactor is shutting down, so the `main` method's Try statement—followed by its Finally clause—is completed.

To Catch or Pass the Buck

When should your code catch an exception and deal with it and when should it pass the buck to whatever code called the method?

If your code has done something completely on its own that results in a thrown exception, it should catch the exception.

For example, your code attempts to open a file and an exception occurs. The act of opening a file is internal to your code. No other code has "asked" your code to open this file. In this case, your code should take care of the exception.

However, if your code was given something to do by some other code and an exception is thrown, the caller should deal with the exception.

For example, your code consists of a method that is called with bad argument data. Within this method, it tries to do something with this data. However, an exception occurs. It is not the responsibility of your code to deal with this failure because your code did not precipitate this failure. Therefore, it should pass the buck to the caller and let the caller worry about how to deal with this failure.

Deriving from `RuntimeException`

It really isn't necessary to derive a class from `RuntimeException`, unless you can think of a new kind of internal failure that isn't specified in Java's extensive list of `RuntimeException` classes.

Some developers get lazy and decide to derive all their exception classes from `RuntimeException`. This is dangerous because their code can call methods that fail based on external failures and treat these failures as if they were internal failures. Because Java does not require internal failures to be handled, these external failures can be ignored. (Your nuclear reactor or rocket explodes and everyone is happy!)

In some sense, we are back to square one. We are ignoring failure and users are paying the price. It would have been better if Java's designers had immediately terminated the JVM when an exception based on `RuntimeException` or one of its subclasses was thrown. The developer would then be forced to fix the internal failure, re-compile the source code, and re-test the program. Relying on `RuntimeException` simply invites the temptation to create bad code. Hopefully, this weakness will be fixed in future versions of Java.

CALC

CALC is a simple four-function calculator application that enables you to multiply, divide, add, and subtract numbers with or without decimal points. You can even work with negative numbers.

Setting Up CALC

To set up CALC, begin by double-clicking your MS-DOS icon (if you are using Windows) and go to a command prompt.

If you created a `projects` directory in Chapter 1, make `projects` your current directory. (If you do not have a `projects` directory, now is as good a time as any to create one.)

Assuming that `projects` is located within `c:\jdk1.2\`, enter the command `cd \jdk1.2\projects` to change to this directory.

From within your projects directory, create a directory called calc (for example, md calc). (If you prefer, you can create this directory entirely in uppercase. For example, you could issue the command md CALC to create this directory. Case does not matter when it comes to directories.)

Download the file calc.java from the Macmillan Web site and place this file in your calc directory.

Compiling CALC

Compilation is a simple process. It involves running the javac.exe program and specifying the name of the source file as an argument to this program.

At the command prompt, enter the following line:

```
c:\jdk1.2\projects\calc>javac calc.java
```

CAUTION

The .java file extension must be specified when compiling an application's source file. The compiler will display an error message if .java is not specified.

If the compiler displays an error message, you might have typed Calc.java or CALC.java instead of calc.java.

CAUTION

You must specify calc.java and not Calc.java, CALC.java, or any other combination of lowercase/uppercase letters. The compiler is very sensitive to case and will display an error message if the class name (calc) does not match the filename (calc).

After compilation is finished, you should end up with a class file called calc.class.

Figure 8.1 shows the compilation process.

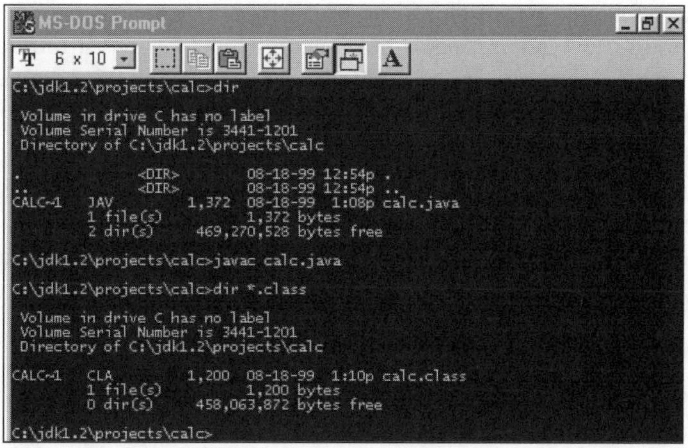

Figure 8.1: Compiling calc.java with the javac.exe compiler.

Running CALC

Congratulations! You successfully compiled calc.java and are now ready to run calc.class. All you need to do is fire up the java.exe program and specify calc.class as an argument to this program.

CAUTION

The .class file extension must not be specified; otherwise, the java.exe program will display an error message.

Figure 8.2 shows the process of running calc.class with java.exe to display usage information.

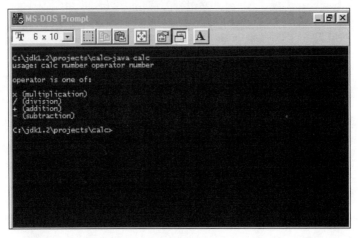

Figure 8.2: *Running* calc.class *with* java.exe *to display usage information.*

Note that the application displays usage information, specifying what arguments need to follow calc on the command line.

The usage information states that three arguments are passed to calc.class when it begins running: a number (with or without a minus sign and with or without a decimal point), an operator (x, /, +, or -), and a second number. Make sure to leave a space between each number and the operator.

Figure 8.3 shows the process of running calc.class with java.exe and passing arguments to calc.class. As you can see, these arguments are specified after calc on the command line.

When you try to divide the number one by the number zero, the application displays Infinity. And when you try to divide negative one by zero, the application displays -Infinity.

✔ For more information on Infinity and -Infinity, see Chapter 3, "Operators, Expressions, and Statements," page 45.

Figure 8.3: Running `calc.class` *with* `java.exe`.

You also might notice that Java's floating-point arithmetic generates slightly inaccurate values. For example, adding 82.9 and 3.26 results in a value of 86.16000000000001 being displayed instead of 86.16. However, this small lack of precision is no different from the lack of precision you would find in other computer languages, such as C and C++.

Potential Problems

What can go wrong with CALC? Hmmm! Try running CALC with the following command line:

```
c:\jdk1.2\projects\calc>java calc a + b
```

You'll notice that the lowercase letter a is displayed. What does this mean? If you examine CALC's source code, you'll see that it calls the parseDouble (String) class method (defined in the Double class). This method throws an exception of data type NumberFormatException when an invalid number is parsed. (The lowercase letter a is not a number.) When the exception is caught, the exception's getMessage () method is called to return a String object that describes the state of the program when the exception occurred. In this case, the state consists of the letter that caused parseDouble (String) to throw an exception (a), which is then displayed.

If you should encounter an error, don't panic. Instead, try to reason out the cause of this error and then take appropriate action.

Enhancing CALC

You can enhance CALC in a number of ways:

- Extend the number of operators that CALC supports. For example, try to provide support for the modulus (%) operator. Remember that this operator requires two integer operands (not a mixture of integer and floating-point operands). (Hint: How about casting?)

- Here's a bigger challenge. Try to enhance CALC so that it can take either three arguments or five arguments. CALC is already handling three arguments. With five arguments, you would specify a number followed by an operator followed by a number followed by a second operator followed by a number. For example, you would now be able to specify expressions such as 6 + 3.5 x 2.

- Here's a puzzler. How would you handle precedence? For example, if you entered the expression 6 + 3.5 x 2, CALC would probably perform the addition operation before multiplication. However, doesn't multiplication have a higher precedence than addition? In a future chapter, we will look at a solution to this problem. This solution presents an application that interprets expressions and uses precedence so that multiplication occurs before addition.

What's Next?

If you are careful about how you write your source code, you can probably reuse it at a later date. Java supports code reuse through its use of packages. The next chapter discusses packages, how to create them, and how to use them. Once you start using packages, you'll find them to be a convenient and very useful tool that can help simplify your development tasks.

Packages

After you start creating Java programs, you'll probably find that your programs contain classes that can be reused in other programs. Rather than duplicate effort, you can take these classes and organize them into packages (that is, your own class libraries).

Creating packages has many benefits. For example, after you have written, compiled, and tested a class, you can save it in a library. The next time you need this class, simply access it from this library. Don't write it again. You'll save yourself development and testing time. You'll also reduce the amount of source code that you need to manage.

Chapter 9 presents the following topics:

- What are packages?
- The package directive
- The import directive
- CLASSPATH
- Package naming conventions
- GRAPHICS

What Are Packages?

Packages are libraries of classes and interfaces. Each library is given its own name space to avoid conflicts between identical class names and interface names.

Consider an example where packages are not used. You are working on a couple of projects at the same time. One of these projects is a Java application for an electronics company and the other project is a financial applet. You find yourself creating `transistor`, `resistor`, and other classes for the electronics application. You also find yourself creating `account`, `mutualFund`, and other classes for the financial applet. For various reasons, you decide to build both projects in the same directory on your hard drive. You compile the source files, and the resulting class files are placed in the same directory as these source files.

You really shouldn't mix your electronics classes with your financial classes because there is a possibility of naming conflicts. Suppose that your electronics application and financial applet contain their own `component` class. You compile the electronics application before the financial applet. The electronics `component` class file is created and then replaced by the financial `component` class file. Although the financial applet runs, the same cannot be said for the electronics application.

This failure occurs because two source files in the same directory use the same name for a class declaration. The compiler compiles each source file and places its resulting class file in the same directory as the source file. Obviously, one of these class files will be replaced by the other class file because a directory can only contain one file with a given name.

If the electronics classes and the financial classes were placed in separate packages, this problem would not occur.

The Package Directive

The package directive is a compiler directive that is placed at the top of a source file and identifies the package where all classes and interfaces that are declared within the source file should be stored.

The format of the package directive is

```
"package" package_name ';'
```

The package reserved word starts the package directive and is followed by *package_name*, an identifier that names the package. This identifier must not be a reserved word.

EXAMPLE

The following code fragment consists of a package directive that identifies a `financial` package:

```
package financial;
```

All class and interface declarations that are contained in the same source file as the `package financial;` directive will be stored in the `financial` package.

The package directive must be specified before any other source code (apart from comments) and only one package directive can be specified in a source file.

CAUTION

Attempting to either declare multiple package directives in the same source file or place source code (apart from comments) before a package directive results in a compiler error.

Packages can contain subpackages that help to further organize classes and interfaces. These subpackages are analogous to subdirectories (that is, directories contained within other directories).

The format of the package directive when subpackage names are included is

```
"package" package_name '.' sub_package_name … ';'
```

The subpackage name (*sub_package_name*) is separated from the package name (*package_name*) by a single period character. The three trailing period characters indicate that additional subpackage names can be specified, as long as each subpackage name is separated from the previous package/subpackage name by a period character. (The three periods are not literally specified in the package directive.)

EXAMPLE

The following code fragment consists of a package directive that specifies an `account` subpackage within the `financial` package:

```
package financial.account;
```

All classes and interfaces located in the same source file as the previous package directive are stored in the `account` subpackage within the `financial` package.

Package names are associated with directory names. In the previous example, the class files generated by the compiler would be placed in either the `financial\account` directory (Windows) or the `financial/account` directory (UNIX).

The package naming convention was designed from a portability point of view. This is why period characters (as opposed to forward slash (/) and back slash (\) characters) are used to distinguish between package names. In the future, package names might not be associated with directory names. They might be associated with something completely different.

Every class or interface is part of some package. If a source file does not contain a package directive, the classes and interfaces declared within that source file are considered part of the unnamed package.

The Import Directive

The import directive "tells" the compiler to import one or more class or interface names from a package. Importing names saves the developer from having to specify a complete package specification for each imported name.

The format of the import directive is

```
"import" package_name '.' class_interface_name ';'
```

The `class_interface_name` refers to a specific class or interface name in the package identified by `package_name`.

EXAMPLE

The following code fragment uses an import directive to import the `rates` class name from the account subpackage that is located within the `financial` package:

```
import financial.account.rates;
```

This import directive allows the developer to specify the following code fragment at some point within a method:

```
rates r = new rates ();
```

Without the import directive, the developer would have to specify package information for each occurrence of the `rates` class name, as in the following code fragment:

```
financial.account.rates = new financial.account.rates ();
```

This extra information makes the code somewhat harder to read.

It would be rather tedious to have to provide a separate import directive for every single class or interface name that is part of a given package. Therefore, Java offers a shortcut import directive.

The shortcut import directive enables the developer to refer to all class and interface names within a package.

The format of the shortcut import directive is

```
"import" package_name '.' '*' ';'
```

The * refers to all class and interface names in the package identified by `package_name`.

EXAMPLE

The following code fragment uses an import directive to import all class and interface names from the account subpackage that is located within the `financial` package:

```
import financial.account.*;
```

This import directive allows the developer to specify the `rates` class name and any other class and interface names that are declared within the account subpackage, without the package information.

Whenever a class or interface name appears in source code, the compiler needs to "know" where the class file related to that name is located. It gets this information in one of two ways. Either the developer prefixes every class or interface name with its complete package name (that is, the package name and any subpackage names) or import directives are specified to supply complete package names in one place.

In either case, the compiler places package information for each referenced class or interface name into the generated class files so that the JVM can locate the class files associated with these referenced names.

Import directives, apart from the package directive and comments, must be specified before any other source code.

CAUTION

Attempting to specify any code (apart from a package directive and comments) before an import directive results in a compiler error.

Suppose that a program contains two import directives that import identical names from two packages. For example, suppose that the `electronics` package contains a `component` class name and the `financial` package also contains a `component` class name, as follows:

```
import electronics.*;
import financial.*;
```

The following statement would be ambiguous:

```
component c = new component ();
```

Which component class is being dealt with? Is it the electronics package version or the financial package version? Because the compiler does not "know," it reports an error. The developer must explicitly supply the correct package information to identify the appropriate class:

```
financial.component c = new financial.component ();
```

or

```
electronics.component c = new electronics.component ();
```

Although this ambiguity is not a common problem, it is something to keep in mind in those situations where you are scratching your head and wondering why the compiler is "complaining."

Java's language classes (such as `String`) are placed in a package called `java.lang` (that is, the `lang` package within the `java` package). The compiler

automatically imports java.lang so it is not necessary to specify an import
java.lang.*; directive at the beginning of a source file that uses String or
other language classes.

CLASSPATH

The JVM runs a Java program by dynamically loading class files as they
are needed. In order to do this, the JVM must be able to locate class files.

Each class file contains the package name(s) for each class or interface that
is referenced from within the class file. If the class or interface is part of
the unnamed package, the class file contains no package information for
that class/interface. Every class file belonging to the unnamed package
must exist in the directory from which the JVM was launched.

The JVM associates package names with directory names. Therefore, when it
comes across a class or interface reference, the JVM obtains the package
name(s) associated with that reference (from the loaded class file of the class
being executed) and searches for the corresponding class file of the referenced
class or interface by locating a directory corresponding to the first package
name followed by subdirectory names corresponding to subpackage names (if
specified). After the class file is found, the JVM loads it into memory and execution continues.

The JVM searches for the first package directory by starting in the directory from which the JVM was launched. What happens if this package
directory is not found in the current directory? In this case, the JVM
obtains the value of the CLASSPATH environment variable and searches each
entry in this path to locate the package directory. After the package directory is found, the directories within the package directory are searched
until the class file is found.

If the package directory cannot be found in the current directory and there
is no CLASSPATH environment variable to continue the search, if subdirectories corresponding to subpackage names cannot be found in the package
directory (or subdirectories), or if the class file does not exist within the
package directory (or a subdirectory), the JVM will throw a
NoClassDefFoundError object.

Package Naming Conventions

Package names must be unique. If they are not unique, the JVM might not
be able to locate the correct package directory. It will stop searching with
the first matching package directory, even if there is another package directory with the same name that contains the class file being sought.

A convention has been established to ensure that package names are unique. This convention makes use of a company's Internet domain name. This name is reversed and then prefixed to a package name. For example, a company called Generic might have an Internet domain name called generic.com. Reversing this name results in com.generic. If Generic has a package called financial, the resulting package name is com.generic.financial (that is, a financial package exists in a generic package that exists in a com package).

GRAPHICS

It's time for an example that brings all these concepts together. To that end, a primitive graphics package has been created.

This graphics package consists of an interface called shape and four classes called point, circle, square, and rectangle.

Listing 9.1 presents the source code to the shape interface.

Listing 9.1: The shape interface.

```
// shape.java

package graphics;

interface shape
{
    void draw ();
}
```

The shape.java source file contains a package directive that places the shape interface in a package called graphics.

The shape interface declares an abstract method called draw (). This method will be implemented by the four shape classes. Because Java's graphical capabilities have not yet been discussed, the four implementations of the draw () method will only display a message to the console that identifies a shape.

The draw () method is a publicly visible method, even though the public reserved word has not been specified. By design, any method declared within an interface is publicly visible, whether or not public prefixes that method. When overridden, the public reserved word will be required to prefix the draw () method declaration in the overriding subclass.

Listing 9.2 presents the source code to the point class.

Listing 9.2: The point class.

```
// point.java

package graphics;
```

Listing 9.2: continued

```
class point
{
    private double x, y;

    point (double x, double y)
    {
        this.x = x;
        this.y = y;
    }

    public double getX () { return x; }

    public double getY () { return y; }
}
```

The point.java source file places point in the same graphics package as shape.

The point class serves as the superclass for the circle subclass. After all, a circle is a point with radius.

Notice that point has not been declared as a public class. This means that point objects cannot be created from outside the graphics package. Even if point had been declared public, it would still not be possible to create point objects because the point (double, double) constructor has package visibility. (The absence of the public, private, or protected reserved words implies package visibility.) Because of this package visibility, point (double, double) can only be called from methods whose classes are declared in the same graphics package as point.

Listing 9.3 presents the source code to the circle class.

Listing 9.3: The circle class.

```
// circle.java

package graphics;

public class circle extends point implements shape
{
    private double radius;

    public circle (double x, double y, double radius)
    {
        super (x, y);

        this.radius = radius;
```

```
    }

    public double getRadius () { return radius; }

    public void draw () { System.out.println ("Circle"); }
}
```

The circle.java source file contains a package directive that places circle in the same package as point and shape.

Unlike point, circle objects can be constructed because the circle class is a public class and the circle (double, double, double) constructor is a public constructor.

Listing 9.4 presents the source code to the square class.

Listing 9.4: The square class.

```
// square.java

package graphics;

public class square implements shape
{
    private double length;

    public square (double length)
    {
        this.length = length;
    }

    public double getLength () { return length; }

    public void draw () { System.out.println ("Square"); }
}
```

The square.java source file contains a package directive that places square in the graphics package.

Like circle, square objects can be constructed because square is a public class and its constructor is a public constructor.

Listing 9.5 presents the source code to the rectangle class.

Listing 9.5: The rectangle class.

```
// rectangle.java

package graphics;

public class rectangle extends square implements shape
{
```

Listing 9.5: continued

```
    private double width;

    public rectangle (double length, double width)
    {
        super (length);

        this.width = width;
    }

    public double getWidth () { return width; }

    public void draw () { System.out.println ("Rectangle"); }

    protected double area () { return width * getLength (); }
}
```

The rectangle.java source file contains a package directive that places rectangle in the graphics package.

Like circle and square, rectangle objects can be constructed because rectangle is a public class and its constructor is a public constructor.

The rectangle class introduces a protected area () method that calculates the area of a rectangle. Normally, this method would be a public method but it has been declared protected to make life difficult and introduce a concept, as will shortly be seen.

The area () method can be called from any method that's class is part of the graphics package. This method also can be called from any method that's class is a subclass of rectangle, regardless of the package in which this subclass is declared.

It's time to build this package.

Building the Package

Under your projects directory, create a graphics directory. Enter the source code from Listings 9.1 through 9.5 into the appropriate source files and save them to the graphics directory. (The graphics directory will correspond to the graphics package.) Figure 9.1 shows the graphics directory with the resulting files.

Compile the rectangle source file from the projects directory, not the graphics directory. You cannot compile this file from inside the graphics directory because the rectangle class references the square class by extending this class and the compiler looks for a graphics directory containing square.java. If the graphics directory is the current directory, the compiler will look for a graphics directory containing square.java within the graphics directory. It will not find this directory and report an error. If projects is the current directory, the compiler will look for a graphics directory within projects. It will find this directory (unless you did not create it) and everything will be fine.

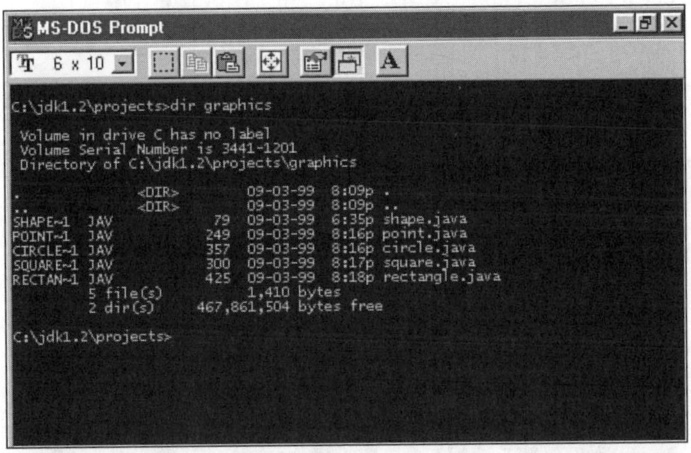

Figure 9.1: *The graphics directory.*

Figure 9.2 shows the results of compiling rectangle.java.

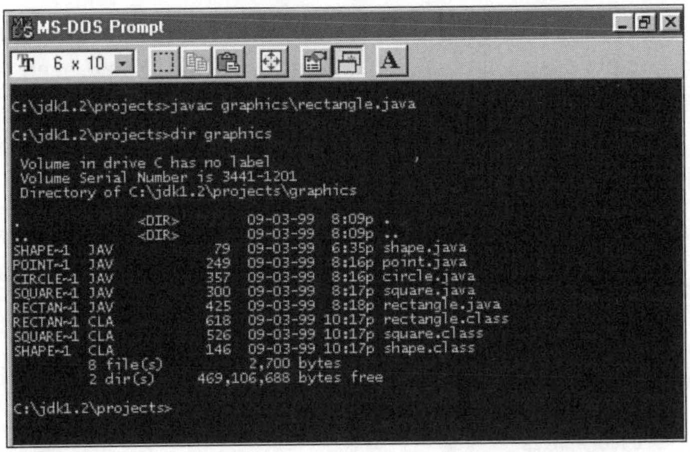

Figure 9.2: *The graphics directory after compiling rectangle.java.*

Notice that class files have been created for shape and square. This happens because the compiler recursively compiles other source files when it detects references to their declared classes and interfaces from within the source file being compiled.

Compile the `circle` source file from the `projects` directory. Figure 9.3 shows the results. In addition to the `circle` class file, a `point` class file also is created.

At this point, you have a `graphics` directory underneath your `projects` directory. The `graphics` directory contains the five source and five class files that constitute this package.

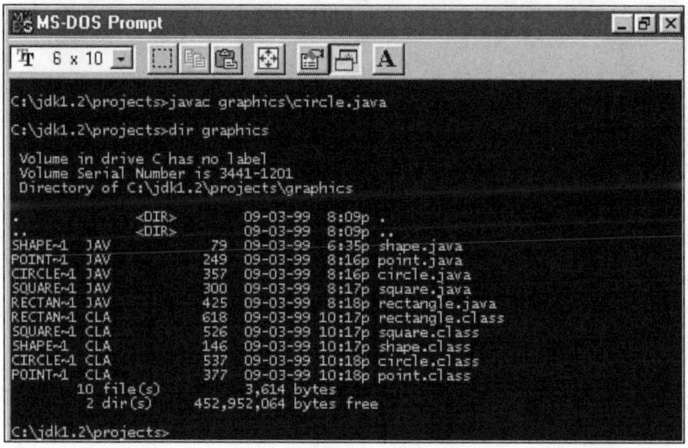

Figure 9.3: The graphics directory after compiling `circle.java`.

You have just built a library of (hopefully) useful graphics tools. Of course, for our purposes, this is just a demonstration. You'll need to add more capabilities to turn this into a useful library.

Now that you have a library, you need an application to make use of this library.

Listing 9.6 presents the source code to the `useGraphics` application.

Listing 9.6: The `useGraphics` application.

```
// useGraphics.java

import graphics.*;

class useGraphics
{
   public static void main (String [] args)
   {
      circle c = new circle (10.5, 20.2, 3.5);
      c.draw ();

      rectangle r = new rectangle (3.2, 32.5);
//       System.out.println (r.area ());
```

```
        areaRectangle ar = new areaRectangle (3.5, 2.6);
        System.out.println ("Area = " + ar.getArea ());
    }
}

class areaRectangle extends rectangle
{
    areaRectangle (double length, double width)
    {
        super (length, width);
    }

    double getArea ()
    {
        return area ();
    }
}
```

Notice the line that attempts to call r.area (). This line is commented out because it will not compile. If you recall from looking at Listing 9.5, the rectangle class declares a protected area () method. This method can be called only from other methods whose classes are declared in the same package as the rectangle class, or from subclasses of rectangle, regardless of package.

Because it would be useful to calculate the area of a rectangle and because some perverse developer (whose name shall not be identified) chose to declare area () as a protected method, useGraphics requires the presence of a rectangle subclass, such as areaRectangle.

The areaRectangle class declares a getArea () method that can legally call area (). This is how useGraphics obtains a rectangle's area—not from the rectangle class but from its areaRectangle subclass.

Copy the code from Listing 9.6 into a source file called useGraphics.java. Save this source file into your projects directory just above your graphics directory.

Compile this source code. You should end up with the class files shown in Figure 9.4.

It's time to use this package.

Using the Package

After you have successfully compiled this application, you are ready to run it. Figure 9.5 shows the results of a sample run.

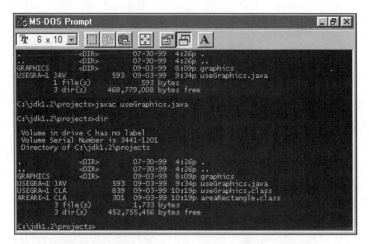

Figure 9.4: *The* useGraphics *application class files.*

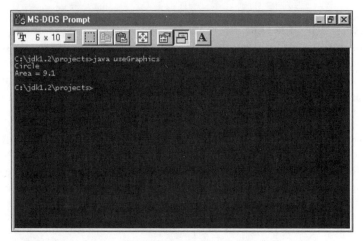

Figure 9.5: *The* useGraphics *application results.*

Now, suppose that you need to move graphics from inside projects to the root directory of the hard drive. Figure 9.6 shows what happens when an attempt is made to run useGraphics.

The JVM cannot find the circle class within the graphics package because it cannot find the graphics package. What do you do?

Remember CLASSPATH! The JVM will search all the directories specified by this environment variable. Modify CLASSPATH so that it points to the root directory. Try running useGraphics a second time. The results are shown in Figure 9.7.

It is usually not a good idea to modify CLASSPATH because it is easy to forget about this environment variable. This forgetfulness can lead to problems.

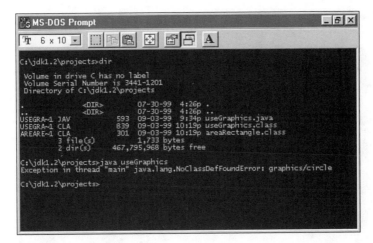

Figure 9.6: *Attempting to run* useGraphics, *but there is no graphics package where it is expected.*

For example, the compiler or JVM might search the CLASSPATH environment variable and locate the wrong package. This happens because you are using the same package name for two different versions of a program. The older version's package directory name appears in CLASSPATH and its class files are referenced. If you had remembered to change CLASSPATH, by replacing this directory name with the new version's directory name, this problem would not have happened.

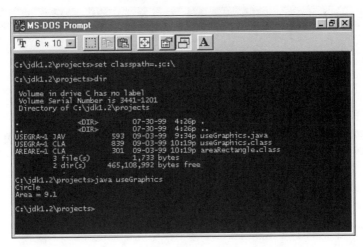

Figure 9.7: *Running* useGraphics *after modifying* CLASSPATH.

The java.exe program allows you to choose a class path that exists for as long as java.exe runs. This class path is specified by using the -classpath option. Figure 9.8 runs useGraphics by using this option.

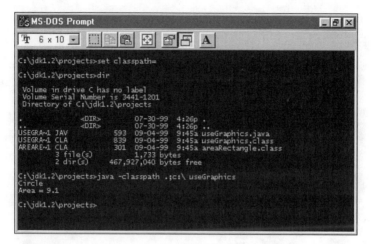

Figure 9.8: Running useGraphics after specifying -classpath.

In Figure 9.8, there is no CLASSPATH environment variable. The only way that the JVM can locate the graphics package is via the -classpath option.

In Figures 9.7 and 9.8, notice that the class path is set to .;c:\. The . represents the current directory and must be specified so that the JVM can locate areaRectangle.class.

And that is all there is to packages. After you get used to organizing your libraries as packages, you'll find them to be really helpful.

What's Next?

Now that you've examined the concept of packages, you've reached the end of one journey (exploring the Java language) and are about to begin a new journey (exploring the class library).

To begin your exploration, I'm going to "string you along" (groan!) in the next chapter where Java's various character and string management classes are covered. You'll learn about character processing along with read-only and read/write string manipulation. Finally, you'll learn about string tokenizing.

Part III

Exploring the Class Library

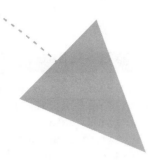

Characters and Strings

Computer programs often process text. These text-processing programs are written in a computer language that supports characters and strings. In this chapter, you will learn about Java's support for characters and strings, and how to use characters and strings in your own Java programs.

Chapter 10 presents the following topics:

- Characters
- Strings

Characters

Chapter 2, "Data Types, Literals, and Variables," introduced you to the concept of characters. You learned that a character is nothing more than a combination of a Unicode binary number and visual symbol data. Furthermore, you saw that Java's char data type is used to create char variables—each variable holding the Unicode value of a character—and learned how to literally specify characters in source code.

EXAMPLE

The following character0 application illustrates assigning a character literal to a char variable and printing out the contents of this variable, as a visual symbol and as a decimal number:

```
// character0.java

class character0
{
    public static void main (String [] args)
    {
        char c = 'A';

        System.out.println (c);
        System.out.println ((int) c);
    }
}
```

OUTPUT

```
A
65
```

Look closely at the two overloaded println method calls. The first println method call takes a char argument and prints out that argument's visual symbol (for example, A). The second println method call takes an int argument and prints out an integer value. It is actually passed a char argument that is cast to an int, via the (int) cast operator, before the method is called. The cast operator causes the Unicode number (for example, 65) associated with the argument's visual symbol to be passed to the method, which is then printed.

These two println method calls illustrate an important point about characters: A character is both a visual symbol and a Unicode number.

The Character Class

Java's class library contains a class called Character. You can use this class to create objects that represent characters. Because Character is located in the java.lang package, you don't need to specify an import java.lang.Character; directive (or even an import java.lang.*; directive) at the top of your source file. (The compiler automatically imports all classes from java.lang.)

Including a `Character` class in the class library might seem to be redundant. After all, you can represent characters by using `char` variables. So why does this class exist? There are two good reasons.

The first reason has to do with the `Vector` data structure class. `Vector` is used to create `Vector` objects that contain other objects. For example, you can create a `Character` object that represents a single character and store this object in the `Vector` object. However, you cannot store a `char` variable in a `Vector` object.

✔ For more information on `Vector`, see Chapter 11, "Data Structures, Part 1," page 261.

The second reason has to do with `Character`'s class methods. These methods allow you to classify their `char` argument values. For example, `Character` declares methods that will tell you if their `char` argument values represent a lowercase letter, a digit, or part of a Java identifier. As you know, methods must be declared in classes, and `Character` is an appropriate place in which to declare these class methods.

A `Character` object is created by first declaring an object reference variable and then assigning it a new instance of the `Character` class, as follows:

```
Character c1 = new Character ('7');
```

The `Character (char)` constructor initializes the `Character` object by storing the value of the `char` argument within the object. In this case, the `char` literal `'7'` is passed to the constructor as its argument.

After a `Character` object has been created, its internal `char` value can be retrieved by calling `Character`'s `charValue ()` instance method, as follows:

```
char ch = c1.charValue ();
```

COMPARING CHARACTERS

`Character` objects can be compared by calling the `compareTo (Character)` instance method. This is illustrated in the following code fragment:

```
Character c2 = new Character ('A');
System.out.println (c2.compareTo (c1));
```

This method works by comparing the Unicode numbers of the `char` values contained in the object that invokes `compareTo (character)` (the invoking object) and the object passed as an argument to this method (the argument object). If the invoking object's `char` value has a Unicode number greater than the Unicode number of the argument object's `char` value, a positive number is returned. If the invoking object's `char` value has a Unicode number less than the Unicode number of the argument object's `char` value, a negative number is returned. If both Unicode numbers are the same, zero is returned.

The following `character1` application illustrates a pair of `Character` objects, a pair of `char` variables, `charValue ()` method calls that extract the `char` values from `Character` objects, and the `compareTo (Character)` method that compares the `char` values in both `Character` objects:

```
// character1.java

class character1
{
    public static void main (String [] args)
    {
        Character c1 = new Character ('6');
        Character c2 = new Character ('7');

        char c3 = c1.charValue ();
        char c4 = c2.charValue ();

        if (c3 < c4)
            System.out.println (c3 + " is less than " + c4);

        if (c1.compareTo (c2) < 0)
            System.out.println (c1 + " is less than " + c4);
    }
}
```

```
6 is less than 7
6 is less than 7
```

CLASSIFYING CHARACTERS

The `Character` class declares class methods that classify `char` arguments. Each method determines if the Unicode value of an argument represents a digit, a letter, or some other entity. A Boolean `true` value is returned if the argument belongs to the classification. Otherwise, a Boolean `false` value is returned.

For example, the `isDigit (char)` method returns true if its `char` argument represents a digit. On the other hand, the `isLetter (char)` method returns true if its `char` argument represents a letter. You can determine if a character represents either a letter or a digit by calling the `isLetterOrDigit (char)` method. This method returns true if its `char` argument represents either a letter or a digit.

The `isLowerCase (char)` and `isUpperCase (char)` class methods determine if their respective `char` arguments represent a lowercase letter or an uppercase letter. The `isLowerCase (char)` method returns `true` if its `char` argument represents a lowercase letter, whereas the `isUpperCase (char)` method returns `true` if its `char` argument represents an uppercase letter.

Want to know if a character represents the start (or just part) of a Java identifier? If you do, check out the `isJavaIdentifierStart (char)` and isJavaIdentifierPart (char) class methods. The isJavaIdentifierStart (char) method returns true if its char argument represents a valid start character for a Java identifier, whereas the isJavaIdentifierPart (char) method returns true if its char argument represents a valid character that serves as part of the identifier's name (after the start character).

The following character2 application illustrates calls to some of the character classification methods:

```
// character2.java

class character2
{
    public static void main (String [] args)
    {
        System.out.println ("Is the Latin symbol 6 a digit? "
                            + Character.isDigit ('6'));

        System.out.println ("Is the Tamil symbol corresponding to " +
                            "Unicode value '\\u0beb' a digit? " +
                            Character.isDigit ('\u0beb'));

        System.out.println ("Is the Greek symbol Omega a digit? " +
                            Character.isDigit ('\u03a9'));

        System.out.println ("Is the Latin symbol A a digit? " +
                            Character.isDigit ('A'));

        System.out.println ("Is the Greek symbol Omega a letter? " +
                            Character.isLetter ('\u03a9'));

        System.out.println ("Is the Latin symbol z a letter? " +
                            Character.isLetter ('z'));

        System.out.println ("Is the Latin symbol z a lowercase letter? " +
                            Character.isLowerCase ('z'));

        System.out.println ("Is the Latin symbol a an uppercase letter? " +
                            Character.isUpperCase ('a'));
    }
}
```

```
Is the Latin symbol 6 a digit? true
Is the Tamil symbol corresponding to Unicode value '\u0beb' a digit? true
Is the Greek symbol Omega a digit? false
Is the Latin symbol A a digit? false
Is the Greek symbol Omega a letter? true
Is the Latin symbol z a letter? true
Is the Latin symbol z a lowercase letter? true
Is the Latin symbol a an uppercase letter? false
```

EXAMPLE

OUTPUT

Figure 10.1 shows the Tamil symbol corresponding to the Unicode value `'u0beb'` and the Greek Omega symbol corresponding to the Unicode value `'\u03a9'`.

Tamil Digit 5   Greek Capital Letter Omega

Figure 10.1: Tamil and Greek symbols.

The Tamil symbol represents the Tamil digit 5 and the Greek symbol represents the Greek uppercase letter Omega.

CONVERTING CHARACTERS

The `Character` class declares a pair of class methods that convert characters representing uppercase letters to lowercase letters and vice versa: `toUpperCase (char)` and `toLowerCase (char)`.

The `toUpperCase (char)` method examines the Unicode number of its `char` argument. If this number corresponds to a lowercase letter, this method returns the uppercase equivalent of that letter. Otherwise, it returns the argument. This is shown in the following code fragment where letter A is converted to letter A:

```
char c = Character.toUpperCase ('a');
```

As with `toUpperCase (char)`, the `toLowerCase (char)` class method also examines the Unicode number of its `char` argument. However, if this number corresponds to an uppercase letter, this method returns the lowercase equivalent of that letter. Otherwise, it returns the argument. For example, the following code fragment converts letter A to letter a:

```
char c = Character.toLowerCase ('A');
```

Strings

Chapter 2 introduced you to the String reference data type and discussed string literals. The String reference data type, implemented by the `String` class (located in the `java.lang` package), is given special treatment by the Java language. For example, Java provides a simplified syntax for creating `String` objects as well as a simplified syntax for concatenating `String` objects.

EXAMPLE

The following `string0` application illustrates both syntaxes:

```
// string0.java

class string0
```

```
{
    public static void main (String [] args)
    {
        String s1 = "abc";
        String s2 = "def";

        System.out.println (s1 + s2);
    }
}
```

abcdef

Behind the scenes, the JVM allocates memory for two String objects. It then initializes the first object to the characters abc and the second object to the characters def.

Suppose that s2 also was assigned abc. In this case the JVM would create only a single String object and assign its reference to both s1 and s2—to conserve memory.

What if you want to change the contents of the s1 object without affecting the contents of the s2 object? You can't do this if both s1 and s2 refer to the same object. However, this is not a problem because the JVM treats String objects as immutable objects. In other words, after a String object has been created, you can NEVER change its contents. If you try to change a String object's contents, the JVM creates a copy of the original object with the new contents.

The following string1 application demonstrates Java's immutable approach to String objects:

// string1.java

```
class string1
{
    public static void main (String [] args)
    {
        String s1 = "abc";
        String s2 = "abc";
        String s3 = "def";

        if (s1 == s2)
            System.out.println ("s1 == s2");

        if (s1 != s3)
            System.out.println ("s1 != s3");

        if (s2 != s3)
            System.out.println ("s2 != s3");

        String s4 = s1.toUpperCase ();
```

```
        if (s4 != s1)
            System.out.println ("s4 != s1");

        System.out.println ("s1 = " + s1);
        System.out.println ("s4 = " + s4);
    }
}
```

```
s1 == s2
s1 != s3
s2 != s3
s4 != s1
s1 = abc
s4 = ABC
```

The first line of output shows that s1 and s2 are referencing the same object. (Remember, the relational operator (==) compares objects by their references, not their contents.) Furthermore, the second and third lines of output show that the object being referenced by s1 and s2 is different from the object being referenced by s3.

The contents of the s1 object are not converted to uppercase by the call to s1's toUpperCase () instance method. Instead, a copy of the s1 object (with lowercase letters converted to uppercase) is created and returned from this method. Assigning this reference to s4 serves as proof. If the contents of s1 were changed, s4 also would reference the same object as s1. (The fourth line of output would show s4 referencing the same object.) However, it clearly shows that s4 references a different object. If this isn't enough proof, look at the fifth and sixth lines of output. These lines show that the contents of s1 and s4 are different.

The String Class

In the previous section, you saw how to implicitly create String objects. However, it also is possible to create these objects by specifying new and calling various String constructors, such as String () and String (String).

The String () constructor creates a String object with no contents, as shown in the following code fragment. (This is analogous to assigning the empty string literal "" to a String object reference variable.)

```
String s = new String ();
```

The String (String) constructor creates a String object and copies the characters from another String object into the newly created String object. The following code fragment illustrates this situation:

```
String s1 = "abc";
String s2 = new String (s1);
```

The object referenced by s2 contains the same contents as the object referenced by s1. However, s1 and s2 reference two different String objects.

OBTAINING A HASH CODE

The String class's overridden hashcode () instance method produces a unique 32-bit integer for each String object that is created by a running program.

The following string2 application illustrates hashCode () method calls:

```
// string2.java
```

EXAMPLE

```
class string2
{
    public static void main (String [] args)
    {
        String s1 = "abc";
        String s2 = "abc";
        String s3 = "def";

        System.out.println ("s1 hash code = " + s1.hashCode ());
        System.out.println ("s2 hash code = " + s2.hashCode ());
        System.out.println ("s3 hash code = " + s3.hashCode ());
    }
}
```

```
s1 hash code = 96354
s2 hash code = 96354
s3 hash code = 99333
```

OUTPUT

If you need any more convincing that s1 and s2 refer to the same object, take a look at the hash codes. The hash codes for s1 and s2 are identical.

✔ For more information on hash codes, see Chapter 12, "Data Structures, Part 2," page 289.

OBTAINING CHARACTERS

The String class declares a charAt (int) instance method that returns a character, from a String object, located at the index specified by the int argument.

For example,

```
char c = "abc".charAt (1);
```

assigns character b to char variable c.

The "abc" literal is first converted to a String object and then the charAt (int) method of this object is called. The number 1 is passed as the index argument to extract character b. (String indexes, like array indexes, always begin at 0.)

Passing a negative number or a number that is greater than or equal to the length of the `String` object's contents results in a `StringIndexOutOfBoundsException` object being thrown.

OBTAINING THE CURRENT LENGTH

The `String` class declares a `length ()` instance method that returns the length of a `String` object (that is, the number of characters stored within the object). This is shown in the following code fragment where 3 is output because the `String` object referenced by s contains three characters: a, b, and c:

```
String s = "abc";
System.out.println (s.length ());
```

CAUTION

Do not confuse `String`'s `length ()` instance method with an array object's `length` instance field. The `length ()` method returns the number of characters in a `String` object, whereas the `length` field returns the number of elements in an array. Confusing `length ()` with `length` leads to a compiler error.

DETERMINING EQUALITY

The `String` class's overridden `equals (Object)` instance method compares the contents of two `String` objects for equality, using a case-sensitive comparison. A Boolean `true` value is returned if both objects have the same contents. If both objects have different contents, a Boolean `false` value is returned. The following code fragment illustrates a call to this method. The word `false` is output because the contents of s1 and s2 are not the same:

```
String s1 = "abc";
String s2 = "def";

System.out.println (s1.equals (s2));
```

The `String` class also declares an `equalsIgnoreCase (String)` instance method that compares the contents of two `String` objects, using a case-insensitive comparison. A Boolean `true` value is returned if both objects have the same contents (based on the case-insensitive comparison); otherwise, a Boolean `false` value is returned. This is illustrated in the following bit of code which outputs the word `true` because the contents of s1 and s2 are the same, from a case-insensitive point of view:

```
String s1 = "A";
String s2 = "a";

System.out.println (s1.equalsIgnoreCase (s2));
```

DETERMINING REGION EQUALITY

The String class declares a regionMatches (int, String, int, int) instance method that compares specific character regions within two String objects, using a case-sensitive comparison. A Boolean true value is returned if both regions have the same contents; otherwise, a Boolean false value is returned.

The first argument specifies the invoking String object's starting index. This index identifies the start of the character region within the invoking String object that will be compared to a character region within the String object that is specified by the second argument. The third argument specifies the starting index of the String object argument's character region. The fourth argument specifies the number of characters that will be compared.

The following code fragment compares the first character at position 0 in s1 with the first character at position 0 in s2. Because both characters are the same, a Boolean true value is returned and true is output:

```
String s1 = "abcde";
String s2 = "aBCDE";
System.out.println (s1.regionMatches (0, s2, 0, 1));
```

If any of the int arguments are invalid, this method does not throw an exception. Instead, it returns a Boolean false value.

The String class also declares an overloaded regionMatches (boolean, int, String, int, int) instance method that takes five arguments. (This overloaded method is called by regionMatches (int, String, int, int).)

The first argument is a boolean argument that controls whether the comparison is case sensitive or case insensitive. If a true value is passed, the comparision is case insensitive. If a false value is passed, the comparison is case sensitive. The other arguments remain the same.

The following code fragment compares the first character at position 0 in s1 with the first character at position 0 in s2. Because true is passed as the first argument, the comparison is case insensitive. Therefore, A is considered identical to a and this method returns a Boolean true value. As a result, true is output:

```
String s1 = "Abcde";
String s2 = "aBCDE";
System.out.println (s1.regionMatches (true, 0, s2, 0, 1));
```

If any of the int arguments are invalid, this method does not throw an exception. Instead, it returns a Boolean false value.

FIRST OCCURRENCE SEARCHING

The String class declares an indexOf (String) instance method that searches for the first occurrence of a string in the invoking String object. A zero-based index of this string is returned, if it is found. If not found, -1 is returned.

For example, the following code fragment searches s for string `"ox"`. The search begins with string `"Th"` at index `0` and continues until string `"ox"` at index `17` is found. This code fragment also searches s for string `"box"` but does not find this string because `"box"` is not present in s. Therefore, `-1` is returned. (Both `17` and `-1` are output.)

```
String s = "The quick brown fox jumped over the lazy ox.";
System.out.println (s.indexOf ("ox"));
System.out.println (s.indexOf ("box"));
```

The `String` class also declares an overloaded `indexOf (String, int)` instance method that takes two arguments. The second `int` argument provides the starting index in the invoking object's contents where the search begins. (This overloaded method is called by `indexOf (String)`.)

The following code fragment searches s for string `"ox"`. The search begins with string `"x "` at index `18` and continues until string ox at index `41` is found. When this happens, `41` is returned by `indexOf (String, int)` and then output:

```
String s = "The quick brown fox jumped over the lazy ox.";
System.out.println (s.indexOf ("ox", 18) );
```

The `indexOf (String, int)` method treats a negative argument value as `0`. Too large of an argument value is treated as one less than the string's length. If the string cannot be found, `-1` is returned.

LAST OCCURRENCE SEARCHING

The `String` class declares a `lastIndexOf (String)` instance method that searches for the last occurrence of a string in the invoking `String` object. If the string is found, a zero-based index is returned. Otherwise, `-1` is returned.

The following code fragment searches s for string `"ox"`. The search begins with string `"x."` at index `42` and continues until string `"ox"` at index `41` is found. This code fragment also searches s for string `"box"` but does not find this string because `"box"` is not present in s. Therefore, `-1` is returned. (Both `41` and `-1` are output.)

```
String s = "The quick brown fox jumped over the lazy ox.";
System.out.println (s.lastIndexOf ("ox"));
System.out.println (s.lastIndexOf ("box"));
```

The `String` class also declares an overloaded `lastIndexOf (String, int)` instance method that takes two arguments. As with `indexOf (String, int)`, the second `int` argument provides the starting index in the invoking object's contents where the search begins. (This overloaded method is called by `lastIndexOf (String)`.)

For example, the following code fragment searches s for string `"ox"`. The search begins with string `" o"` at index `40` and continues until string ox at index 17 is found. When this happens, 17 is returned by lastIndexOf (String, int) and output.

```
String s = "The quick brown fox jumped over the lazy ox.";
System.out.println (s.lastIndexOf ("ox"), 40);
```

As with indexOf (String, int), the lastIndexOf (String, int) method treats a negative argument value as 0. Too large of an argument value is treated as one less than the string's length. If the string cannot be found, -1 is returned.

CONVERTING STRINGS

The String class declares a toUpperCase () instance method that creates a new String object with the same contents as the invoking String object, except that every lowercase letter is converted to uppercase. The following code fragment illustrates converting lowercase letters to uppercase:

```
String s = "abc";
System.out.println (s.toUpperCase ());
```

The String class also declares a toLowerCase () instance method that creates a new String object with the same contents as the invoking String object, except that every uppercase letter is converted to lowercase. The following code fragment shows a call to toLowerCase (), which makes a copy of s and then converts ABC to "abc":

```
String s = "ABC";
System.out.println (s.toLowerCase ());
```

TRIMMING STRINGS

The String class declares a trim () instance method that creates a new String object with the same contents as the invoking String object, except that whitespace characters (spaces, newlines, and tabs) have been removed from the front and end of the new String object. The contents of the invoking String object are not changed.

For example, the following code fragment calculates the length of the original String object s and the new String object. (The length of the original object is 9, whereas the length of the new object is 3.)

```
String s = "  \nabc  \n";
System.out.println (s.length ());
System.out.println (s.trim ().length ());
```

THE VALUE OF A STRING

The String class declares several valueOf class methods that convert their non-String arguments to String objects. For example, the valueOf (double) method converts its double argument to a String object, whereas the valueOf (long) method converts its long argument to a String object.

The following `string3` application illustrates `valueOf` method calls:

```
// string3.java

class string3
{
    public static void main (String [] args)
    {
        String s = String.valueOf (false);
        System.out.println (s);

        s = String.valueOf ('A');
        System.out.println (s);

        char [] c = { 'a', 'b', 'c' };

        s = String.valueOf (c);
        System.out.println (s);

        s = String.valueOf (c, 0, 2);
        System.out.println (s);

        s = String.valueOf (3.5d);
        System.out.println (s);

        s = String.valueOf (2.5f);
        System.out.println (s);

        s = String.valueOf (59);
        System.out.println (s);

        s = String.valueOf (8000l);
        System.out.println (s);
    }
}
```

```
false
A
abc
ab
3.5
2.5
59
8000
```

THE toString () METHOD

The `String` class's overridden `toString ()` instance method returns a `String` object that consists of the `String` object's characters. This might seem redundant but there is a good reason for overriding `toString ()`.

The default version of toString () (that is to say, Object's toString () method) returns a String object consisting of a class name and a hash code. For example, if you had a String object s consisting of the characters a, b, and c, and were to call System.out.println (s);, and String's toString () method had not been overridden, abc would not be printed. Instead, the String class name followed by the @ character followed by a hash code would be printed. Therefore, String must override its own toString () method.

The following code fragment passes a String object to the println (String) method. The String object's toString () method is implicitly called to retrieve its contents and these contents are printed:

```
String s = "abc";
System.out.println (s);
```

The StringBuffer Class

The String class creates objects that are read only. These objects never can be modified. Whenever you call a String method that returns a String object, such as toUpperCase (), a new String object is returned. The String object on which the method was invoked is not modified.

If String objects could be modified, it would be impossible to share references to the same object. However, repeatedly generating new String objects in a loop can result in extra memory allocations and a decrease in performance as objects are repeatedly garbage collected. Fewer objects would be generated if String objects could be modified.

Java has a solution to the need for modifiable strings—the StringBuffer class (located in the java.lang package). This class makes it possible to create objects that represent modifiable strings.

A StringBuffer object contains an internal character array. At any point in time, this array has a certain size that is known as its *capacity*. If this capacity is exceeded, the StringBuffer object can dynamically expand this array to accommodate additional characters.

The StringBuffer () constructor constructs a StringBuffer object and initializes its internal array to hold 16 characters—its initial capacity. The array is empty at this point. The following code fragment does just this:

```
StringBuffer sb = new StringBuffer ();
```

The StringBuffer (int) constructor constructs a StringBuffer object and initializes its internal array to hold int argument characters. If a negative value is passed, a NegativeArraySizeException object is thrown. The array is empty at this point. The following code fragment creates an empty StringBuffer object with an initial capacity of 100 characters:

```
StringBuffer sb = new StringBuffer (100);
```

The StringBuffer (String) constructor constructs a StringBuffer object and initializes its internal array to hold the characters from the String argument plus room for an additional 16 characters. The following code fragment creates a StringBuffer object that holds the characters from the String object "abc". The initial capacity of this StringBuffer object is 19 characters:

```
StringBuffer sb = new StringBuffer ("abc");
```

ENSURING CAPACITY

The StringBuffer class declares an ensureCapacity (int) instance method to guarantee that a StringBuffer object has a minimum capacity. If the object does not have this minimum capacity, it is expanded to this capacity. The int argument specifies the new capacity. If a value less than 16 is passed, the capacity is not changed.

For example, the following code fragment creates a StringBuffer object with an initial capacity of 16 characters. Its ensureCapacity (int) method is called to guarantee that it can contain at least 30 characters, before dynamically expanding its internal array:

```
StringBuffer sb = new StringBuffer ();
sb.ensureCapacity (30);
```

The ensureCapacity (int) method exists for performance reasons. Each time the array needs to expand, a new character array that is larger than the original character array must be created and the contents of the original character array must be copied into this array, which takes time. Expanding the internal character array many times during a program's execution can impact performance.

OBTAINING THE CURRENT CAPACITY

The StringBuffer class declares a capacity () instance method that returns the current capacity of the invoking StringBuffer object.

EXAMPLE

The following stringbuffer0 application illustrates changing a StringBuffer object's capacity and determining the current capacity:

```
// stringbuffer0.java

class stringbuffer0
{
    public static void main (String [] args)
    {
        StringBuffer sb = new StringBuffer ();
        System.out.println (sb.capacity ());
        sb.ensureCapacity (50);
        System.out.println (sb.capacity ());
        sb.ensureCapacity (15);
```

```
      System.out.println (sb.capacity ());
   }
}
```

```
16
50
50
```

OBTAINING THE CURRENT LENGTH

The StringBuffer class declares a length () instance method that returns the number of characters in a StringBuffer object. The following code fragment creates two StringBuffer objects: sb1 and sb2. It then calls the length () method to return the length of each object. The length of sb1 is zero and the length of sb2 is three:

```
StringBuffer sb1 = new StringBuffer ();
System.out.println (sb1.length ());
StringBuffer sb2 = new StringBuffer ("abc");
System.out.println (sb2.length ());
```

SPECIFYING A NEW LENGTH

The StringBuffer class declares a setLength (int) instance method that changes the length of the StringBuffer object. The int argument specifies the new length. This argument must be a positive value. If a negative value is passed, a StringIndexOutOfBoundsException object is thrown.

If the new length is less than the original length, characters are truncated from the array. If the new length is greater than the original length, additional null characters (characters with Unicode zero values) are appended to the end of the array.

The following stringbuffer1 application illustrates the differences between a StringBuffer object's length and its capacity:

```
// stringbuffer1.java

class stringbuffer1
{
   public static void main (String [] args)
   {
      StringBuffer sb = new StringBuffer ("abc");

      System.out.println ("sb = " + sb);
      System.out.println ("Length = " + sb.length ());
      System.out.println ("Capacity = " + sb.capacity ());

      sb.setLength (2);
```

```
                    System.out.println ("sb = " + sb);
                    System.out.println ("Length = " + sb.length ());
                    System.out.println ("Capacity = " + sb.capacity ());

                    sb.setLength (4);

                    System.out.println ("sb = " + sb);
                    System.out.println ("Length = " + sb.length ());
                    System.out.println ("Capacity = " + sb.capacity ());
                }
            }
```

OUTPUT

```
sb = abc
Length = 3
Capacity = 19
sb = ab
Length = 2
Capacity = 19
sb = ab
Length = 4
Capacity = 19
```

Although the length changes, the capacity does not change by calling
setLength (int).

APPENDING CHARACTERS

The StringBuffer class declares several append instance methods that convert different data types to string representations and then append these
representations to the invoking StringBuffer objects. For example, the
append (boolean) method converts its boolean argument to a string representation and appends this representation to the invoking StringBuffer
object's internal array.

EXAMPLE

The following stringbuffer2 application illustrates calls to most of the
append methods:

```
// stringbuffer2.java

class stringbuffer2
{
    public static void main (String [] args)
    {
        StringBuffer sb = new StringBuffer ();

        sb.append (true);

        sb.append ('A');

        char [] carray = { 'a', 'b', 'c' };
```

```
            sb.append (carray);

            sb.append (carray, 0, 1);

            sb.append (3.5d);

            sb.append (2.4f);

            sb.append (45);

            sb.append (900001);

            sb.append ("That's all!");

            System.out.println (sb);
        }
    }
```

OUTPUT

trueAabca3.52.44590000That's all!

The StringBuffer object sb is created with a capacity of 16 characters. After this capacity is reached, the internal array is dynamically expanded so that additional characters can be stored.

DELETING CHARACTERS

The StringBuffer class declares a delete (int, int) instance method that deletes a subset of characters from a StringBuffer object's internal array. The first int argument specifies the index of the first character in the subset of characters to be deleted, and the second int argument specifies the index of the last character to be deleted (plus one). If an invalid value is passed for either argument, a StringIndexOutOfBoundsException object is thrown.

The following code fragment creates a StringBuffer object initialized to abcde and then deletes characters b and c from the internal array. As a result, ade is output:

```
StringBuffer sb = new StringBuffer ("abcde");
sb.delete (1, 3);
System.out.println (sb);
```

INSERTING CHARACTERS

The StringBuffer class declares several insert instance methods that convert different data types to string representations and then insert these representations into the invoking StringBuffer objects. For example, the insert (int, boolean) method converts its boolean argument to a string representation and inserts this representation into the invoking StringBuffer object's array at the specified offset. The first int argument of this method (and all other insert methods) specifies an offset into the array where the representation should be stored. If this argument is not valid, a `StringIndexOutOfBoundsException` object is thrown.

The following `stringbuffer3` application illustrates calls to the `insert (int, boolean)` method:

```
// stringbuffer3.java

class stringbuffer3
{
    public static void main (String [] args)
    {
        StringBuffer sb1 = new StringBuffer ("xy");
        System.out.println (sb1);

        sb1.insert (0, false);
        System.out.println (sb1);

        StringBuffer sb2 = new StringBuffer ("xy");
        System.out.println (sb2);

        sb2.insert (1, true);
        System.out.println (sb2);
    }
}
```

```
xy
falsexy
xy
xtruey
```

The 0 offset in the first `insert (int, boolean)` method call specifies that the string representation of the Boolean `false` value is inserted before x, whereas the 1 offset in the second `insert (int, boolean)` method call specifies that the string representation of the Boolean `true` value is inserted after x but before y. These two cases illustrate that the specified offset "tells" an `insert` method to insert a string representation in front of the character at that offset.

OBTAINING CHARACTERS

The `StringBuffer` class declares a `charAt (int)` instance method that returns a character from the invoking `StringBuffer` object's array. The `int` argument specifies the zero-based index of this character. If a negative value or a value greater than or equal to the length of the array is passed as the index, a `StringIndexOutOfBoundsException` object is thrown.

The following code fragment creates a `StringBuffer` object whose internal array is initialized to abcdef. The `charAt (int)` method is called with 1 as its argument. This method returns character b, which is subsequently printed:

```
StringBuffer sb = new StringBuffer ("abcdef");
System.out.println (sb.charAt (1));
```

REPLACING CHARACTERS

In addition to the charAt (int) method for obtaining a character, the StringBuffer class also declares a setCharAt (int, char) instance method that changes a character within the internal array. The int argument specifies this index. If a negative value or a value greater than or equal to the length of the array is passed, a StringIndexOutOfBoundsException object is thrown.

The following code fragment illustrates changing b to x in StringBuffer object sb:

```
StringBuffer sb = new StringBuffer ("abcdef");
sb.setCharAt (1, 'x');
System.out.println (sb);
```

THE toString () METHOD

The StringBuffer class's overridden toString () instance method returns a String object that contains all the characters in the StringBuffer object's internal array.

The following code fragment creates a StringBuffer object, calls its toString () method, and assigns the resulting String object reference to s. The println (String) method is called to output the string:

```
StringBuffer sb = new StringBuffer ("abc");
String s = sb.toString ();
System.out.println (s);
```

The StringTokenizer Class

Suppose you want to create a Java program that must break up a string into small meaningful pieces. You can use the StringTokenizer class to accomplish this task.

A StringTokenizer object treats a String object as a sequence of tokens (pieces) that are separated from other tokens by delimiter characters. The most commonly used delimiters are the whitespace characters (spaces, tabs, newlines, and carriage returns).

You can create a StringTokenizer object by specifying new and calling one of three constructors to initialize the object: StringTokenizer (String), StringTokenizer (String, String), and StringTokenizer (String, String, boolean).

The `StringTokenizer (String)` constructor initializes a new `StringTokenizer` object with the `String` argument to be tokenized and a default set of delimiters (space character, tab character, newline character, carriage-return character, and form-feed character). The following code fragment creates a `StringTokenizer` object for the `"two tokens"` String object:

```
StringTokenizer st = new StringTokenizer ("two tokens");
```

The `StringTokenizer (String, String)` constructor initializes a new `StringTokenizer` object with the first `String` argument to be tokenized and the set of delimiters specified by the second `String` argument. The following code fragment creates a `StringTokenizer` object for the `"23,32,45"` String object. The `","` String object specifies a single comma-character delimiter:

```
StringTokenizer st = new StringTokenizer ("23,32,45", ",");
```

The `StringTokenizer (String, String, boolean)` constructor initializes a new `StringTokenizer` object with the first `String` argument to be tokenized, a set of delimiters specified by the second `String` argument, and the delimiter-return behavior specified by the third `boolean` argument. If `true` is passed, delimiter characters are returned as tokens. (Each delimiter is returned as a `String` object consisting of the single delimiter character.) If the `boolean` argument is `false`, delimiter characters are skipped and not returned. (The previous two constructors never return delimiters as tokens.)

The following code fragment creates a `StringTokenizer` object for the `"a:b:c"` String object. The `":"` String object specifies a single colon-character delimiter. This character will be returned as a token because `true` is specified as the third argument:

```
StringTokenizer st =
new StringTokenizer ("a:b:c", ":", true);
```

Each `StringTokenizer` constructor sets an internal character index to point to the first character in the `String` object. This character index is advanced during the tokenizing process and helps the `StringTokenizer` object locate tokens.

The `StringTokenizer` class is located in the `java.util` package. You must specify either an `import java.util.StringTokenizer;` directive or an `import java.util.*;` directive at the start of your source file before you can use this class.

TOKENIZING

After a `StringTokenizer` object has been created, various instance methods can be called to count the number of tokens, determine if there are any more tokens to extract, and extract the next token.

The `countTokens ()` instance method returns an `int` that identifies the number of tokens in the `String` object.

The hasMoreTokens () instance method returns true if there are more tokens to extract; otherwise, false is returned. Each time hasMoreTokens () is called, the first thing that it does is skip over leading delimiters (unless delimiters also are being returned as tokens).

The nextToken () instance method returns a String object that holds the next token. Like hasMoreTokens (), each time nextToken () is called, the first thing that it does is skip over leading delimiters (unless delimiters also are being returned as tokens). However, unlike hasMoreTokens (), it then checks to see if there is another token to return. If not, nextToken () throws a NoSuchElementException object.

The nextToken (String) instance method records its String argument as the new set of delimiters and then calls nextToken ().

EXAMPLE

The following stringtokenizer0 application illustrates the tokenizing process:

```
// stringtokenizer0.java

import java.util.*;

class stringtokenizer0
{
    public static void main (String [] args)
    {
        String message = "The quick brown fox jumped over the lazy dog.";

        StringTokenizer st = new StringTokenizer (message);

        System.out.println ("Number of tokens = " + st.countTokens ());

        while (st.hasMoreTokens ())
            System.out.println (st.nextToken ());
    }
}
```

It is a good idea to call hasMoreTokens () before calling nextToken () to prevent the possibility of a NoSuchElementException object being thrown.

OUTPUT

```
Number of tokens = 9
The
quick
brown
fox
jumped
over
the
lazy
dog.
```

Notice the last line of output. The period character is included with the word dog. However, the period character and dog are separate tokens. They really shouldn't be included together as one token. The next example shows how to handle this kind of situation.

EXAMPLE

The following stringtokenizer1 application illustrates the tokenizing process where delimiter characters need to be modified during tokenizing:

```
// stringtokenizer1.java

import java.util.*;

class stringtokenizer1
{
    public static void main (String [] args)
    {
        String phoneNumber = "(204) 555-1234";

        StringTokenizer st = new StringTokenizer (phoneNumber, "()");

        System.out.println ("Number of tokens = " + st.countTokens ());

        System.out.println (st.nextToken ());

        System.out.println (st.nextToken (") -"));

        System.out.println (st.nextToken ());
    }
}
```

In this example, the 204 area code, 555, and 1234 are extracted as separate tokens from the phoneNumber object. This task is complicated by the different delimiter characters that are present: (,), -, and space.

A StringTokenizer object is created with () as the delimiter characters. After this object is created, the first call to nextToken () skips over the (delimiter, recognizes the) character as another delimiter, and returns 204. The subsequent nextToken (") -") call resets the delimiters to), a space character, and a hypen (-) character. The) character is required because the very first character that will be examined by nextToken ()—which is called by nextToken (String)—is the) character. If) is not included in the set of delimiters, the) will be treated as a token. The space character is required because a space appears after) in phoneNumber. If space is not included in the set of delimiters, it will be treated as a token. The hyphen character is required because tokenizing must stop after the third 5 character. The final nextToken () call extracts 1234 as a token. The current delimiter characters are the), space, and hyphen characters. Only the hyphen character is required because the hyphen character in phoneNumber is the first character that is examined when nextToken () is called. If this character is not treated as a delimiter, -1234 will be returned—not 1234, as expected.

```
Number of tokens = 2
204
555
1234
```

Notice that countTokens () returns the wrong value (2) as far as the number of returned tokens are concerned. However, this method is not really returning a wrong value. At the time countTokens () is called, the only delimiter characters that are recognized are (and). They separate the tokens 204 and 555-1234 (including the leading-space character). This indicates that care must be exercised when calling countTokens (). If you plan to change delimiters during the tokenizing process, don't rely on countToken ()'s return value.

What's Next?

Many text-processing programs need to organize text within data structures before this text can be manipulated. For example, a text-sorting application might require text to be stored as String objects in an array or in a Vector data structure object. The next two chapters focus on these and other kinds of data structures, along with common operations that are applied to stored objects.

11

Data Structures, Part 1

Many kinds of data structures have been developed over the years. They can be categorized as either fixed-size data structures or dynamic data structures. Fixed-size data structures cannot grow (that is, no new data items can be added after the limit has been reached). Conversely, dynamic data structures can grow. The only limit to the number of data items that can be added to a dynamic data structure is available memory. This chapter explores fixed-size data structures, from Java's perspective.

Chapter 11 presents the following topics:

- Arrays
- Primitives
- Enumerations
- Vectors
- Bit sets
- SPL

Arrays

Unlike C or C++, Java requires arrays to be dynamically allocated. This is accomplished by using new and assigning the address of the newly allocated memory to a special kind of reference variable—the array variable.

Arrays exist in one or more dimensions. One-dimensional arrays are useful for working with lists of data items. Two-dimensional arrays are useful for working with tables of data items. Three-dimensional (and higher) arrays can be created but they are rarely needed.

Arrays are often used by sorting and searching algorithms to hold the data items to be sorted/searched. This has led to the development of a wide variety of sorting and searching algorithms. Some of these algorithms, as they relate to arrays, are examined in this chapter.

Array Variables

An *array variable* is declared by specifying a data type, an identifier that names the variable, and one or more pairs of square bracket characters ([ ]) that the compiler uses to distinguish an array variable from a scalar variable (a non-array variable). The format of an array variable declaration is

```
data_type identifier '[' ']' … ';'
```

or

```
data_type '[' ']' … identifier ';'
```

where `data_type` identifies each element's data type (that is, boolean, byte, char, double, float, int, long, short, or a reference data type)—not the array variable's data type (which is a special reference data type), identifier identifies the name of the array, and the three dots indicate optional pairs of square brackets following the initial pair. Each pair of square brackets represents one dimension.

TIP

Reserved words cannot be used as array variable names.

An array variable is initialized to null.

EXAMPLE

The following code fragment illustrates the declaration of x and y array variables:

```
int x [];
int [] y;
```

The x and y array variables contain the addresses of blocks of memory that will hold their elements. However, at this point, these variables are initialized to null because these blocks have not yet been allocated. The int data types are the data types of the elements in each array, not the data types of the variables themselves.

Figure 11.1 shows the newly created x and y array variables as they appear in memory.

Figure 11.1: *Newly created array variables x and y as they appear in memory.*

Dynamic Memory Allocation

After an array variable has been created, a block of memory that holds the array's elements can be allocated and a reference to this block assigned to the array variable.

Memory is dynamically allocated by specifying new followed by the array's data type and one or more pairs of square brackets: The number of pairs depends upon the number of the dimensions—one pair per dimension.

CAUTION

The number of square bracket pairs in the array allocation must match the number of square bracket pairs in the array variable declaration. If these numbers do not match, the compiler reports an error.

After memory has been allocated, each element is initialized to zero—interpreted as false, '\u0000', 0, 01, 0.0d, 0.0f, or null (depending on the data type).

One-Dimensional Arrays

The simplest kind of array is a *one-dimensional array*. Each element follows the previous element in linear succession, with the first element being located at position 0. Figure 11.2 shows a conceptual view of a one-dimensional array.

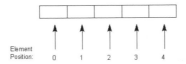

Figure 11.2: *A conceptual one-dimensional array.*

The format of a one-dimensional array allocation and default element initialization is

identifier '=' "new" *data_type* '[' *expression* ']' ';'

where *identifier* is the name of an array variable, *data_type* is the array's data type—which must match the array variable's data type—and *expression* evaluates to a positive integer value that specifies the number of elements in the array.

EXAMPLE

The following code fragment illustrates the creation of a one-dimensional array variable x followed by the allocation of three elements. Each element is given the int data type. Therefore, each element is four bytes in size:

```
int [] x;
x = new int [3];
```

Figure 11.3 shows the newly created x array variable and its memory block as they appear in memory. Each element in this block is initialized to zero.

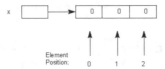

Figure 11.3: *A newly created one-dimensional array variable x and its block of elements as they appear in memory.*

One-dimensional array variables can be declared and their one-dimensional arrays allocated and initialized to default values in a single statement, by using either one of the following two formats:

```
data_type identifier '[' ']' '='
"new" data_type '[' expression ']' ';'
```

or

```
data_type '[' ']' identifier '='
"new" data_type '[' expression ']' ';'
```

After a one-dimensional array has been created, its elements can be accessed by using the array index operator (also known as the array subscript operator).

The array index operator format is

```
identifier '[' expression ']'
```

where *identifier* is the name of an array variable and *expression* is an integer expression that evaluates to a positive integer value, starting at zero.

The value stored in the element at the index represented by *expression* can be replaced by a new value or retrieved. However, a valid index (an index starting at zero and ranging to one less than the length of the array) must be specified or an ArrayIndexOutOfBoundsException object is thrown.

CAUTION

Always specify a valid element index or an `ArrayIndexOutOfBoundsException` object will be thrown.

Every one-dimensional array has a `length` field that returns the number of elements in the array. (The fact that an array variable is a reference to a block of memory and that every memory block is associated with a `length` field leads some to suggest that arrays are special kinds of objects. From one perspective, this is true. From another perspective, it is not. You'll have to form your own opinion.)

The format used to access this field is

```
identifier '.' "length"
```

where *identifier* is the name of an array variable and `length` represents the number of elements in the array. *identifier* and `length` are separated by a single period character.

CAUTION

Do not confuse `length` with `length ()`. The `length` field returns the number of elements in a one-dimensional array, whereas the `length ()` method is declared by the `String` and `StringBuffer` classes, and returns the number of characters in an object created from either class. Mixing `length` with `length ()` will result in compiler errors.

EXAMPLE

The following code fragment illustrates the creation of a one-dimensional array variable x, the allocation of a block of three elements that is assigned to this variable, the array index operator to set and retrieve element values, and the use of `length` and a For loop statement to iterate through this array and print out each value:

```
int [] x = new int [3];

// Assign values to elements 0 through 2 using the array
// index operator.

x [0] = 10;
x [1] = -5;
x [2] = 9000;

// Loop through the array's elements and print out the value
// of each element using the array index operator.  The
// number of iterations is controlled by the number of
// elements returned by the length field.

for (int i = 0; i < x.length; i++)
    System.out.println (x [i]);
```

Figure 11.4 shows the contents of the memory block assigned to x after it has been explicitly initialized.

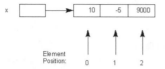

Figure 11.4: *The memory block assigned to x after it has been explicitly initialized.*

✔ For more information on an alternative way of explicitly initializing a one-dimensional array, see Chapter 2, "Data Types, Literals, and Variables," page 29.

Two-Dimensional Arrays

A *two-dimensional array*, also known as a *table*, consists of a one-dimensional array (known as the *row array*) of one-dimensional arrays (known as *column arrays*). Each element of the row array references its own column array. Figure 11.5 shows a conceptual view of a two-dimensional array.

Columns

(0, 0)	(0, 1)	(0, 2)	(0, 3)	(0, 4)
(1, 0)	(1, 1)	(1, 2)	(1, 3)	(1, 4)
(2, 0)	(2, 1)	(2, 2)	(2, 3)	(2, 4)
(3, 0)	(3, 1)	(3, 2)	(3, 3)	(3, 4)
(4, 0)	(4, 1)	(4, 2)	(4, 3)	(4, 4)

Rows

Element Position: (row, column)

Figure 11.5: *A conceptual two-dimensional array.*

The format of a two-dimensional array allocation and default element initialization is

identifier '=' "new" *data_type* '[' *expression* ']' '[' ']' ';'

where *identifier* is the name of an array variable, *data_type* is the array's data type—which must match the array variable's data type—and *expression* evaluates to a positive integer value that specifies the number of row elements in the array. The second square bracket pair must be specified as a placeholder for the column arrays. The compiler does not enable an expression to be placed between this second pair.

CAUTION

Placing an expression between the second pair of square brackets following new and the two-dimensional array's data type results in a compiler error.

At this point, a one-dimensional array has been created. This array represents the number of row elements in the two-dimensional array.

EXAMPLE

The following code fragment illustrates the creation of a two-dimensional array variable x and the allocation of memory for its row array elements:

```
// The following statement declares an array variable
// called x that references a two-dimensional array.

double [][] x;

// The following statement allocates a one-dimensional
// row array of three elements.  Each row element will
// reference a column array.  However, at this point, each
// element is initialized to null.

x = new double [3][];
```

Figure 11.6 shows the contents of the memory block assigned to x. These contents represent the single row array of three reference elements.

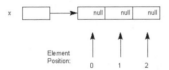

Figure 11.6: *The memory block assigned to x after a single row array of three reference elements has been created.*

Before the two-dimensional array can be used, its column arrays must be created.

EXAMPLE

The following code fragment continues from the previous code fragment and illustrates the creation of a one-dimensional column array for each element of the row array:

```
// The column arrays must be explicitly created.  In this
// example, each column array will be given 5 elements.  A
// For loop statement will be used to create these column
// arrays.

for (int i = 0; i < x.length; i++)
    x [i] = new int [5];
```

Figure 11.7 shows the two-dimensional x array as it appears in memory.

Two-dimensional array variables can be declared and their one-dimensional row arrays allocated and initialized to default null values in a single statement, by using either one of the following two formats:

```
data_type identifier '[' ']' '[' ']' '='
"new" data_type '[' expression ']' '[' ']' ';'
```

or

```
data_type '[' ']' '[' ']' identifier '='
"new" data_type '[' expression ']' '[' ']' ';'
```

After the row array has been allocated, each element must be initialized to a column array. This format is identical to the format of a one-dimensional array allocation and default initialization.

After a two-dimensional array has been created, its elements can be accessed by using the array index operator.

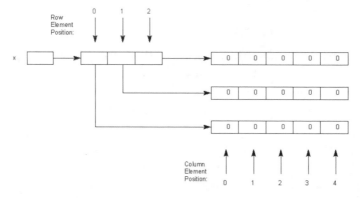

Figure 11.7: *A newly created two-dimensional x array as it appears in memory.*

EXAMPLE

The following code fragment illustrates the creation of a two-dimensional array variable x, a one-dimensional row array, a separate one-dimensional column array for each row array element, and the use of the array index operator to store and fetch int data items to and from various elements:

```
int [][] x = new int [3][];

for (int i = 0; i < x.length; i++)
    x [i] = new int [5];

// The following method call displays the default 0 value
// that is stored in the first element of the column array
// which is stored in the first element of the row array.

System.out.println (x [0][0]);

// The following statement assigns 1 to this element.

x [0][0] = 1;
```

Figure 11.8 shows the results of the memory block assigned to x after it has been manipulated.

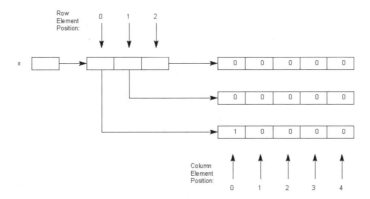

Figure 11.8: *The memory block assigned to x after it has been manipulated.*

One of the more interesting capabilities brought forward by Java's array-of-arrays concept is the fact that each column array can have a different length. This results in memory savings for certain kinds of programs where some rows need fewer columns than other rows. A two-dimensional array that has a different number of columns for each row is known as a *ragged array*.

EXAMPLE

The following code fragment illustrates the creation of a ragged array:

```
int [][] x = new int [3][];

x [0] = new int [5];
x [1] = new int [10];
x [2] = new int [4];
```

Figure 11.9 shows a conceptual view of a two-dimensional ragged array.

Columns

(0,0)	(0,1)	(0,2)		
(1,0)	(1,1)	(1,2)	(1,3)	(1,4)
(2,0)	(2,1)	(2,2)	(2,3)	
(3,0)	(3,1)	(3,2)	(3,3)	(3,4)
(4,0)	(4,1)			

Rows (left label)

Element Position: (row, column)

Figure 11.9: *A conceptual two-dimensional ragged array.*

The same alternative syntax that the compiler offers to one-dimensional arrays is available to two-dimensional (and higher dimensional) arrays. However, this syntax is enhanced to accommodate the extra dimension(s).

The following compareDemo application illustrates creating a two-row by three-column array using the alternative syntax and then the memory allocation syntax. As you'll see, the alternative syntax saves typing:

```java
// compareDemo.java

class compareDemo
{
    public static void main (String [] args)
    {
        int [][] x = { { 1, 2, 3 }, { 10, 20, 30 } };

        for (int row = 0; row < x.length; row++)
        {
            for (int col = 0; col < x [row].length; col++)
                System.out.print (x [row][col] + " ");

            System.out.println ("");
        }

        System.out.println ("");

        int [][] x2 = new int [2][];

        for (int i = 0; i < x.length; i++)
            x2 [i] = new int [3];

        x2 [0][0] = 1;
        x2 [0][1] = 2;
        x2 [0][2] = 3;

        x2 [1][0] = 10;
        x2 [1][1] = 20;
        x2 [1][2] = 30;

        for (int row = 0; row < x.length; row++)
        {
            for (int col = 0; col < x [row].length; col++)
                System.out.print (x [row][col] + " ");

            System.out.println ("");
        }
    }
}
```

As you can see, x.length returns the number of rows in this table. This also could be stated as the number of elements in the one-dimensional array assigned to the x array variable.

For each element in this row array, x [row].length returns the number of columns in that row.

Sorting Arrays

A variety of sorting algorithms have been invented for use with arrays. These algorithms include bubble sort, quick sort, shell sort, heap sort, and selection sort. In this section, we will look at the bubble sort.

The *bubble sort* makes many passes (iterations) over an array of data items. During each pass, adjacent data items are compared to each other to determine which data item has a smaller or greater numerical value. Depending on whether the sort is an ascending sort or a descending sort, the data items are swapped (exchanged) so that the smaller or larger data item appears first. Bubble sort gets its name from the fact that either the smaller or the larger data item "bubbles" to the top of the array (the first element—at index 0) during each pass.

EXAMPLE

The following bSort application illustrates the bubble sort algorithm. An array of double-precision floating point values is sorted into ascending order:

```
// bSort.java

class bSort
{
    public static void main (String [] args)
    {
        double [] x = { 92.3, 45.2, 6.8, -3.6, 10, 9000, -39 };

        System.out.println ("Before the sort...\n");
        for (int i = 0; i < x.length; i++)
            System.out.print (x [i] + " ");
        System.out.println ("\n");

        for (int pass = 0; pass < x.length - 1; pass++)
            for (int i = 0; i < x.length - pass - 1; i++)
                if (x [i] > x [i+1])
                {
                    double temp = x [i];
                    x [i] = x [i + 1];
                    x [i + 1] = temp;
                }

        System.out.println ("After the sort...\n");
        for (int i = 0; i < x.length; i++)
            System.out.print (x [i] + " ");
    }
}
```

```
Before the sort...

92.3 45.2 6.8 -3.6 10.0 9000.0 -39.0

After the sort...

-39.0 -3.6 6.8 10.0 45.2 92.3 9000.0
```

Searching Arrays

Two major search algorithms have been invented for use with arrays: linear search and binary search.

The *linear search* searches through an array for a specific data item by starting at element zero and continuing through successive elements until either the data item is found or the end of the array is reached. The average number of elements that must be examined is one-half of the array's length. For example, an array of ten million elements would require an average of five million element examinations. This could seriously impact performance. Therefore, linear search is best used with small arrays. (Linear search can be used with sorted or unsorted arrays.)

The following lSearch application illustrates the linear search algorithm. An array of double-precision floating-point values is searched for a specific data item:

```java
// lSearch.java

class lSearch
{
    public static void main (String [] args)
    {
        double [] x = { 92.3, 45.2, 6.8, -3.6, 10, 9000, -39 };

        int i;
        for (i = 0; i < x.length; i++)
            if (x [i] == 9000)
                break;

        if (i == x.length)
            System.out.println ("Not found");
        else
            System.out.println ("Found");
    }
}
```

Found

The *binary search* searches through an array for a specific data item by calculating the index of the middle element of an array and then comparing the searched data item with the data item in the middle element. Either the search ends because the data item is found or the middle element of the array's first or second half is used to determine if the data item being sought is in the first half (below the middle element) or in the last half (above the middle element) of the array. The only downside to a binary search is that the array must be sorted before the search can commence.

The maximum number of elements that need to be examined during a binary search is $\log_2 n$. For example, 1,024 elements would take exactly 10 examinations and 1,048,576 elements would take exactly 20 examinations. (Contrast this with an average of 512 examinations and 524,288 examinations, respectively, if linear search was used.)

The following `bSearch` application illustrates the binary search algorithm. An array of double-precision floating-point values is searched for a specific data item:

```java
// bSearch.java

class bSearch
{
   public static void main (String [] args)
   {
      double [] x = { -39, -3.6, 6.8, 10, 45.2, 92.3, 9000 };

      double value = 6.8;
      int lower = 0, upper = x.length - 1;

      while (lower <= upper)
      {
         int middle = (lower + upper) / 2;

         if (value > x [middle])
            lower = middle + 1;
         else
         if (value < x [middle])
            upper = middle - 1;
         else
            break;
      }

      if (lower > upper)
         System.out.println ("Not found");
      else
```

```
                    System.out.println ("Found");
        }
}
```

OUTPUT

Found

Primitives

A *primitive* is a data structure object composed of a single data item that has a primitive boolean, byte, char, double, float, int, long, or short data type. Primitives are created from the Boolean, Byte, Character, Double, Float, Integer, Long, and Short primitive classes. These classes are located in the java.lang package and also are known as *data type classes* or *wrapper classes*.

Primitives exist because the fundamental principle of Java is that everything is an object. From a more practical perspective, Java's Vector class (which you will shortly explore) creates container objects that store other objects. Primitive data items cannot be stored in a Vector object, whereas primitives can be stored.

The Boolean Class

The Boolean class creates primitives that wrap themselves around data items of the boolean data type. The Boolean (boolean) constructor initializes a Boolean primitive to a boolean data item. Boolean's booleanValue () instance method returns this data item.

EXAMPLE

The following application illustrates the creation of a Boolean primitive and the extraction of its boolean data item:

```
// primitive1.java

class primitive1
{
    public static void main (String [] args)
    {
        boolean b = true;
        Boolean b2 = new Boolean (b);
        System.out.println (b2.booleanValue ());
    }
}
```

OUTPUT

true

The Byte Class

The Byte class creates primitives that wrap themselves around data items of the byte data type. The Byte (byte) constructor initializes a Byte primitive to a byte data item. Byte's byteValue () instance method returns this data item.

EXAMPLE

The following application illustrates the creation of a `Byte` primitive and the extraction of its `byte` data item:

```
// primitive2.java

class primitive2
{
   public static void main (String [] args)
   {
      byte by = (byte) 'A';
      Byte by2 = new Byte (by);
      System.out.println (by2.byteValue ());
   }
}
```

OUTPUT

65

The Character Class

The `Character` class creates primitives that wrap themselves around data items of the char data type. The `Character (char)` constructor initializes a `Character` primitive to a char data item. `Character`'s `charValue ()` instance method returns this data item.

EXAMPLE

The following application illustrates the creation of a `Character` primitive and the extraction of its char data item:

```
// primitive3.java

class primitive3
{
   public static void main (String [] args)
   {
      char c = '*';
      Character c2 = new Character (c);
      System.out.println (c2.charValue ());
   }
}
```

OUTPUT

*

The Double Class

The `Double` class creates primitives that wrap themselves around data items of the double data type. The `Double (double)` constructor initializes a `Double` primitive to a double data item. `Double`'s `doubleValue ()` instance method returns this data item.

EXAMPLE

The following application illustrates the creation of a `Double` primitive and the extraction of its double data item:

```
// primitive4.java
```

```
class primitive4
{
   public static void main (String [] args)
   {
      double d = 3.5;
      Double d2 = new Double (d);
      System.out.println (d2.doubleValue ());
   }
}
```

3.5

OUTPUT

The Float Class

The Float class creates primitives that wrap themselves around data items of the float data type. The Float (float) constructor initializes a Float primitive to a float data item. Float's floatValue () instance method returns this data item.

The following application illustrates the creation of a Float primitive and the extraction of its float data item:

```
// primitive5.java
```

EXAMPLE

```
class primitive5
{
   public static void main (String [] args)
   {
      float f = -29.6f;
      Float f2 = new Float (f);
      System.out.println (f2.floatValue ());
   }
}
```

-29.6

OUTPUT

The Integer Class

The Integer class creates primitives that wrap themselves around data items of the int data type. The Integer (int) constructor initializes an Integer primitive to an int data item. Integer's intValue () instance method returns this data item.

The following application illustrates the creation of an Integer primitive and the extraction of its int data item:

```
// primitive6.java
```

EXAMPLE

```
class primitive6
{
```

```
    public static void main (String [] args)
    {
        int i = 17;
        Integer i2 = new Integer (i);
        System.out.println (i2.intValue ());
    }
}
17
```

OUTPUT

The Long Class

The Long class creates primitives that wrap themselves around data items of the long data type. The Long (long) constructor initializes a Long primitive to a long data item. Long's longValue () instance method returns this data item.

EXAMPLE

The following application illustrates the creation of a Long primitive and the extraction of its long data item:

```
// primitive7.java

class primitive7
{
    public static void main (String [] args)
    {
        long l = 100000001;
        Long l2 = new Long (l);
        System.out.println (l2.longValue ());
    }
}
10000000
```

OUTPUT

The Short Class

The Short class creates primitives that wrap themselves around data items of the short data type. The Short (short) constructor initializes a Short primitive to a short data item. Short's shortValue () instance method returns this data item.

EXAMPLE

The following application illustrates the creation of a Short primitive and the extraction of its short data item:

```
// primitive8.java

class primitive8
{
    public static void main (String [] args)
    {
        short s = -1800;
```

```
        Short s2 = new Short (s);
        System.out.println (s2.shortValue ());
    }
}
-1800
```

Enumerations

Enumerations are objects created from classes that implement the Enumeration interface. They are used to enumerate (that is, iterate over) objects in a container object. Enumeration is located in the java.util package.

The Enumeration interface declares two abstract instance methods, hasMoreElements () and nextElement (), that any class implementing this interface must provide.

The hasMoreElements () method returns a Boolean true value if there is at least one more element within the container to retrieve. The nextElement () method returns the Object reference of the current element in the container and advances to the next element. This Object reference must be cast back to the reference of the object that was stored in the container. (The instanceof operator is useful for this task.) If there are no more elements, a NoSuchElementException object is thrown.

You'll work with these methods when you explore the Vector class because Vector implements Enumeration.

Vectors

Vectors are growable array data structure objects. Java's designers created vectors as a dynamic alternative to fixed-size arrays.

Vectors are implemented by Vector objects created from the Vector class. This class is located in the java.util package.

Every Vector object contains an internal fixed-size array of Object references. To support the capability to dynamically grow this array, Vector objects also contain an internal field that identifies the current array capacity and another internal field that specifies by how much the array grows when it is full. This latter field is called *capacity increment*.

The Vector () constructor initializes a Vector object with an internal array capacity of ten objects and a capacity increment of zero. (Zero means that the array will double in size when it needs to grow.) This is illustrated by the following code fragment:

```
Vector v = new Vector ();
```

The Vector (int) constructor initializes a Vector object with an initial array capacity specified by the int argument and a capacity increment of zero. As with Vector (), zero means that the array will double in size when it needs to grow. The following code fragment illustrates this constructor:

```
Vector v = new Vector (20);
```

The Vector (int, int) constructor initializes a Vector object with an initial array capacity specified by the first int argument and a capacity increment specified by the second int argument. The following code fragment creates a Vector object with an internal array capacity of 30 elements. Each time the internal array fills, it will grow by 20 elements:

```
Vector v = new Vector (30, 20);
```

TIP

Every time a Vector object's internal array grows, a new internal array of the appropriate size must be created and the old internal array's elements copied to the new internal array. The old internal array is then destroyed. Internal array creation and copying takes time. If this happens frequently, it will impact performance. Try to choose appropriate capacity increments for your programs to minimize these performance hits.

The addElement (Object) Method

The Vector class declares an addElement (Object) instance method that adds the object referenced by the Object argument to the Vector object. (A reference to a subclass of Object is typically passed as this argument.) The following code fragment adds a new String object to Vector object v:

```
v.addElement ("abc");
```

The removeElement (Object) Method

The Vector class declares a removeElement (Object) instance method that removes the object whose reference is specified by the Object argument from the Vector object. The following code fragment removes the first element from Vector object v:

```
v.removeElement (v.firstElement ());
```

The firstElement () Method

The Vector class declares a firstElement () instance method that returns a reference to the first object in the Vector object. The following code fragment retrieves and displays the first element from Vector object v. The object's toString () method is implicitly called to return a string representation of the object:

```
System.out.println (v.firstElement ());
```

The `lastElement ()` Method

The `Vector` class declares a `lastElement ()` instance method that returns a reference to the last object in the `Vector` object. The following code fragment retrieves and displays the last element from `Vector` object v. The object's `toString ()` method is implicitly called to return a string representation of the object:

```
System.out.println (v.lastElement ());
```

The `isEmpty ()` Method

The `Vector` class declares an `isEmpty ()` instance method that determines if any objects are contained within the `Vector` object. A Boolean `true` value is returned if the `Vector` object is empty. The following code fragment checks to see if `Vector` object v is empty by calling the `isEmpty ()` method. If it is empty, `true` is returned and displayed. If it is not empty, `false` is returned and displayed:

```
System.out.println (v.isEmpty ());
```

The `contains (Object)` Method

The `Vector` class declares a `contains (Object)` instance method that determines if the object specified by the `Object` argument is contained within the `Vector` object. A Boolean `true` value is returned if the object is present. The following code fragment checks to see if `Vector` object v contains the `"abc"` `String` object. (Don't forget, the compiler internally converts `"abc"` into new `String ("abc")`.) If this object is contained in v, `true` is returned and displayed. If this object is not present, `false` is returned and displayed:

```
System.out.println (v.contains ("abc"));
```

The `indexOf (Object)` Method

The `Vector` class declares an `indexOf (Object)` instance method that returns the integer index of the object whose reference is specified by the `Object` argument if this object is contained within the `Vector` object. If the object is not found, a -1 value is returned. The following code fragment searches `Vector` object v's internal array to see if it contains a reference to `"abc"`. If it does, a positive integer that identifies the position is returned and displayed. If it does not, -1 is returned and displayed:

```
System.out.println (v.indexOf ("abc"));
```

The `elements ()` Method

The `Vector` class declares an `elements ()` instance method that creates and returns an enumeration object. This object can iterate over all data items stored within the `Vector` object's internal array. (For those who are curious, elements () creates the enumeration object from an anonymous inner class that implements the Enumeration interface's methods and has access to the Vector object's fields and methods.)

EXAMPLE

The following vectorDemo application illustrates the creation of a Vector object for storing other objects and iterating through this object, via an enumeration, to obtain each stored object:

```java
// vectorDemo.java

import java.util.*;

class employee
{
   private String name;
   private double salary;

   employee (String name, double salary)
   {
      this.name = name;
      this.salary = salary;
   }

   public String toString ()
   {
      return "Name = " + name + ", Salary = " + salary;
   }
}

class vectorDemo
{
   public static void main (String [] args)
   {
      String [] names = { "John", "Sally", "June" };

      double [] salaries = { 50000.0, 40500.0, 60000.0 };

      // Create a Vector object with an initial array capacity of 20.

      Vector v = new Vector (20);

      for (int i = 0; i < 20; i++)
      {
           // Return a random integer from 1 to 2.

           int choice = 1 + (int) (Math.random () * 2);

           Object o = null;
```

```
            switch (choice)
            {
                case 1: int j = (int) (Math.random () * names.length);
                        int k = (int) (Math.random () * salaries.length);
                        o = new employee (names [j], salaries [k]);
                        break;

                case 2: o = new Character ((char) ('A' + i));
            }

            v.addElement (o);
        }

        // Output Vector object v's contents.

        Enumeration e = v.elements ();
        while (e.hasMoreElements ())
        {
            Object o = e.nextElement ();

            if (o instanceof employee)
                System.out.println ((employee) o);
            else
                System.out.println (((Character) o).charValue ());
        }
    }
}
```

OUTPUT

```
A
Name = Sally, Salary = 60000.0
Name = John, Salary = 40500.0
D
E
Name = Sally, Salary = 40500.0
Name = John, Salary = 40500.0
Name = Sally, Salary = 40500.0
Name = June, Salary = 50000.0
Name = John, Salary = 50000.0
K
Name = Sally, Salary = 60000.0
M
Name = June, Salary = 40500.0
O
P
Name = Sally, Salary = 60000.0
R
S
Name = Sally, Salary = 50000.0
```

SPL

Have you ever wondered how to write a program that processes computer languages—such as a compiler or an interpreter? If you have, here is your chance to look "behind the curtain" and see some of what goes on.

SPL (Simple Programming Language) is an application that interprets programs written in the SPL language. This language consists of three statements: VAR, PRINT, and ASSIGNMENT.

The VAR statement declares an integer variable. It has the following syntax:

```
"var" identifier
```

identifier is the variable's name and must follow the rules of any Java identifier.

The PRINT statement prints the names and values of all declared variables. It has the following syntax: `"print"`.

The ASSIGNMENT statement evaluates an expression and assigns the result to a variable. It has the following syntax: *identifier* `'='` *expression*.

identifier is the name of a previously declared variable, via the VAR statement.

expression consists of integer literals, variable names, and a mixture of addition (+), subtraction (-), multiplication (*), and division (/) operators. Multiplication and division occur before addition and subtraction. However, this precedence can be changed by using the parentheses characters.

The following listing presents a sample SPL program.

Listing 11.1: SPL program.

```
var i
i = 10

var j
j = ( 6 + 3 ) * i

print
```

An SPL program consists of a sequence of tokens—consecutive sequences of non-white space characters. Each token must be separated from other tokens by at least one white-space character.

Setting Up SPL

To set up SPL, begin by double-clicking your MS-DOS icon (if you are using Windows) and go to a command prompt.

If you created a `projects` directory in Chapter 1, "Introducing Java," make `projects` your current directory. (If you do not have a `projects` directory, now is as good a time as any to create one.)

Assuming that `projects` is located within `c:\jdk1.2\`, enter the command `cd \jdk1.2\projects` to change to this directory.

From within your `projects` directory, create a directory called `spl` (for example, `md spl`). (If you prefer, you can create this directory entirely in uppercase. For example, you could issue the command `md SPL` to create this directory. Case does not matter when it comes to directories.)

Download the file `spl.java` from the Macmillan Web site and place this file in your `spl` directory.

Compiling SPL

Compilation is a simple process. It involves running the `javac.exe` program and specifying the name of the source file as an argument to this program.

At the command prompt, enter the following line:

`c:\jdk1.2\projects\spl>javac spl.java`

CAUTION

The `.java` file extension must be specified when compiling an application's source file. The compiler will display an error message if `.java` is not specified.

If the compiler displays an error message, you might have typed `spl` with a different combination of uppercase/lowercase letters than the lowercase letters used as SPL's class name (for example, you might have specified something like `javac Spl.java` at the command line when you should have specified `javac spl.java`).

CAUTION

You must specify `spl` and not `Spl`, `SPL`, or any other combination of lowercase/uppercase letters. The compiler is very sensitive to case and will display an error message if the class name (`spl`) does not match the filename (`spl`).

After compilation is finished, you should end up with a class file called `spl.class`.

Figure 11.10 shows the compilation process.

Running SPL

Congratulations! You successfully compiled `spl.java` and are now ready to run `spl.class`. All you need to do is fire up the `java.exe` program and specify `spl.class` as an argument to this program.

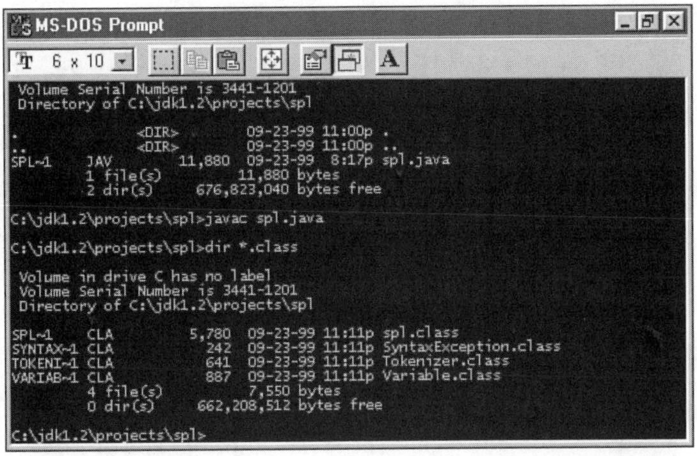

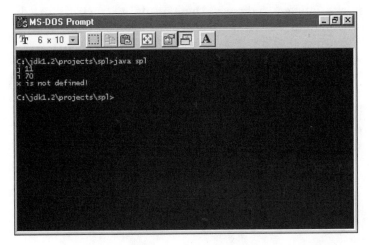

Figure 11.10: *Compiling* `spl.java` *with the* `javac.exe` *compiler.*

CAUTION

The `.class` file extension must not be specified when running SPL; otherwise, the `java.exe` program will display an error message.

Figure 11.11 shows the process of running `spl.class` with `java.exe`.

```
C:\jdk1.2\projects\spl>java spl
j 11
i 70
x is not defined!

C:\jdk1.2\projects\spl>
```

Figure 11.11: *Running* `spl.class` *with* `java.exe`.

SPL shows the output of the small program embedded within the source code. The last line displays an SPL error message because the program tries to access a variable before it is declared.

Potential Problems

What can go wrong with SPL? Here is one possibility.

- Trying to run a program without separating tokens with space characters will result in SPL errors. The reason is that the implementation of StringTokenizer's nextToken () method identifies a token as a consecutive sequence of non-white space characters. For example, 6+3 would be returned as a single 6+3 token instead of individual 6, +, and 3 tokens.

Enhancing SPL

You can enhance SPL in a number of ways:

- Modify the getToken (boolean) method so that it's possible to specify an SPL program without separating each token with space characters.

- Change VAR to INTEGER and add support for other data types (for example, REAL).

What's Next?

Now that you've explored fixed-size data structures, you will get a chance to learn about dynamic data structures—such as linked lists, hash tables, stacks, queues, and trees. Dynamic data structures are discussed in the next chapter.

Data Structures, Part 2

In Chapter 11, "Data Structures, Part 1," you began to explore data structures from Java's perspective. You examined a number of fixed-size data structures, including the premier data structure in this category—the array. This chapter concludes your exploration of data structures by focusing on dynamic data structures, beginning with the linked list.

Chapter 12 presents the following topics:

- Linked lists
- Hash tables
- Stacks
- Queues

Linked Lists

A *linked list* is the direct opposite of an array. Linked lists are composed of dynamically expandable/shrinkable numbers of linked storage locations that are known as *nodes*. These nodes are scattered throughout memory. In contrast, the array data structure is composed of a fixed number of contiguous elements that are located side-by-side.

Linked lists offer performance advantages over arrays. For example, it is "cheaper" to insert a node into the middle of a linked list than it is to insert a new element between existing elements in an array. When an element is inserted into an array, an opening must be created. All elements starting with the element at the insertion point must be moved down one element to create this opening, and this takes time. The same can be said for deletion. Deleting a node from a linked list is faster than deleting an element from an array because all array elements below the deletion point must be moved up one element to close the hole. However, arrays offer memory advantages over linked lists. For example, nodes are larger than elements because they include linking information.

Nodes are dynamically allocated and linked to each other by special reference fields that are known as *link fields*. It is these link fields that make linked lists possible.

There are two kinds of linked lists: *singly linked* and *doubly linked*. A singly linked list's nodes are linked in a forward direction, whereas a doubly linked list's nodes are linked in forward and backward directions.

Linked lists can be sorted and searched. However, linked-list sorting and searching algorithms differ from their counterpart array sorting and searching algorithms.

Nodes

Nodes are created from self-referential classes (classes that declare one or more reference members to refer to objects of the same class data type).

Listing 12.1 presents the source code to a node class that is used as the basis for a singly linked list. (Singly linked lists are discussed later in this chapter.)

Listing 12.1: The node class.

```
class node
{
    private String data;
    private node next;

    node (String data)
    {
```

```
        setData (data);
        setNext (null);
    }

    void setData (String data)
    {
        this.data = data;
    }

    String getData ()
    {
        return data;
    }

    void setNext (node next)
    {
        this.next = next;
    }

    node getNext ()
    {
        return next;
    }
}
```

This class declares a `private String` field called data and a `private node` field called next.

The data field contains the node's data. Although one field is illustrated, many data fields could be present, including array and object reference fields.

The next field contains a reference to an object of data type node. Because a node object can reference another node object, via next, the node class is a self-referential class.

The constructor initializes data to its `String data` argument and next to null. It is common practice to set all link fields to null when creating an object that represents a node because the very first node in a linked list serves as the root node (the first node) and does not yet reference any other nodes—there are no other nodes at this point.

Dynamic Memory Allocation

Nodes are dynamically created, via new, and subsequently attached to other nodes in a linked list by manipulating their link fields.

The following code fragment uses the node class in Listing 12.1 to create a node variable called root and dynamically create a node object with its data field initialized to Some data. A reference to this node object is then assigned to root:

```
node root = new node ("Some data");
```

Figure 12.1 shows the newly created root variable and node object as they appear in memory.

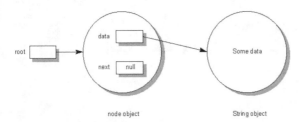

Figure 12.1: *Newly created* root *variable and* node *object as they appear in memory.*

The root variable references the root node object. This object's String data field references a String object that contains Some data. Its next field is null because it does not reference another node object.

Singly Linked Lists

A singly linked list is a linked list of nodes where each node has a single link field. Therefore, these nodes can only link to other nodes in a forward direction. Singly linked lists are commonly used to implement hash table and stack data structures. Figure 12.2 shows a conceptual view of a singly linked list.

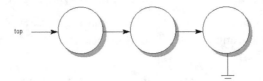

Figure 12.2: *A conceptual singly linked list.*

It's customary to create a variable called top that references the root node in a singly linked list. The last node is shown with an electrical grounding symbol to symbolize that it is the last node.

EXAMPLE

The following sll1 application illustrates the construction of a singly linked list consisting of two nodes:

```
// sll1.java

class node
{
    private String data;
```

```java
      private node next;

      node (String data)
      {
         setData (data);
         setNext (null);
      }

      void setData (String data)
      {
         this.data = data;
      }

      String getData ()
      {
         return data;
      }

      void setNext (node next)
      {
         this.next = next;
      }

      node getNext ()
      {
         return next;
      }
   }

   class sll1
   {
      public static void main (String [] args)
      {
         node top = new node ("Some data");
         top.setNext (new node ("Some more data"));

         while (top != null)
         {
            System.out.println (top.getData ());
            top = top.getNext ();
         }
      }
   }
```

```
Some data
Some more data
```

OUTPUT

Figure 12.3 shows the newly created singly linked list as it appears in memory.

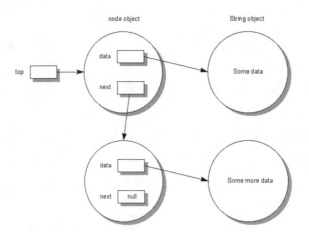

Figure 12.3: *Newly created singly linked list as it appears in memory.*

Nodes can be inserted into a singly linked list before the first node, after the last node, or between two nodes.

A node is inserted before the first node by setting its link field to point to the root node and then setting the top variable to reference the new node. Figure 12.4 shows a conceptual view of inserting a node before the root node.

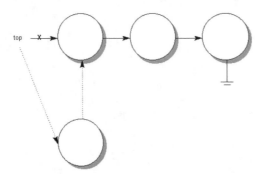

Figure 12.4: *Inserting a node before the root node.*

The X drawn through the arrow between top and the first node means that the link between top and this node is broken. The dashed arrows indicate the newly inserted node.

EXAMPLE

The following sll2 application illustrates inserting a node before the root node in a singly linked list:

```
// sll2.java

class node
{
```

```java
    private String data;
    private node next;

    node (String data)
    {
        setData (data);
        setNext (null);
    }

    void setData (String data)
    {
        this.data = data;
    }

    String getData ()
    {
        return data;
    }

    void setNext (node next)
    {
        this.next = next;
    }

    node getNext ()
    {
        return next;
    }
}

class sll2
{
    public static void main (String [] args)
    {
        node top = new node ("First node data");
        top.setNext (new node ("Second node data"));

        node temp = new node ("Before first node data");
        temp.setNext (top);
        top = temp;

        while (top != null)
        {
            System.out.println (top.getData ());
            top = top.getNext ();
        }
    }
}
```

```
Before first node data
First node data
Second node data
```

A node is inserted after the last node by first finding the current last node and setting its link field to point to the node to be inserted. If the singly linked list is empty, as evidenced by the top variable containing a null reference, the new node becomes the root node and top is set to reference this node. Figure 12.5 shows a conceptual view of inserting a node after the last node.

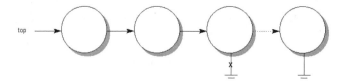

Figure 12.5: *Inserting a node after the last node.*

The following s113 application illustrates inserting a node after the last node in a singly linked list:

```
// sll3.java
```

```java
class node
{
   private String data;
   private node next;

   node (String data)
   {
      setData (data);
      setNext (null);
   }

   void setData (String data)
   {
      this.data = data;
   }

   String getData ()
   {
      return data;
   }

   void setNext (node next)
   {
      this.next = next;
   }
```

```
      node getNext ()
      {
         return next;
      }
   }

class sll3
{
   public static void main (String [] args)
   {
      node top = new node ("First node data");
      top.setNext (new node ("Second node data"));

      node temp = new node ("After last node data");

      // Find last node.

      node last = top;
      while (last != null)
         if (last.getNext () != null)
            last = last.getNext ();
         else
            break;

      if (last != null)
         last.setNext (temp);
      else
         top = temp;

      while (top != null)
      {
         System.out.println (top.getData ());
         top = top.getNext ();
      }
   }
}
```

```
First node data
Second node data
After last node data
```

OUTPUT   A node can be inserted between two other nodes by finding its predecessor node. The newly inserted node's link field will be set to the link field of the predecessor node and the predecessor node's link field will be set to the newly inserted node. Figure 12.6 shows a conceptual view of inserting a node between two nodes.

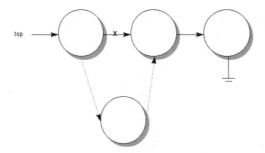

Figure 12.6: *Inserting a node between two nodes.*

EXAMPLE

The following sll4 application illustrates inserting a node between two nodes in a singly linked list:

```
// sll4.java

class node
{
   private String data;
   private node next;

   node (String data)
   {
      setData (data);
      setNext (null);
   }

   void setData (String data)
   {
      this.data = data;
   }

   String getData ()
   {
      return data;
   }

   void setNext (node next)
   {
      this.next = next;
   }

   node getNext ()
   {
      return next;
   }
```

```
    }

    class sll4
    {
        public static void main (String [] args)
        {
            node top = new node ("First node data");
            top.setNext (new node ("Second node data"));
            top.getNext ().setNext (new node ("Third node data"));

            node second = top.getNext ();
            node temp = new node ("Between second and third nodes data");
            temp.setNext (second.getNext ());
            second.setNext (temp);

            while (top != null)
            {
                System.out.println (top.getData ());
                top = top.getNext ();
            }
        }
    }
```

OUTPUT

```
First node data
Second node data
Between second and third nodes data
Third node data
```

Occasionally, nodes need to be removed from a singly linked list. A node is
removed by setting the predecessor node's link field to the link field of the
node to be removed. Figure 12.7 shows a conceptual view of removing a node.

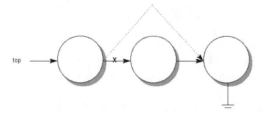

Figure 12.7: *Removing a node.*

EXAMPLE

The following sll5 application illustrates node removal. The second node in
the singly linked list is removed:

```
// sll5.java

class node
{
```

```
        private String data;
        private node next;

        node (String data)
        {
           setData (data);
           setNext (null);
        }

        void setData (String data)
        {
           this.data = data;
        }

        String getData ()
        {
           return data;
        }

        void setNext (node next)
        {
           this.next = next;
        }

        node getNext ()
        {
           return next;
        }
     }

     class sll5
     {
        public static void main (String [] args)
        {
           node top = new node ("First node data");
           top.setNext (new node ("Second node data"));
           top.getNext ().setNext (new node ("Third node data"));

           // Delete node whose data equals "Second node data".

           node curr = top;
           node prev = null;

           while (curr != null)
              if (curr.getData ().equals ("Second node data"))
              {
                 if (prev != null)
                    prev.setNext (curr.getNext ());
```

```
            else
                top = curr.getNext ();

            break;
        }
        else
        {
            prev = curr;
            curr = curr.getNext ();
        }

    while (top != null)
    {
        System.out.println (top.getData ());
        top = top.getNext ();
    }
    }
}
```

First node data
Third node data

Doubly Linked Lists

A doubly linked list is a linked list of nodes where each node has two link fields. Therefore, these nodes can link to other nodes in forward and backward directions. Doubly linked lists are commonly used to implement stack and queue data structures. Figure 12.8 shows a conceptual view of a doubly linked list.

top   bottom

Figure 12.8: *A conceptual doubly linked list.*

A doubly linked list can be thought of as two singly linked lists—a forward list and a backward list. Therefore, it's customary to create a variable called top that references the root node of the forward list and a variable called bottom that references the root node of the backward list. The root node in both singly linked lists is shown with an electrical grounding symbol to symbolize that these nodes are the last nodes in their respective lists.

The following dll1 application illustrates the construction of a doubly linked list consisting of two nodes:

```java
// dll1.java

class node
{
    private String data;
    private node next;
    private node previous;

    node (String data)
    {
        setData (data);
        setNext (null);
        setPrevious (null);
    }

    void setData (String data)
    {
        this.data = data;
    }

    String getData ()
    {
        return data;
    }

    void setNext (node next)
    {
        this.next = next;
    }

    node getNext ()
    {
        return next;
    }

    void setPrevious (node previous)
    {
        this.previous = previous;
    }

    node getPrevious ()
    {
        return previous;
    }
}
```

```
class dll1
{
    public static void main (String [] args)
    {
        // Create top node.

        node top = new node ("Some data");

        // Create bottom node.
        node bottom = new node ("Some more data");

        // Link bottom node after top node (in forward singly linked
        // list).

        top.setNext (bottom);

        // Link top node after bottom node (in backward singly linked
        // list).

        bottom.setPrevious (top);

        // Traverse the doubly linked list in a forward direction.

        while (top != null)
        {
            System.out.println (top.getData ());
            top = top.getNext ();
        }

        // Print a blank line.

        System.out.println ("");

        // Traverse the doubly linked list in a backward direction.

        while (bottom != null)
        {
            System.out.println (bottom.getData ());
            bottom = bottom.getPrevious ();
        }
    }
}
```

OUTPUT

```
Some data
Some more data

Some more data
Some data
```

Figure 12.9 shows the newly created doubly linked list as it appears in memory.

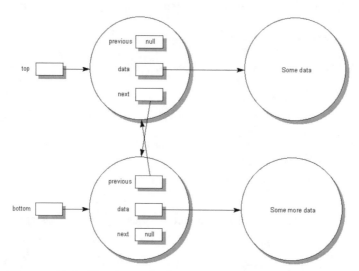

Figure 12.9: *Newly created doubly linked list as it appears in memory.*

Nodes can be inserted and removed from a doubly linked list in a fashion similar to inserting and removing nodes from a singly linked list. However, both the previous and next link fields need to be taken into account when performing an insert or a removal. Figure 12.10 shows a conceptual view of inserting a node into a doubly linked list.

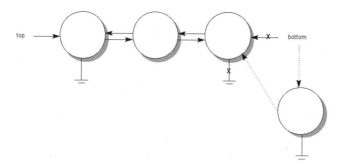

Figure 12.10: *Inserting a node into a doubly linked list.*

The following dll2 application illustrates node insertion. A new node is inserted at the back of the forward singly linked list, which is also the front of the backward singly linked list:

EXAMPLE   // dll2.java

```java
class node
{
   private String data;
   private node next;
   private node previous;

   node (String data)
   {
      setData (data);
      setNext (null);
      setPrevious (null);
   }

   void setData (String data)
   {
      this.data = data;
   }

   String getData ()
   {
      return data;
   }

   void setNext (node next)
   {
      this.next = next;
   }

   node getNext ()
   {
      return next;
   }

   void setPrevious (node previous)
   {
      this.previous = previous;
   }

   node getPrevious ()
   {
      return previous;
   }
}

class dll2
{
   public static void main (String [] args)
```

```
{
   // Create top node.

   node top = new node ("First node data");

   // Create bottom node.

   node bottom = new node ("Second node data");

   // Link bottom node after top node (in forward singly linked
   // list).

   top.setNext (bottom);

   // Link top node after bottom node (in backward singly linked
   // list).

   bottom.setPrevious (top);

   // Create third node.

   node temp = new node ("Third node");

   // Add third node to end of forward singly linked list.

   bottom.setNext (temp);

   // Add third node to front of backward singly linked list.

   temp.setPrevious (bottom);
   bottom = temp;

   // Traverse the doubly linked list in a forward direction.

   while (top != null)
   {
      System.out.println (top.getData ());
      top = top.getNext ();
   }

   // Print a blank line.

   System.out.println ("");

   // Traverse the doubly linked list in a backward direction.

   while (bottom != null)
   {
```

```
                System.out.println (bottom.getData ());
                bottom = bottom.getPrevious ();
            }
        }
    }
```

OUTPUT

```
First node data
Second node data
Third node

Third node
Second node data
First node data
```

Sorting Linked Lists

Sorting a linked list is different from sorting an array because nodes are
not necessarily adjacent to each other. For this reason, it is not possible to
simply index a linked list with an operator similar to the array index operator. Instead, links must be followed.

The insertion sort algorithm is a very efficient algorithm for inserting nodes
into a linked list in either an ascending sort order or a descending sort
order. The idea behind insertion sort is to first locate the insert position
(either in front of the first node, after the last node, or between two nodes)
and then insert the new node.

The following isort application illustrates the insertion sort algorithm:

EXAMPLE

```
// isort.java

class node
{
    private int data;
    private node next;

    node (int data)
    {
        setData (data);
        setNext (null);
    }

    void setData (int data)
    {
        this.data = data;
    }

    int getData ()
    {
        return data;
```

```
        }

        void setNext (node next)
        {
            this.next = next;
        }

        node getNext ()
        {
            return next;
        }
    }

    class isort
    {
        public static void main (String [] args)
        {
            int [] numbers =
            {
                45, -3, 98, 79, 42, 21, 1000, -333, 42, 42, 0, 100000
            };

            // Create a root node containing the first number.

            node top = new node (numbers [0]);

            // For each remaining number...

            for (int i = 1; i < numbers.length; i++)
            {
                // Create a node for each number.

                node data = new node (numbers [i]);

                // Locate the appropriate insert position.

                node curr = top;
                node prev = null;

                while (curr != null)
                    if (curr.getData () > numbers [i])
                    {
                        if (prev == null)
                        {
                            data.setNext (top);
                            top = data;
                        }
                        else
```

```
                    {
                        data.setNext (prev.getNext ());
                        prev.setNext (data);
                    }

                    break;
                }
                else
                {
                    prev = curr;
                    curr = curr.getNext ();
                }

                // curr == null signifies that the appropriate insert
                // position comes after the last node.

                if (curr == null)
                    prev.setNext (data);
            }

            while (top != null)
            {
                System.out.println (top.getData ());
                top = top.getNext ();
            }
        }
    }
}
```

```
-333
-3
0
21
42
42
42
45
79
98
1000
100000
```

Searching Linked Lists

Searching a linked list is similar to searching an array because a linear search algorithm is used. However, instead of searching through adjacent array elements, adjacent nodes are searched. Also, instead of using the array index operator to move from element to element, link fields are followed to move from node to node.

The following `lsearch` application illustrates the linear search algorithm as it applies to linked lists:

```java
// lsearch.java

class node
{
    private int data;
    private node next;

    node (int data)
    {
        setData (data);
        setNext (null);
    }

    void setData (int data)
    {
        this.data = data;
    }

    int getData ()
    {
        return data;
    }

    void setNext (node next)
    {
        this.next = next;
    }

    node getNext ()
    {
        return next;
    }
}

class lsearch
{
    public static void main (String [] args)
    {
        int [] numbers =
        {
            45, -3, 98, 79, 42, 21, 1000, -333, 42, 42, 0, 100000
        };

        // Create a root node containing the first number.
```

```
node top = new node (numbers [0]);

// For each remaining number...

for (int i = 1; i < numbers.length; i++)
{
    // Create a node for each number.

    node data = new node (numbers [i]);

    // Insert node at the front of the linked list.

    data.setNext (top);
    top = data;
}

// Display all nodes.

node temp = top;
while (temp != null)
{
    System.out.println (temp.getData ());
    temp = temp.getNext ();
}

// Display a blank line.

System.out.println ("");

// Search for 79.

temp = top;
while (temp != null)
    if (temp.getData () == 79)
    {
        System.out.println ("79 found");
        break;
    }
    else
        temp = temp.getNext ();

if (temp == null)
    System.out.println ("79 not found");

// Search for -79.

temp = top;
while (temp != null)
```

```
                if (temp.getData () == -79)
                {
                    System.out.println ("-79 found");
                    break;
                }
                else
                    temp = temp.getNext ();

            if (temp == null)
                System.out.println ("-79 not found");
        }
}
```

OUTPUT

```
100000
0
42
42
-333
1000
21
42
79
98
-3
45

79 found
-79 not found
```

Hash Tables

Arrays are good at storing and retrieving objects, as long as some portion of an object directly maps to an array index. However, this isn't always the case. For example, suppose that you own a factory with 200 employees and want to write a program to process the employee payroll.

You design your program with an array that references 200 objects, with each object describing one employee. Because each employee has a unique Social Security number (SSN), you decide to use this number as an array index so that you can quickly locate an employee object by the object's SSN field.

However, there is a problem. In order to use an SSN as an array index, your program would need to allocate an array with one billion elements—because each SSN is a nine-digit number ranging from zero to one less than one billion. Even if you had sufficient memory to hold an array of this size, much of this memory would be wasted because you only need 200 array elements to reference the maximum number of 200 objects.

You can still use the SSN—just not directly. The idea is to map the SSN to a smaller range of numbers. Because there are 200 employees, you must map one billion possible SSNs to 200 entries. Then, you can efficiently retrieve a record without wasting memory. This mapping can be done indirectly via *hashing*.

Hashing is a computer science technique for mapping keys (unique values such as SSNs) to array indexes by scrambling the bits of a key in such a way that not all keys map to the same array index. In other words, hashing scrambles these bits so that key values are uniformly distributed among array indexes. (One billion SSNs mapping to 200 array entries in a uniform distribution would result in five million SSNs mapping to each entry.)

Unfortunately, because the ratio of keys to array indexes can be very large (for example, one billion to 200), collisions (two or more keys mapping to the same array index) are bound to occur.

What do you do when two (let alone five million) keys hash to the same array index? Which value gets stored in this element? There are a variety of solutions to this problem but one of the more popular solutions is to not store a value in an array element. Instead, each array element is treated as a reference to a dynamically growable/shrinkable linked list. Key/value pairs, instead of values only, are stored in these nodes.

Consider this scenario. The employee object associated with a particular SSN is required. The SSN hashes to index 20. The linked list referenced by array element 20 is traversed until a node is found whose key matches the original key, or the node is not found. If the node is found, the value is returned.

The data structured formed by combining array elements and linked lists with appropriate logic is known as a *hash table*. Each array element that references a linked list for hashing purposes is known as a *bucket*.

Figure 12.11 shows a conceptual view of a hash table.

The f(key) = index notation means that a hash function is applied to a key to generate an array index. Hopefully, this index does not collide with an index being used. If it does collide, a new entry is added to the linked list referenced by the indexed array element.

Load factor can affect performance. The closer this ratio gets to 1.0, the greater the number of collisions.

Hashtable Objects

Hash tables are implemented by Hashtable objects created from the Hashtable class. This class is located in the java.util package.

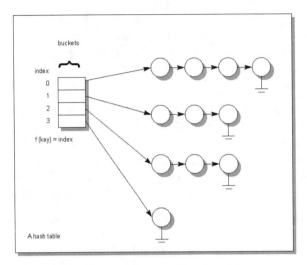

Figure 12.11: *A conceptual hash table.*

Every Hashtable object has an internal growable array of buckets. The total number of buckets is known as the object's capacity and the default load factor is .75. When the number of occupied buckets exceeds the capacity multiplied by the load factor, the bucket array grows.

The Hashtable () constructor initializes a Hashtable object with an internal capacity of 101 elements and a default load factor of .75. As soon as the number of occupied buckets exceeds 101 × .75 (or 75 buckets), the array will grow. For example, the following code fragment creates a Hashtable object with an internal array capacity of 101 buckets:

```
Hashtable h = new Hashtable ();
```

The Hashtable (int) constructor initializes a Hashtable object with an initial capacity specified by the int argument. The load factor remains at .75. For example, the following code fragment creates a Hashtable object with an internal capacity of 200 buckets:

```
Hashtable h = new Hashtable (200);
```

The Hashtable (int, float) constructor initializes a Hashtable object with an initial capacity specified by the int argument and a load factor specified by the float argument. The following code fragment creates a Hashtable object with an internal capacity of 200 buckets and a load factor of .8:

```
Hashtable h = new Hashtable (200, 0.8f);
```

It would be a very unusual situation where the load factor changes because .75 has been found to be optimal under many circumstances.

The put (Object, Object) Method

The Hashtable class declares a put (Object, Object) instance method that maps the first Object argument, the key, to an internal array index. This mapping takes place by calling the object's hashCode () instance method to return a unique hash code. (Remember: Every object has a hashCode () method because this method is inherited from the Object class.) The second Object argument references the object to be stored in the Hashtable object.

This method returns the previous value assigned to this key if the key/value pair was already present in the Hashtable object. Otherwise, this method returns null. The following code fragment puts the course title/Java 101 key/value pair into the Hashtable object referenced by h:

```
h.put ("course title", "Java 101");
```

If course title is not present, a new node is added to the linked list referenced by the internal array element whose index corresponds to the generated hash code. If course title is present, Java 101 replaces the contents of the value in the appropriate node.

The get (Object) Method

The Hashtable class declares a get (Object) instance method that maps the first Object argument, the key, to an internal array index.

This method returns the previous value assigned to this key if the key/value pair was already present in the Hashtable object. Otherwise, this method returns null. The following code fragment gets and prints the value associated with the course title key from the Hashtable object referenced by h:

```
System.out.println (h.get ("course title"));
```

The isEmpty () Method

The Hashtable class declares an isEmpty () instance method that returns true if the Hashtable object is empty or false if there is at least one key/value pair stored within this object. For example, the following code fragment checks the Hashtable object referenced by h to see if it is empty and then prints the result:

```
System.out.println (h.isEmpty ());
```

The containsKey (Object) Method

The Hashtable class declares a containsKey (Object) instance method that returns true if the Hashtable object contains a key/value pair whose key is identified by the Object argument. Otherwise, false is returned. The following code fragment gets and outputs a true/false value if a key/value pair exists with the course title key in the Hashtable object referenced by h:

```
System.out.println (h.containsKey ("course title"));
```

The remove (Object) Method

The Hashtable class declares a remove (Object) instance method that removes the key/value pair from the Hashtable object if a key/value pair, whose key is identified by the Object argument, exists in this object. The value associated with this key is returned. If the key/value pair is not present, null is returned.

The following code fragment removes the key/value pair identified by the course title key from the Hashtable object referenced by h:

```
h.remove ("course title");
```

The keys () and elements () Methods

The Hashtable class declares a keys () instance method that creates and returns an enumeration object. This object can iterate over all the keys in a Hashtable object by using the enumeration's hasMoreElements () and nextElement () instance methods.

The Hashtable class also declares an elements () instance method that creates and returns an enumeration object.

EXAMPLE

The following hashtableDemo application illustrates the creation of a Hashtable object, storing several key/value pairs in this object, and enumerating all keys and all values, via enumeration objects:

```java
// hashtableDemo.java

import java.util.*;

class hashtableDemo
{
   public static void main (String [] args)
   {
      String data;
      String msg;

      // Create a Hashtable object with an initial capacity of 20
      // buckets and a load factor of .75.

      Hashtable h = new Hashtable (20);

      System.out.println (h.put ("one", new Integer (1)));
      System.out.println (h.put ("name", "John Doe"));
      System.out.println (h.put ("date", new Date ()));
      System.out.println (h.put ("one", new Integer (4)));

      // Output all keys.
```

```
            System.out.println ("\nOutputting keys...");
            Enumeration e = h.keys ();
            while (e.hasMoreElements ())
                    System.out.println (e.nextElement ());

            // Output all values.

            System.out.println ("\nOutputting values...");
            e = h.elements ();
            while (e.hasMoreElements ())
                System.out.println (e.nextElement ());
        }
}
null
null
null
1
```

OUTPUT

```
Outputting keys...
date
name
one

Outputting values...
Sun Sep 26 00:31:54 CDT 1999
John Doe
4
```

Stacks

A *stack* is implemented as either an array or linked list data structure where insertions and deletions are made from one end—the top. For this reason, a stack is often referred to as a *last-in, first-out* (LIFO) data structure.

Data items are *pushed* (inserted) onto the top of a stack and *popped* (removed) off of the top. The last item pushed is the first item popped.

Figure 12.12 shows a concetual view of a stack.

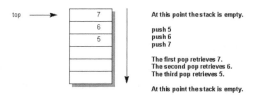

Figure 12.12: A conceptual stack.

Consider the following real-life example. In a cafeteria, dirty trays are pushed onto the top of a stack of dirty trays. The cafeteria worker pops trays from the top of the stack to wash them.

Stacks are used by a variety of applications. For example, when a method is called, the address of the instruction that gets executed when the method returns is pushed on to the stack. If this is not done, the JVM would not know which instruction to execute when the method returns. Stacks also are used to create locals and parameters by pushing storage for these variables onto the top of the stack when a method is called. When the method returns, this storage is popped, which is why locals and parameters disappear. Stacks also are used by compilers during expression evaluation.

A stack data structure could be created by a developer but Java has already taken care of this detail. Java's class library implements stacks by Stack objects created from the Stack class—a subclass of Vector. This class is located in the java.util package.

The Stack () constructor initializes a Stack object. At this point, the stack is empty. For example, the following code fragment creates an empty Stack object:

```
Stack s = new Stack ();
```

The push (Object) Method

The Stack class declares a push (Object) instance method that pushes an object onto a Stack object. The object being pushed is referenced by the Object argument. The following code fragment pushes a new String object onto the Stack object referenced by s:

```
s.push ("abc");
```

The pop () Method

The Stack class declares a pop () instance method that pops an object from a Stack object. A reference to the object being popped is returned from this method. If the stack is empty, an EmptyStackException object is thrown.

The following code fragment pops an object from the Stack object referenced by s and prints this object:

```
System.out.println (s.pop ());
```

The isEmpty () Method

The Stack class declares an isEmpty () instance method that checks to see if a Stack object is empty. A Boolean true value is returned if the Stack object is empty; otherwise, a Boolean false value is returned. For example, the following code fragment checks to see if the Stack object referenced by s is empty. If it is not empty, an object is popped and then output:

```
    if (!s.isEmpty ())
        System.out.println (s.pop ());
```

EXAMPLE

The following stackDemo application illustrates the creation of a Stack object, pushing objects onto the top of this object, popping objects off the top of this object (as long as the Stack object is not empty), and outputting these objects:

```
// stackDemo.java

import java.util.*;

class stackDemo
{
    public static void main (String [] args)
    {
        Stack s = new Stack ();

        s.push (new Integer (-5));
        s.push (new Double (3.14159));
        s.push ("John Doe");
        s.push (new stackDemo ());

        while (!s.isEmpty ())
            System.out.println (s.pop ());
    }

    public String toString ()
    {
        return "This is stackDemo.";
    }
}
```

OUTPUT

```
This is stackDemo.
John Doe
3.14159
-5
```

Queues

Like a stack, a *queue* is also an implemented array or linked list data structure where insertions are made at one end—the tail—and removed from another end—the head. For this reason, a queue is often referred to as a *first-in, first-out* (FIFO) data structure.

Figure 12.13 shows a conceptual view of a queue.

Consider the following real-life example. Customers line up in a bank to wait for an available teller. New customers arrive at the tail of the line and must wait until they get to the head of the line before they can be serviced.

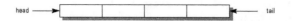

Figure 12.13: *A conceptual queue.*

Queues are used by a variety of applications. Examples include scheduling threads, spooling documents to a printer, and routing packets (small documents) through a network.

EXAMPLE

The following queueDemo application illustrates the creation of a Queue object, inserting objects at the tail of this object, removing objects from the head of this object (as long as the Queue object is not empty), and printing these objects:

```
// queueDemo.java

import java.util.*;

class Queue extends Vector
{
   void insertAtTail (Object o) { addElement (o); }

   Object removeFromHead ()
   {
      Object o = firstElement ();
      removeElement (o);

      return o;
   }
}

class queueDemo
{
   public static void main (String [] args)
   {
      Queue q = new Queue ();

      q.insertAtTail (new Integer (-5));
      q.insertAtTail (new Double (3.14159));
      q.insertAtTail ("John Doe");
      q.insertAtTail (new queueDemo ());

      while (!q.isEmpty ())
         System.out.println (q.removeFromHead ());
   }

   public String toString ()
   {
      return "This is queueDemo.";
```

```
    }
}
```

OUTPUT

```
-5
3.14159
John Doe
This is queueDemo.
```

Queue, like the Stack class, extends Vector. Both classes take advantage of
Vector's isEmpty () method to determine if the underlying Vector layer's
internal array is empty.

What's Next?

In the next chapter, you will explore the Java Foundation Classes, and
learn about its various features. You'll also have a chance to play with
graphical applets.

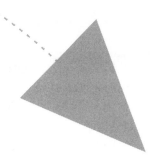

JFC

Many of us are drawn to computers because of the excitement that colorful computer graphics, images, and Graphical User Interfaces (GUIs) generate. Therefore, it should come as no surprise that one of the first things many developers like to do when learning a new computer language is to play with computer graphics, process images, and develop GUIs. The Java Foundation Classes (JFC) provide an opportunity to work with these capabilities.

This chapter explores the five major areas of the JFC: AWT, Swing, Java2D, Accessibility, and Drag and Drop. However, it is not possible to explore every possible detail because it would take an entire book to do justice to the JFC. Instead of a detailed exploration, this chapter provides an overview of the many capabilities that the JFC has to offer.

Chapter 13 presents the following topics:

- The Java Foundation Classes
- Inside the JFC: The AWT
- Inside the JFC: Swing
- Inside the JFC: Java2D
- Inside the JFC: Accessibility
- Inside the JFC: Drag and Drop

The Java Foundation Classes

In the fall of 1995, Sun Microsystems released its first version of the JDK—version 1.0. This version included a set of packages that collectively were called the Abstract Windowing Toolkit (AWT).

The AWT was and is a collection of classes and interfaces that developers use for graphics, image processing, and GUI development in Java. Developers were first introduced to the AWT by way of an applet that animated images of Sun's Java mascot—Duke.

The AWT generated a lot of excitement when it was released. Developers used it to write all kinds of programs. However, it became apparent that the AWT could not offer everything for everybody. It had limitations:

- The AWT relied on the host computer's operating system to provide the visual and interactive GUI components. Therefore, it was not possible to create GUI programs with a consistent "look and feel" across all computers that supported the JVM.

- The AWT had to use the lowest-common-denominator component features. Simply put, operating system–specific features (such as Motif's tear-off menus, which are not defined by Windows) could not be included because they are specific to a certain platform. As a result, GUIs were rather bland in appearance.

These (and other) limitations were not the fault of Java's AWT designers. In order for Java to succeed, some version of the AWT had to be released with the first version of Java. There was only so much time to ready the AWT so it could meet the delivery date. In time, these (and other) features would be added. That time arrived two years after Java's initial release.

In 1997, Java developers were given another AWT to work with. This AWT included everything from the previous AWT plus additional capabilities. This AWT also served as the nucleus for some AWT-related features such as drag and drop. The new AWT and related features were given a new name—the Java Foundation Classes.

The JFC consists of many classes and interfaces. Because there are so many, Table 13.1 lists only the 28 packages that comprise the JFC. (The JDK documentation provides detailed information on the classes and interfaces that are part of each package.)

Table 13.1: AWT Packages

Package Name	Description
java.awt	Contains all the graphics, image processing, and GUI classes and interfaces.
java.awt.color	Contains color space classes.

Package Name	Description
`java.awt.datatransfer`	Contains classes and interfaces for transferring data within and between Java programs.
`java.awt.dnd`	Contains classes and interfaces for supporting drag-and-drop operations.
`java.awt.event`	Contains classes and interfaces that describe the various kinds of AWT events (that is, actions that are initiated by the user as the user interacts with components).
`java.awt.font`	Contains classes and interfaces for working with fonts and font metrics (that is, measurements).
`java.awt.geom`	Contains classes and one interface that support Java2D two-dimensional geometry operations.
`java.awt.im`	Contains classes and one interface used by the input method framework.
`java.awt.image`	Contains classes and interfaces for creating and modifying images.
`java.awt.image.renderable`	Contains classes and interfaces for producing rendering-independent images.
`java.awt.print`	Contains classes and interfaces for complex printing tasks.
`javax.accessibility`	Contains classes and interfaces that define a contract between GUI components and an assistive technology that provides access to those components.
`javax.swing`	Contains classes and interfaces that describe a set of "light-weight" (all-Java) components.
`javax.swing.border`	Contains classes and one interface that make it possible to draw borders around Swing components.
`javax.swing.colorchooser`	Contains classes and one interface that are used by the `JColorChooser` component.
`javax.swing.event`	Contains classes and interfaces that describe the various kinds of events that Swing components can fire.
`javax.swing.filechooser`	Contains classes that are used by the `JFileChooser` component.
`javax.swing.plaf`	Contains classes and one interface that Swing uses to provide its plugable look-and-feel capabilities.
`javax.swing.plaf.basic`	Contains classes and one interface that Swing uses to provide a basic look and feel.
`javax.swing.plaf.metal`	Contains classes that Swing uses to provide a metal look and feel.
`javax.swing.plaf.multi`	Contains classes that Swing uses to provide an auxiliary look and feel (that is, a combination of a basic look and feel with a custom look and feel).

continues

Table 13.1: continued

Package Name	Description
`javax.swing.table`	Contains classes and interfaces that are used by the `JTable` component.
`javax.swing.text`	Contains classes and interfaces that are used by editable and read-only text components.
`javax.swing.text.html`	Contains classes for creating HTML text editors.
`javax.swing.text.html.parser`	Contains classes and one interface for creating an HTML parser.
`javax.swing.text.rtf`	Contains one class for creating a rich-text editor.
`javax.swing.tree`	Contains classes and interfaces that are used by the `JTree` component.
`javax.swing.undo`	Contains classes and interfaces for supporting undo/redo capabilities in an application such as a text editor.

The `java.awt` package (and subpackages) contains classes and interfaces that describe the AWT, Java2D, and Drag-and-Drop capabilities. The `javax.swing` package (and subpackages) contains classes and interfaces that describe Swing capabilities. Finally, the `javax.accessibility` package contains classes and interfaces that describe accessibility capabilities. (The `javax` prefix stands for Java Extension. Any package that is a member of the `javax` package is considered to be a standard extension to Java's core classes and interfaces.)

Inside the JFC: The AWT

The AWT portion of the JFC can be summarized into primitive graphics generation, font manipulation, image processing, printing, and GUI development.

Primitive graphics generation enables basic shapes (for example, arcs, lines, ellipses, and rectangles) to be drawn as outlines or filled-in regions. Also, the drawing color and other drawing attributes can be selected.

Font manipulation enables different fonts to be created and various measurements to be taken so that text can be properly aligned.

Image processing enables images to be created or obtained from external sources (such as files or network connections) and manipulated (for example, blurred, sharpened, cropped, scaled, and so on). (Image processing is an involved topic that is beyond the scope of this book. As a result, it is not discussed.)

✔ For more information on primitive graphics, font manipulation, and images, see Chapter 14, "AWT, Part 1," page 347.

Printing is the AWT's mechanism for printing documents using a "pages and book" metaphor. This mechanism makes it possible to control page setup and page formats, and manage print job dialog boxes. (*JavaWorld Magazine* contains a very well written article that explores the basics of the AWT's printing model. This article is available at the following Web address: `http://www.javaworld.com/javaworld/jw-06-1999/jw-06-step.html`.)

From a Java perspective, GUI development involves several tasks. These tasks include creating components (for example, buttons, list boxes, and menus), organizing these components into *containers* (that is, groups of components), specifying the layout manager object that a container uses to lay out these components on the screen, and registering *event handlers* (that is, objects that respond to events).

✔ For more information on GUI development, see Chapter 15, "AWT, Part 2," page 381.

The AWT views a component as a hybrid of two entities—an object created from an AWT component class, such as `Button`, and a *peer* (that is, host operating system code that creates, displays, and manages a component's visible window). Figure 13.1 illustrates the relationship between a `Button` object and a button peer.

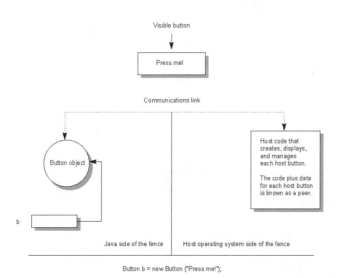

Visible button

Press me!

Communications link

Host code that creates, displays, and manages each host button.

The code plus data for each host button is known as a peer.

Button object

b

Java side of the fence   Host operating system side of the fence

Button b = new Button ("Press me!");

Figure 13.1: *Relating a* `Button` *object to a button peer.*

Whenever something interesting happens to a peer, such as the user pressing a button, a *peer event* (that is, an event defined by the host operating system) occurs. This event is passed from the host operating system side of the fence to the Java side of the fence, where it ends up in the "bowels" of the AWT. The AWT then passes this event to the object associated with the peer. (Each component object has its own peer.) Any objects that have registered themselves as *listeners* (objects who listen to events) with the component object will be forwarded a copy of this event.

EXAMPLE

To give some indication of how to write an AWT program, I've created a simple `JFCDemo1` application.

Figure 13.2 shows `JFCDemo1`'s output. This output consists of a GUI window with a button and a label. Press the button to have a new message appear in the label.

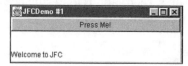

Figure 13.2: The JFCDemo1 GUI.

`JFCDemo1.java` contains the following source code:

```
[ 1] // JFCDemo1.java
[ 2]
[ 3] import java.awt.*;
[ 4] import java.awt.event.*;
[ 5]
[ 6] class JFCDemo1
[ 7] {
[ 8]    static String [] msgs =
[ 9]    {
[10]       "Welcome to JFC",
[11]       "JFC includes the Abstract Windowing Tookit",
[12]       "JFC includes Swing",
[13]       "JFC includes Java2D",
[14]       "JFC includes Accessibility",
[15]       "JFC includes Drag and Drop"
[16]    };
[17]
[18]    final static Label l = new Label (msgs [0]);
[19]
[20]    public static void main (String [] args)
[21]    {
[22]       Frame f = new Frame ("JFCDemo #1");
[23]       f.addWindowListener
[24]       (new WindowAdapter ()
[25]          {
[26]             public void windowClosing (WindowEvent e)
[27]                {
[28]                   System.exit (0);
```

```
[29]                                    }
[30]                   }
[31]           );
[32]
[33]          Panel pane = new Panel ();
[34]          pane.setLayout (new BorderLayout ());
[35]
[36]          Button b = new Button ("Press Me!");
[37]          b.addActionListener
[38]          (new ActionListener ()
[39]                   {
[40]                       public void actionPerformed (ActionEvent ae)
[41]                          {
[42]                             int n = (int) (Math.random () *
[43]                                            msgs.length);
[44]                             l.setText (msgs [n]);
[45]                          }
[46]                   }
[47]           );
[48]          pane.add ("North", b);
[49]
[50]          pane.add ("South", l);
[51]
[52]          f.add (pane);
[53]
[54]          f.setSize (300, 100);
[55]          f.setVisible (true);
[56]      }
[57] }
```

Lines 3 and 4 import two AWT packages: java.awt and java.awt.event. The java.awt package contains component classes, among other things. The java.awt.event package contains event classes.

Lines 6 through 57 declare the JFCDemo1 class.

Lines 8 through 16 declare a String array of messages that will be randomly displayed to the user, via a label peer, every time a button peer is pressed.

Line 18 creates a Label object, 1, and initializes it, via the Label (String) constructor, to the first message in the array. (The Label (String) constructor tells low-level AWT code to communicate with the host operating system to create a label peer.)

Object 1 must be declared as a read-only class field because it will be accessed from an anonymous inner class.

Lines 20 through 56 declare JFCDemo1's main method. This method creates the GUI.

Every GUI consists of components that must be organized into containers. JFCDemo1 is no exception. The first thing that it does is to create a Frame object that serves as a container for components. This object is called f and is created in Line 22. The Frame (String) constructor causes a frame window peer to be created on the host. The String argument is passed to this frame window peer and serves as the title in the frame window peer's title bar.

Eventually, the user will tire of playing with this program and want to close JFCDemo1. The user will probably click the close box on the frame window peer's title bar. By default, nothing will happen. JFCDemo1 will not close.

Clicking the mouse while the mouse pointer is positioned over the close box causes an event to be fired to the host operating system. This event is passed from the host operating system to the AWT. The AWT then forwards this event to the object that corresponds to the peer. In this case, that object is f because f corresponds to the frame window peer.

In order for the peer window to close, some action must be taken on the Java side of the fence. This action will result in a message being sent from the AWT to the host operating system that tells the host to close the window peer.

To respond to window closing events, JFCDemo1 registers an event handler that responds to this kind of event. This is accomplished in lines 23 through 31.

Line 23 calls f's addWindowListener (WindowListener) method. The WindowListener argument that is passed to this method is a reference to any object that implements the WindowListener interface.

The WindowListener interface declares several window event methods, including a window closing event method. If this interface were implemented by the JFCDemo1 class, each WindowListener method would have to be implemented. However, we are only interested in implementing the method that corresponds to the window-closing event. We don't want to implement the other methods.

Java offers a solution by providing a class that implements WindowListener— WindowAdapter. The WindowAdapter class provides default implementations of all methods declared in this interface. However, we cannot use the default version of WindowAdapter's windowClosing (WindowEvent) method to respond to window closing events because the default version does nothing. (We want to exit JFCDemo1.)

If you look closely at lines 23 through 31, you'll notice that an object is being created from an anonymous inner class. Specifically, an object is being created from a class that extends WindowAdapter. This class overrides windowClosing (WindowEvent). The new method calls System.exit (0) to terminate JFCDemo1. (When System.exit (0) is called, the AWT sends a message to the host to have it kill the frame window peer and any component peers contained within.)

Line 33 creates a Panel container object called pane. We will place our components within this object by calling an appropriate method.

Before we add any components to pane, we need to tell pane what layout manager object to use for laying out these components. This is accomplished in Line 34 where a new BorderLayout object is created and installed as pane's layout manager. BorderLayout divides a container into five areas: North, South, East, West, and Center.

Line 36 creates a Button object called b and initializes this object to Press me!. At the same time, a button peer is created. A String object containing Press Me! is passed to the peer.

Lines 37 through 47 create a listener object, via an anonymous inner class, and call b's addActionListener (ActionListener) method to register this object as a listener to action events (events that occur when a button peer is pressed).

When an action event occurs, the registered object's actionPerformed (ActionEvent) method is called. This method's ActionEvent parameter receives a reference to the object that is created to describe a button peer press.

The actionPerformed (ActionEvent) method generates a random number and uses it to index the msgs array. An appropriate String object containing one of these messages is retrieved and assigned to the Label object, l, by calling l's setText (String) method. This method takes the contents of the String argument and sends it to the host operating system. The host sets the label peer to the contents of the String argument.

Line 48 adds the Button object, b, to the North portion of the panel container, pane. Line 50 adds the Label object, l, to the South portion of pane.

Line 52 adds pane to the Frame object, f.

Line 54 sets the size of the frame window peer to 300 pixels (horizontally) by 100 pixels (vertically).

Line 55 sends a message to the frame window peer that tells this peer to make itself visible.

Peers and objects working together serve as the model for how the AWT does its thing.

✔ For more information on the AWT, see Chapter 14, "AWT, Part 1," page 347, and Chapter 15, "AWT, Part 2," page 381.

Inside the JFC: Swing

The Swing portion of the JFC was created to address limitations that exist in the AWT. These limitations include a small number of components, reliance on a host operating system's components (peers), and an inconsistent look and feel across platforms.

Swing adds a rich collection of components to the JFC. These components include labels and buttons that can contain images, trees with images that represent branches, toolbars, tool tips, progress bars, sliders, split panes— and the list goes on.

Swing does not depend upon the host operating system providing these components because Swing creates and manages them entirely within Java.

Because Swing contains all component creation and drawing code, it is possible to provide a consistent look and feel across Windows, Solaris, and other operating systems. This is a real plus.

It also is possible to create a specific look and feel for each platform. (Swing defines Windows, Solaris, Macintosh, and other looks and feels.)

EXAMPLE

I've created a `JFCDemo2` application that illustrates a Swing version of the `JFCDemo1` application. Much of the source code is identical, but there are a few differences.

`JFCDemo2` displays the same GUI as `JFCDemo1`, but enables the look and feel to be changed via a command-line argument.

Figure 13.3 shows `JFCDemo2`'s output. This output consists of a GUI window with a button and a label. Press the button to have a new message appear in the label.

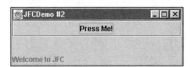

Figure 13.3: *The `JFCDemo2` GUI.*

`JFCDemo2.java` contains the following source code:

```
[  1] // JFCDemo2.java
[  2]
[  3] import javax.swing.*;
[  4]
[  5] import java.awt.*;
[  6] import java.awt.event.*;
[  7]
[  8] class JFCDemo2
[  9] {
[ 10]    static String [] msgs =
[ 11]    {
[ 12]       "Welcome to JFC",
[ 13]       "JFC includes the Abstract Windowing Toolkit",
[ 14]       "JFC includes Swing",
[ 15]       "JFC includes Java2D",
```

```
[ 16]              "JFC includes Accessibility",
[ 17]              "JFC includes Drag and Drop"
[ 18]       };
[ 19]
[ 20]       final static JLabel l = new JLabel (msgs [0]);
[ 21]
[ 22]       public static void main (String [] args)
[ 23]       {
[ 24]           if (args.length != 1)
[ 25]               selectLookAndFeel ("Metal");
[ 26]           else
[ 27]               selectLookAndFeel (args [0]);
[ 28]
[ 29]           JFrame f = new JFrame ("JFCDemo #2");
[ 30]           f.addWindowListener
[ 31]           (new WindowAdapter ()
[ 32]                 {
[ 33]                     public void windowClosing (WindowEvent e)
[ 34]                           {
[ 35]                               System.exit (0);
[ 36]                           }
[ 37]                 }
[ 38]           );
[ 39]
[ 40]           JPanel pane = new JPanel ();
[ 41]           pane.setLayout (new BorderLayout ());
[ 42]
[ 43]           JButton b = new JButton ("Press Me!");
[ 44]           b.addActionListener
[ 45]           (new ActionListener ()
[ 46]                 {
[ 47]                     public void actionPerformed (ActionEvent ae)
[ 48]                           {
[ 49]                               int n = (int) (Math.random () *
[ 50]                                           msgs.length);
[ 51]                               l.setText (msgs [n]);
[ 52]                           }
[ 53]                 }
[ 54]           );
[ 55]           pane.add ("North", b);
[ 56]
[ 57]           pane.add ("South", l);
[ 58]
[ 59]           f.setContentPane (pane);
[ 60]
[ 61]           f.setSize (300, 100);
[ 62]           f.setVisible (true);
[ 63]       }
```

```
[ 64]
[ 65]     private static void selectLookAndFeel (String lnfName)
[ 66]     {
[ 67]         String actualName = null;
[ 68]
[ 69]         if (lnfName.equals ("Metal"))
[ 70]             actualName =
[ 71]                 UIManager.getCrossPlatformLookAndFeelClassName ();
[ 72]         else
[ 73]         if (lnfName.equals ("System"))
[ 74]             actualName =
[ 75]                 UIManager.getSystemLookAndFeelClassName ();
[ 76]         else
[ 77]         if (lnfName.equals ("Mac"))
[ 78]             actualName =
[ 79]                 "com.sun.java.swing.plaf.mac.MacLookAndFeel";
[ 80]         else
[ 81]         if (lnfName.equals ("Windows"))
[ 82]             actualName =
[ 83]                 "com.sun.java.swing.plaf.windows.WindowsLookAndFeel";
[ 84]         else
[ 85]         if (lnfName.equals ("Motif"))
[ 86]             actualName =
[ 87]                 "com.sun.java.swing.plaf.motif.MotifLookAndFeel";
[ 88]
[ 89]         try
[ 90]         {
[ 91]             UIManager.setLookAndFeel (actualName);
[ 92]         }
[ 93]         catch (ClassNotFoundException e)
[ 94]         {
[ 95]
[ 96]             System.err.println ("Unable to find class that " +
[ 97]                                 "specifies " + actualName +
[ 98]                                 " look and feel.");
[ 99]         }
[100]         catch (UnsupportedLookAndFeelException e)
[101]         {
[102]             System.err.println (actualName +
[103]                                 " look and feel not supported.");
[104]         }
[105]         catch (Exception e)
[106]         {
[107]             System.err.println ("Could not get " + actualName +
[108]                                 " look and feel for some reason.");
[109]         }
[110]     }
[111] }
```

Rather than walk through all the source code, only those details that differ from JFCDemo1 will be discussed.

Line 20 creates a JLabel object instead of a Label object. Line 29 creates a JFrame object instead of a Frame object. This pattern continues in lines 40 and 43 where JPanel and JButton objects are created instead of Panel and Button objects. The only difference between creating these objects and the equivalent objects in JFCDemo1 is that each class starts with a J—for Java. (Who knows why the designers chose J instead of something like S—for Swing.) However, the J components have many more features than their AWT equivalents (for example, JButtons can have associated tool tips), not to mention the capability to have different looks and feels.

Another difference is the call to JFrame's setContentPane (Panel) method—instead of Frame's add (Panel) method. (Swing's containers—such as JFrame—always require components to be placed on what are known as panes—essentially nothing more than panels).

A third difference has to do with the selectLookAndFeel (String) method in lines 65 through 110. This method processes the command-line argument that is passed to JFCDemo2 and selects an appropriate package name for the package that contains the classes implementing a particular look and feel. For example, the com.sun.java.swing.plaf.windows.WindowsLookAndFeel package contains the Swing classes that implement the Windows look and feel.

Swing supports the following looks and feels: Metal, System, Mac, Motif, and Windows. The Metal look and feel is the default look and feel that was used when Swing was created. The System look and feel is the look and feel of the host operating system. The Mac look and feel is the look and feel of the MacOS. (This look and feel does not exist for Windows versions of the JDK.) The Motif look and feel is the look and feel of Solaris. Finally, the Windows look and feel is the look and feel of Windows.

Figure 13.3 shows the Metal look and feel. This is the look and feel that's presented when no arguments are passed to JFCDemo2.

Figure 13.4 shows the System look and feel. This is the look and feel that's presented when System is passed as an argument to JFCDemo2. (This just happens to correspond to the Windows look and feel because Windows was the host platform on which this book was written.)

Figure 13.4 *The* JFCDemo2 *GUI with the System look and feel.*

Figure 13.5 shows the Windows look and feel. This is the look and feel that's presented when Windows is passed as an argument to JFCDemo2.

Figure 13.5: *The* JFCDemo2 *GUI with the Windows look and feel.*

Figure 13.6 shows the Motif look and feel. This is the look and feel that's presented when Motif is passed as an argument to JFCDemo2.

Figure 13.6: *The* JFCDemo2 *GUI with the Motif look and feel.*

There is a lot more to be said about Swing. Discussing Swing to its fullest extent is beyond the scope of this book. After all, there are many excellent books that discuss Swing in detail, so I will pass the buck.

NOTE

Swing was christened at the 1997 JavaOne conference in San Francisco. Apparently, Swing engineers used a music-based demonstration to showcase Swing components. Among the jokes that were passed back and forth, one of the engineers suggested that swing was being considered the "in sound" in music. Because the Swing classes did not yet have a name and because its engineers felt that it would be the "in GUI development technology for Java," why not call this unnamed technology Swing! After all, for many developers and users of Java technology, "GUIs don't mean a thing if they ain't got that Swing."

Inside the JFC: Java2D

The Java2D portion of the JFC enriches the paint (Graphics) method that is inherited by applet classes. This method lets objects created from these classes update their drawable areas—those rectangular areas that are visible within Web pages.

The paint (Graphics) method is called by the AWT whenever the drawable area needs to be repainted. This method is called with a single object argument. (This argument identifies what is known as a *graphics context*—a specific video display or printer.) A reference to this object is placed in the Graphics parameter.

Graphics is an abstract class. Objects cannot be created from Graphics. However, objects can be created from nonabstract subclasses of Graphics.

In fact, each kind of video display and printer that is supported by Java has its own specific subclass that describes the actual characteristics of the device. Because of polymorphism, whenever a Graphics method is called, the actual method within the subclass is called. (Now you know from where the AWT gets its name.)

To summarize, whenever the drawable area needs to be repainted, the AWT creates an object from a subclass of Graphics that represents a graphics context. This object is then passed as an argument to paint (Graphics) when this method is called. Because of polymorphism, whenever code in paint (Graphics) calls a Graphics method, the actual method that is called is the method in the subclass.

Graphics declares a wide variety of methods for setting drawing colors and fonts, drawing text, drawing shapes (such as lines, points, arcs, ovals, and rectangles), and copying regions of the drawable area to another area. These capabilities are great but they are only a starting point.

Graphics does not contain methods to draw thick borders around shapes or draw curved surfaces using geometric entities—such as Bézier curves. And this is only the beginning.

Because of limitations in the Graphics class, JFC designers decided to create another class that contains additional features. This class is called Graphics2D.

One feature that is present in Graphics2D is the capability to create transformations that transform the appearance of the drawable area into something quite different. For example, imagine shearing an image. What do I mean by *shearing*? Because a picture is worth a thousand words, take a look at Figures 13.7 and 13.8. Figure 13.7 shows an image of the planet Saturn before shearing and Figure 13.8 shows the same image after shearing. (Talk about a major gravity disruption!)

Figure 13.7: An unsheared Saturn.

Figure 13.8: *Taking the shears to Saturn.*

EXAMPLE

I've created a JFCDemo3 applet to illustrate a simple JFC-Java2D applet. This applet can be used to display an image that is either sheared or not.

JFCDemo3.java contains the following source code:

```
[ 1] // JFCDemo3.java
[ 2]
[ 3] import java.awt.*;
[ 4] import java.awt.geom.AffineTransform;
[ 5]
[ 6] import java.applet.Applet;
[ 7]
[ 8] public class JFCDemo3 extends Applet
[ 9] {
[10]     Image image;
[11]     boolean shear = false;
[12]
[13]     public void init ()
[14]     {
[15]         String imageName = getParameter ("image");
[16]         if (imageName != null)
[17]             image = getImage (getCodeBase (), imageName);
[18]
[19]         String shear = getParameter ("shear");
[20]         if (shear.toLowerCase ().equals ("true"))
[21]             this.shear = true;
[22]     }
[23]
[24]     public void paint (Graphics g)
[25]     {
[26]         Graphics2D g2 = (Graphics2D) g;
[27]
[28]         if (image != null)
[29]         {
[30]             if (shear)
```

```
[31]                    {
[32]                        AffineTransform at = new AffineTransform ();
[33]                        at.shear (0.5, 0.0);
[34]                        g2.setTransform (at);
[35]                    }
[36]
[37]                    g2.drawImage (image, 0, 0, this);
[38]            }
[39]    }
[40] }
```

The init () method in lines 13 through 22 is used to obtain the values of image and shear parameters. The value of the image parameter is the name of an image file to be displayed. The shear parameter is true if the image is to be sheared before being displayed and false if the image should not be sheared prior to display.

Line 26 casts the Graphics subclass object to a Graphics2D object. This new object makes it possible to access the additional features that Graphics2D brings to the party.

If the image is to be sheared, the code in lines 32 through 34 is executed.

Line 32 creates an AffineTransform object. (An *affine transformation* is a mathematical concept whereby straight lines are transformed into straight lines and parallel lines into parallel lines but the distance between points and the angles between lines might be altered.)

After a new AffineTranform object has been created, its shear (double, double) method is called to indicate the amount of horizontal and vertical shearing. This is followed by a call to the Graphics2D subclass object's setTransform (AffineTransform) method that sets the transformation to be used for all future graphics operations—until replaced by another call to setTransform (AffineTransform).

When the image is drawn in Line 37, the previously set AffineTransform object describes the shearing process that is used to display the new image.

The following HTML code is placed in a file called JFCDemo3.html. This code is used to describe an applet that loads an image of Saturn and shears this image before displaying it. (The Saturn.jpg file must be placed in the same directory as JFCDemo3.class and JFCDemo3.html.)

```
<applet code="JFCDemo3.class" width=725 height=260>
  <param name="image" value="Saturn.jpg">
  <param name="shear" value="true">
</applet>
```

To run this applet, type appletviewer JFCDemo3.html at the command prompt. Notice the sheared effect.

If you would like more information on Java2D, please visit Sun Microsystem's Java Tutorial. This excellent tutorial is available at the Web site listed in Appendix D, "Additional Resources."

Inside the JFC: Accessibility

The Accessibility portion of the JFC seeks to make Java software easy to use for everyone, including physically challenged people who are blind, have no arms, have trouble reading, and so on, and work-challenged people who are driving in a car and need to communicate by way of voice (instead of by typing at a keyboard), and so on. Truly, this is a very liberating technology.

Technologies, such as Braille readers and voice recognizers are known as *assistive technologies* because they assist people in working with computers. Accessibility provides the means for plugging the software associated with these technologies into the JFC.

In many cases, a developer need not do anything for an assistive technology to find out useful information about a program—which can help a challenged individual. For example, assistive technologies can automatically retrieve the textual information that is provided by the following Swing code fragment:

```
JButton b = new JButton ("Press Me!");
JLabel l = new JLabel ();
JFrame f = new JFrame ("My application");
```

However, there are some things that a developer should do to make it easier for assistive technologies to retrieve as much information as possible. These things include the following.

If a component does not have a descriptive name (such as Press Me! in the previous JButton object), specify a name by first obtaining the component's accessible context object and then calling that object's setAccessibleName (String) method. The following code fragment does this for the previous JLabel object l:

```
l.getAccessibleContext ().setAccessibleName ("Some label");
```

If a tool tip is not provided for a component, provide the equivalent description by obtaining the component's accessible context and then calling the component's setAccessibleDescription (String) method. The following code fragment does this for the previous JButton object b:

```
b.getAccessibleContext().setAccessibleDescription("Clicking this button is bad
➥for your health! ");
```

Specify keyboard alternatives wherever possible. For example, JButton provides a setMnemonic (int) method that provides an alternative keystroke.

The following code fragment makes it possible to press the Alt and P keys simultaneously to click the previous JButton object b:

```
b.setMnemonic (KeyEvent.VK_P);
```

Whenever a JLabel component describes another component, call the JLabel component's setLabelFor (Component) method to associate the other component with the JLabel component. This enables assistive technologies to find associated components (a text field associated with a label, for example). The following code fragment associates the previous JButton component (identified by JButton object b) with the previous JLabel component (identified by JLabel object l):

```
l.setLabelFor (b);
```

EXAMPLE

I've created a JFCDemo4 application that is virtually identical to JFCDemo2 except for the inclusion of a couple of accessibility features.

Figure 13.9 shows JFCDemo4's output. This output includes a tool tip. Notice that P in Press Me! is underlined. (Underlining the letter P indicates that pressing Alt plus P is the same as pressing the button.)

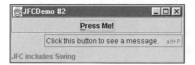

Figure 13.9: *The JFCDemo4 GUI with a tool tip and a keyboard alternative.*

JFCDemo4.java contains the following source code:

```
[  1] // JFCDemo4.java
[  2]
[  3] import javax.swing.*;
[  4]
[  5] import java.awt.*;
[  6] import java.awt.event.*;
[  7]
[  8] class JFCDemo4
[  9] {
[ 10]    static String [] msgs =
[ 11]    {
[ 12]       "Welcome to JFC",
[ 13]       "JFC includes the Abstract Windowing Toolkit",
[ 14]       "JFC includes Swing",
[ 15]       "JFC includes Java2D",
[ 16]       "JFC includes Accessibility",
[ 17]       "JFC includes Drag and Drop"
[ 18]    };
[ 19]
[ 20]    final static JLabel l = new JLabel (msgs [0]);
```

```
[ 21]
[ 22]    public static void main (String [] args)
[ 23]    {
[ 24]        if (args.length != 1)
[ 25]            selectLookAndFeel ("Metal");
[ 26]        else
[ 27]            selectLookAndFeel (args [0]);
[ 28]
[ 29]        JFrame f = new JFrame ("JFCDemo #2");
[ 30]        f.addWindowListener
[ 31]        (new WindowAdapter ()
[ 32]            {
[ 33]                public void windowClosing (WindowEvent e)
[ 34]                    {
[ 35]                        System.exit (0);
[ 36]                    }
[ 37]            }
[ 38]        );
[ 39]
[ 40]        JPanel pane = new JPanel ();
[ 41]        pane.setLayout (new BorderLayout ());
[ 42]
[ 43]        JButton b = new JButton ("Press Me!");
[ 44]        b.setMnemonic (KeyEvent.VK_P);
[ 45]        b.addActionListener
[ 46]        (new ActionListener ()
[ 47]            {
[ 48]                public void actionPerformed (ActionEvent ae)
[ 49]                    {
[ 50]                        int n = (int) (Math.random () *
[ 51]                                        msgs.length);
[ 52]                        l.setText (msgs [n]);
[ 53]                    }
[ 54]            }
[ 55]        );
[ 56]        b.setToolTipText ("Click this button to see a message.");
[ 57]        pane.add ("North", b);
[ 58]
[ 59]        l.setLabelFor (b);
[ 60]        pane.add ("South", l);
[ 61]
[ 62]        f.setContentPane (pane);
[ 63]
[ 64]        f.setSize (300, 100);
[ 65]        f.setVisible (true);
[ 66]    }
[ 67]
[ 68]    private static void selectLookAndFeel (String lnfName)
```

```
[ 69]    {
[ 70]        String actualName = null;
[ 71]
[ 72]        if (lnfName.equals ("Metal"))
[ 73]            actualName =
[ 74]                UIManager.getCrossPlatformLookAndFeelClassName ();
[ 75]        else
[ 76]        if (lnfName.equals ("System"))
[ 77]            actualName =
[ 78]                UIManager.getSystemLookAndFeelClassName ();
[ 79]        else
[ 80]        if (lnfName.equals ("Mac"))
[ 81]            actualName =
[ 82]                "com.sun.java.swing.plaf.mac.MacLookAndFeel";
[ 83]        else
[ 84]        if (lnfName.equals ("Windows"))
[ 85]            actualName =
[ 86]                "com.sun.java.swing.plaf.windows.WindowsLookAndFeel";
[ 87]        else
[ 88]        if (lnfName.equals ("Motif"))
[ 89]            actualName =
[ 90]                "com.sun.java.swing.plaf.motif.MotifLookAndFeel";
[ 91]
[ 92]        try
[ 93]        {
[ 94]            UIManager.setLookAndFeel (actualName);
[ 95]        }
[ 96]        catch (ClassNotFoundException e)
[ 97]        {
[ 98]
[ 99]            System.err.println ("Unable to find class that " +
[100]                                " specifies " + actualName +
[101]                                " look and feel.");
[102]        }
[103]        catch (UnsupportedLookAndFeelException e)
[104]        {
[105]            System.err.println (actualName +
[106]                                " look and feel not supported.");
[107]        }
[108]        catch (Exception e)
[109]        {
[110]            System.err.println ("Could not get " + actualName +
[111]                                " look and feel for some reason.");
[112]        }
[113]    }
[114] }
```

Inside the JFC: Drag and Drop

The drag-and-drop portion of the JFC makes it possible to create programs where the user can select a graphical image (such as a file icon), click the mouse button and hold this button down while dragging the image to another graphical image (such as a wastebasket icon), and then release the mouse button. At this point, some action takes place. The action is associated with the destination image (for example, wastebasket) and will typically modify the file associated with the source image (for example, trashing the file associated with the source image).

Drag and drop is an involved topic. A well-written article that explains drag and drop in detail (including the concepts of data flavors, drag sources, drag gestures, and drop targets) is available at the following *JavaWorld Magazine* Web address—`http://www.javaworld.com/javaworld/jw-03-1999/jw-03-dragndrop.html`.

What's Next?

Computer graphics, images, and GUIs are important contributing factors to the success of software. Fortunately, Java's designers saw fit to develop the JFC, facilitating the development of Java software with powerful graphics, image processing, and GUI capabilities.

Chapters 14 and 15 continue to explore the AWT portion of the JFC. Chapter 14, "AWT, Part 1," focuses on graphics and images, whereas Chapter 15, "AWT, Part 2," focuses on developing GUIs.

AWT, Part 1

If you are like me, you enjoy computer graphics. The ability to create something visual is an exciting experience. The AWT gives you the ability to create and manipulate graphics to your heart's content. You can also use the AWT's imaging capabilities to incorporate images into your programs.

Chapter 14 presents the following topics:

- The AWT Drawing Mechanism
- Colors
- Fonts
- Graphics
- Images
- FIREWORKS

The AWT Drawing Mechanism

Before you let your imagination run loose and attempt to draw some graphics, you should first learn how the AWT's drawing mechanism works. The following discussion emphasizes the drawing mechanism from the perspective of an applet. However, the same mechanism applies to applications with graphical user interfaces.

Every applet has a drawable area. When this area must be redrawn, the AWT calls the applet's update (Graphics) method. The default version of this method, inherited by every applet class, clears the drawable area to a background color and then calls the applet's paint (Graphics) method to do the actual drawing. (The AWT never directly calls paint (Graphics).)

What is this Graphics argument that is passed to both paint (Graphics) and update (Graphics)? To be precise, it is an object created from a Graphics subclass that represents a graphics context.

A *graphics context* is nothing more than an object associated with a drawable area where the actual graphics appear. This drawable area can be a portion of a piece of paper, a portion of the monitor's screen, or a portion of an image buffer.

Drawing is accomplished by calling Graphics methods via the graphics context reference that is passed to paint (Graphics). The subclass from which this graphics context was created "knows" how to output graphics to an image buffer, monitor, or printer. The Java program does not need to be aware of these details. (Polymorphism makes this possible.)

Your applets must never directly call update (Graphics) or paint (Graphics). (However, they can call paint (Graphics) from within an overridden update (Graphics) method.) Instead, when they need to schedule a repaint, they should call the applet's inherited repaint () method. This method schedules a call, made by the AWT, to the update (Graphics) method.

As you progress through this chapter, small examples will be presented that override update (Graphics), paint (Graphics), or both methods, and call various Graphics methods.

Colors

This world would be pretty dull without color. Colors offer excitement and convey meaning. For example, amusement parks and the Las Vegas strip offer excitement to many people, and color has a big role to play in both venues. Also, traffic lights convey meaning. Red means stop, green means go, and yellow indicates caution.

Graphics also would be dull without color. The AWT makes it possible to write graphical programs that use color by way of its `Color` class.

The `Color` Class

The `Color` class, located in the `java.awt` package, controls the color that a graphics context uses to display graphics.

The `Color` class declares a few constructors for initializing objects that represent colors. These constructors include `Color (int, int, int)` and `Color (float, float, float)`.

The `Color (int, int, int)` constructor initializes a `Color` object to a color that is defined by its red, green, and blue components. The first `int` argument represents the red component. The second `int` argument represents the green component. The third `int` argument represents the blue component. All three arguments must be integer values ranging from 0 through 255 inclusive. (Zero represents the darkest shade of the color component and 255 represents the brightest shade.) If either of these arguments is less than 0 or greater than 255, an `IllegalArgumentException` object is thrown. (The least-significant byte from each `int` argument is concatenated with the other least-significant bytes and stored as a single 32-bit integer. The leftmost byte is set to 255.)

The following code fragment creates a `Color` object and uses `Color (int, int, int)` to initialize this object to a medium shade of green:

```
Color green = new Color (0, 128, 0);
```

The `Color (float, float, float)` constructor initializes a `Color` object to a color that is defined by its red, green, and blue components. However, unlike the previous constructor, these components are represented by `float` arguments. The first `float` argument represents the red component. The second `float` argument represents the green component. The third `float` argument represents the blue component. All three arguments must be floating-point values ranging from 0.0f through 1.0f inclusive. (Like the previous constructor, 0.0f represents the darkest shade of the color component and 1.0f represents the brightest shade.) If either of these arguments is less than 0.0f or greater than 1.0f, an `IllegalArgumentException` object is thrown. (The `Color (float, float, float)` constructor converts its `float` values to `int` values that range from 0 through 255 and then calls `Color (int, int, int)` to complete initialization.)

The following code fragment creates a `Color` object and uses `Color (float, float, float)` to initialize this object to a bright shade of red:

```
Color red = new Color (1.0f, 0.0f, 0.0f);
```

THE getRed (), getGreen (), AND getBlue () METHODS

A Color object's internal int values can be retrieved by calling Color's getRed (), getGreen (), and getBlue () instance methods. Take a look at the following code fragment to see how this is done:

```
Color red = new Color (1.0f, 0.0f, 0.0f);
System.out.println (red.getRed ());    // Outputs 255.
System.out.println (red.getGreen ()); // Outputs 0.
System.out.println (red.getBlue ());  // Outputs 0.
```

THE getRGB () METHOD

A Color object's internal int, which contains the three component values, can be retrieved by calling Color's getRGB () instance method.

The retrieved value's left-most byte contains 255. The next-to-left-most byte contains the red component. The next-to-right-most byte contains the green component. Finally, the right-most byte contains the blue component. The following bit of code shows how to extract all three component values at once:

```
Color green = new Color (0, 255, 0);
System.out.println (green.getRGB ());
```

THE brighter () AND darker () METHODS

After a Color object has been created, it can be brightened or darkened by calling Color's brighter () or darker () instance methods. These methods create and return a reference to a new object that represents a brighter or darker version of the calling Color object. A call to the brighter () method can be seen in the following code snippet:

```
Color blue = new Color (0.0f, 0.0f, 0.5f);
blue = blue.brighter ();
```

PRE-CREATED Color OBJECTS

The Color class declares 13 read-only class fields that represent common colors.

Each field is a Color object that was created with a correct mixture of red, green, and blue components to represent the named color. The names of these fields are black, blue, cyan, darkGray, gray, green, lightGray, magenta, orange, pink, red, white, and yellow. The following fragment of code shows the value of the orange field being assigned to a Color variable:

```
Color c = Color.orange.
```

THE Graphics CLASS AND Color OBJECTS

The Graphics class declares a pair of instance methods for setting and fetching the current drawing color: setColor (Color) and getColor ().

The setColor (Color) method takes a Color object argument and sets the current drawing color to the color represented by this object. The getColor () method returns a Color object that represents the current drawing color.

The following paint (Graphics) method sets the current drawing color of its graphics context argument g to Color.green:

```
public void paint (Graphics g)
{
   g.setColor (Color.green);
}
```

Fonts

Fonts add an aesthetic quality to the text of a publication. Quite simply, fonts make it easier to read text.

Fonts are nothing more than sets of type. Each font shares a consistent size and *face* (style). Size is measured in *points* (units of type that are each approximately 1/72 of an inch). Faces include Bold, Italic, Bold and Italic, or neither Bold nor Italic (Plain). When a program draws text, this text always appears in a specific font.

A font is given a *face name* that identifies its typographic design and face. For example, Courier New Bold identifies a font that has the Courier New typographic design and a Bold face.

Every font belongs to a family of fonts that are related by the fact that they share the same typographic design. Those fonts that belong to a family share a common *family name*. For example, Times New Roman Bold and Times New Roman Italic share the common Times New Roman family name.

Creating a Font

The Font class is used to create Font objects that represent instances of fonts from the collection of fonts that are managed by the host operating system. This class is located in the java.awt package.

Font declares a Font (String, int, int) constructor that initializes a Font object. The String argument identifies a font's name. The first int argument identifies a face, whereas the second int argument identifies a size.

The font name passed as a String argument to Font (String, int, int) is a virtual family name. No existing font on the host operating system shares this virtual family name.

The AWT distinguishes the following virtual family names: Dialog, DialogInput, Monospaced, SansSerif, and Serif. (Sans in SansSerif means "without" and Serif means descenders. Therefore, a Serif font has descenders [such as the bottom portion of the lowercase letter j], whereas a SansSerif font disregards these descenders.)

Not all fonts are available on all platforms. Because Java was designed with portability in mind, the AWT maps the family names of appropriate host operating system fonts to the virtual family names. Therefore, the developer only needs to think in terms of `Dialog`, `Monospaced`, and so on, and let the AWT "worry" about mapping these virtual family names to existing font family names. By default, the AWT selects the Courier family name for `Monospaced`, the TimesRoman family name for `Serif`, and the Helvetica family name for `SansSerif`. However, if Courier, TimesRoman, and Helvetica fonts should not be available (highly unlikely), the AWT would attempt to choose reasonable alternatives from whatever fonts are present.

The following code fragment creates a 12-point Dialog Bold `Font` object:

```
Font f = new Font ("Dialog", Font.BOLD, 12);
```

`Font.BOLD` is a read-only class field, declared in the `Font` class, that identifies a font family's Bold face. `Font` also declares `PLAIN` and `ITALIC` read-only class fields that identify a font family's Plain and Italic faces.

`Font.BOLD` and `Font.ITALIC` can be combined to achieve a Bold Italic face by using either the addition operator (+) or the bitwise OR operator (¦).

The following code fragment creates a 36-point Serif Italic Bold `Font` object:

```
Font f = new Font ("Serif", Font.ITALIC ¦ Font.BOLD, 36);
```

THE Graphics CLASS AND Font OBJECTS

The `Graphics` class declares a pair of instance methods for setting and fetching the current font: `setFont (Font)` and `getFont ()`.

The `setFont (Font)` method takes a `Font` object argument and sets the current font to the font represented by this object. All text drawn after setting the font will appear in this font. The `getFont ()` method returns a `Font` object that represents the current font.

The following code fragment sets the current font of the `paint (Graphics)` method's graphics context argument g to a 12-point Monospaced Plain font:

```
public void paint (Graphics g)
{
    g.setFont (new Font ("Monospaced", Font.PLAIN, 12));
}
```

GRAPHICS ENVIRONMENTS

Suppose you are writing a program that you want to run on a particular computer and you know that this computer has a really cool font—such as `Creepy`. You hope to display text using this font. Can this be done? The answer is yes. However, before you can do this, you need to understand the Java 2 graphics environment concept.

Under Java 2, a graphics environment is a set of all graphics devices and fonts that are managed by a host operating system. Java 2 introduces a `GraphicsEnvironment` class that retrieves this information.

`GraphicsEnvironment` declares a `getLocalGraphicsEnvironment ()` class method that returns a `GraphicsEnvironment` object. This object represents the graphics environment of the host operating system. It is easy to retrieve the local graphics environment, as shown by the following code snippet:

```
GraphicsEnvironment ge;
ge = GraphicsEnvironment.getLocalGraphicsEnvironment ();
```

`GraphicsEnvironment` declares a `getAllFonts ()` instance method that returns an array of `Font` objects corresponding to all fonts managed by the host operating system. The following snippet of code builds on the previous code snippet to retrieve the array of `Font` objects:

```
Font [] allFonts = ge.getAllFonts ();
```

The `getAllFonts ()` method has a lot of work to do. Therefore, it is not uncommon for this method to take more than 30 seconds to complete.

The following `showFonts` applet calls `getAllFonts ()` to obtain a complete list of `Font` objects that represent all host operating system fonts, and then proceeds to display `Hello!` using each font:

EXAMPLE

```
// showFonts.java

import java.awt.*;
import java.applet.Applet;

public class showFonts extends Applet
{
   public void paint (Graphics g)
   {
      GraphicsEnvironment ge =
            GraphicsEnvironment.getLocalGraphicsEnvironment ();

      Font [] allFonts = ge.getAllFonts ();

      for (int i = 0; i < allFonts.length; i++)
      {
         Font f = allFonts [i].deriveFont (10.0f);
         System.out.println (f);
         g.setFont (f);

         g.setColor (Color.black);
         g.drawString ("Hello!", 10, 50);
```

```
            try
            {
                Thread.sleep (1000);
            }
            catch (InterruptedException e) {}

            g.setColor (Color.white);
            g.fillRect (0, 0, getSize ().width, getSize ().height);
        }
    }
}
```

Normally, your paint (Graphics) method would not contain long loops and sleep for certain intervals during each loop iteration. The reason is that paint (Graphics) is called many times during the life of an applet and needs to be as responsive as possible. However, as this is only a simple example, please overlook this breach of protocol.

There is one additional item to note. This item is a call to Font's deriveFont (float) instance method.

Each Font object that is returned by getAllFonts () has a size of 1 point. This is too small to display any text in a visible size. Therefore, deriveFont (10.0f) converts this text size to 10 points. After this is done, the Hello! text can be viewed.

To run the showFonts applet, you need an HTML file with the following <applet> tag:

```
<applet code="showFonts.class" width=300 height=100>
</applet>
```

You run this applet from the command line by typing

```
appletviewer showfonts.html
```

Figure 14.1 displays output from showFonts.

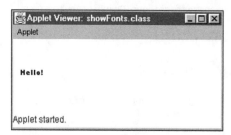

Figure 14.1: *Output from the* showFonts *applet.*

THE getFamily () METHOD

Font's getFamily () instance method returns a String object that contains the family name of a Font object. The following code fragment calls this method to return and display the family name of the 12-point Dialog Bold font:

```
Font f = new Font ("Dialog", Font.BOLD, 12);
System.out.println (f.getFamily ());
```

This code fragment outputs dialog.bold. (Personally, I'm not sure why getFamily () did not return Dialog. I guess there are some mysteries that only Java's designers understand. Who knows! Maybe this a bug!)

THE getFontName () METHOD

Font's getFontName () instance method returns a String object that contains the face name of a Font object. The following code fragment calls this method to return and display the face name of the 12-point Dialog Bold font:

```
Font f = new Font ("Dialog", Font.BOLD, 12);
System.out.println (f.getFontName ());
```

This code fragment, as expected, outputs dialog.bold.

THE getSize () METHOD

Font's getSize () instance method returns an int that contains the size of a font. The following code fragment calls this method to return the size of the 12-point Dialog Bold font:

```
Font f = new Font ("Dialog", Font.BOLD, 12);
System.out.println (f.getSize ());
```

This code fragment outputs 12.

THE isBold () METHOD

Font's isBold () instance method returns a Boolean true value if a Font object has a Bold face. Otherwise, false is returned. The following code fragment calls this method to determine if a 24-point SansSerif Bold Font object has the Bold face:

```
Font f = new Font ("SansSerif", Font.BOLD, 24);
System.out.println (f.isBold ());
```

This code fragment outputs true.

THE isItalic () METHOD

Font's isItalic () instance method returns a Boolean true value if a Font object has an Italic face. Otherwise, false is returned. The following code fragment calls this method to determine if a 16-point Serif Bold Italic Font object has the Italic face:

```
Font f = new Font ("Serif", Font.BOLD + Font.ITALIC, 16);
System.out.println (f.isItalic ());
```

This code fragment outputs true.

THE isPlain () METHOD

Font's isPlain () instance method returns a Boolean true value if a Font object has neither a Bold nor Italic face. Otherwise, false is returned. The following code fragment calls this method to determine if a 10-point Monospaced Font object has the Plain face:

```
Font f = new Font ("Monospaced", Font.PLAIN, 10);
System.out.println (f.isPlain ());
```

This code fragment outputs true.

Font Metrics

Fonts are either fixed-width or proportional. In a fixed-width font (such as Courier), every character has the same width. For example, a lowercase letter i takes up as much width as an uppercase letter X. On the other hand, different characters have different widths in a proportional font (such as Arial). For example, in a proportional font, i would have a narrower width than X.

Text displayed in a proportional font is much easier to read than text displayed in a fixed-width font. However, fixed-width fonts are easier to use from a developer's perspective. For example, it is easier to justify text based on a fixed-width font than to justify this text based on a proportional font.

After you have some text to work with, how do you determine certain measurement details, such as a character's height or the average width of characters in a proportional font? The answer is to use the FontMetrics class.

FontMetrics, like Graphics, is an abstract class. You cannot create FontMetrics objects. Instead, each graphics context has a FontMetrics subclass object associated with the currently installed Font object. You obtain the FontMetrics subclass object by calling the getFontMetrics () instance method, which is declared in the Graphics class. The following bit of code introduces a paint (Graphics) method that obtains the current FontMetrics object:

```
public void paint (Graphics g)
{
   FontMetrics fm = g.getFontMetrics ();
}
```

Each time you set a graphics context's font, a new FontMetrics object is created by the graphics context object and replaces the previous FontMetrics object.

The following code fragment introduces a paint (Graphics) method that obtains the current FontMetrics object and assigns its reference to fm1. However, the current font is changed by a call to setFont (Font). This invalidates the FontMetrics object assigned to fm1. (At this point, fm1 should not be used.) A second call to getFontMetrics () retrieves the new FontMetrics object and assigns its reference to fm2. This FontMetrics object assigned to fm2 can be used until it is replaced—or the paint (Graphics) method ends:

```
public void paint (Graphics g)
{
   FontMetrics fm1 = g.getFontMetrics ();
   g.setFont (new Font ("Dialog", Font.PLAIN, 12));
   FontMetrics fm2 = g.getFontMetrics ();
}
```

Every font is associated with certain measurements. These measurements are illustrated in Figure 14.2.

Figure 14.2: *Font measurements.*

As illustrated in Figure 14.2, measurements are made from a font's baseline. The portion of a character that appears below the baseline is known a *descent*, whereas the portion of a character that appears above the baseline is called an *ascent*. Some characters have extra visual information (such as an acute) appearing above the ascent. This extra information is called *leading* (pronounced ledding). Finally, the combination of descent, ascent, and leading is called *height*.

THE getAscent () METHOD

FontMetrics's getAscent () instance method returns an int that contains the font's ascent in points. Acquiring this information is shown by the following snippet of code:

```
public void paint (Graphics g)
{
   FontMetrics fm = g.getFontMetrics ();
   int ascent = fm.getAscent ();
}
```

THE getDescent () METHOD

FontMetrics's getDescent () instance method returns an int that contains the font's descent in points. The following bit of code calls this method to determine the descent of the current Font object:

```
public void paint (Graphics g)
{
   FontMetrics fm = g.getFontMetrics ();
   int descent = fm.getDescent ();
}
```

THE getHeight () METHOD

FontMetrics's getHeight () instance method returns an int that contains the font's height in points. The following paint (Graphics) method contains a call to getHeight () to return the height of the current Font object:

```
public void paint (Graphics g)
{
   FontMetrics fm = g.getFontMetrics ();
   int height = fm.getHeight ();
}
```

THE getLeading () METHOD

FontMetrics's getLeading () instance method returns an int that contains the font's leading in points. The following example calls this method to determine the leading of the current Font object:

```
public void paint (Graphics g)
{
   FontMetrics fm = g.getFontMetrics ();
   int leading = fm.getLeading ();
}
```

THE stringWidth (String) METHOD

FontMetrics's stringWidth (String) instance method returns an int that contains the combined advance width of all the characters in the String argument. The following code fragment calls this method to determine the combined advance width of String object "Hello", according to the current Font object:

```
public void paint (Graphics g)
{
   FontMetrics fm = g.getFontMetrics ();
   int aw = fm.stringWidth ("Hello");
}
```

The following `centerText` applet calls `stringWidth (String)` to center several text messages on an applet's drawable area:

```java
// centerText.java

import java.awt.*;
import java.applet.Applet;

public class centerText extends Applet
{
   String [] msgs =
   {
      "Duke wants these messages centered!",
      "He wants you to know that he does not drink excessively!",
      "(But don't you believe it.)"
   };

   public void paint (Graphics g)
   {
      FontMetrics fm = g.getFontMetrics ();

      for (int i = 0; i < msgs.length; i++)
      {
         int x = (getSize ().width - fm.stringWidth (msgs [i])) / 2;
         int y = fm.getHeight () * (i + 1);

         g.drawString (msgs [i], x, y);
      }
   }
}
```

The `getSize ()` instance method returns a `Dimension` object (created from the `Dimension` class in the `java.awt` package) that contains the width and height of an applet. The `width` class field returns the width.

The `drawString (String, int, int)` method draws the characters contained within the `String` object argument on to the drawable area. This method is discussed in more detail under the next topic.

To run the `centerText` applet, you need an HTML file with the following `<applet>` tag:

```html
<applet code="centerText.class" width=400 height=200>
</applet>
```

You run this applet from the command line by typing

```
appletviewer centerText.html
```

Figure 14.3 displays output from `centerText`.

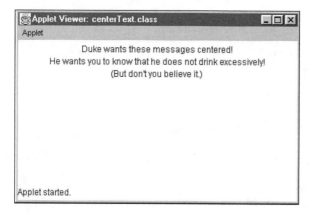

Figure 14.3: Output from the centerText applet.

Graphics

Now that we know what a graphics context is and that the AWT calls an applet's update (Graphics) method to update the applet's drawable area, it's time to learn how to draw. To begin, we need to examine the AWT's coordinate system.

Coordinate System

Every drawable area consists of small colored dots known as *picture elements (pixels)*. The exact number of pixels is controlled by the width and height of the drawable area.

The drawable area is mapped out with a two-dimensional coordinate system that locates every pixel. According to this system, every pixel is identified by a coordinate pair—a pair of integer numbers that identify the horizontal and vertical distances (measured in pixels) from the *origin* (the pixel located in the upper-left corner of the drawable area) to a pixel.

The horizontal distance from the origin is known as an *x-coordinate* and the vertical distance from the origin is known as a *y-coordinate*. The x-coordinate increases through positive values from left to right, whereas the y-coordinate increases through positive values from top to bottom.

Pixels are written out using the (x, y) format: x identifies the x-coordinate and y identifies the y-coordinate. The origin is written out as (0, 0).

Figure 14.4 illustrates the AWT's coordinate system.

Text

The Graphics class declares three instance methods for drawing text: drawString (String, int, int), drawChars (char [], int, int, int, int), and drawBytes (byte [], int, int, int, int).

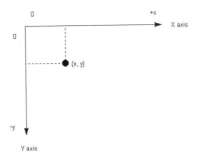

Figure 14.4: *The AWT's coordinate system.*

The drawString (String, int, int) method draws the characters contained within the String object argument on to the drawable area using the current font (via setFont (Font)) and in the current drawing color (via setColor (Color)) with the left-most character starting at the coordinate pair identified by the two int arguments. The first int argument identifies the x-coordinate. The second int argument identifies the y-coordinate. (Note: The y-coordinate identifies the baseline of the text to be drawn.)

The following code fragment illustrates a call to drawString (String, int, int):

```
public void paint (Graphics g)
{
    g.drawString ("Duke rules!", 10, 30);
}
```

Figure 14.5 illustrates an applet's drawable area with the text drawn by the previous code fragment.

Figure 14.5: *An applet's drawable area displaying some text.*

The drawChars (char [], int, int, int, int) method draws the characters within the char [] array on to the drawable area using the current font and in the current drawing color. The first int argument identifies the zero-based offset within this array from where the first character to be drawn will be obtained. The second int argument identifies the number of characters to be drawn. Specifying a negative value for this argument causes an InternalError object to be thrown. The third int argument identifies the x-coordinate of the left-most character and the fourth int argument identifies the y-coordinate of the baseline.

The following code fragment illustrates a call to drawChars (char [], int, int, int, int):

```
public void paint (Graphics g)
{
   char [] c =
   {
      'W', 'a', 't', 'c', 'h', ' ',
      'i', 't', ' ',
      'D', 'u', 'k', 'e', '!'
   };

   g.drawChars (c, 0, c.length, 10, 30);
}
```

The drawBytes (byte [], int, int, int, int) method draws the bytes within the byte [] array on to the drawable area using the current font and in the current drawing color. The first int argument identifies the zero-based offset within this array from where the first byte to be drawn will be obtained. The second int argument identifies the number of bytes to be drawn. Specifying a negative value for this argument causes an InternalError object to be thrown. The third int argument identifies the x-coordinate of the left-most character and the fourth int argument identifies the y-coordinate of the baseline.

The following code fragment illustrates a call to drawBytes (byte [], int, int, int, int):

```
public void paint (Graphics g)
{
   byte [] b =
   {
      0x65, (byte) 'B', 0x66
   };

   g.drawBytes (b, 0, b.length, 10, 30);
}
```

Lines and Points

The Graphics class declares an instance method for drawing lines and points (pixels): drawLine (int, int, int, int).

The drawLine (int, int, int, int) method draws a line or point on to the drawable area in the current drawing color. The line is drawn from the coordinate pair identified by the first pair of int arguments to the coordinate pair identified by the last pair of int arguments. The first int argument of each pair identifies the x-coordinate. The second int argument of each pair identifies the y-coordinate. If both x-coordinates are the same and both y-coordinates are the same, a point is drawn.

The following code fragment illustrates a call to drawLine (int, int, int, int) to draw a line from (10, 15) to (100, 115):

```
public void paint (Graphics g)
{
    g.drawLine (10, 15, 100, 115);
}
```

Figure 14.6 illustrates an applet's drawable area with the line drawn by the previous code fragment.

Figure 14.6: *An applet's drawable area displaying a line.*

Rectangles

The Graphics class declares two instance methods for drawing and filling rectangles: drawRect (int, int, int, int), and fillRect (int, int, int, int).

The drawRect (int, int, int, int) method draws the outline of a rectangle on to the drawable area in the current drawing color. Its upper-left corner is specified by the coordinate pair identified by the first pair of int arguments. The width of the rectangle is specified by the third int argument and the height of the rectangle is specified by the last int argument.

The following code fragment illustrates a call to drawRect (int, int, int, int) to draw a rectangle outline with an upper-left corner at (5, 15), a width of 50 pixels, and a height of 75 pixels:

```
public void paint (Graphics g)
{
   g.drawRect (5, 15, 50, 75);
}
```

The `fillRect (int, int, int, int)` method draws a solid rectangle on to the drawable area in the current drawing color. Its upper-left corner is specified by the coordinate pair identified by the first pair of `int` arguments. The width of the rectangle is specified by the third `int` argument and the height of the rectangle is specified by the last `int` argument.

The following code fragment illustrates a call to `fillRect (int, int, int, int)` to draw a solid rectangle with an upper-left corner at (5, 15), a width of 50 pixels, and a height of 75 pixels:

```
public void paint (Graphics g)
{
   g.fillRect (5, 15, 50, 75);
}
```

Figure 14.7 illustrates an applet's drawable area with the solid rectangle drawn by the previous code fragment.

Figure 14.7: *An applet's drawable area displaying a solid rectangle.*

ROUNDED RECTANGLES

The `Graphics` class declares two instance methods for drawing and filling rectangles with rounded corners: `drawRoundRect (int, int, int, int, int, int)`, and `fillRoundRect (int, int, int, int, int, int)`.

The `drawRoundRect (int, int, int, int, int, int)` method draws the outline of a rectangle with rounded corners on to the drawable area in the current drawing color. Its upper-left corner is specified by the coordinate pair identified by the first pair of `int` arguments. The width of the rectangle is specified by the third `int` argument and the height of the rectangle is specified by the fourth `int` argument. The fifth `int` argument specifies the width of the arc that occupies one-quarter of a circle's circumference and is used for each rounded corner. The sixth int argument specifies the height of the arc that occupies one-quarter of a circle's circumference and is used for each rounded corner.

Figure 14.8 illustrates a rounded rectangle with a height and width as well as rounded corners with arc width and arc height.

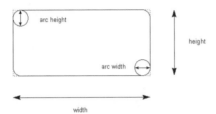

Figure 14.8: A rounded rectangle.

The following code fragment illustrates a call to drawRoundRect (int, int, int, int, int, int) to draw a rounded rectangle outline with an upper-left corner at (5, 15), a width of 50 pixels, a height of 75 pixels, an arc width of 20 pixels, and an arc height of 15 pixels:

```
public void paint (Graphics g)
{
    g.drawRoundRect (5, 15, 50, 75, 20, 15);
}
```

The fillRoundRect (int, int, int, int, int, int) method draws a solid rectangle with rounded corners on to the drawable area in the current drawing color. Its upper-left corner is specified by the coordinate pair identified by the first two int arguments. The width of the rectangle is specified by the third int argument and the height of the rectangle is specified by the fourth int argument. The fifth int argument specifies the width of the arc that occupies one-quarter of a circle's circumference and is used for each rounded corner. The sixth int argument specifies the height of the arc that occupies one-quarter of a circle's circumference and is used for each rounded corner.

The following code fragment illustrates a call to fillRoundRect (int, int, int, int, int, int) to draw a solid rounded rectangle with an upper-left corner at (5, 15), a width of 50 pixels, a height of 75 pixels, an arc width of 20 pixels, and an arc height of 15 pixels:

```
public void paint (Graphics g)
{
    g.fillRoundRect (5, 15, 50, 75, 20, 15);
}
```

Figure 14.9 illustrates an applet's drawable area with the solid rounded rectangle drawn by the previous code fragment.

Figure 14.9: An applet's drawable area displaying a solid rounded rectangle.

THREE-DIMENSIONAL RECTANGLES

The Graphics class declares two instance methods for drawing and filling three-dimensional rectangles: draw3DRect (int, int, int, int, boolean), and fill3DRect (int, int, int, int, boolean).

The draw3DRect (int, int, int, int, boolean) method draws the outline of a three-dimensional rectangle on to the drawable area in the current drawing color. Its upper-left corner is specified by the coordinate pair identified by the first pair of int arguments. The width of the rectangle is specified by the third int argument and the height of the rectangle is specified by the fourth int argument. The boolean argument specifies the raised/sunken appearance of the rectangle. If true is specified, the rectangle has a raised appearance. If false is specified, the rectangle has a sunken appearance.

The following code fragment illustrates a call to draw3DRect (int, int, int, int, boolean) to draw a three-dimensional rectangle outline with an upper-left corner at (5, 15), a width of 50 pixels, a height of 75 pixels, and a sunken appearance. Before the rectangle is drawn, the drawing color is set to yellow to achieve high contrast:

```
public void paint (Graphics g)
{
   g.setColor (Color.yellow);
   g.draw3DRect (5, 15, 50, 75, false);
}
```

Figure 14.10 illustrates an applet's drawable area with the three-dimensional rectangle outline drawn by the previous code fragment.

Figure 14.10: *An applet's drawable area displaying a three-dimensional rectangle outline.*

The fill3DRect (int, int, int, int, boolean) method draws a solid three-dimensional rectangle on to the drawable area in the current drawing color. Its upper-left corner is specified by the coordinate pair identified by the first pair of int arguments. The width of the rectangle is specified by the third int argument and the height of the rectangle is specified by the fourth int argument. The boolean argument specifies the raised/sunken appearance of the rectangle. If true is specified, the rectangle has a raised appearance. If false is specified, the rectangle has a sunken appearance.

The following code fragment illustrates a call to fill3DRect (int, int, int, int, boolean) to draw a solid three-dimensional rectangle with an upper-left corner at (5, 15), a width of 50 pixels, a height of 75 pixels, and a raised appearance:

```
public void paint (Graphics g)
{
    g.fill3DRect (5, 15, 50, 75, true);
}
```

Ovals

The Graphics class declares two instance methods for drawing and filling ovals: drawOval (int, int, int, int), and fillOval (int, int, int, int).

Both methods draw ovals within what is known as a *bounding rectangle* of a certain width and height. The oval is drawn so that each side of the bounding rectangle touches the oval. Figure 14.11 provides an illustration of an oval inside a bounding rectangle.

The drawOval (int, int, int, int) method draws the outline of an oval on to the drawable area in the current drawing color. The upper-left corner of its bounding rectangle is specified by the coordinate pair identified by the first pair of int arguments. The width of the bounding rectangle is specified by the third int argument and the height of the bounding rectangle is specified by the last int argument.

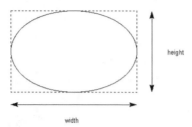

Figure 14.11: *An oval inside a bounding rectangle.*

The following code fragment illustrates a call to drawOval (int, int, int, int) to draw an oval outline with the upper-left corner of its bounding rectangle at (5, 15), a width of 50 pixels, and a height of 75 pixels:

```
public void paint (Graphics g)
{
    g.drawOval (5, 15, 50, 75);
}
```

The fillOval (int, int, int, int) method draws a solid oval on to the drawable area in the current drawing color. The upper-left corner of its bounding rectangle is specified by the coordinate pair identified by the first pair of int arguments. The width of the bounding rectangle is specified by the third int argument and the height of the bounding rectangle is specified by the last int argument.

The following code fragment illustrates a call to fillOval (int, int, int, int) to draw a solid oval with the upper-left corner of its bounding rectangle at (5, 15), a width of 50 pixels, and a height of 75 pixels:

```
public void paint (Graphics g)
{
    g.fillOval (5, 15, 50, 75);
}
```

Figure 14.12 illustrates an applet's drawable area with the solid oval drawn by the previous code fragment.

Arcs

The Graphics class declares two instance methods for drawing and filling arcs: drawArc (int, int, int, int, int, int), and fillArc (int, int, int, int, int, int).

Both methods draw arcs within what is known as a bounding rectangle of a certain width and height. The arc is drawn so that its end points just touch this rectangle. Figure 14.13 provides an illustration of an arc inside a bounding rectangle.

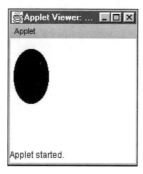

Figure 14.12: *An applet's drawable area displaying a solid oval.*

The drawArc (int, int, int, int, int, int) method draws the outline of an arc on to the drawable area in the current drawing color. The upper-left corner of its bounding rectangle is specified by the coordinate pair identified by the first pair of int arguments. The width of the bounding rectangle is specified by the third int argument. The height of the bounding rectangle is specified by the fourth int argument. The fifth int argument identifies the starting angle of this arc (in degrees). The sixth int argument identifies the ending angle of this arc (in degrees). Positive values for the starting and ending angles cause the arc to be drawn in a counter-clockwise fashion. Negative values for the starting and ending angles cause the arc to be drawn in a clockwise fashion. This is illustrated in Figure 14.14.

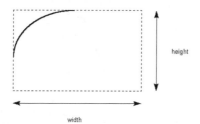

Figure 14.13: *An arc inside a bounding rectangle.*

The following code fragment illustrates a call to drawArc (int, int, int, int, int, int) to draw an arc outline with the upper-left corner of its bounding rectangle at (5, 15), a width of 50 pixels, a height of 75 pixels, a starting angle of 25 degrees, and an ending angle of 165 degrees:

```
public void paint (Graphics g)
{
    g.drawArc (5, 15, 50, 75, 25, 165);
}
```

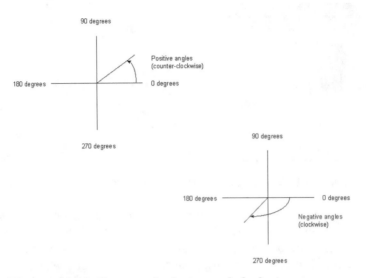

Figure 14.14: *Counter-clockwise and clockwise arcs.*

The `fillArc (int, int, int, int, int, int)` method draws a solid arc on to the drawable area in the current drawing color. The upper-left corner of its bounding rectangle is specified by the coordinate pair identified by the first pair of `int` arguments. The width of the bounding rectangle is specified by the third `int` argument. The height of the bounding rectangle is specified by the fourth `int` argument. The fifth `int` argument identifies the starting angle of this arc (in degrees). The sixth `int` argument identifies the ending angle of this arc (in degrees). Positive values for the starting and ending angles cause the arc to be drawn in a counter-clockwise fashion. Negative values for the starting and ending angles cause the arc to be drawn in a clockwise fashion.

The following code fragment illustrates a call to `fillArc (int, int, int, int, int, int)` to draw an arc outline with the upper-left corner of its bounding rectangle at (5, 15), a width of 50 pixels, a height of 75 pixels, a starting angle of 25 degrees, and an ending angle of 165 degrees:

```
public void paint (Graphics g)
{
    g.fillArc (5, 15, 50, 75, 25, 165);
}
```

Figure 14.15 illustrates an applet's drawable area with the solid arc drawn by the previous code fragment.

Figure 14.15: *An applet's drawable area displaying a solid arc.*

Copying Regions of Drawable Areas

The copyArea (int, int, int, int, int, int) instance method copies one rectangular region of a drawable area to another region on the same drawable area.

The first pair of int arguments identify the x and y coordinates of the upper-left corner of the region to copy. The third int argument identifies the width of this region. The fourth int argument identifies the length of this region. The fifth and sixth int arguments identify a relative displacement from the upper-left corner of the region to be copied to the destination. For example, if the first pair of int arguments identified (6, 10) as the upper-left corner of the region to be copied, and if the fifth int argument was 28 while the sixth int argument was 32, the upper-left corner of the destination would be (6 + 28, 10 + 32) or (34, 42).

The following code fragment illustrates a call to fillArc (int, int, int, int, int, int) to draw an arc outline and copyArea (int, int, int, int, int, int) to make a duplicate of this arc:

```
public void paint (Graphics g)
{
   g.fillArc (5, 15, 50, 75, 25, 165);
   g.copyArea (5, 15, 50, 75, 50, 50);
}
```

Figure 14.16 illustrates an applet's drawable area with the solid arc drawn and copied by the previous code fragment.

Figure 14.16: *An applet's drawable area displaying a solid arc along with a copy of this arc.*

Images

Images (that is, pictures created from tables of colored pixels) add spice to an otherwise dull program. Images are normally used with applets, as opposed to applications.

Java supports two flavors of images: images based on the Graphical Interchange Format (GIF) and images based on the Joint Photographic Experts Group (JPEG) file format.

The Image Class

Images are represented by objects created from subclasses of Java's abstract Image class. This class is located in the java.awt package.

An Image subclass object contains the pixels that represent an image. To obtain an Image subclass object, you must call one of two instance methods that are declared in the Applet class: getImage (URL) and getImage (URL, String). These methods obtain an image from a computer attached to the Internet whose address is specified by a uniform resource locator (URL).

The getImage (URL) method takes a single URL object argument and returns an Image subclass object.

The URL argument contains the Internet address where the image file is located and the name of the image file (for example, http://www.geoff.com/geoff.gif—a fictitious address and filename).

The getImage (URL, String) method takes a URL object argument and a String object argument and returns an Image subclass object.

The URL argument contains the Internet address where the image file is located. It does not contain the name of the image file. Instead, the String argument contains the name of the image file. The getImage (URL, String) method concatenates the name of the image file to the Internet address and then calls getImage (URL).

You can specify a URL object argument by taking advantage of the URL class, in the java.net package, to create a URL object. However, there is a simpler way.

If you place your GIF or JPEG (also known as JPG) files in the same directory as the directory containing your applet's HTML file, you can use the Applet class's getDocumentBase () instance method to return a URL object representing the Internet address of this HTML file document.

After an Image object has been obtained, you can use the drawImage (Image, int, int, ImageObserver) instance method, declared in the Graphics class, to draw the image's pixels on to the drawable area. The two int arguments identify the x and y coordinates of the upper-left corner where the image will be drawn. (The first int argument identifies the x coordinate, whereas the second int argument identifies the y coordinate.) The ImageObserver argument will shortly be explained.

At this point, you might think that either getImage method has loaded an image into an Image subclass object and that drawImage (Image, int, int, ImageObserver) can go ahead and draw this image. However, this is not the case.

The getImage (URL) and getImage (URL, String) methods do not load images. The drawImage (Image, int, int, ImageObserver) method does not draw an image. There is a very good reason for this: applet performance.

It takes time to load images over the Internet. For example, loading a 100,000-byte image via a 28,800–bits per second modem would require approximately 30 seconds to load. If the getImage methods did the actual loading, your applet's users would freak with having to wait before they could use your applet. There has to be a better way.

Suppose that the getImage methods only store the URL and prepare an empty Image object for holding an image. Now suppose that drawImage (Image, int, int, ImageObserver) starts a background thread to load this image into the Image object argument and display this image, and then immediately returns so the applet can keep running. This improves performance.

However, the applet might want to determine certain things about the image, such as its width and height (in pixels). It can't do this while an image is still loading. It can only do this after the image has been loaded. How does it know when the background thread has finished downloading the image? When the background thread is finished, it notifies the ImageObserver object, which updates the Image object previously saved by the call to drawImage (Image, int, int, ImageObserver). If the applet calls Image's getWidth (ImageObserver) and getHeight (ImageObserver) methods, and these methods do not return -1, the applet knows that the image has been loaded.

Every applet object implements `ImageObserver`. Therefore, it is possible to pass the reserved word `this` as the fourth argument to `drawImage (Image, int, int, ImageObserver)`. When the image has been loaded, the background thread will notify the applet that the loading is complete.

EXAMPLE

The following `drawImage` applet calls `getImage (URL, String)` to obtain an `Image` object containing the pixels of the `durango.jpg` JPEG file. This file is located in the same directory as the HTML file that contains the `drawImage` applet. The `drawImage (Image, int, int, ImageObserver)` method is then called to draw this image via a background thread:

```
// drawImage.java

import java.applet.Applet;
import java.awt.*;

public class drawImage extends Applet
{
    Image image;

    public void init ()
    {
        image = getImage (getDocumentBase (), "durango.jpg");
    }

    public void paint (Graphics g)
    {
        if (image != null)
            g.drawImage (image, 0, 0, this);
    }
}
```

To run the `drawImage` applet, you need an HTML file with the following `<applet>` tag:

```
<applet code="drawImage.class" width=280 height=160>
</applet>
```

You run this applet from the command line by typing

```
appletviewer drawImage.html
```

Figure 14.17 displays output from `drawImage`.

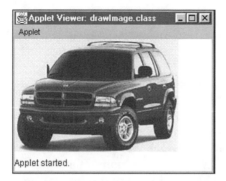

Figure 14.17: *Output from the* drawImage *applet.*

FIREWORKS

Fireworks are fun and exciting to watch. Therefore, this chapter wraps up by showing how to write an applet to create your very own fireworks.

FIREWORKS demonstrates quite a few of the AWT's graphics and image processing capabilities. These capabilities range from calling drawLine (int, int, int, int) to plotting a rocket and rocket fragments to creating colors to double buffering.

Setting Up the Project

To set up FIREWORKS, begin by double-clicking your MS-DOS icon (if you are using Windows) and go to a command prompt.

If you created a projects directory in Chapter 1, "Introducing Java," make projects your current directory. (If you do not have a projects directory, now is as good a time as any to create one.)

Assuming that projects is located within c:\jdk1.2\, enter the command cd \jdk1.2\projects to change to this directory.

From within your projects directory, create a directory called fireworks (for example, md fireworks). (If you prefer, you can create this directory entirely in uppercase. For example, you could issue the command md FIREWORKS to create this directory. Case does not matter when it comes to directories.)

Download the file fireworks.java from the Macmillan Web site and place this file in your fireworks directory.

Compiling FIREWORKS

Compilation is a simple process. It involves running the javac.exe program and specifying the name of the source file as an argument to this program.

At the command prompt, enter the following line:

```
c:\jdk1.2\projects\fireworks>javac fireworks.java
```

C A U T I O N

The .java file extension must be specified when compiling a source file. The compiler will display an error message if .java is not specified.

If the compiler displays an error message, you might have typed fireworks with a different combination of uppercase/lowercase letters than the lowercase letters used as FIREWORK's class name (for example, you might have specified something like javac Fireworks.java at the command line when you should have specified javac fireworks.java).

C A U T I O N

You must specify fireworks and not Fireworks, FIREWORKS, or any other combination of lowercase/uppercase letters. The compiler is very sensitive to case and will display an error message if the class name (fireworks) does not match the filename (fireworks).

After compilation is finished, you should end up with a class file called fireworks.class and a class file called rocket.class.

Figure 14.18 shows the compilation process.

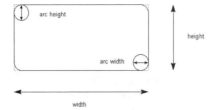

Figure 14.18: *Compiling* fireworks.java *with the* javac.exe *compiler.*

Running FIREWORKS

Congratulations! You successfully compiled fireworks.java and are now ready to run fireworks.class.

Before FIREWORKS can be run, an HTML file needs to be constructed so that appletviewer.exe (or the Web browser) can load the applet's starting class file, start the virtual machine, and get things going.

The following code describes the HTML for the FIREWORKS applet. This HTML is stored in a text file called fireworks.html:

```
[ 1] <applet code="fireworks.class" width=300 height=300>
[ 2] </applet>
```

The <APPLET> tag identifies the applet's starting class file and describes the size of the applet area.

The name of the class file, specified by the code attribute, is fireworks.class. The width of the applet area, specified by the width attribute, is 300 pixels. The height of the applet area, specified by the height attribute, is also 300 pixels.

Figure 14.19 shows the appletviewer.exe tool running the FIREWORKS applet. A separate window displays the image.

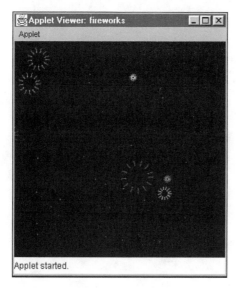

Figure 14.19: *Using* appletviewer.exe *to run the FIREWORKS applet.*

Potential Problems

What can go wrong with FIREWORKS? Practically nothing. It is pretty robust. However, if you modify some of the numeric constants, you might experience strange results. (Or you might end up with a blank screen.)

Enhancing FIREWORKS

You can enhance FIREWORKS in a number of ways. Here is one suggestion:

- Modify FIREWORKS to incorporate different kinds of rockets that produce different explosion effects. For example, the current rockets produce the explosion effect shown in Figure 14.19. However, another kind of rocket could be introduced to model a different kind of explosion effect. Need examples? Think about real-life fireworks. (Hint: For each kind of rocket, consider subclassing rocket and overriding moveAndDraw (Graphics)).

What's Next?

As we've just seen, the AWT makes it possible to create graphical programs, by taking advantage of its many graphics features. However, the AWT also makes it possible to create sophisticated GUIs. The AWT's GUI development capabilities are investigated in the next chapter.

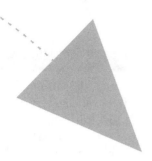

AWT, Part 2

In the previous chapter, you learned about the AWT's graphics capabilities. However, the AWT can also be used to create graphical user interfaces.

Chapter 15 presents the following topics:

- Working with Components
- Working with Containers
- Laying Out Components
- Handling Events

Working with Components

The process of creating and interacting with a component is rather involved, for the following reason: When Java was first released, it needed a quick and dirty tool kit for developing GUIs. This tool kit became known as the AWT. Rather than develop GUI components in Java, the AWT's designers chose to pass the buck and let the host operating system create and manage components, under the direction of the AWT. For this reason, an AWT button looks like a Windows button under Windows and a Motif button under Motif. (It is only with the advent of Swing that it is possible for an upgraded AWT to create and manage components entirely in Java.)

A component is created by first creating an object of a specific component class and then adding this object to another object that serves as a container. After this object is placed in the container (by calling a special container method), the container, in concert with its associated layout manager, informs the host operating system (via the AWT portion of the JVM's runtime system) that it should create a host operating system component, known as a *peer*. The peer is then associated with the Java object that was added to the container. If this object is ever removed from the container, the peer is destroyed.

The host operating system creates the peer and this peer becomes visible to the user. When the user interacts with the peer, various host operating system–specific actions (known as *events*) occur. These events are intercepted by the peer's management logic and forwarded to the AWT portion of the JVM's runtime system. This portion of the runtime forwards these events to the Java program for processing. (To simplify things, a developer usually refers to the Java object as the component and forgets about the peer.)

The Component Class

The AWT provides an abstract Component class that factors out the commonality of all components. (Because Component is abstract, you cannot create objects from this class.) Component is located in the java.awt package.

Component declares a variety of useful methods that make it possible to get and set various attributes of all components, as well as draw the components. All of these methods are inherited by actual component subclasses. Each subclass chooses which methods to override. (More often than not, it is the paint (Graphics) method that is overridden.) The following paragraphs outline some of Component's more useful methods.

Every component has the notion of a foreground and a background. The getForeground (Color) instance method returns a component's foreground color, whereas the setForeground (Color) instance method sets the foreground color to the value of the Color object argument. The getBackground

(Color) instance method returns a component's background color, whereas the setBackground (Color) instance method sets the background color to the value of the Color object argument.

The getFont () instance method returns a component's font (used to display text on the component), whereas the setFont (Font) instance method sets the font to the value of the Font object argument.

The getCursor () instance method returns the current cursor (shape of the mouse pointer) that appears when the mouse pointer moves over the component, whereas the setCursor (Cursor) instance method sets the shape of this cursor to the value of the Cursor object argument.

The repaint () instance method "tells" the AWT to redraw the component. The AWT responds by calling the component's update (Graphics g) instance method to erase the component's background (to the background color) and redraw the component (using the foreground color). The redrawing operation is handled by having the inherited update (Graphics) method call the component's overridden paint (Graphics) method.

Every component has a size. The getSize () instance method returns this size as a Dimension object. (Dimension is located in the java.awt package.) This object contains a pair of fields, width and height, representing the component's current width and height. However, this size also can be changed. The setSize (int, int) instance method sets the component's size to the width specified by the first int argument and to the height specified by the second int argument. However, because a layout manager object (which you will investigate at a later point in this chapter) is responsible for positioning components so that they display appropriately on the screen, it must ensure that changing the size of a component after it has been displayed will not cause problems with the screen positions of other visible components. For this reason, the layout manager object might choose to ignore a setSize (int, int) method call. For this reason, it's best to set a component's size before the component is displayed.

Figure 15.1 provides a class hierarchy of the AWT's non-Swing component classes. The Component and MenuComponent classes are shown in gray because they are abstract classes. (For brevity, MenuComponent and its subclasses are not discussed in this book. If you would like more information about menus, please consult the JDK documentation.)

Button

Of all the various components, buttons are probably the most familiar. For example, a dialog box often contains OK and Cancel buttons to give the user the capability to exit from the dialog box.

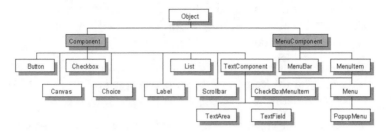

Figure 15.1: *The AWT's non-Swing component class hierarchy.*

The AWT's `Button` class, located in the `java.awt` package, is used to create `Button` objects that represent buttons.

The `Button` class declares a pair of constructors for initializing `Button` objects: `Button ()` and `Button (String)`.

The `Button ()` constructor initializes a `Button` object with no button *label* (descriptive text that appears on the button and identifies the button's purpose). A button peer, created when this `Button` object is added to a container, will not display a button label. (It is possible to add a button label at a later time.) For example, the following code fragment creates and initializes a `Button` object with no button label:

```
Button b = new Button ();
```

The `Button (String)` constructor initializes a `Button` object with the button label provided by the `String` object argument. The following code fragment creates and initializes a `Button` object with the button label `Ok`:

```
Button b = new Button ("Ok");
```

Figure 15.2 illustrates a button (based on the previous code fragment).

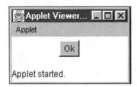

Figure 15.2: *A button.*

Canvas

Artistic developers and users enjoy painting and drawing on canvases. The AWT's `Canvas` class, located in the `java.awt` package, is used to create `Canvas` objects that represent drawable surfaces. Thanks to `Canvas`, Java drawing pad programs can be constructed—so you can express yourself artistically.

TIP

It is not a good idea to draw directly on a button, list box, or other component, because this drawing occurs on a component's background and anything that is drawn on the component's background might disappear after the component has been added to a container.

The Canvas () constructor initializes a Canvas object with no size. A container's layout manager automatically sizes the canvas to an appropriate size when the Canvas object is added to the container.

Canvas inherits Component's update (Graphics) and paint (Graphics) methods. The update (Graphics) method clears the canvas to its background color and then calls paint (Graphics)—which does nothing. If you want to draw something on a canvas, you must extend the Canvas class and override the paint (Graphics) method.

For example, the following code fragment declares a myCanvas class that extends Canvas:

```
class myCanvas extends Canvas
{
   myCanvas (int x, int y)
   {
      setSize (x, y);
   }

   public void paint (Graphics g)
   {
      g.drawString ("Hello", 10, 30);
   }
}
```

A myCanvas (int, int) constructor is provided to specify the width and height of the canvas (in pixels). The constructor will try to set this size by calling the setSize (int, int) method.

The following code fragment obtains the width and height of the current component, creates a myCanvas object, and initializes this object to the obtained width and height:

```
int width = getSize ().width;
int height = getSize ().height;
myCanvas mc = new myCanvas (width, height);
```

Figure 15.3 illustrates a canvas (based on the previous code fragment).

TIP

If you would like a more complete example of canvases, please check out the JPAD application, located on the Macmillan Web site with the rest of this book's source files.

Figure 15.3: A canvas.

Checkbox

Programs often contain check boxes to enable users to select one of two possibilities. When the user clicks the little square that represents a check box, either a check mark will appear to indicate a true state or an already visible check mark will disappear to indicate a false state.

The AWT's Checkbox class, located in the java.awt package, is used to create Checkbox objects that represent check boxes.

The Checkbox class declares a variety of constructors for initializing Checkbox objects. These constructors include Checkbox (), Checkbox (String), and Checkbox (String, boolean).

The Checkbox () constructor initializes a Checkbox object with no check box label. The initial state of this object is false. Therefore, when the check box peer is created, it will not display a check box label identifying the check box and will not display a check mark. For example, the following code fragment creates and initializes a Checkbox object with no check box label and an initial false state:

```
Checkbox cb = new Checkbox ();
```

The Checkbox (String) constructor initializes a Checkbox object with the check box label provided by the String object argument. The initial state of this object is false. The following code fragment creates and initializes a Checkbox object with the Married check box label and an initial false state:

```
Checkbox cb = new Checkbox ("Married");
```

Finally, the Checkbox (String, boolean) constructor initializes a Checkbox object with the check box label provided by the String object argument and an initial state provided by the boolean argument. For example, the following code fragment creates and initializes a Checkbox object with the Credit Card check box label and an initial true state:

```
Checkbox cb = new Checkbox ("Credit Card", true);
```

Figure 15.4 illustrates a check box (based on the previous code fragment).

Figure 15.4: *A check box.*

CheckboxGroup

There are times when you want to design a GUI with a feature similar to the Windows radio buttons. In other words, you want to provide a group of check boxes in which only one of these check boxes can be checked at a given time. The AWT gives you the capability to accomplish this task by taking advantage of the CheckboxGroup class.

The AWT's CheckboxGroup class, located in the java.awt package, is used to create CheckboxGroup objects that represent groups of Checkbox objects.

The CheckboxGroup class declares a constructor for initializing a CheckboxGroup object: CheckboxGroup (). The following code fragment creates and initializes a CheckboxGroup object:

```
CheckboxGroup cbg = new CheckboxGroup ();
```

After you've created a CheckboxGroup object, you need to add some Checkbox objects to the CheckboxGroup object. This is accomplished by taking advantage of the Checkbox (String, boolean, CheckboxGroup) constructor.

The Checkbox (String, boolean, CheckboxGroup) constructor is called after a CheckboxGroup object has been created. When you pass a reference to a CheckboxGroup object, the newly created Checkbox object is placed into the CheckboxGroup object.

For example, the following code fragment creates and initializes a CheckboxGroup object, creates and initializes three Checkbox objects, and adds these objects to the CheckboxGroup object:

```
CheckboxGroup cbg = new CheckboxGroup ();
Checkbox cb1 = new Checkbox ("Left justify", true, cbg);
Checkbox cb2 = new Checkbox ("Center justify", false, cbg);
Checkbox cb3 = new Checkbox ("Right justify", false, cbg);
```

You can indicate which check box is the currently selected check box by calling CheckboxGroup's setSelectedCheckbox (Checkbox) instance method and find out which check box is selected by calling CheckboxGroup's getSelectedCheckbox () instance method.

Figure 15.5 illustrates a check box group (based on the previous code fragment). Only one check box from within this group can be selected at a time.

Figure 15.5: *A check box group.*

Choice

The AWT makes it possible for a developer to create components that serve as drop-down list boxes. The user can click the arrow associated with a list box and open it up to view all textual items. From the list, a selection can be made. In Java-speak, a drop-down list box is known as a *choice*.

The AWT's Choice class, located in the java.awt package, is used to create Choice objects that represent drop-down list boxes.

The Choice class declares a constructor for initializing a Choice object: Choice ().

The Choice () constructor initializes a Choice object to an empty state. You must add textual items to this object before you can use it in a meaningful way. For example, the following code fragment creates and initializes a Choice object. There are no items in this object:

```
Choice c = new Choice ();
```

Choice's add (String) instance method adds the contents of its String object argument to the Choice object. If a null reference is passed to add (String), a NullPointerException object is thrown.

For example, the following code fragment creates and initializes a Choice object, and then adds the contents of two String objects to this object:

```
Choice c = new Choice ();
c.add ("First item");
c.add ("Second item");
```

Choice declares a variety of other methods for inserting and removing items. These methods are described in the JDK documentation.

After the user selects a Choice item, it is possible to identify this item by calling Choice's getSelectedIndex () and getSelectedItem () instance methods. The getSelectedIndex () method returns the zero-based index of the selected item, as an int. (If there are no items in the Choice object, this method returns -1.) The getSelectedItem () method returns a String object containing the textual contents of the selected item. (If there are no items in the Choice object, this method returns null.)

Figure 15.6 illustrates a choice (based on the previous code fragment).

Figure 15.6: A choice.

Label

Labels are commonly used to display text on a GUI. This text serves to identify the purpose of various components. For example, a text entry component that is used to enter a person's first name could be associated with the First name: label text.

The AWT's Label class, located in the java.awt package, is used to create Label objects that represent labels.

The Label class declares three read-only class fields called LEFT, CENTER, and RIGHT. These class fields are useful for aligning the contents of a label's text within the label.

The Label class declares three constructors for initializing Label objects: Label (), Label (String), and Label (String, int).

The Label () constructor initializes a Label object with no descriptive text. A label peer, created when this Label object is added to a container, will not display any text. (It is possible to supply this text at a later time.) For example, the following code fragment creates and initializes a Label object with no descriptive text:

```
Label l = new Label ();
```

The Label (String) constructor initializes a Label object with the descriptive text provided by the String object argument. By default, this text is left aligned. The following code fragment creates and initializes a Label object with descriptive text:

```
Label l = new Label ("First name:");
```

Finally, the `Label (String, int)` constructor initializes a `Label` object with the descriptive text provided by the `String` object argument and an alignment specified by the `int` argument. If the `int` argument is not one of `Label.LEFT`, `Label.CENTER`, or `Label.RIGHT`, an `IllegalArgumentException` object is thrown.

For example, the following code fragment creates and initializes a `Label` object with descriptive text that is centered within the label:

```
Label l = new Label ("Centered text", Label.CENTER);
```

Figure 15.7 illustrates left-aligned, centered, and right-aligned labels.

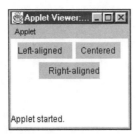

Figure 15.7: *Left-aligned, centered, and right-aligned labels.*

List

Choices represent drop-down list boxes. Lists represent non-drop-down list boxes. In other words, the user does not need to click a small arrow button to see the contents of the list box. (Choices are often used where GUI space must be conserved.)

The user might select one item or multiple items from the list. If the list contains more items than can be displayed on the screen, a scrollbar will be displayed to enable the user to scroll through these items.

The AWT's `List` class, located in the `java.awt` package, is used to create `List` objects that represent lists.

The `List` class declares a constructor for initializing a `List` object: `List ()`.

The `List ()` constructor initializes a `List` object to an empty state. You must add textual items to this object before you can use it in a meaningful way. The following code fragment creates and initializes a `List` object. There are no items in this object:

```
List l = new List ();
```

`List`'s `add (String)` instance method adds the contents of its `String` object argument to the `List` object. If the item already exists in the list, it is added again. For example, the following code fragment creates and initializes a `List` object, and then adds the contents of two `String` objects to this object:

```
List l = new List ();
l.add ("First item");
l.add ("Second item");
```

`List` declares a variety of other methods for inserting and removing items. These methods are described in the JDK documentation.

Assuming that the user can only select a single item from the list, it is possible to identify this item by calling `List`'s `getSelectedIndex ()` and `getSelectedItem ()` instance methods. The `getSelectedIndex ()` method returns the zero-based index of the selected item, as an int. (If there are no items in the `List` object, this method returns `-1`.) The `getSelectedItem ()` method returns a `String` object containing the textual contents of the selected item. (If there are no items in the `List` object, this method returns `null`.)

By default, the user can only select a single item at a time. However, the developer can make it possible for the user to select multiple items. This is accomplished by calling `List`'s `setMultipleMode (boolean)` instance method with a `true` argument. If the developer needs to know the current selection mechanism used by a list, the `isMultipleMode ()` instance method can be called to return the current state of the list—`false` means single selection only.

Assuming that the user can select more than one item from the list, it is possible to identify these items by calling `List`'s `getSelectedIndexes ()` and `getSelectedItems ()` instance methods. The `getSelectedIndexes ()` method returns an array of ints that hold the zero-based indexes of the selected items. (If there are no items in the `List` object, this method returns `null`.) The `getSelectedItems ()` method returns an array of `String` objects that contain the textual contents of the selected items. (If there are no items in the `List` object, this method returns `null`.)

Figure 15.8 illustrates a list (based on the previous code fragment).

Figure 15.8: *A list.*

Scrollbar

Scrollbars are used to scroll through lists and multiple lines of text where not all lines are visible. However, scrollbars also can be used for a different purpose: to select a numeric value from a range of numeric values.

A scrollbar consists of two buttons (labeled with arrows) that delimit the edges of a scrollable region and a slider that identifies the current position within this region. Either button can be pressed to move the slider in the direction of the pressed button.

When the slider is positioned next to one of the buttons, the slider represents the minimum position (the smallest numeric value in a range of numeric values). When positioned next to the other button, the slider represents the maximum position (the largest value in the numeric range).

Scrollbars exist in two varieties: horizontal and vertical. The choice of scrollbar to use depends upon the requirements of a given program.

Figure 15.9 illustrates a horizontal scrollbar and a vertical scrollbar.

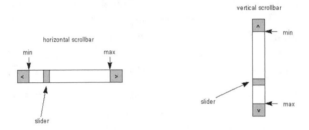

Figure 15.9: *Horizontal and vertical scrollbars.*

The AWT's Scrollbar class, located in the java.awt package, is used to create Scrollbar objects that represent scrollbars.

The Scrollbar class declares two read-only class fields called HORIZONTAL and VERTICAL. These class fields identify the orientation of a scrollbar.

The Scrollbar class declares several constructors for initializing Scrollbar objects.

The Scrollbar (int, int, int, int, int) constructor initializes a Scrollbar object. The first int argument identifies the orientation of a scrollbar. Either Scrollbar.HORIZONTAL or Scrollbar.VERTICAL should be passed. The second int argument identifies the position of the slider. This value should be somewhere between the values specified by the final two arguments. The third int argument identifies the width of the slider. This width typically indicates the amount of material that is visible on the screen. The fourth int argument identifies the minimum value of the scrollbar's numeric range, and the fifth int argument identifies the scrollbar's maximum value (of the same numeric range).

The following code fragment creates a vertical scrollbar that has a numeric range of 0 through 100. The initial position of the slider is 1 and its width is 2:

```
Scrollbar sb = new Scrollbar (Scrollbar.VERTICAL,
                    1, 2, 0, 100);
```

The Scrollbar class provides a variety of useful methods for getting and setting a scrollbar's orientation, size of the slider, slider position, minimum and maximum range settings, and lots more. For example, the following code fragment creates a scrollbar and retrieves information about this scrollbar. After it has been retrieved, the information is displayed:

```
Scrollbar sb = new Scrollbar (Scrollbar.HORIZONTAL, 0, 1, 0,
                    50);

// Get orientation: Scrollbar.HORIZONTAL, Scrollbar.VERTICAL
System.out.println (sb.getOrientation ());

// Get slider width
System.out.println (sb.getVisible ());

// Get numeric range minimum value
System.out.println (sb.getMinimum ());

// Get numeric range maximum value
System.out.println (sb.getMaximum ());

// Get current slider position
System.out.println (sb.getValue ());
```

TextComponent

Programs often require users to enter one or more lines of text via text components. Because there is much commonality in entering one or more lines of text, the AWT factors out this commonality into the TextComponent class.

The TextComponent class contains a setText (String) instance method to set the visible text of a text component to the contents of the String object argument and a getText () instance method to return the currently visible text.

Furthermore, TextComponent makes it possible to select and retrieve portions of text. This is accomplished by enabling the user to press the mouse button at a starting point (within visible text) and drag the mouse cursor across the text. All selected text is displayed in reverse video. Various instance methods, such as getSelectionStart (), getSelectionEnd (), getSelectedText (), setSelectionStart (int), setSelectionEnd (int), and selectAll (), are used to accomplish this task.

Many other useful methods are declared in TextComponent.

TextComponent contains a private constructor. As a result, it is not possible to create TextComponent objects. Instead, the developer must make use of the derived TextField and TextArea classes to create TextField objects (for entering a single line of text) and TextArea objects (for entering multiple lines of text), respectively.

TextField

The AWT's TextField class, located in the java.awt package, is used to create TextField objects that represent text fields.

The TextField class declares several constructors for initializing TextField objects: TextField (), TextField (int), TextField (String), and TextField (String, int).

The TextField () constructor initializes a TextField object with no initially visible text and requests that exactly one character of text be displayed (based on the current font). The following code fragment creates and initializes a TextField object with no initially visible text and a text field width of one character:

```
TextField tf = new TextField ();
```

The TextField (int) constructor initializes a TextField object with no initially visible text and requests that a minimum number of characters (specified by the int argument) be displayed (based on the current font).

For example, the following code fragment creates and initializes a TextField object with no initially visible text and a text field width of at least 20 characters:

```
TextField tf = new TextField (20);
```

The TextField (String) constructor initializes a TextField object with the text specified by the String object argument. An attempt will be made to display all this text. The following code fragment creates and initializes a TextField object with Some text. Every attempt is made to see that all this text is visible:

```
TextField tf = new TextField ("Some text");
```

The TextField (String, int) constructor initializes a TextField object with the text specified by the String object argument and requests that a minimum number of characters (specified by the int argument) be displayed (based on the current font).

For example, the following code fragment creates and initializes a TextField object with Some text and a text field width of at least 20 characters. Every attempt is made to see that at least 20 characters of text are visible:

```
TextField tf = new TextField ("Some text", 20);
```

If you want to dynamically change this text, you can call the inherited setText (String) instance method to change the text to the characters found in the String object argument. For example, the following code fragment creates and initializes a TextField object. It then calls setText (String) to give this text field some text:

```
TextField phone = new TextField ("Current text");
tf.setText ("Replacement text");
```

You can retrieve the current text as a String object by calling the inherited getText () instance method. The following code fragment creates and initializes a TextField object. The getText () instance method is called to retrieve its text and print it, via a call to System.out.println (String):

```
TextField name = new TextField ("John Doe");
System.out.println (name.getText ());
```

TextField provides many other useful methods for interacting with text field components.

Figure 15.10 illustrates a text field.

Figure 15.10: *A text field.*

TextArea

The AWT's TextArea class, located in the java.awt package, is used to create TextArea objects that represent text areas.

The TextArea class declares several constructors for initializing TextArea objects. The most useful constructors include TextArea (int, int) and TextArea (String, int, int).

The TextArea (int, int) constructor initializes a TextArea object that consists of a number of rows (specified by the first int argument) and a number of columns (specified by the second int argument). For example, the following code fragment creates and initializes a TextArea object with no visible text, 10 rows, and 5 columns:

```
TextArea ta = new TextArea (10, 5);
```

The TextArea (String, int, int) constructor initializes a TextArea object with the text specified by the String object argument. Furthermore, the number of rows is specified by the first int argument and the number of columns by the second int argument.

The following code fragment creates and initializes a TextArea object with Some text, 3 rows, and 20 columns:

```
TextArea ta = new TextArea ("Some text", 3, 20);
```

If you do not provide text or want to dynamically change this text, you can call the inherited setText (String) instance method to change the text to the characters found in the String object argument. For example, the following code fragment creates and initializes a TextArea object with no text. It then calls setText (String) to give this text field some text:

```
TextArea notes = new TextArea (10, 55);
notes.setText ("Please enter some notes.");
```

You can retrieve the current text as a String object by calling the inherited getText () instance method.

The following code fragment creates and initializes a TextArea object. The getText () instance method is called to retrieve its text and print it, via a call to System.out.println (String):

```
TextField notes = new TextField ("Enter notes", 5, 4);
System.out.println (notes.getText ());
```

TextArea declares a variety of methods for inserting, appending, and replacing text. These methods are discussed in the JDK documentation.

Figure 15.11 illustrates a text area.

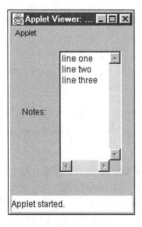

Figure 15.11: A text area.

Working with Containers

After a component object is created, you must add this object to a container object. If you don't do this, the component object's peer will never be created and displayed.

Containers are components that organize other components. They can even organize other containers. This nesting capability makes it possible to create very sophisticated GUIs.

Containers work in partnership with layout managers. Every container object has its own layout manager object. It is this layout manager object that determines how component peers are laid out on the screen.

The Container Class

The AWT provides an abstract Container class that factors out the commonality of all containers. (Because Container is abstract, you cannot create objects from this class.) Container is located in the java.awt package.

Container declares a variety of methods for adding component objects to a container object. For example, the commonly used add (Component) method is declared within this class. Additionally, Container inherits all of Component's methods. As a result, a container object is also a component object.

Figure 15.12 provides a class hierarchy of the AWT's container classes.

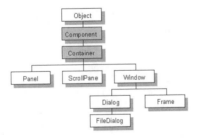

Figure 15.12: *The AWT's container class hierarchy.*

Panel

The AWT provides a Panel class that describes the simplest kind of container. Panel is located in the java.awt package.

The Panel class declares a Panel () constructor that is used to initialize a Panel object. The following code fragment creates a Panel object:

```
Panel p = new Panel ();
```

After a `Panel` object has been created, you can call `Panel`'s inherited add (Component) instance method to add a component to the `Panel` object. The following code fragment adds a `Button` object to `Panel` object p:

```
p.add (new Button ("Ok"));
```

Because the `Applet` class is derived from `Panel`, the drawable area of an applet is really a panel. Therefore, it is possible to mix graphics with components on the same panel.

EXAMPLE

The following `panelDemo1` applet demonstrates drawing on a panel and placing a `Button` component on the same panel by calling the inherited add (Component) method:

```
// panelDemo1.java

import java.awt.*;
import java.applet.Applet;

public class panelDemo1 extends Applet
{
   public void init ()
   {
      Button b = new Button ("Ok");
      add (b);
   }

   public void paint (Graphics g)
   {
      int width = getSize ().width;
      int height = getSize ().height;

      g.setColor (Color.red);
      g.drawLine (0, 0, width - 1, height - 1);
      g.drawLine (0, height - 1, width - 1, 0);
   }
}
```

The following HTML is required to run the `panelDemo1` applet:

```
<applet code="panelDemo1.class" width=170 height=100>
</applet>
```

Figure 15.13 shows `panelDemo1`'s output.

When multiple components are added to a panel, the panel's default layout manager flows these components across the panel in a left-to-right manner.

EXAMPLE

The following `panelDemo2` applet demonstrates flowing multiple buttons across a panel:

```
// panelDemo2.java
```

```
import java.awt.*;
import java.applet.Applet;

public class panelDemo2 extends Applet
{
    public void init ()
    {
        add (new Button ("1"));
        add (new Button ("2"));
        add (new Button ("3"));
        add (new Button ("4"));
        add (new Button ("5"));
        add (new Button ("6"));
        add (new Button ("7"));
        add (new Button ("8"));
        add (new Button ("9"));    }
}
```

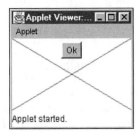

Figure 15.13: *The output from* `panelDemo1`.

The following HTML is required to run the `panelDemo2` applet:

```
<applet code="panelDemo2.class" width=250 height=65>
</applet>
```

Figure 15.14 shows panelDemo2's output.

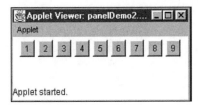

Figure 15.14: *The output from* `panelDemo2`.

Notice that all nine buttons appear on the same row in a left-to-right fashion. Try shrinking the horizontal size of the applet. You should see some of the buttons being displayed on a row beneath the other buttons. This is an example of Panel's layout manager doing its job.

ScrollPane

The AWT provides a ScrollPane class that describes a scrollable container for holding a single component. More components can be added to the scroll pane by placing the component objects into a Panel object and inserting this Panel object into a ScrollPane object. ScrollPane is located in the java.awt package.

The ScrollPane class declares a ScrollPane (int) constructor that is used to initialize a ScrollPane object. The int argument describes the policy that a ScrollPane object uses for displaying scrollbars. If ScrollPane.SCROLLBARS_ALWAYS is passed, both a horizontal and a vertical scrollbar are always displayed (even if scrolling is not required). If ScrollPane.SCROLLBARS_AS_NEEDED is passed, scrollbars are displayed only if the size of the component exceeds the scroll pane's displayable area. If ScrollPane.SCROLLBARS_NEVER is passed, scrollbars are never displayed. The following code fragment creates a ScrollPane object:

```
ScrollPane sp = new ScrollPane
                  (ScrollPane.SCROLLBARS_AS_NEEDED);
```

After a ScrollPane object has been created, you can call ScrollPane's inherited add (Component) instance method to add a component to the ScrollPane object. The following code fragment demonstrates creating a Panel object to hold multiple Button objects and adding this Button object to a newly created ScrollPane object:

```
ScrollPane sp = new ScrollPane
                  (ScrollPane.SCROLLBARS_AS_NEEDED);

Panel p = new Panel ();
for (int i = 0; i < 10; i++)
    p.add (new Button ("Ok" + i));

sp.add (p);
```

EXAMPLE

The following spDemo applet demonstrates creating a ScrollPane object to hold a Panel object containing multiple Button objects:

```
// spDemo.java

import java.awt.*;
import java.applet.Applet;

public class spDemo extends Applet
{
    ScrollPane sp = new ScrollPane (ScrollPane.SCROLLBARS_AS_NEEDED);
```

```
public void init ()
{
   Panel p = new Panel ();

   for (int i = 0; i < 5; i++)
        p.add (new Button ("Button " + i));

   sp.add (p);
   add (sp);

   setBackground (Color.lightGray);
   sp.setBackground (Color.white);
}
}
```

The following HTML is required to run the spDemo applet:

```
<applet code="spDemo.class" width=200 height=200>
</applet>
```

Figure 15.15 shows spDemo's output.

Figure 15.15: *The output from* spDemo.

Usually, you'll create a Canvas subclass object containing an image and insert this subclass object into a ScrollPane object so that you can scroll through this image—especially for large images.

Frame

The Frame class creates Frame objects that represent windows with borders, titles, and Resize, Maximize, Minimize, and Close button gadgets; and optional menu bars. Frame is located in the java.awt package.

The Frame (String) constructor initializes a Frame object with a title specified by the String object argument. This title appears in the title area of
the frame window peer.

Frame is used only by applications. Applets cannot take advantage of this class.

To create an application that contains a frame window, you would extend
the Frame class and add your components to this container.

EXAMPLE

The following frameDemo application demonstrates creating a GUI for an
application, by extending the Frame class:

```
// frameDemo.java

import java.awt.*;

class frameDemo extends Frame
{
   frameDemo (String title)
   {
      super (title);

      Panel p = new Panel ();
      p.add (new Button ("Ok"));
      p.add (new Button ("Cancel"));

      add (p);

      setSize (200, 100);
      setVisible (true);
   }

   public static void main (String [] args)
   {
      new frameDemo ("Frame Demo");
   }
}
```

The frameDemo (String) constructor passes its String object argument to
the Frame (String) constructor via the super (title) call. After this is
done, a Panel object is created to hold a Button object labeled Ok and a
Button object labeled Cancel. After these objects have been added to the
Panel object, the size of the frame is specified by calling the inherited
setSize (int, int) method. The first int argument specifies the horizontal width in pixels and the second int argument specifies the vertical
height in pixels. Finally, the inherited setVisible (boolean) method is
called with a true argument to make the frame window peer visible.

Figure 15.16 shows frameDemo's output.

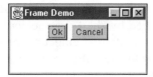

Figure 15.16: *The output from* `frameDemo`.

Dialog

The `Dialog` class creates `Dialog` objects that represent dialog boxes. `Dialog` is located in the `java.awt` package.

Dialog boxes are useful for entering or editing data. These windows usually contain a button labeled `OK` that is clicked to save changes and a button labeled `Cancel` that is clicked to discard changes.

Dialog boxes exist in two flavors: *modal* and *modeless*. When a modal dialog box is displayed, the user must terminate the dialog box before she or he can interact with the rest of the GUI. An example of a modal dialog box is a dialog box for entering new employee information. When a modeless dialog box is displayed, the user can interact with the rest of the GUI before terminating the dialog box. An example of a modeless dialog box is a dialog box for searching through text for a specific phrase.

Dialog boxes are not standalone windows. They exist within the context of a frame window. For example, an application has a `File` menu with an `Open` menu item. When the user selects `Open`, a dialog box is displayed with a list of files from which the user can choose. Because dialog boxes depend on frame windows, all `Dialog` constructors take a reference to a `Frame` object as the first argument.

The `Dialog (Frame)` constructor initializes a `Dialog` object that belongs to the frame window identified by the `Frame` object argument. The resulting dialog box has no title. It is not modal and can be resized. For example, the following code fragment creates a `Dialog` object that belongs to `Frame` object `f`. This dialog box is modeless:

```
Dialog d = new Dialog (f);
```

The `Dialog (Frame, boolean)` constructor initializes a `Dialog` object that belongs to the frame window identified by the `Frame` object argument. This dialog box has no title. The `boolean` argument specifies the dialog box's modality: `true` means modal and `false` means modeless. The dialog box can be resized. For example, the following code fragment creates a `Dialog` object that belongs to `Frame` object `f`. This dialog box is modeless:

```
Dialog d = new Dialog (f, false);
```

The Dialog (Frame, String) constructor initializes a Dialog object that belongs to the frame window identified by the Frame object argument. This dialog box has the title specified by the String object argument. It is not modal and can be resized. For example, the following code fragment creates a Dialog object that belongs to Frame object f. The title of this dialog box is Title. This dialog box is modeless:

```
Dialog d = new Dialog (f, "Title");
```

Finally, the Dialog (Frame, String, boolean) constructor initializes a Dialog object that belongs to the frame window identified by the Frame object argument. This dialog box has the title specified by the String object argument. Its modality is specified by the boolean argument: true means modal and false means modeless. The dialog box can be resized. For example, the following code fragment creates a Dialog object that belongs to Frame object f. Its title is Insert and it is modal.

```
Dialog d = new Dialog (f, "Insert", true);
```

You can control resizing by calling Dialog's setResizable (boolean) instance method. Passing a true argument value results in a resizable dialog box. Passing a false argument value results in a dialog box that cannot be resized. For example, the following code fragment changes the dialog box in the previous code fragment from resizable to not resizable:

```
d.setResizable (false);
```

The following dialogDemo application demonstrates creating a non-resizable dialog box:

```java
// dialogDemo.java

import java.awt.*;

class dialogDemo
{
   public static void main (String [] args)
   {
      Frame f = new Frame ();

      yesNo yn = new yesNo (f, "Is the sky blue?");
   }
}

class yesNo extends Dialog
{
   yesNo (Frame f, String title)
   {
      super (f, title);

      Panel p = new Panel ();
```

```
      p.add (new Button ("Yes"));
      p.add (new Button ("No"));
      add (p);

      setSize (200, 100);
      setResizable (false);
      setVisible (true);
   }
}
```

Laying Out Components

Containers use *layouts* (also known as *layout managers*) to position and size components on the screen in a platform-independent fashion. Without layouts, developers would be forced to specify exact sizes and positions for all components that are to be displayed. The resulting GUI might look fine on one platform. However, the GUI would probably look like a mess on another platform. (Different platforms might choose different component sizes and screen resolutions.)

Layouts are objects created from classes that implement the LayoutManager interface. This interface declares methods that lay out components onto the screen. Two of the more commonly used layouts are BorderLayout and FlowLayout. These layouts will be discussed in this chapter—although other layouts are used by some of the program examples. Please refer to the JDK documentation for information on these other layouts.

BorderLayout

The BorderLayout class creates BorderLayout objects that divide a container into five areas: North, South, East, West, and Center. Each area can hold exactly one component. BorderLayout is the default layout manager used by the Frame and Dialog classes.

You can explicitly provide a BorderLayout layout manager by calling a container object's setLayout (LayoutManager) instance method. For example, you can change Panel's default layout manager to BorderLayout, as follows:

```
Panel p = new Panel ();
p.setLayout (new BorderLayout ());
```

When you want to add a component to a container that uses a BorderLayout layout manager, you can call the container's add (String, Component) instance method. The first argument is one of "North", "South", "East", "West", or "Center". The second argument is a reference to a component object. (This method does not work properly if the container's current layout manager is not BorderLayout.) For example, the following code fragment adds a new button component to the North area of the previously created panel:

```
p.add ("North", new Button ("Ok"));
```

The following blDemo applet demonstrates changing a Panel object's default layout manager to a BorderLayout object and adding Button objects to the container's North, West, Center, East, and South areas:

EXAMPLE

```
// blDemo.java

import java.awt.*;
import java.applet.Applet;

public class blDemo extends Applet
{
   public void init ()
   {
      setLayout (new BorderLayout ());

      add ("North", new Button ("North"));
      add ("West", new Button ("West"));
      add ("Center", new Button ("Center"));
      add ("East", new Button ("East"));
      add ("South", new Button ("South"));
   }
}
```

The following HTML is required to run the blDemo applet:

```
<applet code="blDemo.class" width=175 height=100>
</applet>
```

Figure 15.17 shows blDemo's output.

Figure 15.17: *The output from* blDemo*.*

FlowLayout

The FlowLayout class creates FlowLayout objects that divide containers into sequences of rows. Components are organized along each row in a left-to-right fashion. If a row has no more room to hold another component, the component is added in the left-most position on the row that follows. FlowLayout is the default layout manager used by the Panel class.

The default layout manager can be changed to a FlowLayout layout manager by using the following code:

```
setLayout (new FlowLayout ());
```

The following flDemo applet demonstrates flowing three components across a container via flDemo's default FlowLayout layout manager:

```
// flDemo.java

import java.awt.*;
import java.applet.Applet;

public class flDemo extends Applet
{
   public void init ()
   {
      add (new Label ("label"));

      add (new Button ("button"));

      add (new TextField (20));

      setBackground (Color.lightGray);
   }
}
```

The following HTML is required to run the flDemo applet:

```
<applet code="flDemo.class" width=280 height=100>
</applet>
```

Figure 15.18 shows flDemo's output.

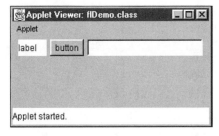

Figure 15.18: *The output from* flDemo.

Combining Layouts

It is not always possible to create the kind of GUI that you want by using a single layout manager. Sometimes, you need to combine multiple layout managers to achieve an appropriate effect. Experimentation with combinations of layout managers is the key to learning what works and what does not work.

EXAMPLE

The following calc applet demonstrates a combination of the BorderLayout layout manager and the GridLayout layout manager to achieve a calculator GUI:

```java
// calc.java

import java.awt.*;
import java.applet.Applet;

public class calc extends Applet
{
   public void init ()
   {
      setLayout (new BorderLayout ());

      add ("North", new Label ("0", Label.RIGHT));

      Panel p = new Panel ();
      p.setLayout (new GridLayout (4, 4));

      p.add (new Button ("7"));
      p.add (new Button ("8"));
      p.add (new Button ("9"));
      p.add (new Button ("/"));
      p.add (new Button ("4"));
      p.add (new Button ("5"));
      p.add (new Button ("6"));
      p.add (new Button ("x"));
      p.add (new Button ("1"));
      p.add (new Button ("2"));
      p.add (new Button ("3"));
      p.add (new Button ("-"));
      p.add (new Button ("0"));
      p.add (new Button ("."));
      p.add (new Button ("C"));
      p.add (new Button ("+"));

      add ("Center", p);
   }
}
```

The following HTML is required to run the `calc` applet:

```
<applet code="calc.class" width=175 height=140>
</applet>
```

Figure 15.19 shows `calc`'s output.

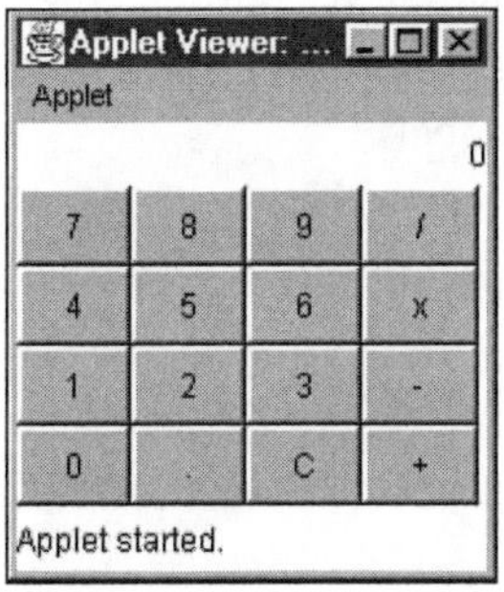

Figure 15.19: *The output from* `calc`.

Handling Events

Events (notifications) occur when users press buttons, scroll through lists of textual items, make selections from menus, move the mouse, and even press keys.

When an event occurs, the component object associated with the component peer to which the event is targeted must be notified, so that it can take whatever action is required to handle the event.

Java provides two event notification models from which a Java program's components can choose: the hierarchical model and the delegation model.

The Hierarchical Model

The *hierarchical model* is a "hard-wired" event notification model, in which an event is passed to every component that has the potential to handle the event. For example, a button click event would automatically be sent to a button component so that this component could handle the event.

Under the hierarchical model, events are represented by instances of the `Event` class.

The hierarchical model is the older of the two models. It has been around since the very first version of Java. This model has been shown to be inflexible and inefficient. As a result, the delegation model was introduced. Developers are encouraged to use the delegation model. Because the hierarchical model will undoubtedly be phased out, it will not be discussed any further.

The Delegation Model

The *delegation model* was introduced in Java 1.1. Under this model, an object that wants to be notified when a component object receives event information from its component peer, via the AWT, must register itself with the component object. The object that registers itself with the component object is known as a *listener object* because it "listens" for events from the component object. Figure 15.20 illustrates the process of sending an event from a component peer to a listener object.

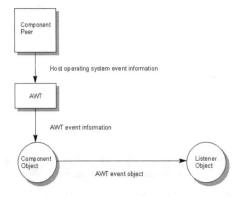

Figure 15.20: *Sending an event to a listener object.*

An object becomes a listener to a component object's events by doing two things. First, it must be created from a class that implements a listener interface. Second, it must call a special component object method to add its reference to the component object's list of listeners.

EXAMPLE

The following `listener1` applet demonstrates implementing a listener interface and registering a listener object with a component object:

```
// listener1.java

import java.awt.*;
import java.awt.event.*;
import java.applet.Applet;

public class listener1 extends Applet implements ActionListener
{
    public void init ()
    {
        // Create button component object.

        Button b = new Button ("Ok");

        // Register listener object as a listener
```

```
        // for action events.

        b.addActionListener (this);

        // Add button component object to listener
        // object container.  The button component
        // peer is created at this time.

        add (b);
    }

    public void actionPerformed (ActionEvent e)
    {
        System.out.println ("Button pressed");
    }
}
```

When the user clicks the Button peer, the host operating system sends an event notification to the AWT. The AWT forwards this information (in a repackaged format) to the Button object that corresponds to this peer. The Button object creates an ActionEvent object with appropriate data and sends this object to every registered listener by calling the actionPerformed (ActionEvent) method for every listener object whose reference is stored in a data structure internal to the Button object.

This scheme works because of Button's addActionListener (ActionListener) instance method. When this method is called, the object passed to this method must implement ActionListener. If it does not, a compiler error occurs. (To implement any interface, all method headers declared in that interface must be re-declared in the class implementing the interface, and this means that code bodies for the interface methods must be provided in that class.)

The ActionListener interface declares an actionPerformed (ActionEvent) method. This is the only method declared in this interface. However, some listener interfaces declare multiple methods. Each method must be implemented or a compiler error will occur.

Sometimes, it is only desirable to implement one or two listener interface methods. In these situations, you can take advantage of an adapter class that implements the listener interface. The adapter class provides a default do-nothing implementation for every method in a particular listener interface. By extending the adapter class with a subclass and overriding only those methods that you are interested in, you can save yourself some typing. Also, you can take advantage of anonymous inner classes to save yourself some more typing. However, anonymous inner classes can be tricky and should be used very carefully. (Some of the GUI examples in this book take advantage of anonymous inner classes for creating a listener object that is registered with a component object.)

EXAMPLE

The following `listener2` application demonstrates creating an object from an anonymous inner class that extends the `WindowAdapter` class. It also demonstrates overriding `WindowAdapter`'s `windowClosing (WindowEvent)` method to exit the application when the user clicks the window's Close box:

```
// listener2.java

import java.awt.*;
import java.awt.event.*;

class listener2 extends Frame
{
   listener2 ()
   {
      addWindowListener (new WindowAdapter ()
                     {
                         public void windowClosing (WindowEvent e)
                         {
                            System.exit (0);
                         }
                     });

      setSize (200, 200);
      setVisible (true);
   }

   public static void main (String [] args)
   {
      new listener2 ();
   }
}
```

If `WindowAdapter` were not used, `listener2` would have to implement the `WindowListener` interface and provide implementations for all the methods declared within this interface.

Under the hierarchical model, events were objects created from the `Event` class. Under the delegation model, events are objects created from subclasses of `AWTEvent`.

Figure 15.21 provides a class hierarchy of the AWT's delegation model event classes. The `AWTEvent` and `InputEvent` classes are shown in gray because they are abstract classes.

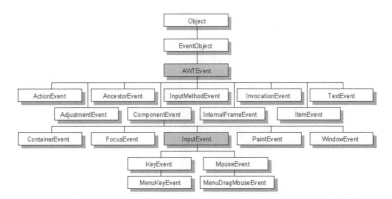

Figure 15.21: *The AWT's delegation model event class hierarchy.*

Under the delegation model, there is a naming convention that is used to keep track of event class names, listener interface names, and the various add*event*Listener methods declared as part of component classes.

An event class begins the name of the event followed by the word Event (for example, ActionEvent). An object from this class is passed to an event handling method. A listener interface begins with the name of the event followed by the word Listener (for example, ActionListener). A class must implement a listener interface before it can include the corresponding add*event*Listener method. An add*event*Listener method begins with the word add followed by the name of the event followed by the word Listener (for example, addActionListener). Keep this in mind when working with event handling. You'll find this naming convention makes it easier to remember different aspects of event handling.

What's Next?

In Chapter 14, "AWT, Part 1," Java's multithreading capabilities were used to animate the FIREWORKS applet. The topic of multithreading will be explored in the next chapter, where you'll learn how to use multiple threads to improve the performance of your Java programs.

Multithreading

The FIREWORKS example, in Chapter 14, "AWT, Part 1," provided a brief look at threads. Although threads were not discussed in detail, the use of a thread made it possible to animate some fireworks.

What are threads and how are they used? What problems can arise when working with threads? These and other questions are answered in this chapter.

Chapter 16 presents the following topics:

- Threads
- Runnables
- Synchronization
- PHILOS

Threads

What comes to mind when you encounter the word thread? Do you think of the phrase "a needle pulling thread" from the *Sound of Music*? Or do you think of a microprocessor interpreting a sequence of instructions? Just as threads are important to fabric, they are also important to computer programs.

Threads are very useful because they serve to improve a program's performance. This idea could be extrapolated into the real world where a human body exists with a heart beating thread, operating independently of the respiration thread, operating independently of the brain thinking thread, and so on.

The capability to run multiple threads, either at the same time (if each thread is given its own processor) or almost at the same time (if all threads share a single processor), is known as *multithreading*.

Every thread has a certain degree of importance, which is relative to the importance of other threads. This importance is known as *priority*. For example, a nuclear power plant is monitored by a software program running on a computer. This program consists of two threads: one thread monitors the temperature of the nuclear core and the other thread monitors a soft drink dispenser. The thread that monitors the nuclear core is a very important thread. If it doesn't do its job, the temperature of the core could become so great that a core meltdown—leading to a nuclear disaster—would occur. Therefore, the thread monitoring the nuclear core should have a greater priority than the thread monitoring the soft drink dispenser. In other words, the thread monitoring the nuclear core should run more often than the thread monitoring the soft drink dispenser.

The Java language provides multithreading capabilities at the language level by using reserved words, classes, and interfaces. However, these capabilities are built on top of already existing multithreading capabilities that are part of the host operating system. Java wraps itself around the host operating system's multithreading capabilities to simplify and provide a consistent multithreading interface to Java programs—an interface that hides the details of what goes on in the host operating system.

The host operating system—not Java—manages threads. For each thread, a special data structure (known under Windows 95, 98, and NT as a *thread information block*) is created. This data structure contains pertinent information about a thread, such as a unique name (to differentiate one thread from another thread) and the contents of the processor registers. These data structures are inserted into a queue data structure so that the host operating system can keep track of which thread is currently running, which thread is the next thread to run, which thread is the next thread after that thread to run, and so on. Figure 16.1 displays a queue of threads.

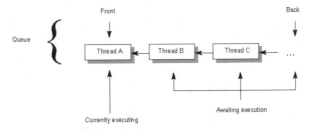

Figure 16.1: *A queue of threads.*

In Figure 16.1, Thread A, whose data structure is at the front of the queue, is currently executing. After it finishes, its data structure will be moved to the back of the queue and Thread B will be given its turn. This will continue with Thread C, and so on, until all threads have executed.

When a thread is running, it is said to be in the running state. When a thread is ready to run (such as Thread B in Figure 16.1), it is in the ready state. When a thread finishes running, it is said to be in the dead state.

A running thread of a certain priority can be interrupted by a thread with a higher priority. When this happens, the lower-priority thread is booted off the processor by the higher-priority thread and the higher-priority thread does its thing. Continuing from the previous nuclear power plant example, suppose that the soft drink dispenser thread is running. This thread cannot be allowed to run for too much time because the nuclear core thread must keep monitoring the temperature of the nuclear core. Therefore, the host operating system keeps interrupting the soft drink dispenser thread so that the nuclear core thread can run.

The host operating system manages several queues of threads. Each queue contains thread data structures for those threads of a certain priority. All threads in the highest-priority queue are given a chance to complete execution before those threads in the next-highest-priority queue can execute.

Wait a minute! In our nuclear power plant example, the nuclear core thread, with a higher priority than the soft drink dispenser thread, always runs. How will the soft drink dispenser thread ever get a chance to run? The answer is that the nuclear core thread periodically yields control to the soft drink dispenser thread. However, because of priority, the operating system ensures that the soft drink dispenser thread does not run too long.

If a higher-priority thread runs all the time and a lower-priority thread never has a chance to run, the higher-priority thread indefinitely postpones the lower-priority thread. This is known as either *indefinite postponement* or *starvation*.

A problem somewhat related to indefinite postponement occurs when two or more threads are running and each thread "grabs hold" of a resource that another thread needs. Like spoiled children, each thread "refuses" to give its resource to another thread until that other thread first gives up its resource. This situation is known as *deadlock*. Neither thread can proceed because it is "selfish" and won't take the first step to break the deadlock.

Java's reliance on how the host operating system implements multithreading can lead to multithreading differences between Java platforms.

For example, older Solaris Java platforms ran a thread of a given priority until the thread either completed or a thread with a higher priority preempted the currently running thread. In contrast, Windows 95, 98, or NT threads of the same priority each run for an identical amount of time, known as a *quantum*. (Unlike older versions of Solaris, Windows threads do not run until they complete.) After this quantum expires, the currently executing thread is interrupted and forced to wait while every other thread of the same priority is given its chance to execute. After all these threads have had their chance to execute, the original thread can continue executing. This execution of threads in a round-robin fashion is known as *time slicing*.

Like Solaris, Windows threads can have priorities. Also, like Solaris, threads of higher priorities can pre-empt threads of lower priorities.

The Thread Class

The Thread class is used to create Thread objects, which are associated with host operating system threads. (One Thread object is associated with one and only one thread.) This class is located in the java.lang package.

When a Thread object is created, a message is sent to the host operating system to create an actual thread. This thread is placed in a ready state. In other words, it does not start immediately after being created. An association is formed between the Thread object and the thread. This makes it possible for various Thread methods to cause messages to be sent to the host operating system to control the thread.

Thread declares several constructors for initializing Thread objects. The simplest of these constructors is Thread ().

The Thread () constructor initializes a Thread object and gives it a default name.

The following code fragment creates a Thread object and initializes it with a default name by way of the Thread () constructor:

```
Thread t = new Thread ();
```

You can supply your own name by taking advantage of the Thread (String) constructor. The String argument provides this name.

The following code fragment creates a `Thread` object and initializes it by way of the `Thread (String)` constructor. This object is christened My Thread:

```
Thread t = new Thread ("My Thread");
```

The other constructors are used with runnables. You'll get a chance to examine runnables together with the pertinent `Thread` constructors later in this chapter.

After a `Thread` object is created, an internal thread is also created and placed in a ready state. This thread will not start to run until the `Thread` object's `start ()` method is called.

THE `start ()` METHOD

The `Thread` class declares a `start ()` instance method that starts the thread associated with the calling `Thread` object. This method does not return anything (its return data type is `void`).

The following code fragment creates a `Thread` object called `Duke's thread` and starts the associated thread:

```
Thread t = new Thread ("Duke's thread");
t.start ();
```

THE `run ()` METHOD

The `Thread` class declares a `run ()` instance method that gets called as a result of the `start ()` method being called. The `run ()` method contains the code that gets executed by a thread.

It is important to stress that your code never calls the `run ()` method. This method is called by the JVM.

The default version of `run ()`, declared in the `Thread` class, does nothing. For this reason, you must derive a class from `Thread` and override the `run ()` method to do something useful.

EXAMPLE

The following `simpleThreadDemo` application shows how easy it is to create a multithreaded application:

```
// simpleThreadDemo.java

class simpleThreadDemo
{
    public static void main (String [] args)
    {
        simpleThread st = new simpleThread ();
        st.start ();
    }
}
```

```
class simpleThread extends Thread
{
   public void run ()
   {
      System.out.println ("I am a thread.");
   }
}
```

I am a thread.

The simpleThreadDemo application declares two classes: The simpleThreadDemo class declares the main method that drives this application and the simpleThread class describes a Thread subclass object. As you can see, simpleThread overrides its inherited run () method. All this method does is print I am a thread..

After creating the simpleThread object st with a default name, the main method starts the associated host-created thread by calling start (). (In reality, the start () method communicates with the JVM and associated runtime code. This results in a message being sent to the host operating system to start the associated thread. This thread is then used by the JVM to interpret another sequence of byte code.)

When the main method is called, a single JVM thread is running. As soon as start () is called, a second thread starts running. The main method (by way of its thread) terminates, but the application does not exit because this other thread is running. After this newly created thread terminates, the application will exit.

THE setName (String) METHOD

The Thread class declares a setName (String) instance method that sets the name of a Thread object to the String object argument.

The following code fragment creates a simpleThread object and then sets its name by calling setName (String):

```
simpleThread st = new simpleThread ();
st.setName ("Simple Thread");
```

THE getName () METHOD

The Thread class also declares a getName () instance method that returns a Thread object's name.

The following code fragment creates a simpleThread object and then gets its default name by calling getName (String). This name is then printed. Under Windows, you might see something like Thread-0:

```
simpleThread st = new simpleThread ();
System.out.println (st.getName ());
```

THE sleep (long) METHOD

The Thread class declares a sleep (long) class method that causes the thread associated with the calling Thread object to sleep for the number of milliseconds that is specified by the long argument. When the thread sleeps, it loses its quantum (under Windows and newer versions of Solaris), enabling another thread to run. Because sleep (long) can throw an InterruptedException object, this method must be placed within a Try statement.

The following code fragment uses sleep (long) to delay execution for 500 milliseconds:

```
try
{
    Thread.sleep (500);
}
catch (InterruptedException e)
{
}
```

THE currentThread () METHOD

The Thread class declares a currentThread () class method that returns a Thread object describing the current thread.

The following code fragment uses currentThread () to obtain the current Thread object:

```
Thread current = Thread.currentThread ();
```

THE setPriority (int) METHOD

The Thread class declares a setPriority (int) instance method that sets the priority of the calling Thread object's associated thread. This priority is specified by the int argument, which must range between Thread.MIN_PRIORITY and Thread.MAX_PRIORITY. If the argument is outside of this range, an IllegalArgumentException object is thrown. (When a Thread [or Thread subclass] object is created, its initial priority is specified as Thread.NORM_PRIORITY.)

The following code fragment creates a Thread object and advances its priority by one:

```
Thread t = new Thread ();

int priority = Thread.NORM_PRIORITY + 1;
if (priority > Thread.MAX_PRIORITY)
    priority = Thread.MAX_PRIORITY;

t.setPriority (priority);
```

THE getPriority () METHOD

The Thread class declares a getPriority () instance method that gets the priority of the calling Thread object's associated thread. This method returns this priority as an int.

The following code fragment returns and prints the priority of a newly created Thread object:

```
Thread t = new Thread ();
System.out.println (t.getPriority ());
```

EXAMPLE

The following threadDemo application illustrates creating a couple of myThread objects (derived from Thread), starting their corresponding threads, and calling various methods declared in the Thread class:

```
// threadDemo.java

class threadDemo
{
   public static void main (String [] args)
   {
      MyThread mt1, mt2;

      mt1 = new MyThread ("Fred");
      mt2 = new MyThread ("Charlie");

      mt1.start ();
      mt2.start ();
   }
}

class MyThread extends Thread
{
   private int sleepInterval;

   public MyThread (String name)
   {
      super (name);

      sleepInterval = (int) (Math.random () * 3500);

      System.out.println ("Thread " + getName () + " will sleep for " +
                          sleepInterval + " milliseconds.");
   }

   public void run ()
   {
      System.out.println (Thread.currentThread ());
```

```
        try
        {
            Thread.sleep (sleepInterval);
        }
        catch (InterruptedException e)
        {
            System.err.println (e);
        }

        System.out.println (getName ());
    }
}
```

OUTPUT

```
Thread Fred will sleep for 2284 milliseconds.
Thread Charlie will sleep for 814 milliseconds.
Thread[Fred,5,main]
Thread[Charlie,5,main]
Charlie
Fred
```

The threadDemo class creates two MyThread objects and then calls their start () methods to start their corresponding threads.

The MyThread class extends the Thread class. MyThread declares a myThread (String) constructor, which takes a single String argument. This argument provides a name for the newly created MyThread object.

The myThread (String) constructor passes its String argument to the Thread layer by way of super. This name is managed by the Thread layer and can later be retrieved by calling the inherited getName () method.

After determining how long a thread will sleep, a message that identifies this value (in milliseconds) along with the name of the thread, via getName (), is printed. The constructor then terminates.

After the two MyThread object threads are started, via calls to the start () method, each thread runs code within the run () method. This method calls the currentThread () method to return a Thread object that describes the current thread. The Thread object is passed to the System.out.println (Object) method where its toString () method is called to obtain a String object that provides a human-readable representation of the Thread object. This String object is then output.

The sleep (long) method is called to give each thread a chance to sleep. When the thread sleeps, it gives up its use of the processor. Because sleep (long) can throw an InterruptedException object, this method must be placed in a Try statement.

After a thread has finished sleeping, getName () is called a second time to show which thread finished first.

Runnables

The mechanics of a multithreaded applet are quite different from the mechanics of a multithreaded application. Before you learn how to write a multithreaded applet, take a look at the following multithreaded application:

```
// runnable1.java

public class runnable1 extends Thread
{
   public static void main (String [] args)
   {
      runnable1 r = new runnable1 ();
      r.start ();
   }

   public void run ()
   {
      System.out.println ("I am running.");
   }
}
```

The runnable1 class extends Thread and provides its own main method. The main method thread creates a runnable1 object and calls this object's inherited start () method. After doing this, the main method thread terminates. The run () method then starts running, via a second thread, and displays I am running. before terminating. When this second thread terminates, the entire application exits. Simple! How much harder can a multithreaded applet be to write? Take a look at runnable2:

```
// runnable2.java

import java.awt.*;
import java.applet.Applet;

public class runnable2 extends Applet, Thread
{
   public void init ()
   {
      this.start ();
   }

   public void run ()
   {
      while (true)
         repaint ();
   }
}
```

```
   public void update (Graphics g)
   {
      paint (g);
   }

   public void paint (Graphics g)
   {
      g.setColor (new Color (rnd (256), rnd (256), rnd (256)));
      g.drawString ("Hello", 10, 30);
   }

   int rnd (int n)
   {
      return (int) (Math.random () * n);
   }
}
```

The runnable2 "applet" approximates the runnable1 application. However, it must take certain differences into account. For example, an applet has an init () method instead of a main method.

What is wrong with runnable2? Why won't this source code compile? The problem is that runnable2 is trying to inherit from both Applet and Thread. (Remember, Java does not support multiple inheritance.)

So how can a multithreaded applet be created if the applet class cannot inherit from Thread? The solution is to have the applet class implement the Runnable interface and use an appropriate Thread constructor to bind an object created from the applet class to a newly created Thread object. Objects created from classes that implement Runnable are known as *runnables*.

The Runnable Interface

Java supplies an interface called Runnable that declares a single public void run () method. To turn an applet into a runnable, the applet class implements Runnable by providing a body for the run () method.

The applet can then use its start () and stop () life-cycle methods to control the creation and destruction of a thread that runs the code within this run () method.

The following runnable3 applet shows how the runnable3 Applet subclass implements Runnable, creates a private Thread variable (t), creates a Thread object and starts the associated thread from within the applet's start () method, and destroys the thread by assigning null to t from within the applet's stop () method:

```
// runnable3.java

import java.awt.*;
```

```java
import java.applet.Applet;

public class runnable3 extends Applet implements Runnable
{
   private Thread t;

   public void start ()
   {
      if (t == null)
      {
         Thread t = new Thread (this);
         t.start ();
      }
   }

   public void stop ()
   {
      t = null;
   }

   public void run ()
   {
      while (true)
         repaint ();
   }

   public void update (Graphics g)
   {
      paint (g);
   }

   public void paint (Graphics g)
   {
      g.setColor (new Color (rnd (256), rnd (256), rnd (256)));
      g.drawString ("Hello", 10, 30);
   }

   int rnd (int n)
   {
      return (int) (Math.random () * n);
   }
}
```

Notice something unusual about the statement that creates the Thread object: The reserved word this is being passed to a Thread constructor—Thread (this). What's going on?

If you look through the JDK documentation that describes the Thread class, you will come across a constructor called Thread (Runnable). This constructor is called with a reference to a runnable. This reference is what binds the run () method declared within the runnable's class to the Thread object. Instead of calling its default run () method, the Thread object will call the run () method declared within the runnable. The end result is a multithreaded applet.

Synchronization

When two or more running threads have access to shared data, some really strange things can happen. For example, two threads called X and Y are running. Both threads can set the values of the name and salary instance fields within a shared object called s. X sets name to John and salary to 30000.0, whereas Y sets name to Alice and salary to 45000.0. Then, each thread prints out the values assigned to these fields. You would expect the X thread to print the values John and 30000.0. You would also expect the Y thread to print the values Alice and 45000.0. However, you might see John and 45000.0 printed, or Alice and 30000.0 printed. Don't believe me? Check out the following useShared1 application and its output.

EXAMPLE

The following useShared1 application illustrates two threads overwriting each other's values:

```
// useShared1.java

class shared
{
    public String name;
    public double salary;
}

class useShared1 extends Thread
{
    static shared s;

    public static void main (String [] args)
    {
        s = new shared ();

        useShared1 us1 = new useShared1 ("X");
        useShared1 us2 = new useShared1 ("Y");

        us1.start ();
        us2.start ();
    }
```

```
useShared1 (String name)
{
   super (name);
}

public void run ()
{
   while (true)
   {
      if (getName ().equals ("X"))
      {
         s.name = "John";

         try
         {
            // Sleep randomly from 0 through 99 milliseconds.

            Thread.sleep ((long) (Math.random () * 100));
         }
         catch (InterruptedException e) {}

         s.salary = 30000.0;
      }
      else
      {
         s.name = "Alice";

         try
         {
            // Sleep randomly from 0 through 99 milliseconds.

            Thread.sleep ((long) (Math.random () * 100));
         }
         catch (InterruptedException e) {}

         s.salary = 45000.0;
      }

      System.out.println (getName () + " name = " + s.name);
      System.out.println (getName () + " salary = " + s.salary);
   }
}
```

OUTPUT

```
X name = Alice
X salary = 30000.0
Y name = John
Y salary = 45000.0
```

```
X name = Alice
X salary = 30000.0
X name = John
X salary = 30000.0
Y name = John
Y salary = 45000.0
Y name = Alice
Y salary = 45000.0
```

To conceptualize the useShared1 application, keep in mind that two threads are running and setting the values of a pair of fields via the shared s object. Each thread runs for a quantum and then the other thread gets a chance to run. One thread might have set the value of the name field to Alice or John but not had a chance to set the value of the salary field before its quantum expired. During its absence, the other thread ran and set both the name and salary fields before its quantum expired. Then, the previous thread gets a new quantum and picks up from where it left off. It updates salary (without realizing that name has already been overwritten) and then prints out the values of both fields. As a result, inconsistent data is displayed.

How do we change this program so that each thread has a chance to set both of the shared fields and display the results before the other thread gains access to these fields (as the result of a quantum expiration)? There is a solution—take advantage of Java's synchronization capabilities.

Java's synchronization capabilities are based on a concept of synchronization that was developed by computer scientist C. A. R. Hoare in a 1974 paper that he authored. This concept was called a *monitor*.

When you create a synchronized block of code, this block is associated with an object that the JVM can lock or unlock (a monitor). Only one thread at a time is permitted access to the code within this block. After the monitor is locked, all other threads that want access to this block must wait on the monitor until it is unlocked.

The following syntax is used to create a synchronized block of code:

```
"synchronized" '(' object_identifier ')'
'{'
    // synchronized code
'}'
```

A synchronized block is identified by specifying the synchronized reserved word followed by the name of an object, object_identifier (between parentheses), that serves as a monitor.

When a thread enters this block, the object identified by object_identifier is locked. All other threads that want to access this block are forced to wait until the thread executing within this block exits the block. The first of these waiting threads can then enter the block.

The best way to understand this concept is to see a second iteration of useShared1 that contains a synchronized block—useShared2.

EXAMPLE

The following useShared2 application illustrates two cooperating threads that do not overwrite shared object fields:

```java
// useShared2.java

class shared
{
   public String name;
   public double salary;
}

class useShared2 extends Thread
{
   static shared s;

   public static void main (String [] args)
   {
      s = new shared ();

      useShared2 us1 = new useShared2 ("X");
      useShared2 us2 = new useShared2 ("Y");

      us1.start ();
      us2.start ();
   }

   useShared2 (String name)
   {
      super (name);
   }

   public void run ()
   {
      while (true)
      {
         synchronized (s)
         {
            if (getName ().equals ("X"))
            {
               s.name = "John";

               try
               {
                  // Sleep randomly from 0 through 99 milliseconds.
```

```
                     Thread.sleep ((long) (Math.random () * 100));
                 }
                 catch (InterruptedException e) {}

                 s.salary = 30000.0;
             }
             else
             {
                 s.name = "Alice";

                 try
                 {
                     // Sleep randomly from 0 through 99 milliseconds.

                     Thread.sleep ((long) (Math.random () * 100));
                 }
                 catch (InterruptedException e) {}

                 s.salary = 45000.0;
             }

             System.out.println (getName () + " name = " + s.name);
             System.out.println (getName () + " salary = " + s.salary);
         }
     }
}
```

```
X name = John
X salary = 30000.0
Y name = Alice
Y salary = 45000.0
X name = John
X salary = 30000.0
Y name = Alice
Y salary = 45000.0
X name = John
X salary = 30000.0
Y name = Alice
Y salary = 45000.0
X name = John
X salary = 30000.0
```

The shared object, s, is used with the synchronized reserved word as a monitor. After a thread is within the synchronized block of code that is guarded by this monitor, it is enabled to complete execution within this block before another thread can enter—even if it loses its quantum. (In this case, the other thread would be forced to wait out its quantums until the thread executing within this synchronized block exits.) Does this synchronization succeed? The output "speaks" for itself.

CAUTION

When using an object as a monitor, both threads must share the object. It must not be unique to one thread. For example, if two threads create their own object and the name of this object is used with `synchronized`, the block of code will not be synchronized.

Blocks of code are not the only entities that can be guarded by using monitors. It turns out that entire methods also can be guarded by placing the synchronized reserved word to the left of a method's return data type. In this case, an entire object created from the class that contains a synchronized method becomes a monitor. You'll have a chance to see this in the next section.

Producers and Consumers

One common example that is used to illustrate the need for synchronization is the producer/consumer example.

A producer produces an item. The consumer consumes this item. The producer is not enabled to produce another item before the first item is consumed. This prevents the producer from producing multiple items before even one of these items has been consumed. The consumer is not enabled to consume more than one item because there is only one item. However, without synchronization, this relationship fails miserably.

EXAMPLE

The following pcDemo1 application illustrates a producer thread and a consumer thread doing their own thing. The producer thread produces items without regard for their consumption. The consumer thread consumes items before they have been produced.

```
// pcDemo1.java

class pcDemo1
{
    public static void main (String [] args)
    {
        shared s = new shared ();

        producer p = new producer (s);
        consumer c = new consumer (s);

        p.start ();
        c.start ();
    }
}
```

```
class shared
{
   private int s = -1;
   private boolean anyMoreData = true;

   public void setShared (int s) { this.s = s; }
   public int getShared () { return s; }
   public boolean anyMoreData () { return anyMoreData; }
   public void setAnyMoreData (boolean b) { anyMoreData = b; }
}

class producer extends Thread
{
   private shared s;

   producer (shared s)
   {
      this.s = s;
   }

   public void run ()
   {
      for (int i = 0; i < 15; i++)
      {
         try
         {
            // Sleep from 0 to 3999 milliseconds.

            Thread.sleep ((int) (Math.random () * 4000));
         }
         catch (InterruptedException e)
         {
            System.err.println (e);
         }

         s.setShared (i);
         System.out.println (i + " produced by producer.");
      }

      s.setAnyMoreData (false);
   }
}

class consumer extends Thread
{
   private shared s;

   consumer (shared s)
   {
```

```
            this.s = s;
        }

        public void run ()
        {
            while (s.anyMoreData ())
            {
                try
                {
                    // Sleep from 0 to 3999 milliseconds.

                    Thread.sleep ((int) (Math.random () * 4000));
                }
                catch (InterruptedException e)
                {
                    System.err.println (e);
                }

                System.out.println (s.getShared () + " consumed by consumer.");
            }
        }
    }
```

OUTPUT

```
-1 consumed by consumer.
0 produced by producer.
1 produced by producer.
2 produced by producer.
2 consumed by consumer.
3 produced by producer.
4 produced by producer.
4 consumed by consumer.
5 produced by producer.
6 produced by producer.
7 produced by producer.
7 consumed by consumer.
8 produced by producer.
8 consumed by consumer.
9 consumed by consumer.
9 produced by producer.
10 produced by producer.
10 consumed by consumer.
```

This is a mess. We need some serious synchronization.

The following pcDemo2 application illustrates a producer thread and a consumer thread "in sync." The producer thread produces an item before this item is consumed and it waits until the consumer thread has consumed this item before producing the next item. Furthermore, the consumer thread does not try to consume an item until it has been produced.

EXAMPLE

```
// pcDemo2.java

class pcDemo2
{
   public static void main (String [] args)
   {
      shared s = new shared ();

      producer p = new producer (s);
      consumer c = new consumer (s);

      p.start ();
      c.start ();
   }
}

class shared
{
   private int s = -1;

   private boolean anyMoreData = true;
   private boolean writeable = true;

   public synchronized void setShared (int s)
   {
      while (!writeable)
         try
         {
            wait ();
         }
         catch (InterruptedException e)
         {
            System.err.println (e);
         }

      this.s = s;
      writeable = false;
      notify ();
   }

   public synchronized int getShared ()
   {
      while (writeable)
         try
         {
            wait ();
         }
         catch (InterruptedException e)
```

```
            {
                System.err.println (e);
            }        writeable = true;

        notify ();
        return s;
    }

    public boolean anyMoreData () { return anyMoreData; }

    public void setAnyMoreData (boolean b) { anyMoreData = b; }
}

class producer extends Thread
{
    private shared s;

    producer (shared s)
    {
        this.s = s;
    }

    public void run ()
    {
        for (int i = 0; i < 15; i++)
        {
            try
            {
                // Sleep from 0 to 3999 milliseconds.

                Thread.sleep ((int) (Math.random () * 4000));
            }
            catch (InterruptedException e)
            {
                System.err.println (e);
            }

            s.setShared (i);
            System.out.println (i + " produced by producer.");
        }

        s.setAnyMoreData (false);
    }
}

class consumer extends Thread
{
    private shared s;
```

```
consumer (shared s)
{
    this.s = s;
}

public void run ()
{
    while (s.anyMoreData ())
    {
        try
        {
            // Sleep from 0 to 3999 milliseconds.

            Thread.sleep ((int) (Math.random () * 4000));
        }
        catch (InterruptedException e)
        {
            System.err.println (e);
        }

        System.out.println (s.getShared () + " consumed by consumer.");
    }
}
}
```

```
0 produced by producer.
0 consumed by consumer.
1 produced by producer.
1 consumed by consumer.
2 produced by producer.
2 consumed by consumer.
3 produced by producer.
3 consumed by consumer.
4 produced by producer.
4 consumed by consumer.
5 produced by producer.
5 consumed by consumer.
6 produced by producer.
6 consumed by consumer.
7 produced by producer.
7 consumed by consumer.
8 produced by producer.
8 consumed by consumer.
9 produced by producer.
9 consumed by consumer.
10 produced by producer.
10 consumed by consumer.
```

```
11 produced by producer.
11 consumed by consumer.
12 produced by producer.
12 consumed by consumer.
13 produced by producer.
13 consumed by consumer.
14 produced by producer.
14 consumed by consumer.
```

In pcDemo2, the producers and consumers are synchronized. However, the println method calls are not contained in synchronized methods. Therefore, the output may not necessarily appear as shown. (However, the previous output was shown when run under the Windows 95 version of Java.)

All of the synchronization takes place in the shared class. This class contains a pair of synchronized methods: getShared () and setShared (int). Because these methods are synchronized, the single shared object s serves as a monitor. When the producer thread is executing the setShared (int) code, the consumer thread is forced to wait. When the consumer thread is executing the getShared () code, the producer thread is forced to wait. This waiting is automatically initiated by the JVM, and guarantees either that the producer thread finishes executing in the setShared (int) method before the consumer thread is enabled to execute the getShared () method or that the consumer thread finishes executing the getShared () method before the producer thread is enabled to execute the setShared (int) method.

However, this is not enough to guarantee that the producer always produces an item before the consumer retrieves that item. In other words, the consumer thread could enter its getShared () method before the producer thread has produced an item.

As you learned in a prior chapter, the Object class introduces five methods that are inherited by every other class: notify (), notifyAll (), wait (), wait (long), and wait (long, int).

The three wait methods are called by a thread to voluntarily wait. Looking back at pcDemo2's shared class, the consumer thread voluntarily waits within its getShared () method as long as the writeable flag is true (indicating that the producer has not produced an item). Also, the producer thread voluntarily waits within its getShared () method as long as the writeable flag is false (indicating that the consumer thread has not consumed a previously produced item). When either wait method is voluntarily called, the thread calling this method is not automatically woken up when the other thread leaves its synchronized method. Instead, the other thread must notify the waiting thread that it is safe to proceed. This happens via the notify () method calls in getShared () and setShared (). By cooperating, the producer thread always produces exactly one item before this item is consumed.

PHILOS

As you know, two problems that can arise if threads are not synchronized are *indefinite postponement* (also known as *starvation*) and *deadlock*. Down through the years, these problems have been illustrated to many computer science students by way of "The Dining Philosophers," a story of intrigue as five philosophers seek to think and eat while avoiding starvation and deadlock. The story goes something like this...

Once upon a time, five philosophers got together to think about the issues of life and eat spaghetti. They entered a room and sat around a table containing five plates heaped with spaghetti in a delicious sauce. (There might have been some breadsticks on the table but anthropologists have not reached any definite conclusions.) One (and only one) fork was placed between each plate.

The dining philosophers were very proper people. The only way in which they would eat spaghetti was to first grab the fork on their left (with their left hand) and then grab the fork on their right (with their right hand). Without both forks, a philosopher would not eat. (It should be obvious that the dining philosophers, although wise, were also a bunch of pigs. After all, each philosopher did not care that the philosopher on either side would have placed a fork in his or her mouth. That same fork would be shared between two mouths!)

Unfortunately, some of the philosophers were greedy and ate more often than the other philosophers. This got to the point where some philosophers would have to wait so long to eat that they starved to death. For some inexplicable reason, these dead philosophers would come back to life and continue to eat and think.

The philosophers continued to think, eat, starve, die, and come back to life until a catastrophic event happened. After several years, all five philosophers grabbed exactly one fork. Because of their selfishness, no philosopher would give up a fork so that another philosopher could eat. Instead, each would wait hoping that the adjacent philosophers would first put down their forks. This never happened. As a result, they all died. None of these philosophers ever came back to life. And so the story ends.

PHILOS is a Java application that introduces five fictitious philosophers: Fred, John, Alice, Wanda, and Pete. Figure 16.2 illustrates how these philosophers are arranged around a table.

Oh, by the way, there are definitely no breadsticks on this table. Also, the forks look like chopsticks because my artistic skills are not worth a hill of beans.

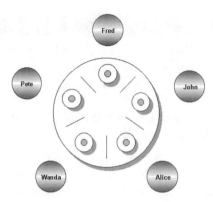

Figure 16.2: Fred, John, Alice, Wanda, and Pete.

Setting Up the Project

To set up PHILOS, begin by double-clicking your MS-DOS icon (if you are using Windows) and go to a command prompt.

If you created a `projects` directory in Chapter 1, "Introducing Java," make projects your current directory. (If you do not have a `projects` directory, now is as good a time as any to create one.)

Assuming that `projects` is located within `c:\jdk1.2\`, enter the command `cd \jdk1.2\projects` to change to this directory.

From within your `projects` directory, create a directory called `philos` (for example, `md philos`). (If you prefer, you can create this directory entirely in uppercase. For example, you could issue the command `md PHILOS` to create this directory. Case does not matter when it comes to directories.)

Download the file `philos.java` from the Macmillan Web site and place this file in your `philos` directory.

Compiling PHILOS

Compilation is a simple process. It involves running the `javac.exe` program and specifying the name of the source file as an argument to this program.

At the command prompt, enter the following line:

```
c:\jdk1.2\projects\philos>javac philos.java
```

CAUTION
The `.java` file extension must be specified when compiling an application's source file. The compiler will display an error message if `.java` is not specified.

If the compiler displays an error message, you might have typed
`Philos.java` or `PHILOS.java` instead of `philos.java`.

CAUTION

You must specify `philos.java` and not `Philos.java`, `PHILOS.java`, or any other combination of lowercase/uppercase letters. The compiler is very sensitive to case and will display
an error message if the class name (`philos`) does not match the filename (`philos`).

After compilation is finished, you should end up with class files
`philos.class`, `philosopher.class`, and `fork.class`.

Figure 16.3 shows the compilation process.

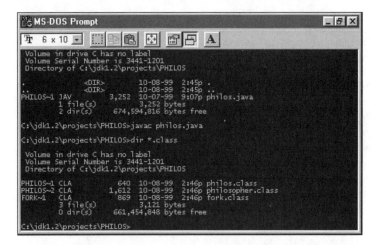

Figure 16.3: *Compiling* `philos.java` *with the* `javac.exe` *compiler.*

Running PHILOS

Congratulations! You successfully compiled `philos.java` and are now ready
to run `philos.class`. All you need to do is fire up the `java.exe` program and
specify `philos.class` as an argument to this program.

CAUTION

The `.class` file extension must not be specified; otherwise, the `java.exe` program will
display an error message.

To run PHILOS at the command line, simply type `java philos` and press the
Enter key. The following is a sample of the output when running PHILOS:

```
Philosopher pete is thinking.
Philosopher john is thinking.
Philosopher fred is thinking.
Philosopher alice is thinking.
```

```
Philosopher wanda is thinking.
Philosopher wanda is hungry.
Philosopher wanda got the left fork.
Philosopher wanda got the right fork.
Philosopher fred is hungry.
Philosopher fred got the left fork.
Philosopher fred got the right fork.
Philosopher john is hungry.
Philosopher john got the left fork.
Philosopher john is starving!
Philosopher alice is hungry.
Philosopher alice is starving!
Philosopher pete is hungry.
Philosopher pete is starving!
Philosopher wanda is eating.
Philosopher fred is eating.
Philosopher wanda putting down the left fork.
Philosopher wanda putting down the right fork.
Philosopher wanda is thinking.
Philosopher alice got the left fork.
Philosopher alice is starving!
Philosopher wanda is hungry.
Philosopher wanda got the left fork.
Philosopher wanda is starving!
Philosopher fred putting down the left fork.
Philosopher fred putting down the right fork.
Philosopher fred is thinking.
Philosopher john got the right fork.
Philosopher pete got the left fork.
Philosopher pete is starving!
Philosopher fred is hungry.
Philosopher fred is starving!
Philosopher john is eating.
Philosopher john putting down the left fork.
Philosopher john putting down the right fork.
```

The five philosophers begin by thinking. Sooner or later, each gets hungry. A hungry philosopher attempts to pick up the left fork. If another philosopher has this fork, the hungry philosopher must wait. If the philosopher waits for awhile, he or she begins to starve. However, because these philosophers cooperate, a philosopher does not starve very much. After a bit, the philosopher gets the left fork and then tries for the right fork. As soon as the right fork is acquired, the philosopher eats. The philosopher then puts down the left fork followed by the right fork and goes back to thinking. This cycle repeats.

Now suppose that the put () method in lines 103 through 107 was replaced with the put () method in lines 98 through 101 and the get (String) method in lines 126 through 146 was replaced with the get (String) method in lines 109 through 124. After recompiling philos.java and then running philos.class, what would happen? Basically, you would get a chance to see just how selfish these philosophers can be—and experience deadlock.

Potential Problems

This program is pretty robust. As far as I can tell, there are no problems with PHILOS. Still, if you should encounter a problem, try to come up with a solution.

TIP

Solving problems can really enhance your Java knowledge and boost your skills!

Enhancing PHILOS

You can enhance PHILOS in a number of ways:

- As the code stands, you are required to comment out one pair of get (String) and put () methods while un-commenting the other pair to switch from selfish to cooperative behavior (and vice versa). This is by design. How would you re-write this program so you didn't have to do this? (Hint: Think about passing a command-line argument that identifies selfish or cooperative behavior and stash this value in the fork class. Also, instead of using synchronized get (String) and synchronized put () methods, try using synchronized code blocks from within these methods. Then, you could combine both get (String) methods into one get (String) method and both put () methods into one put () method.)

- If you want a bigger challenge, think about modifying this program to use graphics and images so that you can watch these philosophers stuff spaghetti into their mouths. If you do accomplish this task, congratulate yourself. Just don't show me the program because these philosophers can get pretty gross.

What's Next?

In the next chapter, you will learn how to organize your data into files, read data from files via objects known as streams, and write data to files via streams. Along the way, you'll find out how two threads can send data to each other in a synchronized fashion by using a tool known as a pipe stream.

Files and Streams

Computers process data stored in Random Access Memory (RAM). This memory is very fast: The amount of time to store data in RAM or retrieve data from RAM is typically measured in nanoseconds (billionths of a second). However, this memory is temporary: Removing a computer's power results in the RAM losing stored data. For data to be reused, it needs to be stored in a more permanent kind of memory—such as magnetic disks. (Although more permanent than RAM, magnetic disk memory also is much slower than RAM.)

Data is not just thrown onto a disk in a jumbled heap: It is organized into files. Java programs channel data into files and channel data out of files by way of streams. Of course, there are security issues to keep in mind—if the Java program is an applet.

Chapter 17 presents the following topics:

- Files
- Streams
- Object serialization
- JED

Files

Intuitively, we all know what files and directories are. However, before diving into the "meat and potatoes" of this chapter, a quick refresher on file/directory concepts couldn't hurt.

A file data structure associates a name and other attributes (such as a creation time, read-only status, and so on) with a sequence of bytes. The organization of these bytes into something meaningful is left up to the program that created the file. Some files contain information (such as names and attributes) about other files. These special files are known as *directories*.

Because directories can contain other directories (in addition to files), a path is used to traverse these directories until either the desired directory is found or the desired file is found. This path can be either *absolute* or *relative*. An absolute path begins with a special starting directory, known as the *root directory*, whereas a relative path begins with the current directory (which might be the root directory).

The root directory has a name that differs from files and other directories. This name typically consists of a single character. However, each platform usually defines its own character for this name. For example, Solaris uses a forward slash character / as the name of its root directory, whereas Windows uses the back slash character \ as the name of its root directory. The character used to identify the root directory also is used to separate one directory from another directory when specifying a path. As we will shortly see, this character is a platform dependency that can be elegantly handled by Java.

Files (including directories) are identified by name and extension. The name identifies the contents of the file (for example, account) and the extension classifies these contents by type (for example, txt would mean text file, class would mean class file, java would mean Java source file, and so on). The name and extension are typically separated by a single period character (for example, account.dat—a data file called account).

Figure 17.1 provides a conceptual view of a file.

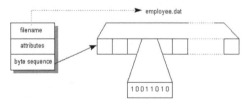

Figure 17.1: *A conceptual file.*

The File Class

The File class obtains information about files and directories. This class is located in the java.io package.

File declares a separatorChar class field that identifies the character used to name the root directory and separate one directory from another directory. This class field returns this character as a char value. File also declares a separator class field that returns this character as a String object.

TIP

You should take advantage of separatorChar and not hardcode backslash or forward slash characters in string literals that specify paths and/or files. Using separatorChar will help to make your code more portable.

File declares several constructors for initializing File objects, including File (String) and File (String, String).

The File (String) constructor initializes a File object to the contents of its String object argument. This argument provides an optional path along with a filename or a final directory name.

Take a look at the following code fragment. It creates a File object and initializes it with the accounts.dat file, located in the root directory:

```
File f = new File (File.separator + "accounts.dat");
```

This would look like \accounts.dat under Windows or /accounts.dat under Solaris.

The File (String, String) constructor initializes a File object to the contents of two String object arguments. The first argument provides an absolute or relative path to a file or directory and the second argument provides the filename or directory name.

The following code fragment creates a File object and initializes it with the jan.dat file in the 1999 directory, just below the root directory:

```
File f = new File (File.separator + "1999", "jan.dat");
```

This would look like \1999\jan.dat under Windows or /1999/jan.dat under Solaris.

THE exists () METHOD

The File class declares an exists () instance method that returns a Boolean true value if the file or directory represented by the calling File object exists. Otherwise, false is returned.

For example, the following code fragment creates a File object and initializes it with autoexec.bat. It calls exists () to determine if autoexec.bat exists in the current directory and outputs the resulting value:

```
File f = new File ("autoexec.bat");
System.out.println (f.exists ());
```

THE canRead () AND canWrite () METHODS

The File class declares canRead () and canWrite () instance methods that return a Boolean true value if the file or directory represented by the calling File object is readable or writable, respectively. Otherwise, false is returned. (Both methods return false if the file or directory does not exist.)

For example, the following code fragment creates a File object and initializes it with x.java. It calls canRead () to determine if x.java is readable and outputs the resulting value:

```
File f = new File ("x.java");
System.out.println (f.canRead ());
```

THE isFile () AND isDirectory () METHODS

The File class declares isFile () and isDirectory () instance methods that return a Boolean true value if the calling File object represents a file or directory, respectively. Otherwise, false is returned.

Examine the following code fragment. It creates a File object, initializes it with the temp directory name (below the root directory), and calls isDirectory () to determine if temp is a directory. The resulting Boolean value is then output:

```
File f = new File (File.separator + "temp");
System.out.println (f.isDirectory ());
```

THE isAbsolute () METHOD

The File class declares an isAbsolute () instance method that returns a Boolean true value if the calling File object contains an absolute path. Otherwise, false is returned.

The following code fragment creates a File object and initializes it with the accounts.dat filename. This code fragment outputs false because the path associated with accounts.dat is relative (no root directory and any other directories that need to be traversed to reach accounts.dat have been specified):

```
File f = new File ("accounts.dat");
System.out.println (f.isAbsolute ());
```

THE getAbsolutePath () METHOD

The File class declares a getAbsolutePath () instance method that returns a String object containing the absolute path of the file/directory information, that is itself contained within the calling File object.

As an example, the following code fragment creates a `File` object identifying `jan.dat` as a file located underneath the 1998 directory:

```
File f = new File ("1998", "jan.dat");
System.out.println (f.getAbsolutePath ());
```

If 1998 is located immediately below the root directory, the absolute path that is printed under Windows is `c:\1998\jan.dat`. (Windows uses drive letters to differentiate one disk drive from another. I'm assuming that the current drive is the drive associated with `c:`.)

THE getName () METHOD

The `File` class declares a `getName ()` instance method that returns a `String` object containing the name portion of the file/directory information, that is itself contained within the calling `File` object.

The following code fragment creates a `File` object identifying `dec.dat` as a file located underneath the 1998 directory. The `getName ()` method returns `dec.dat`:

```
File f = new File ("1998", "dec.dat");
System.out.println (f.getName ());
```

THE getPath () METHOD

The `File` class declares a `getPath ()` instance method that returns a `String` object containing the relative path portion of the file/directory information, that is itself contained within the calling `File` object.

For example, the following code fragment creates a `File` object identifying `mar.dat` as a file located underneath the 1998 directory. The `getPath ()` method returns `1998/mar.dat` (assuming Solaris) or `1998\mar.dat` (assuming Windows):

```
File f = new File ("1998", "mar.dat");
System.out.println (f.getPath ());
```

THE getParent () METHOD

The `File` class declares a `getParent ()` instance method that returns a `String` object containing the parent directory of the final file or directory, as specified in the file/directory information contained within the calling `File` object. If there is no parent directory, `null` is returned.

Check out the following code fragment. It creates a `File` object identifying `feb.dat` as a file located underneath the 1999 directory. The `getParent ()` method returns `1999` as the parent directory of `feb.dat`:

```
File f = new File ("1999", "feb.dat");
System.out.println (f.getParent ());
```

THE length () METHOD

The File class declares a length () instance method that returns the length of the file specified in the file/directory information contained within the calling File object. If this object represents a directory, zero is returned.

For example, the following code fragment creates a File object identifying aug.dat as a file located underneath the 1999 directory. The length () method returns the length of this file:

```
File f = new File ("1999", "aug.dat");
System.out.println (f.length ());
```

THE lastModified () METHOD

The File class declares a lastModified () instance method that returns a long integer containing the time at which the file or directory was last modified.

The following code fragment creates a File object identifying aug.dat as a file located underneath the 1999 directory. The lastModified () method returns the time at which this file was last modified:

```
File f = new File ("1999", "aug.dat");
System.out.println (f.lastModified ());
```

If you display this value, you will only see an integer number. This is not meaningful from a human perspective. However, there is a way in which to convert this value to something more meaningful: Take advantage of the Date class.

The Date class, part of the java.util package, is used to create objects that represent the current date. This class provides a Date (long) constructor that can initialize a Date object with a long integer representing a point in time. Calling Date's toString () method results in a String object being returned that contains a standard representation of this time. The previous code fragment could display this value, as follows:

```
File f = new File ("1999", "aug.dat");
System.out.println (new Date (f.lastModified ()));
```

Of course, the compiler chooses the System.out.println (Object) method to call. This method contains code that calls toString () to return a String object with the human-readable date representation. The contents of this object are then printed.

THE list () METHOD

The File class declares a list () instance method that returns an array of String objects containing the names of files and directories located in the directory specified by the contents of the calling File object. If the File object refers to a file (and not a directory), null is returned.

The following code fragment prints out the names of all files and directories located in the root directory:

```
File f = new File (File.separator);
String [] names = f.list ();
for (int i = 0; i < names.length; i++)
    System.out.println (names [i]);
```

Types of Files

There are many kinds of files in existence: audio, video, text, data, and executable—to name a few.

Data files are typically divided into a sequence of fixed-length chunks called *records*. Each record is then divided into a sequence of fixed length chunks called *fields*. Each field contains a unit of data. For example, an employee data file might contain a sequence of records—one per employee. Each employee record might contain first name, last name, salary, and other fields of interest.

Figure 17.2 shows a file of employee records where each record is divided into first name, last name, and salary fields.

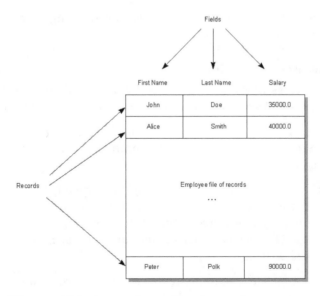

Figure 17.2: *An employee file of records.*

Files can be accessed in one of two ways: sequentially or in a random fashion.

SEQUENTIAL ACCESS FILES

If you need to open a file for reading or writing (but not both), you need to use a *sequential access file*. A sequential access file is read from in a linear fashion by reading the first record and continuing to read records, one after another, until the last record has been read. Conversely, a sequential access file is written to by writing the first record and continuing to write records until the last record has been written. An example of a sequential access file is an audio file that has been opened to read, interpret, and play its contents. After the entire file has been read, the file can be closed.

Java provides `FileInputStream`, `FileOutputStream`, `FileReader`, and `FileWriter` classes for working with files in a sequential access manner. These classes will be discussed in more detail when we look at streams.

RANDOM ACCESS FILES

If you need to open a file and then perform a variety of read/write operations on this file before it is closed, you need to use a *random access file*. With random access files, a portion of the file can be read from, followed by a write to another portion of the same file—the file does not have to be re-opened between reading and writing. An example of a random access file is an employee data file that has been opened to insert new employee records, delete existing employee records, and update existing employee records. After all these operations have been performed, the file is closed.

Java provides a `RandomAccessFile` class for working with files in a random access manner.

THE `RandomAccessFile` CLASS

Random access files can be accessed by taking advantage of Java's `RandomAccessFile` class. This class is located in the `java.io` package.

`RandomAccessFile` objects are created by calling either the `RandomAccessFile (File, String)` constructor or the `RandomAccessFile (String, String)` constructor.

The `RandomAccessFile (File, String)` constructor initializes a `RandomAccessFile` object to a `File` object argument that describes the file and a `String` object argument that describes the *file mode* (reading/writing capabilities) of this object. This mode can be r (for reading only) or rw (for reading and writing).

The following code fragment creates a random access file object, `raf`, from `File` object `f`:

```
try
{
    File f = new File ("newfile");

    RandomAccessFile raf = new RandomAccessFile (f, "rw");
}
```

```
catch (IOException e)
{
   System.out.println (e);
}
```

Because RandomAccessFile (File, String) can throw an IOException object, the constructor call is placed inside a Try statement.

The RandomAccessFile (String, String) constructor initializes a RandomAccessFile object to the name of a file, via the first String object argument, and the file mode, via the second String object argument.

The following code fragment creates a random access file object, raf, from a String object argument:

```
try
{
   RandomAccessFile raf = new RandomAccessFile ("newfile",
                                                  "rw");
}
catch (IOException e)
{
   System.out.println (e);
}
```

The file mode argument passed to a RandomAccessFile constructor determines what this constructor does if the file already exists or does not exist. For example, if r is passed and the file exists, the file is opened for reading. If r is passed and the file does not exist, a FileNotFoundException object is thrown. If rw is passed and the file exists, the file is opened for reading and writing. The contents are not erased. If rw is passed and the file does not exist, a new file of length 0 is created.

The RandomAccessFile constructor ensures that the file associated with the RandomAccessFile object is open. After this object is no longer required, the file associated with the RandomAccessFile object should be closed by calling the close () instance method.

For example, the following code fragment expands on the previous code fragment to close newfile:

```
try
{
   RandomAccessFile raf = new RandomAccessFile ("newfile",
                                                  "rw");

   // Statements to manipulate this file.

   raf.close ();
}
```

```
catch (IOException e)
{
    System.out.println (e);
}
```

RandomAccessFile declares a collection of instance methods for reading.
These methods include readFloat () (to read a float), readInt () (to read
an int), and readUTF () (to read a string of characters). RandomAccessFile
also declares a collection of instance methods for writing. These methods
include writeUTF (String) (to write a String object's characters),
writeBoolean (boolean) (to write a boolean), and writeDouble (double)
(to write a double-precision floating-point number).

In addition to its support for reading and writing, RandomAccessFile keeps
track of the current reading/writing position by using an internal file
pointer. This position can be obtained by calling the getFilePointer ()
instance method to return the current position as a long integer. This position can be set by calling the seek (long) instance method to set the position to the value of the long integer argument.

EXAMPLE

The following RAFDemo application illustrates the creation of a
RandomAccessFile object that is tied to a file called employee.dat. This file
will contain a single record composed of three employee fields—two String
files (first name and last name) and a double salary field:

```
// RAFDemo.java

import java.io.*;

class RAFDemo
{
    public static void main (String [] args) throws IOException
    {
        // Create RandomAccessFile object raf.  A physical
        // employee.dat file is created if it does not exist.
        // Otherwise it is opened.  The file pointer is
        // positioned to the start of the first (and only)
        // record.  The file mode is set to rw for both
        // reading and writing.

        RandomAccessFile raf =
                new RandomAccessFile ("employee.dat", "rw");

        // Display employee.dat's current length.

        System.out.println ("employee.dat length = " +
                            raf.length ());
```

```
          // Write employee's first name.

          raf.writeUTF ("John");

          // Write employee's last name.

          raf.writeUTF ("Smith");

          // Write employee's yearly salary.

          raf.writeDouble (45000.0);

          // Set file pointer to start of file.

          raf.seek (0L);

          // Read employee's first name.

          String fname = raf.readUTF ();

          // Read employee's last name.

          String lname = raf.readUTF ();

          // Read employee's yearly salary.

          double salary = raf.readDouble ();

          // Output employee details.

          System.out.println ("First name = " + fname);
          System.out.println ("Last name = " + lname);
          System.out.println ("Salary = " + salary);

          // Close employee.dat.

          raf.close ();
      }
}
```

```
employee.dat length = 0
First name = John
Last name = Smith
Salary = 45000.0
```

Another useful instance method that is declared by RandomAccessFile (and is introduced in this example) is length (). This method returns the length of the file as a long integer.

Streams

Java supports many kinds of streams, by providing a variety of stream classes. Each stream class name identifies the stream as either an input stream (data flowing from a source) or an output stream (data flowing to a destination).

Furthermore, when Java was first introduced, the stream classes only channeled data from a source to a destination in 8-bit quantities. This was fine for graphics, audio, and video data. However, this was not so fine if the data was textual in nature. (Because Java supports Unicode text and each character of Unicode text occupies two bytes, it makes more sense to treat each character as a 16-bit quantity than two 8-bit quantities.) As a result, a new set of classes was created to channel data from a source to a destination in 16-bit quantities.

If you wander through the JDK documentation, you will come across a pair of abstract classes that serve as the ultimate superclasses for 8-bit input streams and 8-bit output streams. These classes are called InputStream and OutputStream. Also, you will come across a pair of abstract classes that serve as the ultimate superclasses for 16-bit input streams and 16-bit output streams. These classes are called Reader and Writer.

Types of Streams

There are many different kinds of streams. However, only three kinds will be discussed in this section: file streams, data streams, and pipe streams. (A fourth kind of stream, known as an object stream, is discussed in the section "Object Serialization," later in this chapter.)

FILE STREAMS

File streams are streams whose sources or destinations are files.

Objects created from the FileInputStream and FileOutputStream classes read 8-bit quantities from or write 8-bit quantities to files, whereas objects created from the FileReader and FileWriter classes read 16-bit quantities from or write 16-bit quantities to files. These classes are located in the java.io package.

FileInputStream and FileReader declare a read () instance method that reads the next 8-bit quantity (FileInputStream) or 16-bit quantity (FileReader) as an int from the file stream. If there are no more quantities, -1 is returned. This method throws an IOException object if an input/output error occurs during the read.

FileOutputStream and FileWriter declare a write (int) instance method that writes the 8-bit quantity (FileOutputStream) or 16-bit quantity

(FileWriter) contained in the int argument to the file stream. This method throws an IOException object if an input/output error occurs during the write.

The file stream class constructors and methods can throw IOException objects.

EXAMPLE

The following copy application demonstrates the creation of FileInputStream and FileOutputStream objects as well as the read () and write (int) methods to copy the contents of the file associated with the file input stream to the file associated with the file output stream:

```
// copy.java

import java.io.*;

class copy
{
    public static void main (String [] args) throws IOException
    {
        if (args.length != 2)
        {
            System.out.println ("usage: java copy srcfile dstfile");
            return;
        }

        // Create file input stream attached to args [0] file.

        FileInputStream fis = new FileInputStream (args [0]);

        // Create file output stream attached to args [1] file.

        FileOutputStream fos = new FileOutputStream (args [1]);

        int ch;

        // While not eof (-1), read all characters from fis and
        // write these characters to the file associated with
        // fos.

        while ((ch = fis.read ()) != -1)
            fos.write (ch);

        // Close file associated with file input stream.

        fis.close ();

        // Close file associated with file output stream.

        fos.close ();
```

```
        }
}
```

You run this program by typing java copy *src dst* at the command line (where *src* is the name of the source file and *dst* is the name of the destination file). For example,

```
java copy copy.java copy.bak
```

copies copy.java to the backup copy.bak file.

DATA STREAMS

Data streams are streams whose sources or destinations are other streams.

Data streams filter 8-bit quantities into non-byte primitive values (for example, doubles, ints, floats, and so on) on input and filter non-byte primitive values into 8-bit quantities on output.

Objects created from the DataInputStream class filter 8-bit quantities from a stream into non-byte primitive values, whereas objects created from the DataOutputStream class filter non-byte primitive values into 8-bit quantities that are sent to a stream. These classes are located in the java.io package.

EXAMPLE

The following dosdis application demonstrates chaining a DataInputStream object to a FileInputStream object and a DataOutputStream object to a FileOutputStream object along with some DataInputStream/DataOutputStream methods for reading/writing non-byte primitive values (such as readInt () and writeFloat (float)):

```
// class dosdis.java

import java.io.*;

class dosdis
{
    public static void main (String [] args) throws IOException
    {
        // Create file output stream attached to data.dat file.

        FileOutputStream fos = new FileOutputStream ("data.dat");

        // Create data output stream chained to fos.

        DataOutputStream dos = new DataOutputStream (fos);

        // Write the integer value 256 to the data output stream.
        // This gets sent to the file output stream.

        dos.writeInt (256);
```

```
// Write the float value 32.5f to the data output stream.
// This gets sent to the file output stream.

dos.writeFloat (32.5f);

// Close the file associated with the output stream.

fos.close ();

// Create file input stream attached to data.dat file.

FileInputStream fis = new FileInputStream ("data.dat");

// Create data input stream chained to fis.

DataInputStream dis = new DataInputStream (fis);

// Read the previously output integer.

int i = dis.readInt ();

// Display this integer.

System.out.println (i);

// Read the previously output floating point value.

float f = dis.readFloat ();

// Display this floating point value.

System.out.println (f);

// Close the file associated with the input stream.

fis.close ();
    }
}
```

256
32.5

OUTPUT

PIPE STREAMS

Pipe streams are streams whose sources and destinations are threads.

Objects created from the PipedInputStream class read 8-bit quantities from objects created from the PipedOutputStream class (by other threads), whereas objects created from the PipedReader class read 16-bit quantities from objects created from the PipedWriter class (by other threads). This makes it possible for one thread to send lots of data to another thread. These classes are located in the java.io package.

The pipe stream class constructors and methods can throw IOException objects.

EXAMPLE

The following pipeDemo application demonstrates creating a piped communications system between two threads. The src thread uses a PipedWriter object to send messages to the dst thread, which picks up these messages and displays them. (The dst thread is started 2 seconds after the src thread to ensure that there is information in the pipe when dst starts. Otherwise, dst exits as soon as it starts.)

```java
// pipeDemo.java

import java.io.*;

class pipeDemo extends Thread
{
    static PipedReader pr;
    static PipedWriter pw;

    public static void main (String [] args) throws IOException
    {
        pipeDemo pd1 = new pipeDemo ("src");
        pipeDemo pd2 = new pipeDemo ("dst");

        pw = new PipedWriter ();
        pr = new PipedReader (pw);

        pd1.start ();

        try
        {
            Thread.sleep (2000);
        }
        catch (InterruptedException e) {}

        pd2.start ();
    }

    pipeDemo (String name)
    {
        super (name);
    }
```

```
public void run ()
{
    int ch;

    try
    {
        if (getName ().equals ("src"))
            for (int i = 0; i < 15; i++)
                pw.write (getName () + " A" + i + '\n');
        else
            while ((ch = pr.read ()) != -1)
                System.out.print ((char) ch);
    }
    catch (IOException e) {}
}
}
```

OUTPUT

```
src A0
src A1
src A2
src A3
src A4
src A5
src A6
src A7
src A8
src A9
src A10
src A11
src A12
src A13
src A14
```

Standard I/O

Throughout this book, you've seen references to something called System.out.println. This method has been called to output the contents of its argument to the DOS window. If you have been wondering how this method works, here is your chance to find out.

In 1970, the UNIX operating system was officially released. Among its many useful features, UNIX sported a flexible input/output mechanism called standard I/O.

A program that uses standard I/O views the operating system as providing a standard input device and a standard output device. All input comes from the standard input device and all output goes to the standard output device. The standard input device can be either the keyboard or a file, whereas the standard output device can be either the screen or a file.

Redirection (the use of the command-line characters < and > to switch the standard input device from the keyboard to a file or device and the standard output device from the screen to a file or device) makes it possible to change the input source and output destination without requiring a program to be rewritten. This is very powerful—and very useful.

In addition to standard output, the concept of standard error was introduced to provide a place to send error messages. The standard error device is the screen, and cannot be redirected to a file.

The `print` and `println` methods (of `System.out`) are instance methods of a class called `PrintStream`, by way of `System`'s out class field. Internally, this is a special `PrintStream` object that is initialized by the JVM.

If you look at the JDK documentation for `PrintStream`, you will find several overloaded `print` methods and several overloaded `println` methods. Each method outputs its argument to the standard output device. In the case of `println`, a newline character is output after the argument to advance to the next line. Here are some examples:

```
System.out.print ('A');
System.out.print ('B');
System.out.println (32);
System.out.println ("ABC");
```

This outputs

```
AB32
ABC
```

to the standard output device.

If you change out to err (for example, `System.err.print` or `System.err.println`), you will output to the standard error device (always the screen) instead of the standard output device.

Standard input is represented by the read instance method of a concrete subclass (initialized by the JVM) of the abstract `InputStream` class, by way of `System`'s in class field. Here is an example:

```
int ch = System.in.read ();
```

When `System.in.read ()` is called, it either reads one keystroke from a host operating system keystroke buffer or one byte from a file (if standard input has been redirected to a file).

When `System.in.read ()` reads from the keystroke buffer, the following scenario occurs. If there is at least one keystroke in the buffer, `System.in.read ()` removes and returns this keystroke. If this buffer is empty, `System.in.read ()` waits until the user has typed zero or more characters, followed by typing the Enter key. As soon as Enter is typed, this method removes and returns the first character from this buffer.

When the Enter key is typed, two characters are stored in the buffer: a carriage-return character followed by a newline character (also known as a line-feed character). The carriage-return character is represented by the `'\r'` character literal and the newline/line-feed character is represented by the `'\n'` character literal.

EXAMPLE

The following `echo` application demonstrates echoing standard input to standard output:

```
// echo.java

import java.io.*;

class echo
{
   public static void main (String [] args) throws IOException
   {
      int ch;

      System.out.print ("Please enter some text: ");

      while ((ch = System.in.read ()) != '\n')
         System.out.print ((char) ch);
   }
}
```

You run this program by typing `java echo` at the command line. For example,

```
java echo
```

This program displays

```
Please enter some text:
```

Type some text followed by the Enter key. You'll see this text echoed to the screen. However, you can use the < and > redirection symbols on the command line to change standard input and/or standard output to a file. For example,

```
java echo <echo.java >echo.bak
```

will copy all characters up to and including the first newline character from `echo.java` to `echo.bak`. If you wanted to copy all characters, you would need to change the expression in the While loop statement from `!= '\n'` to `!= -1`. Of course, if you tried inputting from the keyboard after making this change, you would not exit this program after typing Enter. (You would keep looping.) Oh well, nothing's perfect.

Object Serialization

Imagine the following scenario. You are interacting with a Java program on your laptop computer. All of a sudden, your computer's battery low indicator light comes on. Your Java program detects this condition, saves the state of its objects to some kind of permanent memory, and shuts down. Shortly thereafter, the computer shuts down. You plug your computer into a recharging device and leave it alone for a few hours. Later, you come back and turn on your computer. The computer returns to "life" and the Java program that was interrupted automatically picks up from where it left off. No data has been lost. Science fiction? No. The capability to save objects and restore these objects at a later time is part of Java, and is known as *object serialization*.

Object serialization is a Java technology, implemented by a pair of classes and an interface, that makes it possible to save the properties of a program's objects to some destination (such as a file) and re-create these objects from these saved properties at a later time.

Object serialization consists of a serialization process and a deserialization process. *Serialization* is the act of writing an object's class name, attributes (public, final, and so on), and field values to a stream. *Deserialization* is the act of reading an object's class name, attributes, and field values; creating a new object from the class name and attributes; and assigning the field values to the new object's fields.

Java's ObjectOutputStream class, located in the java.io package, is designed to handle the serialization process.

The ObjectOutputStream (OutputStream) constructor is used to initialize a new ObjectOutputStream object. The OutputStream object argument identifies the stream where the object will be written.

ObjectOutputStream's writeObject (Object) instance method is responsible for the actual writing process. A reference to the object which is to be written is passed via the Object argument. This object must be created from a class that implements the empty Serializable interface; otherwise, a NotSerializableException object will be thrown. Because of polymorphism, a reference to any object can be passed, via Object, as long as its class implements Serializable.

The writeObject (Object) method only writes the values of non-transient instance fields to the destination stream. Class fields are not written because they are not part of an object. Fields prefixed with the transient reserved word are not written because they are intended to mark data that is meaningless after being re-created, such as the value of a dynamic counter field (constantly updated by a thread).

Java's ObjectInputStream class, located in the java.io package, is designed to handle the deserialization process.

The ObjectInputStream (InputStream) constructor is used to initialize a new ObjectInputStream object. The InputStream object argument identifies the stream from where the serialized object will be read.

ObjectInputStream's readObject () instance method is responsible for the actual reading process. This method reads a serialized object, creates a new object of the data type identified by the serialized class name, assigns the serialized non-transient instance field values to this object, and returns a reference to the object. Transient instance fields are initialized to default zero values.

EXAMPLE

The following example illustrates serialization and deserialization by way of three source files: timer.java, shutDown.java, and startup.java.

The timer.java source file declares a timer class that implements the Serializable interface. This class consists of three instance fields: name, counter, and stopped. Of these three fields, only name is not a transient field. The reason is that, when we serialize a timer object, we want to preserve its name but not the counter or stopped values. After all, when we deserialize a timer object, we will want the counter to start at its default zero value. Also, we don't want to take the chance that the timer will start up automatically after it has been deserialized. (This would happen if stopped was not transient and contained a false value when serialized.)

```
// timer.java

import java.io.*;

class timer extends Thread implements Serializable
{
   private String name;

   private transient long counter;
   private transient boolean stopped;

   timer (String name)
   {
      this.name = name;
   }

   public void run ()
   {
      long time = System.currentTimeMillis ();

      while (!stopped)
```

```
    {
        try
        {
            // Sleep for exactly 10 milliseconds.

            time += 10;
            Thread.sleep (Math.max (0, time -
                                System.currentTimeMillis ()));
        }
        catch (InterruptedException e) {}

        // Do not change counter while its value is being retrieved.

        synchronized (this)
        {
            counter++;
        }
    }
}

void begin ()
{
    stopped = false;
    start ();
}

void end ()
{
    stopped = true;
}

long getCounter ()
{
    long temp;

    // Ensure that counter is not changed while its value is
    // being retrieved - in case main thread's quantum expires.

    synchronized (this)
    {
        temp = counter;
    }

    return temp;
}

String getTimerName ()
{
```

```
        return name;
    }
}
```

The shutdown.java source file declares a shutdown class with a main method.
This application creates a timer object (from the timer class), starts this timer,
outputs some values, sleeps, and serializes the timer object to a file called
objects.tmp. Only the value of the timer object's name field is serialized.

```java
// shutdown.java

import java.io.*;

class shutdown
{
    public static void main (String [] args)
        throws ClassNotFoundException, IOException
    {
        // Create and start a timer.

        timer t = new timer ("Timer A");
        t.begin ();

        // Sleep for a bit to give the timer thread a chance to
        // increment the counter.

        try
        {
            Thread.sleep (2000);
        }
        catch (InterruptedException e) {}

        t.end ();

        // Print out the current timer name and counter.

        System.out.println ("Timer name = " + t.getTimerName ());
        System.out.println ("Timer counter = " + t.getCounter ());

        // Create an objects.tmp file and connect it to the
        // FileOutputStream object fos.

        FileOutputStream fos = new FileOutputStream ("objects.tmp");

        // Chain fos to the newly created ObjectOutputStream object oos.

        ObjectOutputStream oos = new ObjectOutputStream (fos);
```

```
            // Write the timer object t to this stream.

            oos.writeObject (t);

            // Flush the ObjectOutputStream object to objects.tmp.

            oos.flush ();

            // Close the FileOutputStream object.

            fos.close ();
        }
    }
```

```
Timer name = Timer A
Timer counter = 199
```

The startup.java source file declares a startup class with a main method.
This application deserializes a timer object from objects.tmp, prints out the
timer object's name and counter values, starts the timer, displays some
counter values, and stops the timer. As expected, the deserialized timer
name matches the serialized name and the deserialized counter value is
zero.

```
// startup.java

import java.io.*;

class startup
{
    public static void main (String [] args)
        throws ClassNotFoundException, IOException
    {
        // Open objects.tmp and connect it to the FileInputStream
        // object fis.

        FileInputStream fis = new FileInputStream ("objects.tmp");

        // Chain fis to the newly created ObjectInputStream object ois.

        ObjectInputStream ois = new ObjectInputStream (fis);

        // Read the timer object t from this stream.

        timer t = (timer) ois.readObject ();

        // Close the FileInputStream object.

        fis.close ();
```

```
        // Display serialized name and counter.

        System.out.println ("Timer name = " + t.getTimerName ());
        System.out.println ("Timer counter = " + t.getCounter ());

        // Begin the timer.

        t.begin ();

        // Print out some counter values.

        for (int i = 0; i < 10; i++)
        {
            System.out.println (t.getCounter ());

            // Sleep for a while.

            try
            {
                Thread.sleep (100);
            }
            catch (InterruptedException e) {}
        }

        // End the timer.

        t.end ();
    }
}
```

OUTPUT

```
Timer name = Timer A
Timer counter = 0
0
11
23
30
44
52
62
74
84
94
```

For those who are curious, this is what the contents of the 64-byte objects.tmp file looks like after it has been created by shutdown.class—not a pretty sight!

```
AC ED 00 05 73 72 00 05-74 69 6D 65 72 56 08 5F    ....sr..timerV._
1E 0A 4C BF 06 02 00 01-4C 00 04 6E 61 6D 65 74    ..L.....L..namet
```

```
00 12 4C 6A 61 76 61 2F-6C 61 6E 67 2F 53 74 72    ..Ljava/lang/Str
69 6E 67 3B 78 70 74 00-07 54 69 6D 65 72 20 41    ing;xpt..Timer A
```

The left side shows hexadecimal values. The right side shows ASCII characters ranging from 32 through 126 or periods for those ASCII characters that are outside of this range. (The DOS Debug program was used to produce this output. Debug uses ASCII.)

JED

JED is a text editor that serves as a practical example of files and streams. This application creates a GUI by deriving a class called jed from the Frame class and executing GUI construction code in the jed (String) constructor.

JED's GUI consists of a window with a menu, a file contents text area, and a status line. The menu consists of a single File item with Open..., Save, Save As..., and Exit commands. The Open... command opens a text file. The Save command saves the contents of the text area to the current file. The Save As... command saves the contents of the text area to a new file. The Exit command causes JED to quit. Finally, the Save and Save As... menu items are grayed out (disabled) if there is nothing to save.

Setting Up JED

To set up JED, begin by double-clicking your MS-DOS icon (if you are using Windows) and go to a command prompt.

If you created a projects directory in Chapter 1, "Introducing Java," make projects your current directory. (If you do not have a projects directory, now is as good a time as any to create one.)

Assuming that projects is located within c:\jdk1.2\, enter the command cd \jdk1.2\projects to change to this directory.

From within your projects directory, create a directory called jed (for example, md jed). (If you prefer, you can create this directory entirely in uppercase. For example, you could issue the command md JED to create this directory. Case does not matter when it comes to directories.)

Download the file jed.java from the Macmillan Web site and place this file in your jed directory.

Compiling JED

Compilation is a simple process. It involves running the javac.exe program and specifying the name of the source file as an argument to this program.

At the command prompt, enter the following line:

```
c:\jdk1.2\projects\jed>javac jed.java
```

> **CAUTION**
>
> The .java file extension must be specified when compiling an application's source file. The compiler will display an error message if .java is not specified.

If the compiler displays an error message, you might have typed Jed.java or JED.java instead of jed.java.

> **CAUTION**
>
> You must specify jed.java and not Jed.java, JED.java, or any other combination of lowercase/uppercase letters. The compiler is very sensitive to case and will display an error message if the class name (jed) does not match the filename (jed).

After compilation is finished, you should end up with a class file called jed.class.

Figure 17.3 shows the compilation process.

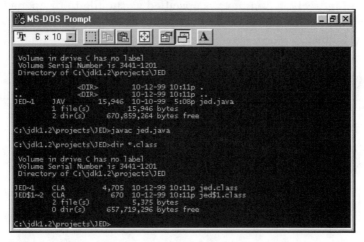

Figure 17.3: Compiling jed.java with the javac.exe compiler.

Running JED

Congratulations! You successfully compiled jed.java and are now ready to run jed.class. All you need to do is fire up the java.exe program and specify jed.class as an argument to this program.

> **CAUTION**
>
> The .class file extension must not be specified, otherwise the java.exe program will display an error message.

Figure 17.4 shows the process of running jed.class with java.exe.

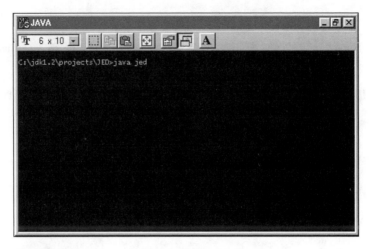

Figure 17.4: *Running* `jed.class` *with* `java.exe`.

In Figure 17.4, `jed.java` is specified as the file to be opened. A separate window appears displaying the contents of `jed.java`. This window is shown in Figure 17.5.

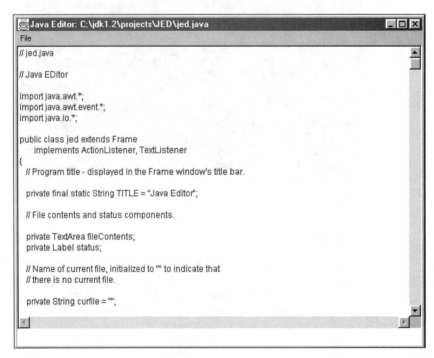

Figure 17.5: *JED's GUI window with a portion of* `jed.java` *displayed.*

Potential Problems

This program is pretty robust. This does not mean that you might not run into problems—especially if you are using a version of the JDK that predates version 1.2. If you should come across a problem, don't panic. Try to think logically about where the source of the problem occurs. You can always press the Ctrl and Break keys simultaneously to terminate JED when the DOS window running JED is active.

TIP

Whenever you need to break out of a Java program that just won't end, simultaneously press the Ctrl and Break keys!

Enhancing JED

You can enhance JED in a number of ways:

- JED does not display a dialog box prompting you to save changes. Instead, it displays a line in the status area at the bottom of its window. You might consider adding a Save Changes? dialog box to present an OK button so that the user can more clearly be informed when text needs to be saved. When the user presses OK, the dialog box disappears. You also might want to display other dialog boxes that appear when an exception occurs—such as when a file cannot be opened.

- The user should have the option of saving or not saving changes when exiting. As it stands, the user must save changes before exiting. Try modifying the Save changes? dialog box to present Yes and No buttons. Pressing Yes results in changes being saved. Pressing No results in changes being ignored.

What's Next?

As far as learning new Java concepts is concerned, we are at the end of our journey. Although many other concepts remain to be explored (such as networking, internationalization, Java Database Connectivity (JDBC), cryptography, and Swing), these concepts must wait for the next iteration of this book. You are strongly encouraged to investigate these other concepts for yourself, by taking advantage of the resources that you'll find within Appendix D, "Additional Resources."

Chapter 18, "Contact Manager," presents a case study that takes you on a journey through the process of developing a Java program, beginning with the design phase and moving through coding and testing phases. This program is called Contact Manager and can help you manage information about your business contacts.

Part IV

Case Study

Chapter 18: Contact Manager

Contact Manager

Suppose you land a job as a Java developer and the boss tells you to develop a large Java program from scratch. It is up to you to create a successful product. How would you go about developing the product, and where would you start? To give you some help, this chapter walks you through the process of developing a Java-based contact manager program. Many concepts from the previous 17 chapters are used.

Chapter 18 presents the following topics:

- Developing a contact manager
- Setting up the project
- Compiling CM
- Running CM
- Potential problems
- Enhancing CM

Developing a Contact Manager

What is a contact manager? How does a developer go about putting one together? These are good questions and this section provides the answers. As you'll discover, the task of developing a contact manager is just as important as the resulting product.

What Is a Contact Manager?

If you want to succeed in a world that gets busier with each passing day, being able to quickly get in touch with the movers and shakers of your business (via contact information) is just as important as reading, writing, and basic arithmetic.

A contact manager program helps you maintain a list of your business contacts. For each contact, you record the contact's name, phone number, fax number, email address, and other pertinent information.

Gathering Requirements

The first step in creating a contact manager (or any other kind of Java program) is not to take the "seat of the pants" approach to developing the program. In other words, you do not sit down at the computer and blindly type keys on the keyboard. It doesn't work. (At least, it never worked for me.)

If you want to create a successful program, the first thing you should do is gather requirements. Find out what the users of the program expect the program to accomplish, and how they envision interacting with this program.

For our contact manager, let's assume that our users want a very simple program that enables them to add new contacts, remove existing contacts, and update existing contacts. As far as contact information is concerned, the information that they want captured is a contact's first name, last name, phone number, fax number, and email address. Oh, by the way, they really want this program to have a graphical interface.

Designing the GUI

Most programs that are developed for users contain graphical user interfaces. After all, a picture is (usually) worth a thousand words of explanation.

Any developer can create a GUI. However, there is more to creating an effective GUI than throwing components on the screen and splashing colors all over the place. Creating usable GUIs is an art.

For example, suppose that your user is colorblind. She or he cannot distinguish color from black, white, and shades of gray. How would your user be able to effectively use your GUI if you intermixed a lot of green and red (which look very similar when viewed as shades of gray)? If you attempt to use color to convey important information, this will be lost on colorblind individuals.

Flow Charts

After you know what the user requires, you should organize this information into a rough approximation of how it fits together as a program. The decisions that need to be made, the statements that must be iterated over, and other details should be clearly understood. To help you visualize this stage of development, you can take advantage of *flow charts* (visual symbols used to identify the flow of data through a program, as well as various decisions and iterations that might affect this flow).

Flow charts use special symbols to identify statements, decisions, and iterations. Figure 18.1 shows some of these symbols.

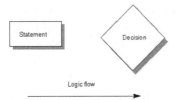

Figure 18.1: Flowchart symbols.

Although flowcharts, if properly drawn, can convey a lot of useful information, they have disadvantages. First, it takes time to draw a flowchart. After all, the flowchart might contain many symbols (such as square boxes illustrating assignment statements and method calls, diamond-shaped boxes illustrating If-else decision statements, arrows, and so on). A second disadvantage (somewhat related to the first disadvantage) is the static nature of a flowchart. Because they take time to draw, flowcharts don't reflect dynamic changes to a developer's view of the program. In other words, they are usually not up to date.

Figure 18.2 shows a flowchart corresponding to the following If-else decision statement:

```
if (x > 3)
    System.out.println ("x > 3");
else
    System.out.println ("x < 3");
```

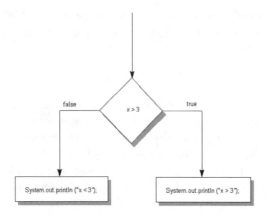

Figure 18.2: *A sample flowchart.*

Pseudocode

If you are not a fan of flowcharting, you can take advantage of pseudocode. Pseudocode is English-oriented (or whatever language you are most comfortable using) text that approximates a program's source code. You aren't concerned with syntax at this point. Instead, you want to specify something close to a program's source code that is easy to translate into source code.

Figure 18.3 shows pseudocode that corresponds to the flowchart in Figure 18.2.

```
if x is greater than 3 then
    print x > 3
else
    print x < 3
```

Figure 18.3: *Pseudocode equivalent of a flowchart.*

Source Code

If you've correctly gathered requirements, created a usable GUI, and either flowcharted or pseudocoded the program, you are now ready to write the program's source code.

Listing 18.1 provides the contact manager source code. This source code is heavily commented so the code will not be explained in any additional detail, except for one item at the end of this chapter.

Listing 18.1: cm.java.

```
// cm.java

import java.awt.*;
import java.awt.event.*;
import java.io.*;
```

```
import java.util.*;

// ============================================================
// Class: cm
//
// This class drives the contact manager.  It contains the
// main method which gets called as soon as this application
// begins to run.
// ============================================================

class cm extends Frame implements ActionListener
{
   // Container of contact objects (one object per business
   // contact).

   private Vector contacts = new Vector (100);

   // List of names component.  (Must specify java.awt in
   // front of List to distinguish the List class in the
   // java.awt package from the List class in the java.util
   // package.)

   private java.awt.List names = new java.awt.List ();

   // Delete and update button components.

   private Button delete;
   private Button update;

   // Default constructor.

   public cm ()
   {
      // Assign Contact Manager to title bar of frame window.

      super ("Contact Manager");

      // Add a listener that responds to window closing
      // events.  When this event occurs (by clicking on the
      // close box in the title bar), save contacts and exit.

      addWindowListener (new WindowAdapter ()
                        {
                                public void windowClosing
                                            (WindowEvent e)
                        {
                            saveContacts ();
```

Listing 18.1: continued

```
                              System.exit (0);
                    }
          });

// Place an empty label in the north part of the frame
// window.  This is done to correct an AWT positioning
// problem.  (One thing that you'll come to realize as
// you work with the AWT is that there are lots of bugs.)

Label l = new Label ();
add ("North", l);

// Place the names component in the center part of the
// frame window.

add ("Center", names);

// Create a panel object to hold four buttons.

Panel p = new Panel ();
Button b;

// Add an Insert button to the Panel object and register
// the current cm object as a listener for button events.

p.add (b = new Button ("Insert"));
b.addActionListener (this);

// Add a Delete button to the Panel object and register
// the current cm object as a listener for button events.

p.add (delete = new Button ("Delete"));
delete.addActionListener (this);

// The Delete button should be disabled until there is at
// least one contact to delete.

delete.setEnabled (false);

// Add an Update button to the Panel object and register
// the current cm object as a listener for button events.

p.add (update = new Button ("Update"));
update.addActionListener (this);

// The Update button should be disabled until there is at
// least one contact to update.
```

```
        update.setEnabled (false);

        // Add a Finish button to the Panel object and register
        // the current cm object as a listener for button events.

        p.add (b = new Button ("Finish"));
        b.addActionListener (this);

        // Add the panel object to the frame window container.

        add ("South", p);

        // Set the background of the frame window container to
        // lightGray (to give a pleasing effect).

        setBackground (Color.lightGray);

        // Set the size of the frame window container to 400
        // pixels horizontally by 200 pixels vertically.

        setSize (400, 200);

        // Do not allow the user to resize the frame window.

        setResizable (false);

        // Load all contacts.

        loadContacts ();

        // Make sure that the frame window is visible.

        setVisible (true);
    }

    public void actionPerformed (ActionEvent e)
    {
        if (e.getActionCommand ().equals ("Delete"))
            delete ();
        else
        if (e.getActionCommand ().equals ("Finish"))
        {
            saveContacts ();
            System.exit (0);
        }
        else
        if (e.getActionCommand ().equals ("Insert"))
```

Listing 18.1: continued

```
        insert ();
    else
        update ();
}

public Insets getInsets ()
{
    // Return an Insets object that describes the number of
    // pixels to reserve as a border around the edges of the
    // frame window.

    return new Insets (10, 10, 10, 10);
}

public static void main (String [] args)
{
    // Create a new cm object and let it do its thing.

    new cm ();
}

private void delete ()
{
    // Obtain index of selected contact item from the names
    // component.

    int index = names.getSelectedIndex ();

    // If no item was selected, index is -1.  We cannot update
    // a contact if no contact item in the names component was
    // selected - because we would have nothing to work with.

    if (index != -1)
    {
        // Remove the contact item from the names component.

        names.remove (index);

        // Remove the Contact object from the contacts Vector
        // object.

        contacts.remove (index);

        // If there are no more contacts ...

        if (contacts.size () == 0)
        {
```

```
                delete.setEnabled (false);
                update.setEnabled (false);
        }
        else

        // Make sure that the first contact item in the names
        // list is highlighted.

        names.select (0);
    }
}

private void insert ()
{
    // Create an Insert data entry form to enter information
    // for a new contact.

    DataEntryForm def = new DataEntryForm (this, "Insert");

    // If the bOk Boolean flag is set, this indicates the user
    // exited the form by pressing the Ok button.

    if (def.bOk)
    {
        // Create a Contact object and assign information from
        // the form to its fields.

        Contact temp = new Contact ();
        temp.fname = new String (def.fname.getText ());
        temp.lname = new String (def.lname.getText ());
        temp.phone = new String (def.phone.getText ());
        temp.fax = new String (def.fax.getText ());
        temp.email = new String (def.email.getText ());

        // Add a new contact item to the names component.

        names.add (temp.lname + ", " + temp.fname);

        // Add the Contact object to the contacts Vector
        // object.

        contacts.add (temp);

        // Make sure that the Delete and Update buttons are
        // enabled.

        delete.setEnabled (true);
        update.setEnabled (true);
```

Listing 18.1: continued

```
    }

    // Destroy the dialog box.

    def.dispose ();

    // Make sure that the first contact item in the names list
    // is highlighted.

    names.select (0);
}

// ============================================================
// Load all contacts from contacts.dat into the contacts
// Vector object.  Also, make sure that the last name/first
// name from each contact is combined into a String object and
// inserted into the names component - as a contact item.
// ============================================================

private void loadContacts ()
{
    FileInputStream fis = null;

    try
    {
        fis = new FileInputStream ("contacts.dat");

        DataInputStream dis = new DataInputStream (fis);

        int nContacts = dis.readInt ();

        for (int i = 0; i < nContacts; i++)
        {
            Contact temp = new Contact ();

            temp.fname = dis.readUTF ();
            temp.lname = dis.readUTF ();
            temp.phone = dis.readUTF ();
            temp.fax = dis.readUTF ();
            temp.email = dis.readUTF ();

            names.add (temp.lname + ", " + temp.fname);
            contacts.add (temp);
        }

        if (nContacts > 0)
        {
```

```
                  delete.setEnabled (true);
                  update.setEnabled (true);
            }
      }
      catch (IOException e)
      {
      }
      finally
      {
         if (fis != null)
             try
             {
                  fis.close ();
             }
             catch (IOException e) {}
      }

      // Make sure that the first contact item in the names list
      // is highlighted.

      names.select (0);
}

// ===========================================================
// Save all Contact objects from the contacts Vector object
// to contacts.dat.  The number of contacts are saved as an
// int to make it easy for loadContacts () to do its job.
// ===========================================================

private void saveContacts ()
{
   FileOutputStream fos = null;

   try
   {
      fos = new FileOutputStream ("contacts.dat");

      DataOutputStream dos = new DataOutputStream (fos);

      dos.writeInt (contacts.size ());

      for (int i = 0; i < contacts.size (); i++)
      {
            Contact temp = (Contact) contacts.elementAt (i);

            dos.writeUTF (temp.fname);
            dos.writeUTF (temp.lname);
            dos.writeUTF (temp.phone);
```

Listing 18.1: continued

```
                dos.writeUTF (temp.fax);
                dos.writeUTF (temp.email);
        }
    }
    catch (IOException e)
    {
        MsgBox mb = new MsgBox (this, "CM Error",
                                    e.toString ());
        mb.dispose ();
    }
    finally
    {
        if (fos != null)
            try
            {
                fos.close ();
            }
            catch (IOException e) {}
    }
}

private void update ()
{
    // Obtain index of selected contact item from the names
    // component.

    int index = names.getSelectedIndex ();

    // If no item was selected, index is -1.  We cannot update
    // a contact if no contact item in the names component was
    // selected - because we would have nothing to work with.

    if (index != -1)
    {
        // Obtain a reference to the Contact object (from the
        // contacts Vector object) that is associated with the
        // index.

        Contact temp = (Contact) contacts.elementAt (index);

        // Create and display an update entry form.

        DataEntryForm def = new DataEntryForm (this, "Update",
                                        temp.fname,
                                        temp.lname,
                                        temp.phone,
                                        temp.fax,
```

```
                                            temp.email);

        // If the user pressed Ok...

        if (def.bOk)
        {
            // Update the contact information in the contacts
            // Vector object.

            temp.fname = new String (def.fname.getText ());
            temp.lname = new String (def.lname.getText ());
            temp.phone = new String (def.phone.getText ());
            temp.fax = new String (def.fax.getText ());
            temp.email = new String (def.email.getText ());

            // Make sure the screen reflects the update.

            names.replaceItem (temp.lname + ", " + temp.fname,
                                    index);
        }

        // Destroy the dialog box.

        def.dispose ();

        // Make sure that the first contact item in the names
        // list is highlighted.

        names.select (0);
    }
  }
}


// ========================================================
// Class: Contact
//
// This class describes the contents of a business contact.
// ========================================================

class Contact
{
    public String fname;
    public String lname;
    public String phone;
    public String fax;
    public String email;
}
```

Listing 18.1: continued

```
// =============================================================
// Class: DataEntryForm
//
// This class provides a data entry form for entering contact
// information.
// =============================================================

class DataEntryForm extends Dialog implements ActionListener
{
    // bOk is a boolean flag.  When true, it indicates that
    // the Ok button was pressed to terminate the dialog box
    // (as opposed to the Cancel button).

    public boolean bOk;

    // The following components hold the text that the user
    // entered into the visible text fields.

    public TextField fname;
    public TextField lname;
    public TextField phone;
    public TextField fax;
    public TextField email;

    public void actionPerformed (ActionEvent e)
    {
        // If the user pressed the Ok button, indicate this
        // by assigning true to bOk.

        if (e.getActionCommand ().equals ("Ok"))
            bOk = true;

        // Destroy the dialog box and return to the point
        // just after the creation of the DataEntryForm object.

        dispose ();
    }

    public DataEntryForm (Frame parent, String title)
    {
        // Call the other constructor.  The current constructor
        // is used for insert operations.  The other constructor
        // is used for update operations.

        this (parent, title, "", "", "", "", "");
    }
```

```
public DataEntryForm (Frame parent, String title,
                      String fname, String lname,
                      String phone, String fax,
                      String email)
{
   // Initialize the superclass layer.

   super (parent, title, true);

   // Choose a grid bag layout so that components can be more
   // accurately positioned.  (It looks nicer.)

   setLayout (new GridBagLayout ());

   // Add appropriate first name, last name, phone, fax, and
   // email components to the current DataEntryForm container.
   // (Remember, DataEntryForm is a subclass of Dialog.
   // Dialog is a container.  Therefore, DataEntryForm
   // inherits the ability to be a container.)

   addComponent (this, new Label ("First name: "), 0, 0, 1, 1,
                 GridBagConstraints.NONE,
                 GridBagConstraints.WEST);

   this.fname = new TextField (15);
   addComponent (this, this.fname, 1, 0, 1, 1,
                 GridBagConstraints.NONE,
                 GridBagConstraints.CENTER);

   if (title.equals ("Update"))
       this.fname.setText (fname);

   addComponent (this, new Label ("Last name: "), 0, 1, 1, 1,
                 GridBagConstraints.NONE,
                 GridBagConstraints.WEST);

   this.lname = new TextField (15);
   addComponent (this, this.lname, 1, 1, 1, 1,
                 GridBagConstraints.NONE,
                 GridBagConstraints.CENTER);

   if (title.equals ("Update"))
       this.lname.setText (lname);

   addComponent (this, new Label ("Phone number: "), 0, 2, 1, 1,
                 GridBagConstraints.NONE,
                 GridBagConstraints.WEST);
```

Listing 18.1: continued

```
this.phone = new TextField (15);
addComponent (this, this.phone, 1, 2, 1, 1,
              GridBagConstraints.NONE,
              GridBagConstraints.CENTER);

if (title.equals ("Update"))
    this.phone.setText (phone);

addComponent (this, new Label ("FAX number: "), 0, 3, 1, 1,
              GridBagConstraints.NONE,
              GridBagConstraints.WEST);

this.fax = new TextField (15);
addComponent (this, this.fax, 1, 3, 1, 1,
              GridBagConstraints.NONE,
              GridBagConstraints.CENTER);

if (title.equals ("Update"))
    this.fax.setText (fax);

addComponent (this, new Label ("Email address: "), 0, 4, 1, 1,
              GridBagConstraints.NONE,
              GridBagConstraints.WEST);

this.email = new TextField (15);
addComponent (this, this.email, 1, 4, 1, 1,
              GridBagConstraints.NONE,
              GridBagConstraints.CENTER);

if (title.equals ("Update"))
    this.email.setText (email);

addComponent (this, new Label (""), 0, 5, 1, 1,
              GridBagConstraints.NONE,
              GridBagConstraints.CENTER);

addComponent (this, new Label (""), 1, 5, 1, 1,
              GridBagConstraints.NONE,
              GridBagConstraints.CENTER);

Button b;

// Add an Ok button to this container.

addComponent (this, b = new Button ("Ok"), 0, 6, 1, 1,
              GridBagConstraints.NONE,
              GridBagConstraints.CENTER);
```

```
        b.addActionListener (this);

        // Add a Cancel button to this container.

        addComponent (this, b = new Button ("Cancel"), 1, 6, 1, 1,
                      GridBagConstraints.NONE,
                      GridBagConstraints.CENTER);
        b.addActionListener (this);

        // Set the size of the dialog window to 250 pixels
        // horizontally by 200 pixels vertically.

        setSize (250, 200);

        // Do not allow users to resize the dialog window.

        setResizable (false);

        // Make sure that the dialog window is visible.

        setVisible (true);
    }

    private void addComponent (Container con, Component com,
                               int gridx, int gridy,
                               int gridw, int gridh, int fill,
                               int anchor)

    {
        // Get the current layout manager.  It is assumed to
        // be a GridBagLayout object.

        LayoutManager lm = con.getLayout ();

        // Create a GridBagConstraints object to make it
        // possible to customize component positioning.

        GridBagConstraints gbc = new GridBagConstraints ();

        // Assign the x and y grid positions.

        gbc.gridx = gridx;
        gbc.gridy = gridy;

        // Assign the number of grid blocks horizontally and
        // vertically that are occupied by the component.

        gbc.gridwidth = gridw;
```

Listing 18.1: continued

```
        gbc.gridheight = gridh;

        // Specify the component's resize policy (fill) and
        // the direction in which the component is positioned
        // when its size is smaller than available space (anchor).

        gbc.fill = fill;
        gbc.anchor = anchor;

        // Set the new constraints that the grid bag layout
        // manager will use.

        ((GridBagLayout) lm).setConstraints (com, gbc);

        // Add the component to the container.

        con.add (com);
    }
}


// ============================================================
// Class: MsgBox
//
// This class displays a message box to the user.  The message
// is usually an error message.  The user must press the Ok
// button to terminate the message box.
// ============================================================

class MsgBox extends Dialog implements ActionListener
{
    public void actionPerformed (ActionEvent e)
    {
        // Terminate the dialog box in response to the user
        // pressing the Ok button.

        dispose ();
    }

    public MsgBox (Frame parent, String title, String msg)
    {
        // Initialize the superclass layer.

        super (parent, title, true);

        // Store the msg argument in a Label object and add
        // this object to the center part of the dialog window.
```

```
        Label l = new Label (msg);
        add ("Center", l);

        // Create a Button object and add it to the south part
        // of the dialog window.

        Button b = new Button ("Ok");
        add ("South", b);

        // Make the current object a listener to events that
        // occur as a result of the user pressing the Ok
        // button.

        b.addActionListener (this);

        // Make sure that the Ok button has the focus.

        b.requestFocus ();

        // Do not allow users to resize the dialog window.

        setResizable (false);

        // Allow the layout manager to choose an appropriate
        // size for the dialog window.

        pack ();

        // Make sure that the dialog window is visible.

        setVisible (true);
    }
}
```

Because CM's source code is heavily commented, it will not be reviewed in any further depth, with one exception.

A Contact object represents a single business contact. These objects are stored in the contacts Vector object by appending them to the end of this object—via Vector's add (Object) instance method. It is not enough to store this object in a Vector. The user needs visual feedback that shows this addition. This is accomplished by creating a String object composed of a last name and a first name. The source code refers to this String object as a contact item. Contact items are appended to the end of the names List component. Because the contacts Vector object and the names List object both store objects in an internal array and use 0 to represent the position of the first object, we can be assured that these two objects reflect each other. For example, the first element in the names object maps to the first element in the contacts object.

Setting Up the Project

To set up CM, begin by double-clicking your MS-DOS icon (if you are using Windows) and go to a command prompt.

If you created a `projects` directory in Chapter 1, "Introducing Java," make `projects` your current directory. (If you do not have a `projects` directory, now is your last opportunity to create one.)

Assuming that `projects` is located within `c:\jdk1.2\`, enter the command `cd \jdk1.2\projects` to change to this directory.

From within your `projects` directory, create a directory called `cm` (for example, `md cm`). (If you prefer, you can create this directory entirely in uppercase. For example, you could issue the command `md CM` to create this directory. Case does not matter when it comes to directories.)

Download the file `cm.java` from the Macmillan Web site and place this file in your `cm` directory.

Compiling CM

Compilation is a simple process. It involves running the `javac.exe` program and specifying the name of the source file as an argument to this program.

At the command prompt, enter the following line:

```
c:\jdk1.2\projects\cm>javac cm.java
```

CAUTION

The `.java` file extension must be specified when compiling a source file. The compiler will display an error message if `.java` is not specified.

If the compiler displays an error message, you might have typed `cm` with a different combination of uppercase/lowercase letters than the lowercase letters used as CM's class name (for example, you might have specified something like `javac Cm.java` at the command line when you should have specified `javac cm.java`).

CAUTION

You must specify `cm` and not `Cm`, `CM`, or any other combination of lowercase/uppercase letters. The compiler is very sensitive to case and will display an error message if the class name (cm) does not match the filename (cm).

Don't panic if the compiler displays error messages. Note the line number(s) associated with these messages and fire up your editor. Go to the offending line(s) and compare the code with the code in Listing 18.1. Make the needed correction(s), save the file, return to the command prompt, and re-try the compilation step.

After compilation is finished, you should end up with the following class files: cm.class, cm$1.class, Contact.class, DataEntryForm.class, and MsgBox.class.

Figure 18.4 shows the compilation process.

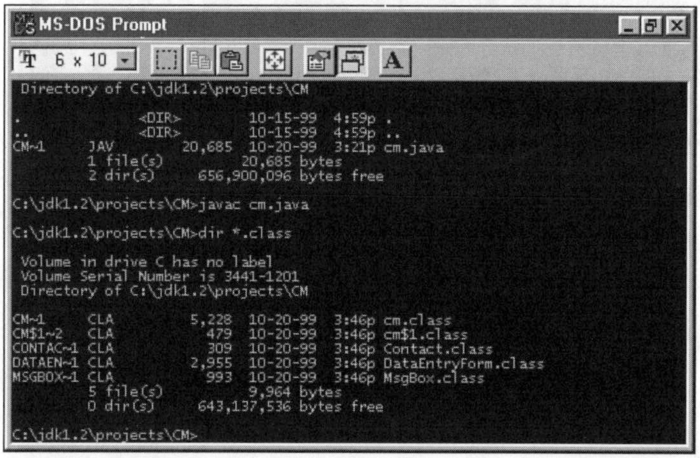

Figure 18.4: *Compiling* cm.java *with the* javac.exe *compiler.*

Running CM

Congratulations! You successfully compiled cm.java and are now ready to run cm.class. All you need to do is fire up the java.exe program and specify cm.class as an argument to this program.

CAUTION

The .class file extension must not be specified when running CM; otherwise, the java.exe program will display an error message.

Figure 18.5 shows the process of running cm.class with java.exe.

CM's main window is shown in Figure 18.6.

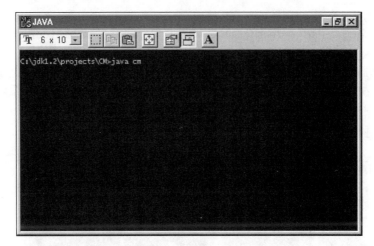

Figure 18.5: *Running* `cm.class` *with* `java.exe`.

Figure 18.6: *CM's main window.*

Potential Problems

What can go wrong with CM? A corrupt data file is one possibility. You might want to add error checking to the `loadContacts ()` method to display an error message if a negative number is returned for the number of contacts saved in the file.

Although this program has been extensively tested, it is very possible that something might have been missed. If you come across such a problem, try and solve it—and increase your Java knowledge in the process.

Enhancing CM

The contact manager source code is just "begging" to be enhanced. For example, you could add sorting logic to make sure that all contact items are displayed in ascending order of last name. Also, you could expand CM to support other fields, such as address fields.

Here is a small enhancement that you should be able to add in about one hour. If you press the Delete button, a contact item (and associated contact Vector object) is deleted. You are not prompted with an Are you sure? message. You might want to create a dialog box to prompt the user for a Yes/No response. Also, you might want to use this dialog box when terminating the program. You could then ask the user if the user wants changes saved prior to exit.

I'm sure you'll be able to think up many other enhancements to this program.

What's Next?

CM is the largest program presented in this book. And yet, it is a toy program in comparison to what could be built. Before you attempt to make significant changes to CM, you should master the concepts that are presented in this book. Not only will you save yourself a lot of frustration, but you also will take pleasure in the creative process, thanks to your Java knowledge.

If you want more information on developing Java software, please turn to Appendix D, "Additional Resources." This appendix serves as a starting point to help you branch off into the world of Java.

I wish you all the best in your future Java endeavors. Goodbye!

Part V

Appendixes

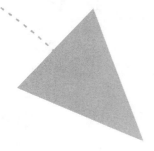

Appendix A

Reserved Words

Reserved words are part of the Java language syntax. They cannot be used as names for variables, methods, classes, interfaces, or packages. Table A.1 lists Java's reserved words.

Table A.1: Reserved Words

abstract	boolean	break	byte	case
catch	char	class	const	continue
default	do	double	else	extends
false	final	finally	float	for
goto	if	implements	import	instanceof
int	interface	long	native	new
null	package	private	protected	public
return	short	static	strictfp	super
switch	synchronized	this	throw	throws
transient	true	try	void	volatile
while				

Java does not currently implement the following reserved words: const and goto.

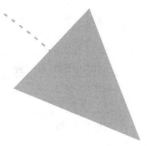

Appendix B

Operator Precedence

Table B.1 lists Java's operators in decreasing order of precedence. Operators with the same precedence are grouped together (and separated from other groups by horizontal lines).

Table B.1: Operator Precedence

Operator	Description	Evaluation Order
()	parentheses	left to right
[]	array index	left to right
++	preincrement	right to left
++	postincrement	right to left
--	predecrement	right to left
--	postdecrement	right to left
+	unary plus	right to left
-	unary minus	right to left
!	logical NOT	right to left
	Boolean NOT	
~	bitwise complement	right to left
(data type)	cast	right to left
*	multiplication	left to right
/	division	left to right
%	modulus	left to right
+	addition	left to right
-	subtraction	left to right
<<	bitwise shift left	left to right
>>	bitwise shift right (sign extension)	left to right

continues

Table B.1: continued

Operator	Description	Evaluation Order
>>>	bitwise shift right (zero extension)	left to right
<	relational less than	left to right
<=	relational less than or equal to	left to right
>	relational greater than	left to right
>=	relational greater than or equal to	left to right
instanceof	reference data type checking	left to right
==	relational equal to	left to right
!=	relational not equal to	left to right
&	bitwise AND	left to right
	Boolean AND	
^	bitwise exclusive OR	left to right
	Boolean exclusive OR	
|	bitwise inclusive OR	left to right
	Boolean inclusive OR	
&&	logical AND	left to right
||	logical OR	left to right
?:	conditional	right to left
=	assignment	right to left
+=	addition plus assignment	right to left
-=	subtraction plus assignment	right to left
*=	multiplication plus assignment	right to left
/=	division plus assignment	right to left
%=	modulus plus assignment	right to left
&=	bitwise AND plus assignment	right to left
	Boolean AND plus assignment	
^=	bitwise exclusive OR plus assignment	right to left
	Boolean exclusive OR plus assignment	

Operator	Description	Evaluation Order
|=	bitwise inclusive OR plus assignment	right to left
	Boolean inclusive OR plus assignment	
<<=	bitwise shift left plus assignment	right to left
>>=	bitwise shift right with sign plus assignment	right to left
>>>=	bitwise shift right with zero plus assignment	right to left

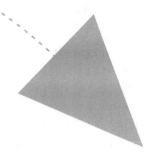

Appendix C

JAR File Management

JAR (Java ARchive) is a platform-independent archival file format that specifies how to bundle multiple files into a single file. The resulting file is known as a *JAR file*.

A JAR file is commonly used to distribute an applet by encapsulating the applet's class and resource files (for example, image files, sound files, and text files) into a single file.

A JAR file reduces the amount of time that it takes for a Web browser to download an applet, because the Web browser only needs to open a single network connection to a remote computer (where the JAR file is located) and download just the JAR file. Without a JAR file, the browser would open a separate network connection for each one of the applet's files and download that file. The process of opening a connection and downloading a single file is a slow process. Multiply this amount of time by the number of applet files and you can see why JAR files are beneficial.

A JAR file can be compressed, further reducing the time it takes to download an applet.

jar.exe

The JDK supplies a tool for creating and working with JAR files. This tool is called jar.exe.

jar.exe is a general-purpose archiving tool. This tool, like other JDK tools, is run from a command line.

jar.exe has the following command-line format:

```
jar [commands] [manifest] [archive] [input]
```

Any argument between square brackets ([ ]) is optional.

If no arguments follow jar, a list of commands (along with command usage examples) is displayed.

A group of commands might be specified after jar. Commands tell jar what to do (for example, create a JAR file, extract files from a JAR file, list the contents of a JAR file, and so on). The presence or absence of jar arguments depends upon what commands are specified.

A command is specified by prefixing it with a hyphen (-) character. Commands can be concatenated into a group and the group prefixed with a single hyphen. Table C.1 provides a list of commands.

The name of a manifest file might be specified. A *manifest file* describes the contents of an archive.

The name of an *archive file* might be specified. This is the file being created or manipulated.

The names of one or more *input files* might be specified. These are the files that are stored into or extracted from the archive.

Table C.1: JAR Commands

Command	Description
-c	Create a new archive
-t	List a table of contents for the archive
-x	Extract named (or all) files from the archive
-u	Update the existing archive
-v	Generate verbose output on standard output
-f	Specify the archive filename
-m	Include manifest information from specified manifest file
-0	Store only; use no zip compression
-M	Do not create a manifest file for the entries
-C	Change to the specified directory and include the following file

Examples

The following examples show how to use jar.exe to work with JAR files. These examples assume a JDK installation directory called c:\jdk1.2 and the presence of the Java source code JAR file called src.jar within this directory:

1. Display jar.exe usage information:

```
c:\jdk1.2>jar
```

2. List the contents of `src.jar`:

   ```
   c:\jdk1.2>jar -tf src.jar
   ```

3. Extract all files from `src.jar`. (An `src` directory is created underneath the JDK installation directory. Directories are created underneath `src` and all archived files are extracted into these directories.)

   ```
   c:\jdk1.2>jar -xf src.jar
   ```

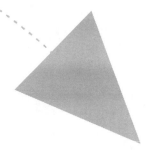

Appendix D

Additional Resources

Our journey has come to an end. So where do you go from here? Fortunately, you have many options to increase your Java skills and assist you in landing a job as a Java developer. These options include the following:

- Visit Sun's Java software Web site
- Join Sun's Java developer connection
- Work through Sun's online Java tutorial
- Read quality Java books from Sun and O'Reilly
- Read quality online and print Java magazines
- Interact with other developers through newsgroups
- Obtain certification to increase employment options

Visit Sun's Java Software Web Site

Sun Microsystems has a Web site dedicated to all things Java. This Web site provides access to the JDK and other toolkits that you can freely download. Also, you can join Sun's Java developer connection to learn more about advanced Java features, participate in various activities, learn how to achieve certification, learn about Sun's various books that explore different aspects of Java, and work through an online tutorial to improve your understanding of this technology.

Sun's Java Web site is located at `http://www.javasoft.com`.

Join Sun's Java Developer Connection

Sun provides an online resource for developers that showcases many articles on different aspects of the Java language. If you are a first-time visitor to this resource, you will be asked to register. Registration is free and only takes a couple of minutes. However, it is a worthwhile endeavour.

The Java developer connection Web site is located at `http://developer.java.sun.com/developer/`.

Work Through Sun's Online Java Tutorial

Various authors have come together to produce an online tutorial that explores many areas of Java technology. This "hands on" tutorial can help you come up to speed with Java technology in short order.

The Java tutorial Web site is located at `http://java.sun.com/docs/books/tutorial/`.

Read Quality Java Books from Sun and O'Reilly

Sun Microsystems offers a quality series of Java books called *The Java Series* that explores Java in a tutorial fashion. This series even includes a book that describes how the virtual machine works—very helpful in learning what goes on "under the hood."

The Java Series Web site is located at `http://java.sun.com/docs/books/`.

O'Reilly and Associates is a book publishing house that offers a wide selection of quality books on many topics. They have produced a very successful line of incredibly useful books on Java technology. Whether you want to learn more about JDBC, multithreading, 3D graphics, or even cryptography, you've come to the right place when you visit O'Reilly.

The O'Reilly Web site is located at `http://www.ora.com`.

Read Quality Online and Print Java Magazines

The Internet offers many online magazines that are dedicated to Java technology. One of the most influential (and freely available) magazines is called *JavaWorld*. This magazine will keep you up to date on what is happening in the Java community, and can help you to improve your Java development skills.

The JavaWorld Web site is located at `http://www.javaworld.com`.

Interact with Other Developers Through Newsgroups

Sometimes, you have a Java question that needs a quick answer but there is no one around the office who can help. What do you do? How about visiting some of Java's many newsgroups. You'll find thousands of questions and hundreds of answers.

Three of the more useful newsgroups include

`comp.lang.java.databases`

`comp.lang.java.gui`

`comp.lang.java.programmer`

Obtain Certification to Increase Employment Options

Finally, if you want to get a really good job with Java technology, you can improve your chances by obtaining certification. Companies will prefer developers who have this designation to those who do not. (It's analogous to having a degree in Computer Science.)

To learn about the certification process, visit the Java developer connection's Web site and point your browser to `http://developer.java.sun.com/ developer/technicalArticles/Interviews/Certification/index.html`.

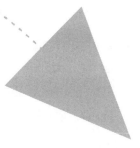

Glossary

Abstract Windowing Toolkit (AWT)   A collection of classes and interfaces that developers use for graphics, image manipulation, and GUI development in Java.

accessor method   A method that gets or sets the value of a private field. (Accessor methods that get values are usually prefixed with the word "get," whereas accessor methods that set values are usually prefixed with the word "set.")

Affine Transformation   A mathematical concept whereby straight lines are transformed into straight lines and parallel lines into parallel lines but the distance between points and the angles between lines might be altered.

American Standard Code for Information Interchange (ASCII)   A seven-bit character set standard that maps 128 binary numbers (with values that range from 0 through 127) to 128 symbols.

anonymous inner class   An inner class without a name.

applet   A Web browser–dependent Java program consisting of one or more class files.

applet parameter   An HTML name/value pair that is accessible to an applet so that an applet can modify its behavior. (Applet parameters make it possible to modify the applet without requiring source code recompilation.)

application   A standalone Java program consisting of one or more class files.

argument   The result of an expression that is passed to a method when the method is called.

array   A data structure composed of a fixed number of sequential storage locations (known as elements).

array variable   A reference variable that points to an array.

ASCII   See *American Standard Code for Information Interchange*.

assistive technologies   Technologies that assist people in working with computers. For example, a Braille device makes it possible for a blind person to read a computer's screen in Braille.

AWT   See *Abstract Windowing Toolkit*.

block   A region of source code surrounded by brace characters.

bucket   An array element that references a linked list for hashing purposes.

byte code   Instructions that are interpreted by the Java virtual machine.

call by reference   The mechanism that passes a variable's reference (address) to a method when that method is called.

call by value   The mechanism that passes the value of a variable to a method when that method is called.

capacity increment   An integer value that specifies by how much a Vector object grows when it is full.

case-sensitive language   A language in which identifiers that differ only in the case of their letters are treated as distinct.

character   The combination of a binary number and a symbol's visual data.

character set   A group of characters that completely define a written language's symbols.

checked exception   An exception that is based upon an external failure.

class   A source code blueprint that describes the state structure and behavior for all objects created from this blueprint.

class field   A field that is shared by all class instances (objects).

class field initialization block   A block, declared within a class and prefixed with the static reserved word, that is used to initialize class fields.

class file   A file with a .class file extension that contains a compiled class.

class instance   See *object*.

class library   One or more packages of useful classes (such as networking and database classes) with each class stored in a separate class file.

class method   A method that can access only class fields declared within the same class as the method.

collision   Two or more keys mapping to the same array index in a hash table.

command-line tools   Programs run from a DOS, UNIX, or other operating system command window.

comment   Textual information that describes source code and contributes towards the understanding of that source code.

component   A GUI building block (such as a button or a list box). A component is represented by a Java object and host operating system code.

composition   The capability to include objects as members of other objects.

compound statement   Zero or more statements surrounded by a pair of brace characters. (Usually, braces surround two or more statements.)

constructor   A "special" method that is only used to initialize an object.

container   An AWT data structure that contains one or more components.

coordinate pair   A pair of integer numbers that identify the horizontal and vertical distances (measured in pixels) from the origin (the pixel located in the upper-left corner of the drawable area) to a pixel.

daemon thread   A thread that runs in the background when processor time is available—time that would otherwise go to waste.

data stream   A stream whose source or destination is another stream.

data structure   A container (implemented as an object) that stores data items.

data type   The classification of a data item.

dead state   The state of a thread after it has died.

deep cloning   The duplication of an object's primitive and reference field values (along with the primitive field values of all objects that are referenced by those reference fields).

demotion rule   A rule that governs the conversion of a primitive data type with a larger size to a primitive data type with a smaller size, via the cast operator.

deserialization   The act of reading an object's class name, attributes, and field values; creating a new object from the class name and attributes; and assigning the field values to the new object's fields.

doubly linked list   A linked list of nodes where each node has two link fields.

drawable area   A rectangular area on a Web page where an applet's graphical output is displayed.

dynamic method binding   The mechanism that the virtual machine uses to locate and call either a superclass method or the correct overridden superclass method in a subclass, via a reference data type.

empty string   A string literal without characters.

encapsulation   The integration of state and behavior into a single object.

enumeration   An object created from a class that implements the Enumeration interface.

error   An exception that represents serious problems with the virtual machine (such as no more memory).

escape sequence   Multiple characters that denote a single character.

event   An action that is initiated by a GUI program's user, by interacting with a component.

event handler   Java code that handles an event.

exception   An object that encapsulates the failed state of a program, at the point where a failure occurred.

exception handler   Code that handles an exception.

expression   A combination of multiple operators and operands (or even just a single operand).

external failure   A failure resulting from the inability to acquire a resource.

field   A variable that holds a unit of state. A meaningful portion of a record (such as the first name of an employee in an employee record).

field initializer   An expression whose value is assigned to the field and has the same data type as the field's data type.

file mode   The reading/writing capabilities of an open file.

file pointer   A system variable that identifies the next reading/writing position in a file.

file stream   A stream whose source or destination is a file.

final variable   A read-only simple variable.

finalizer   A "special" object method that the virtual machine calls just before it destroys the object.

graphics context   An object, created from a subclass of AWT's abstract Graphics class, that represents a specific display device (such as an image buffer, monitor, or printer).

graphics environment   A set of all graphics devices and fonts that are managed by the host operating system.

GUI   Graphical User Interface.

hash code   An integer number that uniquely identifies an object.

hash table   The data structure formed by combining array elements and linked lists with appropriate logic.

hashing   A computer science technique for mapping keys to array indexes by scrambling the bits of a key in such a way that not all keys map to the same array index.

helper method   A hidden method that assists non-hidden methods in the performance of their tasks.

identifier   A sequence of consecutive non-white space characters (no embedded spaces or tabs) that are used to name reserved words, variables, methods, classes, interfaces, and packages.

image   A picture created from a table of colored pixels.

import directive   A directive to the compiler to import one or more class or interface names from a package.

indefinite postponement   Preventing a thread from running because a thread with a higher priority has exclusive use of the processor.

inheritance   The capability to relate one object to another object based on the classes from which these objects were created.

initializer   A method that initializes either class fields or instance fields.

inner class   A class declared within another class (or method).

instance field   A field that is unique to each class instance (object).

instance field initialization block   A block, declared within a class, that is used to initialize instance fields.

instance inner class   A class that is declared within another class, without the static reserved word. Code within this class can access the outer class's instance and class fields.

instance method   A method that can access all instance and class fields declared within the same class as the method.

interface   A named collection of abstract methods and read-only fields.

internal failure   A failure resulting from flawed code.

Java   A software technology that enables the development of portable, object-oriented, and secure computer programs.

Java Development Kit (JDK)   Sun's toolkit for creating Java software. The Java Development Kit contains development tools, documentation, and examples.

Java Foundation Classes (JFC)   The new AWT and related features (including Java2D, Swing, Drag and Drop, and Accessibility).

Java Native Interface (JNI)   A mechanism that "connects" class files to C/C++ libraries.

Java Runtime Environment (JRE)   A runtime version of the Java Development Kit. The Java Runtime Environment contains no development tools, documentation, or examples.

JIT compiler   See *just in time compiler*.

JNI   See *Java Native Interface*.

just in time (JIT) compiler   A program that translates byte code into device code while the Java virtual machine is running a program.

key   A unique integer value (used in hashing, indexing, and so on).

key word   See *reserved word*.

layout   The pattern by which a container's components are displayed on the screen.

layout manager   An object, associated with a container, that is responsible for laying out the container's components on the screen.

lifetime   The duration of a variable.

link field   A special reference field that is used by a node to link itself to another node.

linked list   A data structure composed of a dynamically expandable/shrinkable number of linked storage locations that are known as nodes.

literal   A data item literally embedded within source code.

load factor   The ratio of the number of occupied buckets—buckets referencing linked lists—to the total number of buckets.

local variable   A non-parameter variable declared within a method.

local variable initializer   An expression that is evaluated to a value (with the same data type as the variable) and then assigned to the local variable.

loop   A repetitive sequence of statements. This sequence is controlled by either a Do-while loop statement, a While loop statement, or a For loop statement.

main class file   The class file within an application or applet whose method byte code "gets first crack" at running.

main method The method within an application whose code "gets first crack" at running.

message A bundle of information sent from one object to another object.

method A named group of statements that specifies a behavior.

method call stack A sequence of method call return addresses where the most recent method call return address appears at the top and the least recent method call return address appears at the bottom.

monitor A locking mechanism that prevents access to a block of code when locked and grants access when unlocked.

multithreading The capability to run multiple threads, either at the same time (if each thread is given its own processor) or almost at the same time (if all threads share a single processor).

node An object that represents a linked list storage location.

object A software entity that combines state and behavior.

object serialization A Java technology, implemented by a pair of classes and an interface, that makes it possible to save the state of a program's objects to some destination (such as a file) and recreate these objects from this saved state at some later time.

operand A data item that is transformed by an operator into a new data item.

operator A combination of symbols that identifies an operation.

overloaded method A method declared within the same class as another method with the same name but with a different parameter list.

package A library of classes and interfaces.

package directive A compiler directive that is placed at the top of a source file and identifies the package where all classes and interfaces declared within the source file are stored.

parameter list A comma-delimited list of variable names and their data types.

parameter variable A variable declared within a method's parameter list.

peer Host operating system code that creates, displays, and manages a component's visible window.

pipe stream A stream whose source or destination is a thread.

polymorphism   The capability to use a superclass object reference variable to invoke subclass versions of overridden superclass methods.

precedence   The natural evaluation order of expressions containing multiple operators and operands.

primitive   A data structure object composed of a single data item that has a primitive Boolean, byte, char, double, float, int, long, or short data type. The class from which a primitive is created also is known as a data structure class or a wrapper class.

primitive data type   A language-defined data type.

promotion rule   A rule that governs the conversion of a primitive data type with a smaller size to a primitive data type with a larger size. The cast operator is not required because no information is lost.

quantum   The amount of time in which a thread can run before the operating system interrupts it and selects another thread to run.

queue   An array or linked list data structure where insertions are made at one end—the tail—and removed from another end—the head.

random access file   A file that is opened for reading and writing at the same time.

ready state   The state of a thread when it is ready to run.

record   A sequence of bytes that is stored in a file and describes an entity.

recursion   An iteration technique by which a method calls itself.

redirection   The use of the command-line characters < and > to switch the standard input device from the keyboard to a file or device and the standard output device from the screen to a file or device.

reference   The address of an object or array.

reference data type   A class or array data type.

reference variable   A variable that holds a reference to a region of memory.

reserved word   An identifier that only can be used to describe a language element.

return data type   The data type of values returned from a method.

runnable   An object that contains a `public void run ()` method and serves as the target of a `start ()` method call.

running state   The state of a thread when it is running.

runtime   Code that serves as a virtual machine operating system.

scalar variable   A non-array variable. (See also *simple variable*.)

scope   The visibility of a variable.

secure program   A Java program that is analyzed before it is allowed to run on a computing device.

self-referential class   A class that declares one or more reference fields to refer to objects of the same class data type.

sequential access file   A file that is opened either for reading or for writing but not for both.

serialization   The act of writing an object's class name, attributes (public, final, and so on), and field values to a stream.

shallow cloning   The duplication of an object's primitive field values.

short-circuiting   The technique of not always evaluating the rightmost operand of a logical AND or logical OR operator.

side effect   Extraneous code that is executed during the evaluation of an operand.

simple statement   A single statement.

simple variable   A single storage location that holds a data item. Synonymous with scalar variable.

singly linked list   A linked list of nodes where each node has one link field.

source code   The textual representation of a Java program.

stack   An array or linked list data structure where insertions and deletions are made from one end—the top.

standard I/O   A mechanism that provides a program with flexible input and output.

starvation   See *indefinite postponement*.

statement   A sequence of tokens that performs an action. This sequence is terminated with a semicolon character.

static inner class   A class that is declared within another class, via the static reserved word. Code within this class can access only the outer class's class field(s).

stopping condition   A Boolean expression that is evaluated and, when true, causes recursion to cease.

stream   A flow of data from a source to a destination.

string   A sequence of characters treated as a single data item.

synchronization   The mechanism by which two threads are prevented from interfering with each other.

system color   A color that is used by the host operating system to draw peers.

thread   A path of execution through byte code.

throwing an exception   The task of passing an exception to the virtual machine.

time slicing   The execution of threads in a round-robin fashion.

token   A meaningful sequence of characters (such as an integer literal or an identifier).

tokenize   The process of extracting tokens from a string or a stream.

unchecked exception   An exception that is based upon an internal failure.

Unicode   A sixteen-bit character set standard that maps up to 65,536 binary numbers (with values that range from 0 through 65535) to a maximum of 65,536 symbols.

unnamed package   The package to which all classes and interfaces are placed if the source file in which they are declared does not have a package directive.

variable   A storage location that holds one or more data items and is manipulated by programs.

vector   A growable array data structure object.

virtual machine   A computer program that simulates a computing device.

Index